The Possibilities of Sense

The Possibilities of Sense

Edited by

John H. Whittaker

First published 2002 by
PALGRAVE
Houndmills, Basingstoke, Hampshire RG21 6XS and
175 Fifth Avenue, New York, N. Y. 10010
Companies and representatives throughout the world

PALGRAVE is the new global academic imprint of
St. Martin's Press LLC Scholarly and Reference Division and
Palgrave Publishers Ltd (formerly Macmillan Press Ltd).

ISBN 0–333–97149–3

This book is printed on paper suitable for recycling and
made from fully managed and sustained forest sources.

A catalogue record for this book is available
from the British Library.

Library of Congress Cataloging-in-Publication Data
The possibilities of sense : essays in honour of D. Z. Phillips
/ edited by John Whittaker.
        p. cm.
    Includes bibliographical references and index.
    ISBN 0–333–97149–3
    1. Ethics. 2. Religion–Philosophy. 3. Phillips, D. Z. (Dewi
Zephaniah) I. Phillips, D. Z. (Dewi Zephaniah) II. Whittaker,
John H., 1945–

    BJ1012.P69 2001
    192–dc21
                                                        2001036883

    10   9   8   7   6   5   4   3   2   1
    11   10   09   08   07   06   05   04   03   02

Printed and bound in Great Britain by
Antony Rowe Ltd, Chippenham, Wiltshire

Contents

Acknowledgements

For help in preparing the typescript, thanks are due to Louisiana State University and the College of William and Mary; and for helping to manage its progress, to Helen Baldwin at the University of Wales, Swansea. Margaret Humphris deserves special appreciation for the long hours they spent in copyreading it.

Basil Blackwell kindly gave permission for the use of Raimond Gaita's 'Critical Notice of Phillips's *Interventions in Ethics*', which appeared in *Philosophical Investigations* 17:4, October 1994, pp. 613–28.

Peter Winch's essay 'Lessing and the Resurrection' was originally written for this volume and is used with permission of the Trust for the Peter Winch Archive.

Notes on the Contributors

James Conant is Professor of Philosophy at the University of Chicago. He is the author of articles on Kant, Nietzsche, Kierkegaard, Frege, William James, Carnap and Wittgenstein.

Ilham Dilman is Emeritus Professor of Philosophy at the University of Wales, Swansea. He has published numerous books, the latest of which are *Language and Reality: Modern Perspectives on Wittgenstein*; *Love: Its Form, Dimensions, and Paradoxes*; and *Free Will*.

John T. Edelman is Professor of Philosophy at Nazareth College of Rochester and the author of *An Audience for Moral Philosophy*?

M. Jamie Ferreira is Professor of Philosophy of Religion at the University of Virginia. She has written *Doubt and Religious Commitment*; *Scepticism and Reasonable Doubt*; and *Transforming Vision: Imagination and Will in Kierkegaardian Faith*.

Antony Flew is an Emeritus Professor of Philosophy at the University of Reading, and author of *An Introduction to Western Philosophy*; *The Logic of Mortality*; and *Atheistic Humanism*.

Raimond Gaita is a member of the Institute of Advanced Research at Australian Catholic University and of King's College, London, and the author of *Good and Evil: an Absolute Conception*.

Walford Gealy is Emeritus Senior Lecturer in Philosophy, University of Wales, Aberystwyth and is the author of *Wittgenstein* (in Welsh) and co-author of *Efrydiau Athronnydol*.

Lars Hertzberg is Professor of Philosophy at Åbo Academy, Finland. He is the author of *The Limits of Experience*, and has published essays on the philosophy of mind, ethics and Wittgenstein in several journals and collections.

Ieuan Lloyd read Philosophy at Swansea and taught Philosophy of Education at London and Birmingham before he joined the Department of Philosophy at Swansea in 1991. His main interest has been the relating of Wittgensteinian thought to Education. He is the author of *Philosophy*.

Colin Lyas is the author of *Aesthetics*. He has also written *Philosophy and Linguistics* and has translated Croce's *Estética*.

B.R. Tilghman is Professor Emeritus at Kansas State University. He has written *But is it Art?*; *Wittgenstein, Ethics and Aesthetics*; and *Introduction to the Philosophy of Religion*.

Michael Weston is lecturer in Philosophy at the University of Essex and the author of *Kierkegaard and Modern Continental Philosophy*.

John H. Whittaker is Professor of Philosophy and Religious Studies at Louisiana State University. He has written *Matters of Faith and Matters of Principles: Religious Truth Claims and Their Logic*; and *The Logic of Religious Persuasion*.

Rowan Williams is Bishop of Monmouth in Wales, and a former Professor of Divinity at Oxford. He is the author of several books, including most recently *On Christian Theology*; and *Lost Icons: Reflections on Cultural Bereavement*.

Peter Winch (d. 1997) was Emeritus Professor of Philosophy at King's College, London, and Professor of Philosophy at the University of Illinois, Urbana-Champaign. His books include *The Idea of a Social Science*, *Ethics and Action*, *Trying To Make Sense*, and *Simone Weil – The Just Balance*. He taught at University of Wales, Swansea, from 1951 to 1964 where D.Z. Phillips was one of his first honours students.

Editor's Introduction

The essays in this volume cover a wide range of philosophy – ethics, logic, the philosophy of religion, the philosophy of literature and the philosophy of education. For those who know D.Z. Phillips, this range of interest should not be surprising, since Phillips's own work ranges over these fields and others as well. Indeed, for him, all philosophy is in one sense one subject. In this special sense, the essays in this collection also belong to the same subject, whose unity has more to do with a shared conception of what philosophy is and does than with what it has to do with common problems.

The idea that philosophy, despite the differences in the problems that it addresses, reflects a unified approach comes largely from Ludwig Wittgenstein. As a mature thinker, Wittgenstein came to believe that philosophical problems were the products of a certain lack of clarity in the way in which they were formulated, and that this lack of clarity has its roots in confused ways of extracting sense from language. From his student days, Phillips was gradually won over to this way of thinking and he remains one of its foremost representatives to this day. Today, in fact, he is the editor of a major journal, *Philosophical Investigations*, which takes its name and its orientation from Wittgenstein's most famous work. Yet the full impact of Wittgenstein's methods was brought home to him, not by Wittgenstein himself, but by one of his closest associates, Rush Rhees, whom Phillips met along with J.R. Jones, Peter Winch and Roy Holland when he arrived at the Philosophy Department at the University of Swansea in the 1950s. When he returned to that same department as a lecturer in 1965, his philosophical acquaintances naturally grew, but it was these men, especially Rhees, whose seriousness as philosophers exemplified the rigour of Wittgenstein. Eventually he became Head of Department at Swansea, and though now retired from teaching, he is editing the 16,000 pages of philosophical papers that Rhees left at Swansea when he died. (At the same time he serves for one semester each year as the Danforth Professor of Religion at Claremont Graduate Center in California.) There is something particularly fitting about this. Rhees, after all, had been a student of Wittgenstein and became one of his literary executors. Now Phillips is doing the same for Rhees.

In large part the inspiration for this volume came from the man who succeeded Phillips as Head of Department, R.W. Beardsmore. Tragically, however, Dick Beardsmore died in 1997. It is to him, though, that we owe the present design of the volume. The contributors' essays are divided into three parts, the first on Phillips's contribution to moral philosophy, the second on his philosophy of religion, and the third on his work in the philosophy of literature and education. These parts are framed by two engaging accounts that put Phillips into perspective as a thinker. In the first of these, Ieuan Lloyd introduces Phillips biographically, explaining the profound effect that his early experience, first as a student and then as a minister, had on his development. In the second – the last essay in the collection – Walford Gealy puts Phillips into context as a *Welsh* philosopher, assessing his place alongside other important figures in the history of Welsh letters.

The title for the whole collection, *The Possibilities of Sense*, reflects the characteristic approach to philosophy that Phillips has always commended. On the one hand, it suggests that the resources of understanding that we need to think our way through philosophical perplexities are ingredients in the grammatical strictures of our speech, which both limit and enable our understanding of concepts. On the other hand, it suggests that there are forms of understanding that lie outside the familiar territory of *our* speech, being governed by their own grammatical limits. Many of the contributors concern themselves with the extent to which, and the conditions under which, these initially alien ways of speaking can be grasped. Yet it must be said that many of these *seemingly* alien ways of understanding are not as remote as they seem. More often than not, we have simply forgotten these possibilities of sense in trying to simplify our understanding, taking the intuitions that belong to one conceptual setting and generalizing them as if they applied to another. Thus, we approach one set of problems – e.g. about the rationality of religious belief or the self-interest involved in ethics – according to over-extended models of what it means to be reasonable. The cure for the problems that accrue by trying to force our thinking in this way is to remember that our ways of understanding range far beyond the privileged models that form our expectations. As Wittgenstein said, we need to remember differences, and to learn this from a 'wider diet of examples'.

Because feeding on a 'wider diet of examples' means recognizing the manifold possibilities of sense available to us, refocusing on the heterogeneity of these possibilities frustrates the attempt to simplify problems in philosophy by generalizing about them theoretically. In moral philosophy, for example, Phillips often points out exceptions to rules designed to make ethics *systematic*; and so it is no wonder that those who are committed to theorizing in ethics regard his conceptual reminders as something of a nuisance. Yet one cannot help but feel that the messiness that a wider diet of examples leaves behind in ethics is more honest than the theoretical generalizations that it undermines. For the exceptions – the forgotten possibilities of sense – that he brings out seem *intuitively* correct; and that means that they *too* are grounded in a grammatical mastery of concepts that most of us, in our rush towards theory, have been led to ignore.

These last few remarks, of course, only introduce the essays to follow, which will flesh out these comments. In Part I Raimond Gaita discusses Phillips's *Interventions in Ethics*, initially by acknowledging the importance of the theoretical exceptions that Phillips brings to our attention; but then he suggests that an exclusive concentration on differences in people's ethical sensibilities can blind us to a shared form of understanding that all moral thinking presumes. Many of the moral exceptions which Phillips points out, he says, are intelligible only because we share a rough sense of what it is to be human. We do not always consciously make use of this in our moral practice (we can, after all, treat one another in very inhumane ways); but we can be awakened to the variety of moral responses, *as moral responses*, only because we share a primitive recognition of other human beings as such. This common understanding is the field in which *anything* that is recognizably moral arises. It gives sense to the distinction between moral shallowness (which has little of the *humane* in it) and moral depth. Part of the job of the moral philosopher, then – according to Gaita – is to draw out this somewhat ragged sense of what it means to be a human being and to make some ethical use of it. The very possibility of moral insight presumes something opening beneath our feet, as it were, allowing us to be struck – morally struck – by behaviour whose moral character we had not previously recognized. That is something that the moral philosopher needs to acknowledge.

Gaita's essay provides a good introduction to several of the essays that follow. Lars Hertzberg's 'On Being Neighbourly' takes up a dispute between Phillips and Peter Winch over the role of the Good Samaritan story as a goad to conscience. What is required of us if we are to react to the parable in this way? And what does it say about us if we do *not* regard the story in this way? Those who find the Samaritan's behaviour out of reach (e.g., who simply find it curious) cannot be accused of making a moral *mistake*, as if they have violated a moral premise to which they were already committed. Such people do not belong to the world of moral possibilities that most of us inhabit, but it is one thing to say that, and another to accuse them of making an epistemic mistake. Here the sense that believers have typically found in the Good Samaritan story reflects the moral character that their lives have assumed, but other reactions to the traveller who fell among robbers can certainly be contemplated. Between these reactions, Hertzberg suggests, the story can *also* be understood as making a kind of appeal. To those whom we respect enough to think that their moral understanding might grow, the story can provide both incentive and guidance.

The case that John Edelman takes up in 'The Availability of Wisdom' invites us to consider similar limits to moral understanding. Instead of asking how the story of the Good Samaritan might draw others into a moral world that is familiar to us, he asks what is required of us if we are to extend our understanding to the morally distant teaching of Socrates that a good man cannot be harmed. Most of us dimly recognize this Socratic saying as a kind of wisdom, just as we look upon the parable of the Good Samaritan as a kind of wisdom. And yet it is extraordinarily difficult to explain why. Edelman struggles with this, only to wonder what an adequate explanation would look like, and what the conditions for understanding it would be. In the end, he suggests that it is only those whose lives have been transformed by love and beauty as sublime ideals who will be fully able to understand the wisdom of Socrates. For hard as it might be for philosophers to accept, moral understanding might not be equally available to all rational thinkers; and so the difficulties that we have in making sense of Socrates's words might not be due to *his* failures as much as they are due to *our* being people of the sort that are not yet able to receive this wisdom.

On this last point Gaita, Hertzberg and Edelman agree with Phillips: limitations in the moral form of our lives manifest themselves in limited possibilities of moral appreciation. But the question is whether, philosophic-ally, this is the end of the matter. Ilham Dilman does not think so. In 'Good and Evil: Love and Egocentricity' Dilman admits that the possibility of explaining one's moral position to someone else depends on the appeal to moral judgements that seem intuitively clear to that person. What if this moral common ground is lacking? Phillips says that in such cases it is often misleading to accuse those who disagree with us on this level of being inconsistent or irrational. They might be wrong, of course; or at least we might think so. But if we say that they are wrong, this judgement only *expresses* difference between our point of view and theirs. It does not signal an argumentative victory, merely the *end* of argumentative possibilities. Yet Dilman claims that moral philosophy need not end with such bedrock disagreements. Perhaps these differences reveal the hopelessness of con-structive, mutually intelligible, arguments; and yet somehow a selfless life in which certain values – especially love – are recognized as moral ideals deserves our credence, even apart from our ability to justify this life to every disbeliever. Here it is too simple to say that the power of love's appeal varies with the moral character of one's sensibilities, and that those who have no room for love in their lives cannot be expected to recognize its appeal. For there are considerations of wholeness, self-realization and maturity to be taken into account, and this enables at least a *kind* of defence to be given for a life that is open to love and free of selfishness.

This last essay, like the earlier ones, presumes a discussion that has long since been underway. But the final essay in Part I introduces a comparatively new issue. In 'On Going the Bloody *Hard* Way in Philosophy' James Conant stresses the connection that Wittgenstein made between the character of a philosophical work and the philosopher's moral character. Wittgenstein was surprisingly insistent about this. Being a philosopher with integrity means 'going the bloody hard way' in one's thinking, but the difficulty in going this way is ethical as well as intellectual. As Conant explains it, this is because, for Wittgenstein, philosophical attention requires an unflinching earnestness about the problems at hand. The ability to see these problems clearly *as problems*, and to face them honestly, demands a moral character that is utterly free of self-deception. Conant, however, does not make this point solely in relation to Wittgenstein's treatment of existential subjects, where one might expect a certain earnestness to arise. He turns instead to Wittgenstein's early struggles with logical questions. In the particular case that Conant discusses, Wittgenstein was struggling with fundamental questions about how *meaning something* differs from *asserting that something is the case*. Bertrand Russell's logical theories had foundered on this problem, but Russell refused to yield his theory of reference in the face of difficulties that he knew were greater than he admitted. That was unthinkable to Wittgenstein. To fail to think difficulties *through*, or at least honestly to confess one's failures, surrenders not only the rigour of philosophy but the integrity of the philosopher.

Directly or indirectly, all these essays were inspired by Phillips. Or at least they show his influence. Yet for all of his influence in moral philosophy, Phillips has had an even greater impact in the philosophy of religion, where his views are widely known and yet poorly understood. Philosophy, as he sees it, plays no role at all in grounding religious claims – e.g. in proving that religious beliefs refer (or do not refer) to a genuine reality, or that religious arguments qualify (or do not qualify) as rational justifications, or that some religious views (or anti-religious views) are superior to others, or in anything of the sort. Yet the assumption that philosophers *must* appraise religious claims in some such way belongs so much to the heart of traditional philosophy of religion that many of his readers misconstrue the force of his thinking. Thus, when Phillips speaks of the groundlessness of religious belief, his critics suppose that he is making a negative judgement about it, as if he were criticizing religious claims for lacking logical features that every rational assertion should have. But that is not his point at all. He means only to distinguish religious claims from the sort of claims that logically *qualify* for judgement as rational claims and that can be appropriately criticized as such. He means to show, that is, only that the rational standards appropriate to other types of belief are not appropriate to most religious beliefs, and that the indiscriminate attempt to justify religious claims by these inappropriate standards *distorts the very meaning of religious ideas*. None of this means that religious claims lack *any* sense as credible beliefs or that they cannot be appropriately held. That is not the issue. Phillips simply wants his readers to see religious claims for what they are, so that they might become more conscious of the ways that these claims are distorted in the effort to be philosophically critical about them.

Phillips, in other words, cannot be accurately described as either a friend or a foe of religion, except in so far as it lies in the interest of religion to have its teachings understood in a logically discriminating way. The contributors to the present volume are well aware of this modesty in Phillips's approach to religion, and they are far less likely than his critics to use contextually unbridled conceptions of reason, truth and reality in their discussions of his work. Instead of simply correcting misunderstandings in the popular under-standing of Phillips's work as a philosopher of religion, they have moved on to other topics. In some cases, they stick close to his work; in other cases, they move further afield.

Among the essays of the first type is the editor's contribution, 'At the End of Reason Comes Persuasion' – a title lifted from one of Wittgenstein's remarks in *On Certainty*. This essay begins with the observation that believers and non-believers often lack not only a common set of religious premises but also a common sense of what it means to think responsibly about religious issues. They share words, perhaps, but not *concepts* and the appro-priate *mode of judgement that goes with them*. The result is that they often talk past one another in their disagreements. The consequence of this is not necessarily the collapse of religious issues into relativism: the failure to share conceptions of judgement in religious matters means only that the possibility of argument must fail, not that there is nothing sensible to be done in the absence of argument. Persuasion, in such cases, can take the place of argument. Yet it is unclear what such persuasion might involve or whether it has any relevance to a wider sense of good judgement. Whitta-ker's thesis is that there is a logically due form of persuasion that applies to such cases, and that it is built on *an increase in appreciation* rather than on an *increase in justificatory grounds*. The power of such persuasion does not come from dressing up weak arguments rhetorically; it comes from the possibility (as Gaita noted in his remarks on moral situations) of displaying a depth in one or another *religious* reaction to life. One appreciates this kind of depth when one sees what it would mean to affirm a religious idea – namely, when one sees that accepting the belief *entails* a transformation, so that believing and *abiding in one's beliefs* come to the same thing. The more one under-stands this in relation to particular beliefs, the more one appreciates the *meaning* – the *point* or the *power* – of such beliefs as transformative ideas. Though this does nothing to furnish evidential or inferential grounds for belief, it none the less might enhance the credibility of such beliefs by linking them to the interest that one might have in amending, and so deepening, his or her life.

M. Jamie Ferreira, in 'An Inheritance Reconsidered', also follows Phillips's work quite closely, although her purpose is not to extend the implications of Phillips's work (as the purpose of the previous essay was) but to compare his thinking to the legacy of David Hume. Phillips, she says, wrongly distances his views from those of Hume, particularly as these are expressed in the *Dialogues Concerning Natural Religion*. But closer attention to the *Natural History of Religion* reveals a side of Hume that Ferreira says could have come from Phillips himself. For there Hume's central concern is not the speculative argument that moves from the nature of the world to its cause; there his primary concern is to present the belief in God as a means of coping with life. Whether or not such religious coping strategies can be

xvi   *John H. Whittaker*

rationalized after the fact, they arise *prior* to the effort to arrive at the existence of God as the product of inference. Here Hume does not distort or reduce the character of religion by forcing it into the mould of a speculative enterprise; he is a spokesman for an *alternative* conception of the very sort that Phillips suggests. As for religious beliefs that are superstitions, there is a moral dimension in Hume's recognition of their character; and here too there is a similar, though implicit, aspect in Phillips's treatment of the same subject.

The remaining essays in this part address problems independently of their connection to Phillips's work, and yet there is an obvious resemblance between the approaches that they take and the aim of grammatical studies. Ben Tilghman, in 'Free Will Defences and Foundationalism', takes issue with traditional 'solutions' to the problem of evil in a way that is very much in keeping with the spirit of Phillips's own remarks on the subject. Challenging the adequacy of traditional treatments of the problem of evil, Tilghman doubts the common assumption that a solution must be found which explains how it is possible for God to be maximally perfect and yet at the same time be the direct or indirect author of evil. In many versions of the popular free will defence, we are asked to imagine different possible worlds, some in which people are not free and others in which they are. In the latter category, we are to imagine that the potentially harmful consequences of our freedom are miraculously corrected before these harms result. Presumably it is possible to imagine such things, but is the contrast between our world and this one really intelligible? Supposedly we can form conceptions of all these worlds and see that this world is superior to the others – and hence that the creator of this world is as good as can be. But Tilghman asks what sense we can make of comparing these worlds. His point is not to deny that religiously meaningful responses to suffering are possible; it is only to deny that the meaningfulness of these responses can be brought out theoretically. What really matters – and here his remarks resemble Phillips's – is not an intellectual solution to the problem but an ungrounded resilience to despair in the face of evils that cannot be understood.

Then, in an impressive commentary on Lessing and the so-called Wolfenbuttel controversy, the late Peter Winch turns his attention to an even darker and more theological issue: the claim that Jesus rose from the dead. His overall purpose is to distinguish this claim from *other* claims about the past that are subject to the usual canons of historical judgement. The resurrection claim, he says, *is* a claim about something that happened in the past. That is not in dispute. But this claim is bound up with religious import in a way that insulates its truth or falsity from determination on historical grounds. For in this case, certain questions (queries about further evidence, the reliability of witnesses, etc.) that would otherwise be asked are *not to be raised*. They are logically impermissible because of the religious significance of the claim at issue. Judging the resurrection appropriately requires one to refocus this issue, so that the proper significance of the claim might come into view. The point here is a fine one, and believers who illustrate it walk, as it were, on a tightrope. Winch follows them out on the same tightrope philosophically, and the resulting essay takes the discussion of the resurrection well beyond the level on which it is typically seen, both in philosophy and in religious studies.

In 'Is it the Same God?', Rowan Williams aims his comments at another theological issue that might be clarified conceptually. He is concerned with the preservation of religious traditions in the midst of inevitable change and growth, particularly with respect to the pressures exerted by feminist theology. He starts with the very Wittgensteinian point that the meaning of Christian claims was never anchored in words themselves, as if this meaning were forever secured by a context-independent reference to things. Ultimately, the meaning of Christian concepts is tied to the life of believers, who are the caretakers of their meaning. Thus, such terms do not have meaning because they first have a reference; it is the other way around: believers afford them a meaning by affording them a normative *use* in their own lives, including a referring use. Williams's point, again, is that there is nothing unchangeable about meaning of religious concepts. If I might explain by borrowing a concept that is used in Winch's discussion of Lessing, the meaningfulness of such concepts depends, in effect, on the *regulae fidei*, the rule-like ways of living, within which religious understanding is measured. To be reminded of this does not make Williams's question of how to preserve theological continuity any easier, since it does nothing to provide an independent guide to acceptable changes in the tradition. But it is difficult to see how theology's self-understanding could be divorced from the sobering reflection that those who speak the language of faith are also those who preside over its proper understanding.

If these essays comprise a testimony to the powerful stimulus that Phillips – and Wittgenstein – have provided in the philosophy of religion, the final essays do the same for the philosophy of literature and education, in which this influence is, for the most part, yet to be felt. As a former Vice-Principal of the University College of Swansea, a former director of the Taliesin Arts Centre there, and a former college concentrator in English, it was only natural that Phillips turn his philosophical interest in these directions. In two works on literature, *Through a Darkening Glass* and *From Fantasy to Faith*, he provides example after example of the conceptual insights that fiction often reveals. For the present volume Michael Weston and Colin Lyas explore the value of these insights. Weston's essay, 'The Mediation of Sense in Literature', might have been included among the essays on ethics, since the literary lessons involved in his discussion of *Through a Darkening Glass* are ethical in nature. Yet because it is literature that Phillips uses to 'intervene' in ethical disputes, Weston's comments are included in this third part of the book to underscore the significance that both he and Phillips find in *this* expression of grammar. For those philosophers whose vision has been stunted by an exclusive preoccupation with theoretical questions, exploring the world of literature can be like getting an arm or a leg out of a cast; and though the freer movement that this opens up in the world of ethical possibilities makes it difficult to formulate theories, the net gain is unmistakable. To give an example, Weston shows that the portrayal of ethical sensibilities in Edith Wharton's novels brings out the fact that the connection between reasons and values is not – as in much ethical theorizing – that reasons provide an independent ground for ethical judgements, but that people's ethical values *are* their reasons. Against that view, the search for a universal ground that might justify ethics appears naive, a lesson that Weston credits to the mediation of (Wharton's) literature. Yet towards the end of his essay Weston explores another possibility, the fact that some literary figures – he mentions Beckett, Schlegel and Nietzsche – might *challenge* the familiar forms of grounding ethical judgements in ethical values by pressing what is ethically recognizable to its limits.

It is precisely at this point, where one examines a literary portrayal of some powerful or curiously deep feeling – even of a somewhat alien feeling – that Colin Lyas in 'That's it Exactly!' stops to reflect. Sometimes in reading a work of literature, after all, we do say, 'That's it – that's what I wanted to say'. But how can we know that these insights, awakened in us by literary forms of expression, capture a sense of things that we had all along, *prior* to reading? How is it, in other words, that one can recover in literature a sense of things that otherwise remain inchoate or obscure? Are there insights that one recognizes as one's own only when they are articulated by another? The matter hardly ends here though, since Lyas goes on to ask how one can *revise* an earlier opinion by saying, 'I once thought as if that (the literary expression of a feeling or a judgement) were *it*, but now I see that I was wrong'. What are such recognitions like? Moved to these questions in part by reading Phillips, but not finding the answers he sought, Lyas turns to Wittgenstein. The result is a defence of the capacity to be moved in such ways as an identifying characteristic of literary appreciation.

In a concluding essay, Antony Flew draws attention to the use to which conceptual clarification can be put in educational issues. In 'Excellence and Elites: Sincerity, Rationality and Monitoring', he endorses a crucial distinction that Phillips makes between the respect to which people are entitled as people, and the respect that they are due because of their achievements. Unlike Phillips, he doubts that there is an internal relation between these achievements and the fact that they are *hard won*. But that is a minor disagreement, and Flew is more concerned with the concept of elitism and the confusions that it has caused in school systems. In fact, his essay turns out to be a pointed critique of the political and social history of education, particularly in Britain. Some of his views are controversial, such as his contention that educational 'output' – the success of the educational system – has never been shown to depend on class size. Overall, however, his remarks have the virtue of reminding us that philosophical distinctions of the sort that Phillips would call 'grammatical' can have powerful implications in very down to earth and politically contentious areas.

The final essay by Walford Gealy, like the biographical introduction by Ieuan Lloyd, stands back from Phillips's accomplishments to place them in perspective. Gealy's purpose is to assess Phillips's place in the history of Welsh letters. Those of us who know Phillips as an English-speaking philosopher might be excused for ignoring the fact that he is, after all, a Welshman. And they might be excused again for not knowing that several of his books have appeared in Welsh. Yet all these publications, both the ones in Welsh and the ones in English, are noteworthy accomplishments, especially so when seen against the backdrop of his Welsh predecessors. The history of philosophy in Wales is neither as ancient nor as full as the history of philosophy in other countries, but neither is there much doubt about the prominent place that Phillips deserves in that story. Gealy's essay offers a remarkably detailed look at Phillips in this context and so provides a fitting conclusion to the philosopher that this collection honours.

*

Before closing this introduction, I want again to thank Dick Beardsmore for his help in getting this project started. For that, and for his friendship, I am deeply grateful.

John H. Whittaker
Lousiana State University

A Personal Tribute

Ieuan Lloyd

Dewi Phillips was born near a chapel. For that matter everyone in Wales was born near a chapel. The chapel was the centre of community life; it was the centre of the universe. In fact, relatively few people did not attend some place of worship. Dewi's chapel was Horeb in Morriston, a town with a population of 8,000, which boasted twenty-eight places of worship with all but five nonconformist. Preaching, teaching and singing were central to its traditions. In its pulpits preachers expounded their faith with scholarship, illustration and unrivalled eloquence. Some of the preachers were actors and would regularly enthral their congregations with hour-long sermons. As E.H. Young in his book *The Chapel* writes:

> They could wring the heart-strings, they could invest their sermons with drama and humor, they could fire their congregations with hope and determination.

But their sermons were not without substance. Nonconformist ministers were often educated better than the priests of the churches, for they had studied Hebrew, Greek and theology. The Sunday school, which had been responsible for making the general population literate long before the provision of state schooling, was a major part of chapel life. Everyone attended Sunday school, old and young alike. There were classes for men and classes for women. In these classes the bible would be dissected and analysed. It is no exaggeration to say that theological arguments would start here and continue at home and in the workplace.

There was, as elsewhere in Wales, a high regard for things intellectual. Access was easy to the many libraries that had been built for the express purpose of providing those who in some cases had had to leave school by the age of twelve with an opportunity to learn of a world beyond coal and steel. The holdings of those libraries were not utilitarian as one might have expected but were mainly of the humanities, where philosophy and theology were major subjects. One miners' library had the best non-university collection in Britain. More enterprising workers would compile their own small libraries. Whilst worship was central to the life of the chapel, study and discussion informed by wider reading also played an important part.

The chapel Dewi attended might be called liberal not only theologically but with respect to the arts. Other chapels frowned on it, and on others like it, for bringing 'worldly' activities within its four walls. Yet Horeb chapel would unashamedly embrace both drama and opera and regularly invited artists of national fame. E.E. Kellet writes of the chapel he attended:

> It took, by itself, the place now hardly filled by theatre, concert-hall, cinema, ballroom, and circulating library put together. Here were all things required for social intercourse; recitals, songs, lectures with or without the lantern, authorized games and talk. It was a liberal education. Politics were freely discussed, books criticized and lent, music other than sacred appraised. It was, in fact, the nearest approach I can think to the agora of Athens, where Socrates posed his questions and the Acharinian charcoalburners compared the chaos of war and peace. It may have been a small and narrow society but it was one which pulsed with life.

Chapel was both enjoyable and instructive.

Morriston was built in the eighteenth century on the edge of Swansea in south Wales. It was a product of the industrial revolution, its street grid system manifesting its sudden birth. Most of the male population were employed directly or indirectly in the various heavy industrial works that blighted the landscape. Noise, sweat and shift work were part of the daily task. Mr Phillips senior, a gentle but strong and thoughtful man, worked all his life in the tin plate works. Money was hard earned and the employers were hard taskmasters. Religion made the hardship of one's living tolerable, even for one able to rise above it. This was the close community that Dewi was born into, a community where physical work was demanding but which was enriched by its vibrant religious life. His immediate family offered an emotionally secure home, his parents giving him every encouragement. His two older brothers had left home, one to become a clergyman and the other to serve in the Second World War. It is a long way in both time and space from Morriston to Claremont, California, where Dewi now holds the Danforth Chair in Philosophy of Religion. But he would be the first to recognize the debt he owes to his formative years in his Welsh environment.

An illustration of the effect that this climate had on the growing son of a tinplate worker was when I and others called at his home on a Sunday evening. We usually had to wait until a second service at Dewi's home had finished. This was the service he took at the age of eight, standing on a wheelback chair whilst his aunts and uncles were the congregation listening to him deliver the sermon that had been delivered earlier that evening by the resident minister. He usually remembered it verbatim (he has an eidetic memory). Apparently, his own delivery was often an improvement. It might be said of him that in the beginning was the word.

Writing, too, came naturally to him. In those early years he would write stories in Dickensian parts. Before the photostat machine had been invented, he would write multiple copies, which we, his friends, then slid under the doors of our neighbours. Regrettably, none of the issues survives.

Among his peers he was seen as an organizer as well as a player. He still enjoys playing tennis with the same healthy competitive spirit. On the street or at his home, when it was raining, games were instantly invented when the equipment of common games would not be available. He brought colour into those times, as he does now. What would otherwise have been dull and grey was transformed by the potential he seemed to find in any situation.

His interests at Swansea Grammar School, founded in 1635 by Bishop Gore, were, as might be expected, mainly in the Arts rather than the Sciences: nor does he have much interest in practical things, though is full of admiration for those who do. And as for modern technology – he has written every word he has ever published with a fountain pen. Some of us deceive ourselves into thinking that sophisticated equipment will make us write more. But I am reminded of Wittgenstein's remark: 'When I hear that someone has bought some new boots for climbing, I wait to see what he does with them.' Dewi continued writing throughout his time at school and published some of his pieces in the school magazine, to which Dylan Thomas had contributed a few years earlier. English was his first love, and the subject he chose to study for his degree at the University College of Swansea. Students at Welsh colleges were compelled to study four subjects in their first year. This was often to the advantage of philosophy in that students were prepared to try their hand at this subject, but could fall back on any of the other subjects should they find no interest in it. In Dewi's case, it was the reverse. He chose philosophy as a second subject but found that he could not give it up. So he first obtained a degree in English and then a year later obtained his first class honours in philosophy. In those heady days, the department consisted of Professor J.R. Jones, R.F. Holland, Peter Winch and Rush Rhees, who was to have an enormous influence on Dewi, as he had on staff and students alike. Then student ratios meant little. There were five staff and only five students taking the unique four-year philosophy course. He was bitten. He stayed on to study for an MA, and his subject was 'Moral and Religious Conceptions of Duty'. It combined his interest in religion and philosophy, an interest which remains with him and with which his name is most commonly associated, though his interests are far wider than that, as his publications manifestly show.

The Philosophical Society at Swansea deserves a mention. Attendance at its weekly meetings was regarded as so important that to miss 'phil.soc' was a greater sin than to miss lectures. Here was philosophy at work and discussion at its best (shades of the Sunday school at Horeb). Eminent people would read papers which were coolly but fiercely discussed. It had the reputation of being a lions' den. Rush Rhees was formidable on these occasions, but exceedingly sympathetic to any contributions that a student might make.

Dewi then moved to Oxford to study for the BPhil. Disillusioned with the kind of philosophy he met there, he changed to the BLitt. and wrote on the 'Language of Talking to God', which was later published as the *Concept of Prayer*. Gilbert Ryle read his MA, accepting a chapter for publication in *Mind*. As a result, he suggested that Dewi should study for a DPhil. rather than a BLitt., but Rhees, not untypically, and perhaps unwisely, discouraged Dewi on the grounds that he did not need it. His supervisor at Oxford was Michael Foster, a deep but tormented man who, sadly, later that year took his own life. Ian Ramsey (later Bishop of Durham), a more outgoing and ebullient character, took his place.

While at Oxford, Dewi took up his original intention of becoming a full-time minister. He had been lay preaching to large congregations since he was in his teens. Though he had not studied theology, the Congregational Church allowed for this by adopting ministers on a probationary basis. So in 1958 Dewi became minister at Fabian's Bay Congregational Chapel, Swansea, which was adjacent to the docks where he and Monica, now his wife, were received warmly. Styles of ministry differ. He was welcomed by one lady who said that some ministers sent their congregations to hell and others were constantly hugging and kissing them. She expressed the hope that he would be somewhere in between. She was not disappointed. Professor J.R. Jones, the head of department at Swansea, preached at his induction service. Their time there was greatly appreciated. Dewi gave great authority to the pulpit and Monica found expression for her natural and patient understanding of people. He had been impressed with the liturgical movement at Mansfield College, Oxford. On alternate Sundays he attended Pusey House. As a result, he felt that the communion service in nonconformist worship had too insignificant a place. Surprisingly, the congregation welcomed the change.

Although he found something satisfying in the preaching and the pastoral work, underneath there was part of him that was not being fulfilled. There was no opportunity to pursue some of the philosophical questions which still interested him. He had by this time completed his BLitt. In 1961 he applied for a post at Queen's College, Dundee, then part of the University of St Andrews, and was surprised to be offered it. He spent two very happy years there, but the pull of Wales was strong. He took up a post in the University College of North Wales, Bangor, in 1963 and a short while later completed his return to Wales by being appointed to a post in Swansea in 1965. Vacancies had occurred because Roy Holland had moved to Leeds and Peter Winch to Birkbeck College, London. His dream had come true. For him Swansea was not just his natural home but his philosophical home. It also gave him the space to develop. But there has been a price to pay for this. The attitude of the Welsh towards those of their own who have 'got on' is mixed. In the presence of those other than their own, the Welsh will often exaggerate a person's achievements; but to those who live amongst them, they seem more reluctant than most to honour their own prophets. Internationally, especially in the philosophy of religion, Dewi has had considerable acclaim, as his recent honorary doctorate from Åbo Akademi, Finland, indicates. The significance of his contributions to philosophical literature in the Welsh language is amply shown by Walford Gealy in this book's final chapter.

There was a rapid promotion for him in Swansea, as he became a Senior Lecturer in 1967. J.R. Jones had become seriously ill and Dewi became acting head. Soon after, in 1971, he was appointed to the chair. It was to be a baptism by fire. The troublesome period of the 1960s in universities was still alive and well in certain pockets, and Swansea was one. During that period Dewi continued to maintain the reputation of the department such that in the first two government Research Assessment Exercises it was given high praise. When the mindless decision to close two Welsh philosophy departments by their respective colleges was taken, it was partly softened by Dewi taking on two members from Bangor and one from Aberystwyth. The department was designated a centre for excellence in Wales. In 1990 a Centre for Philosophy and Health Care joined the department. This was not met with approval by a minority of members of the department. The next five years were to be the most unpleasant in its history. There were tensions within the department which led to unwelcome publicity. Philosophers elsewhere were only too ready to take sides without taking the trouble to find out the facts, some later regretting their precipitative judgements. The whole story has not been told and this is not the place to tell it. Suffice it to say that it is nothing short of a miracle that, largely through Dewi's efforts, the department has survived, albeit sorely bruised. Without these events it would have continued to be amongst the largest and strongest in the country.

Even throughout these debilitating times, which took a physical toll on people, Dewi continued to write. It was in many ways a healthy distraction from the worries of the department. In 1992 he accepted the Danforth Chair in Philosophy of Religion at Claremont Graduate School in Claremont, California, previously occupied by John Hick. Dick Beardsmore, for whom Dewi had considerable respect, took his place in the department and continued until his sad and untimely death in 1997. Dewi took early retirement from Swansea in 1996, relinquishing his chair, but was appointed Rush Rhees Research Professor for five years in the same year – a part-time post.

Dewi had had a wider involvement with the college at Swansea. He had been a Vice-Principal and had enjoyed the politics of it all. My guess is that if his interest in philosophy were not so strong, a part of his nature would have been attracted to the challenge of being in charge of another institution. He shares with Thales of Miletus not only an ability in philosophy but also, as was evident in those early years, a commercial enterprising spirit. For example, the Taliesin Arts Centre at the college, consisting of a bookshop, art gallery and theatre, was built largely under his enthusiastic leadership. He, with Monica, regularly scoured Wales to display and sell the works of art in the Ceri Richards Gallery, where he was responsible for the exhibitions. In many instances he did the selling himself, moving easily from lecturing on the rhetoric of Gorgias to charming customers into buying paintings and sculptures, for which the impecunious artists were eternally grateful.

Of many philosophers it could be said that they enjoy teaching, discussing or writing. Dewi is rare in enjoying all three, an enjoyment that remains undiminished over the years. When teaching larger audiences, he has a presence and an eloquence which he has retained from early years in the pulpit. His consuming interest in philosophy is conveyed through a style which is deceptively uncomplicated and which uses illustrations liberally. It makes him a formidable lecturer. In discussion he has the enviable ability to get to the heart of the issues, and usually leaves students, be they full-time, extramural or postgraduate, with a fresh interest in the problems. Time and again I have witnessed, especially at international conferences, his ability to extract the main issues from papers of varying traditions and persuasions. When he has arranged conferences himself, he manages to persuade people of quite different philosophical temperaments and convictions to talk with one another. It is one of his qualities that he likes people no matter what their differences, and he creates an atmosphere for discussion that is without rancour or malice. He himself, though pressing and direct in argument, is always without animosity. For him the problem is the most important thing. This is evident in the generosity he shows when anyone consults him. His capacity for writing is legendary. He can go for days writing almost continuously with a minimum of sleep. His concentration and involvement in what he is doing, together with an unfathomable source of energy, had made him produce, individually, over the years what some departments cannot boast collectively. To date he has written sixteen books, fifty-eight contributions to books, and over a hundred journal articles.

Rush Rhees's influence on Swansea staff and students was considerable. In his latter years, Rhees returned to Swansea from Cambridge, and though they had been in contact over the intervening years by correspondence, Dewi was pleased that he had opportunity to discuss philosophy with Rhees again. Rhees died in Swansea in 1988. There was no question where his papers should go. Dewi secured the purchase of some 16,000 pages of Rhees's manuscripts. Rhees had written a great deal but published little. Each lecture was prepared no matter how many times he had given it before. Dewi sees it as one of the most fortunate events that he has had the opportunity of editing Rhees's works. He has found the whole business exciting if humbling. After reading some of Rhees's notes recently, he said to me 'How can you write after reading something like that?' To date he has edited seven books of Rhees's papers, four volumes of which have been published.

More recently, Peter Winch, his one-time teacher and close friend, died; and Dewi has again arranged that his papers be held in Swansea and has taken on the onerous task of ensuring that his work is also published.

What of Dewi's religious beliefs now? He is no longer a member of a church. His views have changed and widened and the intellectual change has not found him a home. He does not regard himself as an unbeliever, for he believes the circle of believers is wider than the circle of worshippers. What he means by this is that those for whom God plays a part in their lives are not confined to those who form part of a church. In his own case, for example, he would not claim his interest in philosophy is just academic, even though he would defend the view that philosophy should not be a form of advocacy. He believes one should show how religion and its various conceptions are important in people's lives. He does not see his life as divided by the professional and the personal in any clear way. In this sense, his views on the philosophy of religion are markedly different from many of his academic colleagues in philosophy of religion. He sees them as being too concerned with reasoning and not enough with imagination. He believes that philosophy of religion and theology have distorted what the believer believes. I remember one occasion in Rome when the nature and place of theodicies were being discussed. Someone was defending the view that the quantity of evil was less than the good that it produced. Dorothy Solle (whose parents had suffered in a concentration camp) found this objectionable for the same reason that Dewi showed in his paper. Both found this rationalist position deeply offensive, and neither thought that belief was in any way dependent on it. On the other hand, many think that he misrepresents what the believer is saying. Yet it is not uncommon that many a non-academic believer finds that Dewi's writings have a deepening effect on their understanding.

Throughout, his concern has been one of trying to clarify what kind of belief *religious* belief is: what is meant by truth in religion and how religious ideas have enlightened human life. Liberalism and idealism had influenced faith among the Welsh, and although some have seen this as an unfortunate period in Welsh history, it has had its benefits, opening the minds of people to problems that otherwise would have been ignored. What Dewi came to see is the need to see why those questions were asked.

I have concentrated largely on Dewi's academic life. It would be a mistake to give the impression that he does not have wider interests. Indeed, anyone who reads his writings could infer that from the variety of examples he uses. His interest in the visual arts has already been mentioned and his home is replete with items bought over the years. Films and music are part of his recreational life. Outside of the arts his taste is catholic. He always has been interested in sport. He has supported since 1968 Swansea City Soccer Club for whom success has not always been something of which they could boast. He still plays tennis regularly. He has been involved over the years with trying to ensure that conditions for the survival of the Welsh language obtain. He has fought for Welsh-speaking schools in the locality. Indeed, his children and grandchildren speak Welsh as their first language. This is of course a deeper interest than the others I have just mentioned. Then, like Kant, he is an excellent host, ensuring, not fortunately with the same precision as Kant, that his guests enjoy themselves. But the reason for concentrating on the influences, domestic and academic, which have helped to shape Dewi's life, is that he is one of a rapidly contracting number of people of whom one wants to say that philosophy is his life. His relationship with the subject is not just professional, however laudable that adjective may be, because that would imply that he can put the subject down at will. The idea of a vocation is now not in currency, and this says something about our times. But no other expression captures the relationship between himself and the subject. The relationship has no duties or rights; rather, he gives himself to the subject unstintingly and there is not retirement from it. This he shares with his teacher Rush Rhees.

University of Wales

Part I
Ethics

1
Intervening in Ethics[1]

Raimond Gaita

The power of the essays in D.Z. Phillips's *Interventions in Ethics* comes partly from the sustained polemic which is inspired and guided by Wittgenstein's admonition to philosophers, 'I'll teach you differences'. If it came only from that, then the reader might be overwhelmed by a predominantly negative tone. However, Phillips's vigorous criticism is informed by things positive – two in particular. First, his concern is not merely to remind philosophers of variety in order to diminish their 'craving for generality'. His reminders are efforts to keep alive possibilities that might disappear. They are, quite literally, exercises of justice. Second, much of his writing is marked by a particular sense of absolute value. It is clear that Phillips is not merely presenting it as though it were something whose grammar he was appreciative of at a distance. Both these dimensions of Phillips's work contribute to its impressiveness, but they are, I think, in some tension with his conception of the nature of philosophy.

He says that the essays were written in the spirit of 'interventions' in ethics, and he says that 'it is extremely difficult to be content with philosophical interventions in ethics' (p. xv). He means that philosophers are almost irresistibly tempted to construct theories, or to seek to underwrite an ethical perspective by appeals to human nature or to metaphysics. And even if one is not vulnerable to those temptations, the 'craving for generality' may show itself in other ways. Phillips argues that Peter Winch fails in his essay 'Who is My Neighbour?' to bring out what is distinctive in the response of the Good Samaritan, because he wrongly emphasizes one kind of 'attitude to a soul' at the expense of others. And he says that in her efforts to reveal the importance to moral philosophy of the concept of a human being, Cora Diamond forgets that 'there is little less ragged than the heterogeneity of the human' (p. xiv).

Phillips's 'interventions' cover a large range of topics. Some of the essays deserve to be called classics because of the place they occupy in past debates. I have in mind, for example, 'On Morality's Having a Point' (written with H.O. Mounce), 'Does it Pay to be Good?' and 'In Search of the Moral "Must":

Mrs. Foot's Fugitive Thought'. But other, more recent essays are equally impressive. 'The Presumption of Theory' is a devastating reply to Onora O'Neil's attack on 'Wittgensteinian Ethics' and the prominence in it of literary examples. 'What Can We Expect from Ethics?' carries some of the same polemic to the more subtle arguments of Bernard Williams in his *Ethics and the Limits of Philosophy*. And Williams (together with Thomas Nagel) comes under wounding fire in 'How Lucky Can You Get?'. In most of these essays Phillips displays an exhilarating energy – indeed joy – in his 'interventions'. The range and depth of his learning are unobtrusively evident in most of them. His tone ranges from the satirical (even the mischievous) to the grave, and *his* prose – always clear – ranges from coolly analytical to the lyrical and rhetorical. Even if we were to put to one side Phillips's huge philosophical output, this collection alone should convince any fair-minded reader that he is a major figure in analytical moral philosophy. It is a source of shame to British moral philosophy that, because of hostility to Wittgenstein and more particularly to his pupil Rush Rhees and to philosophers inspired by him, Phillips has often been denied that fair-minded reading.

Phillips's interventions are most interesting when they are against philosophers with whom he is generally in deep sympathy. In this collection the essays like that are 'My Neighbour and My Neighbours', in which he criticizes Peter Winch, and 'Philosophy and the Heterogeneity of the Human', in which he criticizes Cora Diamond. I will concentrate my discussion on these essays, for they raise interesting difficulties for Phillips's understanding of philosophy as conceptual analysis.

In his essay 'Who is My Neighbour?' Peter Winch develops points he made in a previous essay, 'Eine Einstellung zur Seele', in order to shed philosophical light on certain aspects of the parable of the Good Samaritan. Winch says that in seeing the man in the ditch as his neighbour, the Samaritan saw him as a 'fellow human being', and that we may see more clearly what *that* amounts to if we reflect on what Wittgenstein meant when he said 'My attitude towards him is an attitude towards a soul. I am not of the opinion that he has a soul.'[2] Phillips believes that Winch is, for the most part, mistaken. He summarizes his objection like this: 'I do not believe that our lack of doubt that we live in a human neighbourhood, does throw much light on the Samaritan's response to a neighbour on the road from Jerusalem to Jericho' (p. xiii).

Phillips acknowledges the interdependence between certain uses of the concept 'human being' and the concepts with which we characterize the responses which are 'an attitude to a soul'. But, for two reasons, he is sceptical about the relevance of that acknowledgement to ethics. First, he believes that the relevance to ethics of that interdependence is severely limited by the fact that its character is determined by the role it plays in Wittgenstein's response to scepticism of 'other minds'. Second, he repeatedly says that an attitude to a soul is not one substantive response. He becomes particularly suspicious when priority is given to sympathetic responses such as pity. He believes that this is likely to lead to – or that it may be the expression of – a morally driven 'homogeneous conception of human life'. He does, of course, acknowledge that we commonly use the expression 'human being' in ways that accord priority to sympathetic responses. But he says that these are moral uses which should not be confused with the constitutive role the variety of attitudes to a soul play in the formation of the concept of a human being that emerges from Wittgenstein's preoccupations in the *Investigations*.

Presumably it cannot be known *a priori* that certain responses are not more basic than others in the constitution of particular conceptions of human being. Phillips emphasizes the need for philosophy to acknowledge diversity: 'The philosopher, if he wants to give a perspicuous representation of human life, in reflecting on what human life is like, will have to take account of this diversity. His task will be to teach us differences' (p. 271). But it is not sufficient to note the diversity: philosophers must reflect on what to make of the differences they mark. Phillips, of course, does not deny this, but he rather overstates things when he says: '*There is no way of showing* that the sympathetic relations are the paradigmatic form of "recognising a human being"' (p. 255; emphasis added). I suspect that reflection would lead him to acknowledge that he had not shown that.

In 'Eine Einstellung zur Seele' and also in 'Who is my Neighbour?'[3] Peter Winch gives a number of examples of sympathetic responses to suffering which, he says, partly build up our concept of pain and other forms of suffering. Other responses also play their part. Phillips agrees that it is natural for us to move towards those whom we see to be suffering in order to offer what help we can, but he observes that it is also natural to turn away. He takes the latter response to express an attitude contrary to pity. However, if we take it, as the context of his remarks invites us to, as the response of someone who finds unbearable the suffering he or she is witness to, then it seems to be a response similar in kind to pity. We would not admonish such a person for their lack of sympathy. We would not say anything like: 'Don't you see what it means to suffer in that way'.

There are, to be sure, other ways of walking away. Some express indifference as in the case of the priest and the Levite. Perhaps Phillips would say that such responses are also natural, and that considered merely as an attitude to a soul, they are on a par with pity. However, it seems not to be so, for we feel the need to explain such behaviour. Simone Weil says somewhere in her notebooks that if a person in a desert comes across someone dying of thirst, then he will share his water with him if he has enough in his canteen. She says that such behaviour is 'automatic'. Certainly it requires no explanation, but we do require an explanation if, having enough water in his canteen, he simply walked past, ignoring the other person's pleas. In such cases the need for explanation appears to arise for reasons which are more basic than would be implied by the claim that it emerges from a moral perspective.

Phillips is right to point out that there are important differences between the use to which Wittgenstein puts his observation about an attitude to a soul and the ways we speak in ethical contexts of human beings. However, I think the differences are not quite as he sees them. If he is wrong about this, then it is partly because his polemical interest in their differences distracts his attention from their connections. Winch says in an essay that follows 'Who is my Neighbour?':

> [W]hat is required is an account of our knowledge and understanding of other human beings which will itself make it possible to see how such knowledge and understanding can of itself impose moral bounds on our will. An account that would achieve this, one which makes recognition of such moral bounds on the will a criterion for the knowledge and understanding of the human beings, that is in question.[4]

He thinks that what Wittgenstein says about an attitude towards a soul, and the perspective it offers on other themes in the *Investigations*, will help us towards achieving such an account. Phillips shows little interest in these epistemic concerns. His focus is on the constitutive role such attitudes play in the formation of our concepts.

That is understandable. Indeed, it may seem strange at first that Winch should seek help in understanding certain epistemic concepts from a passage in the *Investigations*, whose radical import is to deny traditional assumptions about their relevance. Wittgenstein's lesson is that we do not conjecture, believe or know that there are other human beings. It is even misleading to say that we are certain that there are other human beings, or as Phillips says, that it is *obvious* that there are (p. 238). We have no idea of what it would be seriously to doubt whether there are other human beings, and the illusion that we do arises from a failure to understand the nature of our psychological concepts and what it is to come to possess and to master them. That failure leads us to mistake the nature of the various forms of our experience and the forms of our intersubjectivity – it leads us to think of them as conditional upon our possession of a special epistemic capacity which enables us to know, with unshakeable certainty, that there are other human beings.

Thus, although the problem of other minds and of scepticism makes sense only within the history of philosophy, both its traditional statement and its 'solutions' (or the despair at achieving one) rest upon a characterization of the difference between philosophy and life which functions to the detriment of both. The tendency to treat scepticism of other minds as purely (merely) philosophical scepticism has distracted attention from its dependence on a conception of experience and practice that was tailor made for it.

From some perspectives, these (apparently) radical forms of scepticism represent the glory of philosophy. I think there is no doubt that they take us to some of its deepest problems. None the less, from another perspective, they represent and depend upon distortions of experience and thought which, for reasons that are systemic and deep, and which Wittgenstein exposed better than anyone, philosophy was ill equipped to understand. The repercussions go well beyond scepticism – to our understanding of the nature of radical and critical thinking and (together with that) to an edifying idealization of reason which partly informs our sense of the worth and importance of the life of the mind. That makes scepticism of other minds and of the external world part of the subject matter of ethics as much as of logic, epistemology and the philosophy of mind. I have remarked on this at some length because it is an example of something like what Diamond calls disassociation. She says: 'someone's philosophical view may be subject to the criticism that it rests on a failure in the relation between his experience and his thought, of a kind which, on his philosophical view there is no intelligible room for. Philosophical views which make certain forms of disassociation invisible, may themselves be described by others as cases of disassociation' (quoted by Phillips, p. 257). Phillips is critical of the use she makes of the notion of disassociation, but I think she is, on the whole, right. I have tried to bring out the way that thought can connect the characteristic concerns of ethics with some of the preoccupations of the *Investigations*.

Phillips is right to say that there is no one substantive attitude which is the attitude to a soul. It is also true that the most important purpose of Wittgenstein's remarks about an attitude to a soul is to wean us from the illusion that we cannot seriously be sceptical that there are other human beings, because we *know* that they exist or because it is *obvious* that they exist. None the less, his remarks also have important epistemic implications. I think that Phillips neglects their importance for Winch's discussion. I do not (cannot) know that you are a human being, but I can know that you are in pain. But we distort our sense of what such knowledge amounts to if, as is traditional in philosophy, we look to propositional knowledge for its prototype. This is why Winch gives prominence to Wittgenstein's quite extraordinarily radical remark that pity 'is a form of conviction that someone else is in pain'.[5] Immediately before, in the same passage, Wittgenstein says '[I]f someone has a pain in his hand, then the hand does not say so (unless it writes it) and one does not comfort the hand, but the sufferer: one looks into his face. How am I filled with pity for *this man?* How does it come out what the object of my pity is?' 'When we notice the reliance on the human form – on its characteristic inflexions and expressions – of the attitudes we call attitudes to a soul, then we will see how the concept of a human being will figure essentially in the answer to the question "How does it come about what the object of my pity is?"' However, as Phillips emphasizes, it is essential to the concept of a human being as it functions in such contexts that it does not select between human beings. Even so, not all selective uses are (as he seems to believe) essentially moral.

We may see this if we reflect on another of the examples that Phillips discusses. Winch writes:

> Suppose you and I are present when a man is being given some terrible news – the death of someone he loves, perhaps. I say 'Poor man! How he will suffer' and you ask, 'What makes you think he will suffer?' That would be a strange question and I would naturally assume at first that he had not grasped the situation, did not realise what was going on, what he was being told, etc.[6]

It would be equally strange to ask whether the man in Winch's examples is the kind of being who could reflect on his suffering, such that the reflection and the suffering could go deep. That seems obvious. The reason I remark on it emerges if we notice what we assume when we take for granted that he is capable of such reflection, or when we take for granted that even if he is too shallow to reflect in any serious way on his sufferings, he might change and deepen. Indeed, the thought that he might be shallow makes sense only if we assume that he can appropriately be called upon to rise to something different, however unlikely it might actually be that he will. And often, if they are from a culture so different from ours that their responses bewilder us, then, even so, we can imagine that it could have been different, that they could have grown in our culture and been intelligible to us. Or rather, our being able to imagine that marks one kind of case whose importance I shall presently discuss. All this is taken for granted, and that fact determines one kind of answer to 'How does it come out what the object of my pity is?' – and here, as in the examples discussed by Wittgenstein, the concept of a human being is essential to the characterization of the object. The objects are different, however, and the reason has to do with the way the concept of a human being in this second case is selective between human beings.

I said that if we are radically bewildered by the behaviour of people from another culture in ways that have essentially to do with the fact that they are from an alien culture, then we can imagine them as having been brought up in our culture. I said that marks one kind of case. This is not an empirical point. It is, rather, a point about what underlies the kind of common understanding that is presupposed when we respond, as Winch (rightly) expects, to his example. It marks the common understanding within which we can take those responses for granted. A racist slave owner (to take an example raised by Winch and discussed by Phillips) does not think that his black slave could, contingently, have been born as a white person, and this is not because he has theories about genetics and their relation to identity. Most accounts of racism assume that if a racist were sincerely (if self-deceivingly) mistaken about what, for example, are the objective characteristics of Blacks or Asians, and if that error is connected with how (physically) they appear to him, then their appearances constitute only a psychological obstacle to his objective appreciation of how things really are. However, it would seem a mistake to think that Negro faces, as they were caricatured in the *Black and White Minstrel Show*, were caricatures which revealed how many white Americans saw Negro faces. Those faces, as reflected in their caricatures, did not appear to white racists as only accidentally incapable of expressions of depth of suffering, as would the face of a white person who was terribly transfigured in an accident. The racist's thought is that is how *they* look, and the fact that they look like that is fundamental to what makes them 'them' and to what makes it inconceivable to a racist that they should be treated as 'one of us'. When thinking of the way Wittgenstein speaks of an attitude to a soul we may think that it teaches us that we cannot doubt that there are other human beings, with thoughts and feelings *essentially like ours*. We can see why that would need serious qualification.

Cavell calls this kind of racism a form of 'soul blindness'.[7] 'Soul' is the right word, as I am sure Phillips would acknowledge. It is conceptually tied – in its non-speculative, non-metaphysical sense – to suffering and to the ways it may go deep; ways which, as I have already noted, are possible because we are able to reflect upon our suffering and to take attitudes to it because of that reflection. Dostoevsky prayed that he should be worthy of his sufferings. If a slave owner could imagine his slave doing the same, then the latter's days as a slave would be numbered. Such a prayer reveals how suffering may go deep, or what is involved here in speaking of depth; and it shows, therefore, if he could attribute it to his slaves, he would be threatened by the realisation of what he has made them suffer.

We sometimes say that each person is a unique perspective on the world. When we speak of treating human beings as though they were things, when our attitude to them is not, in the sense I am now invoking, an attitude towards a soul, then the kind of individuality expressed in the thought that they are a unique perspective on the world has become invisible to us. Simone Weil said that if we see that other human beings are perspectives on the world, just as we are, then we could not treat them unjustly. That is not quite right, but she is right to connect our sense of justice with our sense that others are a unique perspective on the world, and the connection is mediated by the realization that the acknowledgement of the distinctive individuality of human beings shows itself in the distinctive way they are a limit to our will. Clearly, therefore, when we say that human beings are a unique perspective on the world, we do not merely mean that they are distinct centres of consciousness. That thought is too meagre to capture what we mean. We have in mind their capacity to make something of their experiences. More strongly, we have in mind a particular understanding of experience and its place in ethical understanding, experience as, for example, it connects with wisdom. It is importantly connected with the fact that the most ethically salient of our experiences present to us under concepts which make a distinction between the real and the sham in ways that require lucidity of us under pain of superficiality. This, together with the qualities of mind that are necessary to achieve such lucidity, is what gives content to this way of speaking of depth and shallowness.

I said earlier that there is a sense of 'soul' that is conceptually tied to suffering. The inner life, as I am suggesting we think of it, is partly constituted by the attitudes we take to certain defining facts of human life – facts such as that we are mortal, that we are vulnerable to suffering, that we may be destroyed by our passions, and so on. Winch called them 'limiting notions' and said that they 'determine the "ethical space" within which the possibilities of good and evil in human life can be exercised', and that 'these notions, along no doubt with others, give shape to what we understand by a human life'.[8] They determine our sense that we belong with others to a common kind whose character is marked by the fellowship whose character and tone we register when we speak of the human condition as a common fate. Much reflection that is, in a broad sense, ethical or spiritual, and much of our art and literature, is, as Diamond emphasizes, in response to such facts and to the ways our reflective attitudes to them enter our sense of common humanity. I call them defining facts of human life, because our responses to them define our sense of belonging to a common kind in ways that condition some of what we mean when we speak of human beings and mean more than that they belong to the species *homo sapiens*; and of what we mean when we speak of a shared humanity against whose background we understand one another. None of this is underwritten by the facts of human nature; nothing metaphysical or biological dictates that it must be so.

What is the significance of all this for Phillips's discussion? First, it is striking that expressions such as 'inner life', or 'a perspective on the world', which have uses in the discussions that preoccupy Wittgenstein in the *Investigations*, are used quite differently in the context in which I introduced them. The differences bring with them different senses of 'soul'. In the case where talk of the soul connects with talk of an inner life (as we mean it when we say that persons are unique perspectives on the world), privacy of the kind that concerned Wittgenstein in what is called 'the private language argument' is not an issue. The slave owner may say that his slaves do not have souls, but that is not a form of scepticism of other minds. Phillips is, therefore, right to mark differences. But, as Cavell and Winch argue, there is also the question of what we may learn from the similarities. Winch hoped that reflection on the way some responses are interdependent with the concepts that characterise their objects, might reveal the ways in which that interdependence underlies a distinctive concept of sensibility, in which feeling, character and response combine in a form of understanding. He hoped that it would give a better philosophical grasp of the distinctions we draw in ethical contexts between understanding and *really* understanding, or between knowing in one's head and knowing in one's heart.

The example of racially based slavery which I have used to do quite a lot of work is, I admit, an example of a special kind. Other cases of slavery are not like it. Slavery in ancient Greece was not. And the Holocaust, which is another of Phillips's examples, is different from both and different again from war crimes of the kind committed, for example, in Bosnia. I do not claim that the example of racially based slavery serves as a prototype for understanding these things, nor even for anything that might reasonably be called 'soul blindness'. But the example shows, I believe, how one may extend Wittgenstein's remarks about an attitude to a soul to examples where we naturally say that the humanity of some people is not fully acknowledged. The examples are often of people who are treated unjustly, sometimes to an horrific extent, but the way the concept 'human being' works in those examples is not essentially morally driven. The slave owner cannot find it intelligible that his slaves should share with him (and with those whom he would not dream of enslaving, however much he may hate or even despise them) a common humanity whose character is conditioned by the kinds of responses those who share in it find intelligible and take to be the defining facts of the human condition. That is why it is literally unintelligible to him that slavery should constitute the injustice we know it to be, and why it rests upon his failure fully to acknowledge his common humanity with his slaves. Winch remarks that 'treating a person justly involves treating with seriousness his own conception of himself, his own commitments and cares, his own understanding of his situation and of what the situation demands of him'.[9] That implies that to take seriously a person's conception of his or her own commitments and cares is to be able to find it intelligible that they could have rich or impoverished inner lives. Failing that, we can have, at best, only an attenuated sense of what it is seriously to wrong them.

I will try to make myself clearer by exploring a different example of how someone might be placed outside that common understanding whose character I have been trying to delineate. Aristotle marked a form of it when he said of Socrates that only someone who was determined to argue for a thesis at all costs could say that a good man could not – that is, could never be – harmed. Aristotle was, I think, saying that Socrates' insensibility (as Aristotle saw it) to the way affliction might, and at a certain extreme must, destroy a life, placed him outside the framework of a common understanding whose common-ness was, in crucial part, constituted by the sympathetic acknowledgement of our vulnerability. To be sure, that vulnerability is not brute; I mean that it is essential to the way that our responses to it condition that common understanding, and that we reflect on it and take attitudes to it because of that reflection. For example, we do not merely fear death. We reflect on that fear, on when it is appropriate and when it is not, on when it is too much and when too little, and so on. We may even conclude that in some circumstances death is no evil, not because we welcome it to relieve our sufferings, but because, for example, we may believe that to die for the sake of justice is no evil. And there are other possibilities. Phillips makes such points, sometimes with devastating effect, against opponents such as Phillipa Foot. Aristotle was aware of their force; indeed he relies on it in the passages in *The Nicomachean Ethics* where he discusses whether misfortune can destroy *eudaimonia*. But none of this – he would say – should lead one to suggest (as did Socrates in the *Apology*, just before he claimed that a good man cannot be harmed) that perhaps death is never an evil. To wonder, flatly, whether death is an evil is not to develop to an extreme point the thought that death need not always be an evil. It is to disengage from the context which gives the latter thought, and the ethical perspectives that inform it, their character. That context is the soil in which the critical concepts with which we appraise such thoughts are rooted.

Consider another example. In a television programme on religious thinkers, Malcolm Muggeridge stood in the remains of one of the Nazi death camps and wondered whether the Allied war effort had been worth it. His reason? He was disgusted by the porn shops and the materialism he found in (what was then) West Germany. The trouble with such remarks is not that they are banal and offensive while pretending to be profound. It is that because of their inhumanity (as we would naturally put it), they threaten to disengage from what gives sense to judgements of depth and shallowness. They are, as is the speech of Negroes to white racists, although for different reasons, outside the conceptual space in which the person who makes them can hope to teach us something, to show us real possibilities that we had not considered, or even to show us sense where we had not considered it to be possible. That is why our radical bewilderment is not bewilderment that someone could say something so obviously false, or so stupid, or so wicked. We do not treat such remarks as expressing some extreme point of a recognizable cognitive or moral failure. Rather, we seem to think that if we were to take them seriously, then that would place those who make them at such a distance from us that we would wonder whether we share a common life with them. If we say something in response, then it is generally a rhetorical manoeuvre to bring them back to common ground where we can once again find our feet with them. That is what Aristotle did. He presented no argument against Socrates. He asked rhetorical questions – not in order to show that Socrates was obviously mistaken, but as a means to reclaiming the space in which discussion would again be possible.

'Our sense of the human is held by differences and distances, as well as by similarities and proximities' (p. 255). The differences Phillips speaks of here are differences we understand and appreciate. They are differences from which we may learn because they are within the space of the kind of common understanding I have been trying to characterize. Far from being incompatible with the acknowledgement of differences, the 'sharedness of human life' that Phillips criticizes in his essay on Diamond enables those differences to speak to us, to have the power to move us, to reveal to us depth where we had not seen it before and sense where we had not thought it possible. Otherwise these different perspectives will be mute, because the humanity in them will be not fully present to us, rather as the slave's humanity is not present to his master and for similar reasons. To be alive to the differences and distances, to the similarities and proximities that make *our* sense of the human, is, quite literally, to be able to be just to them, to hear in them the distinctive voice of a unique perspective on the world.

Phillips says, 'I recognize that philosophical misunderstandings are not always misunderstandings of the logic of the language the philosophers use when not philosophizing. The misunderstandings may be a sign that the language in question means nothing to the philosophers concerned. I also recognize that prestigious philosophical accounts may help to erode moral perspectives they are blind to' (p. 260). When he contrasts 'misunderstandings of the logic of language' with a blindness to moral perspectives, he speaks as though it were relatively clear what these amounted to and how they are related. However, Diamond's denial that we are clear about this is one of the issues between her and Phillips. One of the things she is questioning is whether linguistic philosophy and its relative conceptual analysis take sufficiently seriously (in the way they draw a sharp difference between philosophical and other forms of thinking) the fact that to understand a concept is to be 'able to participate in life-with-the concept'. Do they acknowledge the limits that places on the ways philosophical thought about morality can disengage from moral thinking? She argues that philosophy conceived as conceptual analysis rests on an inadequate sense of what it is to grasp a concept, just as philosophy conceived as linguistic philosophy rests on an inadequate understanding of language. Of course, Phillips knows this. But sometimes he appears to write as though he doesn't. He sometimes writes as though it is contingent that philosophers are sometimes 'blind to the meaning' of moral perspectives, as though it is contingent that disagreement is not always the consequence of confusion in the 'logic of the language' philosophers use when they are not philosophizing.

Diamond says that there is 'an assumption in much of philosophy that philosophical thinking does not call on a responsiveness involving the whole mind'. In a later essay in her collection *The Realistic Spirit* she says, commenting on Iris Murdoch, 'Mistrust of language is a reluctance to see all that is involved in using it well, responding well to it, meeting it well, reluctance to see what kind of failure it may be to use it badly. How do our words, thoughts and descriptions let us down? How do they, used at full stretch – and in what spirit or spirits – illuminate? Moral philosophy may no longer call itself "linguistic" (it rarely called itself that anyway), but the narrowness of focus has not changed.'[10] If she is right (and I think that she is), then these remarks, when taken together, show that it is hardly contingent that moral philosophy is often characterized by a kind of meaning-blindness. Not only does it seldom exhibit the use of 'the whole mind', it explicitly thinks of the powers of mind relevant to philosophy in ways that leave out, or that mischaracterize, a large part of what makes up the 'whole mind'.

Moral thinking is an imaginative achievement. The philosophical engagement with it that would reclaim neglected perspectives, must share some of the same imaginative character. The relevant kind of imaginativeness is not a means to securing thoughts whose cognitive character can be characterized independently of it. Central to Diamond's concern with literature is her claim that philosophers will misunderstand the importance of the literary imagination to philosophy, if they think of it as a means of yielding to them a richer and more diverse cognitive harvest than they could acquire by themselves, but upon which they can then get to work with an unchanged and relatively thin conception of the forms of thought that are distinctively philosophical.

That takes me back to Diamond's remarks about 'a responsiveness involving the whole mind', about 'how... our words, thoughts and descriptions let us down', and her question 'How do they, used at full stretch – and in what spirit or spirits – illuminate?' The answers to that last question will vary according to what one is thinking about. R.F. Holland said about moral philosophy: 'A stance has to be taken, unless it goes by default, towards the difference between judgements that are of the highest significance for ethics and those that are not'.[11] Amongst the 'judgements that are of the highest significance for ethics', Holland (and Phillips) would include Socrates' claims that a good man cannot be harmed and that it is better to suffer evil than to do it. They would also include Wittgenstein's attempt, in his 'Lecture on Ethics', to give his audience a sense of what he meant by absolute value. In this connection Wittgenstein said that he had to speak personally. Clearly his response to the experiences he spoke of was, as Diamond puts it, 'with the whole mind', and that is internal to them being the kind of experiences they are. The same must be said about any adequate response to that part of Wittgenstein's lecture. Phillips has interesting things to say on Socrates and Wittgenstein, and the sense of absolute value conveyed by them informs many of his 'interventions'. Phillips has taken the stance that Holland says must be taken. It is obvious in most of what he writes. Oddly, some of his thoughts about the nature of philosophy compel him to deny it.

He says, 'What is general in ethics is struggling with conceptual puzzlement, and attempting to provide conceptual clarification and elucidation.

This concern is general insofar as it is not personal. These puzzles may occur for anyone since they arise from characteristic ways in which people speak of moral considerations' (p. xiv). That needs considerable qualification if it is to include what Wittgenstein did in his lecture. Was he doing philosophy when he spoke personally? I do not say that the answer is obvious. But even if one answers that he was not, it would be wrong to say that he merely provided material for conceptual analysis. The reason is the one I gave earlier. Any adequate engagement with Wittgenstein's remarks will require qualities of mind, imagination and character that resist any sharp division between philosophical and other forms of reflection about morality.

Australian Catholic University and King's College, London

Notes

1   This essay is substantially the same as a critical notice of D.Z. Phillips's *Intervening in Ethics* (Basingstoke: Macmillan, 1992), which appeared in *Philosophical Investigations* 17:4, October 1994. It is published here with the publisher's permission.
2   Ludwig Wittgenstein, *Philosophical Investigations*, ed. G.E.M. Anscombe and R. Rhees, trans. G.E.M. Anscombe (Oxford: Basil Blackwell, 1953), Part 2, IV.
3   Peter Winch, *Trying to Make Sense* (Oxford: Basil Blackwell, 1987).
4   Ibid., p. 173.
5   Ibid., p. 164; see *Philosophical Investigations*, Part 1, Nos. 286–7.
6   Ibid., p. 151.
7   Stanley Cavell, *The Claim of Reason* (Oxford: Clarendon Press, 1979), p. 376.
8   Peter Winch, *Ethics and Action* (London: Routledge and Kegan Paul, 1972), p. 43.
9   Winch, *Trying to Make Sense*, p. 177.
10 Cora Diamond, *The Realistic Spirit* (Cambridge, Mass.: MIT Press, 1991), p. 380.
11 R.F. Holland, *Against Empiricism* (Oxford: Basil Blackwell, 1980), p. 2.

2
On Being Neighbourly

Lars Hertzberg

Jesus' parable of the Good Samaritan as rendered in Luke 10: 25–37 is brief and laconic: a man is robbed and left lying by the wayside. A priest and then a Levite pass him by without stopping to help. Next comes a foreigner, a man from the despised neighbouring Samaria, who stops, tends to the wounds of the robbery victim and brings him to an inn, paying for his care and promising to settle any outstanding costs when passing by next. A lawyer asks Jesus, 'Who is my neighbour?' Rather than answering his question Jesus tells the parable and then returns the question to his inter-locutor, 'Which of these three, thinkest thou, was neighbour unto him that fell among the thieves?' On receiving the answer, 'He that shewed mercy on him', Jesus says, 'Go and do thou likewise.'[1]

But how are we to go about doing 'likewise'? Our response to this question depends on what we make of the differences in the three men's reactions. Peter Winch and D.Z. Phillips have given differing accounts of the differ-ences between them. Winch concludes his essay, 'Who is My Neighbour?' as follows:

> the priest and the Levite saw something different from what the Samar-itan saw when they came upon the injured man in the roadway. We might say: they did not see a neighbour in him. Perhaps it would be odd to say that they did not recognize him as a fellow human being... But in some contexts we *do* speak like this. Consider the attitudes of Europeans and white Americans to slaves in the seventeenth and eight-eenth centuries. It was sometimes said of them – indeed, they sometimes said of themselves – that they did not regard slaves as humans... My central point is that in questions concerning our understanding of each other our *moral* sensibility is indeed an aspect of our *sensibility*, of the way we see things, of what we make of the world we are living in.[2]

Winch's view, I take it, may be paraphrased as follows: no extra premise was needed to take the Samaritan from the thought, 'Unless I do something that man will suffer terribly, maybe die', to 'I have to help him.' Had he shown no inclination to help, on the other hand, we would, according to Winch, have reason to question whether what lay in front of him was a human being in need of help. As Winch says,

> it is an important fact about us that our reactions to each other are in all sorts of ways quite different from our reactions to anything else. In the present context its importance lies in its connection with *our understanding of the kinds of creature* we are having commerce with.[3]

And later,

> the practical modalities [i.e. the necessity or impossibility of acting in a certain way] to which we respond in our dealings with each other – responses which may of course be modified, blunted or intensified in particular circumstances – are akin to what Wittgenstein called 'rules of grammar': perhaps even a special case of these.[4]

Putting this point somewhat bluntly: just as, to use an example of Wittgenstein's, it is part of the grammar of the word *chair* that *this* is how you sit in a chair, it is in some sense part of the grammar of the words *human being* that *this* (i.e. coming to the rescue) is how you act when a human being is in distress. But if we argue thus, it is not clear just how close the analogy should be taken to be. As we saw, Winch admits that one's response to another human being may be blunted or modified in particular circumstances,[5] and accordingly, someone who has learnt the grammar of the word *human* may yet fail to respond in the appropriate way. That is connected with the fact that there is such a thing as being *tempted* to ignore the demands posed by the distress of another; which means that considerations of character enter in. There is hardly any analogue for this in the case of sitting in a chair.

Phillips wrote the essay 'My Neighbour and My Neighbours'[6] in criticism of Winch. According to Phillips, in giving prominence to benevolent or sympathetic responses such as coming to the rescue of someone in an emergency, clutching one's own thumb in sympathy when someone else strikes his with a hammer (or, to mention an example not considered by Winch, forbearing to strike down a conquered enemy soldier cowering at one's feet), Winch fails to do justice to the actual variety of ways in which we may characteristically respond to other human beings. As we all know, people will also respond to each other in unsympathetic and callous, even invidious, ways, as in recoiling in disgust from someone who is hurt, in being relieved that the one who is racked by gout is someone else, or in rushing in to kick someone when he's down. Accordingly, Phillips argues, it is misleading to account for the Samaritan's response by saying that he acted the way he did simply because he realized that what he had before him was a human being in distress, since the responses of the priest and the Levite might equally be thought to come under that description.

In fact, it is not easy to imagine a situation in which a person's conduct would lead us to conclude that he did not realize that those around him were human beings. This would seem to require something more bizarre than simply failing to help someone in an emergency, perhaps a situation like the following: the passer-by stops by the prostrate body, observes it carefully, then points to a plant growing five inches from the victim's head: 'Look, a foxglove! I've never seen them this far south!' (Or, for a different type of example, someone meeting a man with a dog and turning to the dog to ask for directions.) These are probably the sorts of consideration that made Phillips observe that the room for doubting whether the beings who surround us are indeed human beings is severely limited: 'We do not question the fact that we live in a human neighbourhood. We do not entertain the possibility that we are surrounded by automata.'[7]

As for Winch's admission that the sympathetic responses may be blunted or stifled, Phillips finds this way of putting the point misleading since it implies that responses like that of the Samaritan are what is to be expected in such cases, whereas failing to respond in these ways is the exception, or at least is what calls for special explanation.[8] Not only does Phillips deny that this is so, he goes further and argues that responses like that of the Samaritan, in so far as they are morally admirable, are extremely rare. He invokes Simone Weil in this connection, pointing out that, for her,

the seeds of the divine are found in those extremely rare occasions, when, out of pure generosity of spirit, a person forbears to use the power at his disposal against a victim ... For Simone Weil, supernatural virtue is the exception rather than the rule, unreflective and natural in a person though its exercise may be. That is why such naturalness is an occasion for wonder, challenge and judgement.[9]

Even aside from this last issue, Phillips is undeniably right in pointing to a tension in Winch's reading of the parable: the tension between the suggestion that what the Samaritan did was what any normal person could be counted on to do in a case like this, and the notion that there was something extraordinary about his action, as is brought out, for instance, by the way Winch speaks about 'the *purity* of the compassion which the parable depicts'.[10]

According to Phillips, the latter alternative is clearly the right one. We have to realize that something *extra* is required if we are to account for the Samaritan's response. Considering the fact that he was in enemy country, his action could, for instance, be taken to show his adherence to something like Christ's disruptive teaching, 'Love your enemies, bless them that curse you, do good to them that hate you and pray for them which despitefully use you, and persecute you.'[11]

Phillips's disagreement with Winch is in fact linked to a more general concern in his thinking about morality: his sustained criticism of the sort of wishful thinking that he has sometimes referred to, in discussion, as 'moral optimism'. I understand this to be the mistake of supposing that nature, or at least *human* nature, can somehow be counted upon to be 'on the side of' morality, and that accordingly sympathetic reactions to other human beings must be thought to be in some sense more basic, natural, immediate or frequent than reactions of the opposite kind, or that there must at least be thought to be natural limits to the degree of brutality that one human being will be prepared to inflict on another. Moral optimism, I take it, may also assume the form of supposing that the human capacity for *reasoning* has an inherent tendency to lead us to the good.

In warning against moral optimism Phillips is, of course, reminding us of something important: any belief that nature or the capacity for thought is on the side of the good is gratuitous, and a moral philosophy which blinds itself to the human possibilities of evil or of moral corruption or callousness, whether from a lack of imagination or out of a misconceived sense of what is required by loyalty to the good, will thereby fail to give a truthful account of the role of moral phenomena in our lives. Hence, it might be said, moral philosophy must be done from a horizon from which the ways of thinking of those who are good and of those who are evil can equally be seen as possibilities (though not as equal *moral* possibilities).[12] (This, of course, is not to deny that in the course of our lives, we will encounter cases in which we should fail in our loyalty to the good by failing to believe in the good. Also, we should not overlook the fact that the contemplation of the depths of human evil may have a sinister charm of its own that may tempt us to distort matters in the opposite direction.)

I have no doubt that Winch would agree with Phillips on this score.[13] However, his own purpose was different from that of Phillips. One of his main concerns throughout his work in moral philosophy, however, was the criticism of what seems to have been the received view of the role of moral thought in contemporary philosophy. On this view, moral considerations are external to the situations to which they apply. We make moral decisions by projecting norms or standards onto situations that are in themselves morally neutral, the norms or standards we employ being determined by the moral convictions we happen to hold. A consequence of this is that a person's willingness to adopt moral considerations is something that calls for explanation or justification. Against this, Winch consistently emphasized that our understanding of the situations to which we respond is itself morally conditioned. Moral excellence is exceptional but comprehensible; on the other hand, it is difficult or impossible[14] to imagine what a total absence of moral understanding would involve: there would, for instance, be a problem of describing the situations that a person totally lacking in moral understanding would be facing. This, we might say, is a point of grammar rather than a commitment to moral optimism.

Now it might be thought that, in his critique of Winch, Phillips is siding with the received view on this issue. However, I believe this to be a misleading appearance. Their concerns are simply different. Phillips is not discussing the nature of moral understanding but rather is addressing the question of what makes an action truly admirable. His point is that Winch is conflating these issues in his discussion of the Parable of the Good Samaritan.

Winch connects his own discussion with a remark made by Wittgenstein concerning the nature of our attitude towards other people's suffering. The point Wittgenstein was making was that it is misleading to think about the pity I may feel for another's suffering as somehow grounded in the *belief* or *opinion* that she has a soul (or mind) and thus is capable of suffering; rather my capacity for pity and my inclination to act accordingly are what gives content to my thought that she is suffering (this, one could say, is what might show, for instance, whether I am *sincere* in my belief that someone is suffering), and thus are part of what gives content to my thought that she is a human being. Wittgenstein sums up this point by saying: 'My attitude towards him is an attitude towards a soul. I am not of the *opinion* that he has a soul.'[15]

Wittgenstein's remark is part of a discussion of solipsism. If, for all I know, the beings surrounding me might not be human beings with feelings and sensations, but automata, it seems quite arbitrary for me to accord these beings a special significance in my dealings with the world: why should hurting or killing one of these human-like creatures be such a momentous thing if we cannot even be sure whether they can feel pain or grief or fear? It seems, accordingly, that the problem of solipsism must be solved before we can proceed in moral philosophy. What Wittgenstein's remark suggests is that this way of approaching the issue gets the problem the wrong way round: it is the importance we accord to our fellow human beings that gives content to our attributions of feeling and sensation, and not the other way round.

Both Winch and Phillips concur with this shift of perspective. The disagreement between them concerns the way in which this perspective is to be applied. Phillips emphasizes that our characteristic responses to other people range from self-sacrifice and generosity over the various trivial ways in which we attend to friends or strangers in our everyday dealings, to indifference, irritation, embarrassment, callousness or even brutality. These different ways of relating to a being are compatible with, even expressive of, the fact that we regard that being as human (or, in some of the cases, at least as a living being); they show what it means to take up 'an attitude toward a soul'. Winch, Phillips claims, is simplifying matters by singling out benevolent or noble responses like that of the Samaritan. Thereby, Phillips claims, he makes it appear as if the insight that we are confronted with a human being will guarantee a benevolent attitude (except in the case in which these ways of responding have been modified or stifled).[16]

Thus, Winch apparently gives Wittgenstein's remark about 'an attitude toward a soul' what might be called a narrow, positive reading, whereas Phillips gives it a wider, neutral reading. There is a similar ambiguity in the following remark by Simone Weil, which Winch quotes in a different context:

> The human beings around us exert just by their presence a power which belongs uniquely to themselves to stop, to diminish, or modify, each movement which our bodies design. A person who crosses our path does not turn aside our steps in the same manner as a street sign, no one stands up, or moves about, or sits down again in quite the same fashion when he is alone in a room as when he has a visitor.[17]

Elizabeth Wolgast, in an essay on primitive reactions, takes exception to Weil's remark. She goes further than Phillips: according to her there are *no* limits to the ways in which we may relate to other human beings. Thus, she also rejects the wider, neutral reading of Wittgenstein's remark. She writes that what Weil says 'seems patently false':

> A person in a family comes to behave *in certain situations* as if others are not around, and people often do this with their servants, or even other customers in places of business. Sometimes we recognize other people's presence and sometimes we do not, sometimes it is a matter of absent-mindedness . . . it is quite true that when we have a *visitor*, we behave differently, but having a visitor is an occasion . . . when the visitor eventually departs, she may leave us with those we ignore without a qualm.[18]

I believe that Wolgast's criticism of Weil contains a misunderstanding that may throw light on the disagreement between Winch and Phillips. Wolgast evidently considers the whole issue empirical. She asks herself whether there are any distinctive features that characterize our dealings with other human beings, and she concludes that she is unable to catch sight of any such features. For any situation in which she behaves in some distinct fashion in relation to others (having visitors, for instance) she can imagine other situations in which those characteristic forms of behaviour would be lacking (being alone with servants). Wolgast would hardly, though, deny observations like the following: I catch a glimpse of my wife through the doorway and from her expression I can immediately see that she is not alone; or, I sit and read alone in the room, as I believe, and then I am startled to discover that there has been someone in the room with me all the time. Nevertheless, she is surely right in claiming that we can hardly draw any general conclusions from examples such as these concerning the way the presence of others will influence a person's behaviour. The reason this is problematic is not only, as she seems to suppose, that counter-examples will be found to all generalizations we might come up with, but rather that it is not clear even what instances these generalizations are supposed to cover. If we wanted to put Weil's claim to a strictly scientific test, we should on this view organize a great number of different situations and observe the ways in which individuals behave in them. But what situations are relevant to our question? Are they situations in which someone is within a certain measurable distance, within sight, hearing or reach, or situations in which one person is actually touching another? Considered as an empirical hypothesis, Weil's description is too vague to be subjected to testing. But this should alert us to the fact that she may be trying to make an entirely different point.

That this is so should be evident from the context of Weil's remarks. In fact, the passage just quoted provides the background for a description of Achilles' treatment of Priam, the old king who has come to beg for the surrender of his son Hector's body. Achilles pushes off the old man. Weil comments: 'It was merely a question of his being as free in his attitudes and movements as if, clasping his knees, there were not a suppliant but an inert object.'[19] That is, like Wolgast she herself gives a counter-example to the above description of our ways of relating to others, in fact the 'counter-example' is what is crucial in this context: what makes Achilles' way of acting so striking is precisely its being an exception to what we normally expect: a form of behaviour that takes account, in one way or another, of the difference between a human being and a lifeless object. The point is that when Achilles pushes off Priam *as if he were* a lifeless object, the character of his action is entirely different from what it would have been if what he had pushed off had in fact *been* a lifeless object.[20]

This reading of the passage from Weil also suggests the possibility of an alternative way of reading Wittgenstein's remark about 'an attitude towards a soul'. The reading I have in mind could perhaps be spelled out as follows: the way in which what a person does or fails to do affects someone else *imposes a certain grammar* on the agent's conduct; it has consequences for the alternative actions logically available to her. However, it does not determine what she will *make* of those alternatives: she may be attentive to those touched by her actions or she may ignore them, comply with their wishes, neglect them or defy them, etc.

If the point made by Weil and Wittgenstein is understood in this way, it is borne out rather than contradicted by Wolgast's formulations: '*ignoring others without a qualm*', or '*acting as if others were not present*' are also descriptive of ways of relating to others, ways of relating whose peculiar character is dependent on the alternative ways of acting that we expect in the situation.

On the other hand, it can hardly be denied that the physical presence of others will often in practice have a palpable effect on how we act in various situations. This is why the phrase 'acting as if others were not present' will in many cases be a way of characterizing a person's conduct, while the phrase 'acting as if there were no horses (fish, turtles) present' would require a much more specific setting to convey anything at all. We might say: but for these and similar facts of human nature (and culture), the specific grammar we use in characterizing a person's conduct towards others would not have taken root.[21] But this observation does not involve a commitment to any testable claim.

Who will be deemed to be affected by someone's acting or failing to act depends on how the situation is viewed. On this score, the perspective of the agent may differ from that of a spectator (or that of someone putatively affected by the action), and they would accordingly describe the action in different terms. A spectator might think the agent is neglecting certain demands that she herself does not acknowledge or of which she is not aware. Consider, for instance, the case of an academic who greets the cleaning woman time and again because he does not realize that she is the same woman he greeted before: failing, as it were, to take in the identities of cleaning women. Our describing his conduct as showing lack of attention would be dependent precisely on the fact that he himself was blind to that perspective on his manner of acting.[22]

1

At this stage, the following objection might be raised: 'If all you are saying is that the way a person's behaviour affects other people has consequences for the ways in which that behaviour can be described, the point is trivial, indeed tautologous: after all, the fact that an action involves X has consequences for the way in which it can be described *no matter what X stands for* – whether "dollar bills", "sleight of hand", "a dull knife" or "people". And if, on the other hand, you insist that the involvement of other people differs from the other cases through the fact that *this* element will *always* be significant, why should that insistence not be considered the imposition of an ideal that anyone is free to reject if she chooses?'

Someone who argued like this would, however, be missing out on an important point. In order to see this more clearly, we have to do some sorting out. We may note, first of all, that there is a vocabulary that can be used to characterize different ways of failing to be responsive to others, a vocabulary comprising terms such as 'neglectful', 'uncompliant', 'stubborn', 'insensitive', 'tactless', 'reckless', 'brutal', 'inconsiderate', 'callous', 'thoughtless', 'indifferent', 'rude', 'impolite', etc. This vocabulary is not neutral, but is normally used to admonish others, to apportion blame or to express remorse, etc. (On the other hand, there are terms we use to criticize someone who is *too* sensitive to other people's wishes or reactions.)

In taking note of the existence of this vocabulary, one is not, of course, taking a moral stand on anything, or imposing an ideal. One may even recognize that such a vocabulary does exist and that it has a critical use, and yet for all that refuse to use one or another of these terms oneself: thus, I might never call anyone impolite and might just shrug my shoulders when others called *her* that. The word *impolite*, as it were, would simply mean nothing to me, although I might have a fairly good idea of the circumstances in which others would apply it.[23] (Some of these terms are easy to 'think away'; others less so. Could we also imagine someone turning her back *altogether* on this kind of vocabulary? It is hard to see what would be involved in imagining such a thing.)

We might say, accordingly: *language* cannot force someone to employ one of these words or to take up the corresponding attitude. (Besides, even among those who share this vocabulary there is some room for disagreement concerning its application to particular cases.) What cannot be coherently described, on the other hand, is the case of someone using these words *the way* everybody else does and yet at the same time using them *without* their force (as if she could cancel their critical force, as it were, by means of a spiritual reservation): using them as others do *is* using them with their ordinary force (except when the *circumstances of speaking* show that their force has been cancelled or reversed, as in irony). The remark 'I thought what you did was highly inconsiderate; however, that is no reflection on you' seems to require quite a peculiar setting to be intelligible.

The force with which a word is used must not be confused with the speaker's feelings in using it. We may well imagine that when the lawyer answers Jesus' question by saying that the Samaritan was neighbour to the robbery victim, he gives his answer through clenched teeth. But this does not remove the force of the answer; rather, if he clenches his teeth it is because he cannot honestly avoid giving an answer that has that force, although he does not want to do so.

Let us compare this situation, once more, with the case of the grammar of the word *chair*: although knowing what a chair is involves knowing what it is to sit in a chair, this does not mean that if I know that something is a chair I shall have to sit in it, nor does it mean that if I use it I can only use it for sitting in; what it does mean is simply that *if* I propose to sit in it, then there are limits to the position I may take up while holding on to my decision.[24] So far, the situation is analogous with that of realizing that there are limits to the ways in which I may deal with the people who surround me if I am not to be considered tactless. The cases are different, however, in the following way: the question whether a person's conduct is or is not to be called tactless (insensitive, etc.) is bound up with other ways of reacting to him in a way in which the question whether a posture can be called sitting is normally not (although it may be thus bound up in special cases, e.g. in a situation in which remaining seated would be tactless). This is part of a description of the way these words are used.

Applying this to the Parable of the Good Samaritan, it means that the reactions of the three passers-by are not symmetrically related to one another. We would describe the conduct of the priest and the Levite in critical terms, that of the Samaritan in terms of praise. Jesus assumes that the lawyer, too, will respond to the parable in this way. On the other hand we can imagine someone who does not share this perspective: someone who praises the priest and the Levite for their steadfastness and thinks the Samaritan's response is a sign of sentimentality. We are, however, free to say that such a person is blind to something. In saying so we would be agreeing with Winch that the Samaritan was the only one whose actions showed that he recognized that the man who had fallen among thieves was a human being.

2

I assume that both Winch and Phillips would agree with the points made in the previous section. How, then, are we to understand their disagreement? Phillips writes:

> Winch gives the impression that reactions, such as that of the Samaritan are, within a certain moral perspective, part of our normal expectations in our dealings with each other; expectations which leave us in no doubt about what we ought to do when confronted by a human being in distress. [He] ... gives the clear impression that fulfilled expectations and reactions, in this respect, are the rule.   (p. 250)

This passage calls for some clarification. We often speak of 'normal expectations' roughly in the sense of things we have a right to demand, and this clearly is the sense Phillips has in mind in the first sentence, since he speaks about expectations *within a moral perspective*, and says that those expectations leave us in no doubt about what we *ought to do*. I take it he is not in disagreement with Winch on this score. Rather, his disagreement seems to concern what is expressed in the second sentence, where he speaks about the extent to which those expectations are actually *fulfilled*: Winch apparently supposing that they will, as a rule, be fulfilled, while Phillips, as we have seen, claims that this is the exception.

Here it might be thought that Phillips, like Wolgast, understands the disagreement as turning on an empirical issue (although the question here is not the same). It all seems, in the end, to boil down to a matter of statistics: how do people for the most part respond in encountering fellow beings in distress? Are they more likely to reach out a hand or to turn their back? But even if we were to treat this as an issue of statistics, it is too loosely described so far for it to be meaningfully put to the test. Presumably, there will be a host of different cases: there will be cases in which almost everyone would give assistance, and cases in which rushing in would be held to be saintly or heroic to a degree defying comprehension; and all sorts of cases in between. The story told by Jesus simply does not give us enough details to enable us to decide what a normal reaction would be in a case like this – and this may well be intentional. For there is a way of reading the parable that would push all questions of comparison and statistics to one side as irrelevant.

On this reading the point of the parable does not lie in its inviting us to pass judgement on the different reactions of the passers-by. That would not be in keeping with Christ's teaching 'Judge not, that ye be not judged' (Matt. 7: 1). What should concern us, after all, is not what the priest and the Levite did at some time in the past, but what *you'll* do the next time *you* are confronted with a human being in distress – in what might be an entirely different situation. This reading would explain why Jesus never does supply the lawyer with the criteria he had requested for deciding who is his neighbour; that would, in effect, have meant telling him in what cases he could feel free to ignore fellow human beings in distress. What he is saying is rather that it is up to each one of us to be neighbour to our fellow beings. The parable simply draws our attention to the internal connection between perceiving someone as your neighbour and responding to him in a certain way.

As for living up to that recognition, it could perhaps be said that most of us are most of the time in most respects at one with the priest and the Levite, in the sense that in some respect we are constantly failing to be a neighbour to someone. Seen in that light, there may be a truth in Phillips's claim that falling short is 'normal'. However, that truth is not to be spelled out in statistical terms, but rather expresses a perspective on life: it acknowledges that we are all imperfect.

According to Phillips, some religious teaching such as Christ's exhortation that we should love our enemies appears to play an indispensable part in our understanding of the Samaritan's response. Winch, on the contrary, argues that it is our access to such responses that prepares us for an understanding of the divine commandment: 'The responses to moral modalities that we share with the Samaritan . . . are amongst the seeds from which, in some people, grow the conception of divinity and its laws.'[25] Let us consider these claims.

Phillips's view that Christ's teaching is indispensable, I take it, should be understood in two ways: Christ might be taken to have *established an external relation* between the injunction and the response, or to have *drawn attention to an internal relation* between them. To think of the relation as external is to think of it as arbitrary, in the sense in which Christ's injunction to the disciples to eat the bread and drink the wine in his memory could be said to have been arbitrary: he might as well have instituted some other by which they were to remember him. We could imagine one of the disciples forgetting how the ceremony was to be carried out, and having to be reminded of Christ's words.[26]

Now suppose the injunction to help one's enemies were arbitrary for someone in the same way. He might ask a friend: 'I remember there was something to do with one's enemies too, but I don't remember what it was: were you supposed to love them or to get back at them?' For him, then, the only authority for doing one thing rather than the other would be whatever Christ had commanded: the spirit of the command was lost on him. If we are to think about the Samaritan's response along these lines, what is impressive about it seems to vanish.

However, there is a sense of explanation in which explaining the response does *not* diminish it. We might imagine someone like the Samaritan encountering the teachings of Christ and finding that they awaken an internal response in him. In this case, his going on in this way is not dependent on his ability to retain the words of Christ: in a sense, what he is given through them is not something he could forget. Thus, a reference to his having learnt this in the past is not required to make his present actions intelligible. (However, I could understand it if someone claimed that only Christ could open someone's heart in this way. I would consider such a conviction not as a theory of human nature but as a part of her Christian faith.)

According to Phillips:

> what the parable does is to extend these reactions [more familiar acts of common decency] radically. Teaching the parable does not presuppose the possession of what it shows. It is at least possible that, on this occasion, the parable creates the possibility of a possession for the first time in the lawyer.   (p. 248)

This seems to mean that the lawyer's relation to the demand to which the Samaritan is responding could be an external one. However, this seems hard to accept: his answer to Christ's question 'Who was neighbour to that man?' is hardly to be understood as a lucky guess: he could not have given the answer he did unless he himself was able to see the Samaritan's action as a natural extension of the injunction to love one's neighbour.

It should be obvious that if the Samaritan's response is to have the kind of moral purity that both Winch and Phillips attribute to it, *he* could not have thought of it as constituting a radical extension of neighbourly love. That would have presupposed that in acting he was aware that he did more than could be expected. This means in turn that he did not need an extra premise to take him from the proposition 'This is a human being in distress' to 'I have to do something'.[27]

What appears to underlie Phillips's line of argument is an unspoken assumption that there is a determinate distinction to be made between the responses that are currently possible for someone and what would constitute an extension of those possibilities. However, our possibilities for responding are evidently characterized by a degree of openness or indeterminacy. Though in a given instance I may be insensitive to the needs of someone in distress, nevertheless I *might* have responded differently; for instance, someone else might have described the situation in terms that opened my eyes to her predicament. On the other hand, if such an extension did not lie within my current *possibilities* of responding, neither would I be capable of responding to the parable itself as a challenge.

Sometimes we admonish someone with the words, 'In your heart of hearts you know what you have to do.' If we say this, it does not mean that I take an optimistic view of his character. These words are not to be understood as some sort of hypothetical prediction of how he would react in a given range of circumstances.[28] The notion of possibility involved here is not to be understood on the analogy, say, of an object being within a person's reach. In uttering the words, 'In your heart of hearts you know what you have to do', we are not asserting a fact about him; rather, we are uttering a peculiar kind of appeal.[29]

Even though the words 'In your heart of hearts you know...' do not express a prediction, they are not meant as a figure of speech. There are people to whom one would *not* say this. Saying it to someone is an expression of respect, however rudimentary; of the conviction that the other is capable of extending her responses; the conviction that we share, as it were, a world of moral possibilities. By addressing his question to the lawyer, Jesus showed that he had not given up on him.[30]

Åbo Academi, Finland

Notes

1 It is probably not beside the point that the man who was testing Jesus with his questions was a lawyer, i.e., someone who himself held a position in the religious hierarchy. It may also be of some importance to note that the word *neighbour* in the parable corresponds to an Old Testament word meaning *kinsman*. So in effect Jesus is getting the lawyer to admit that only the Samaritan proved himself a true kinsman to the robbed Jew. I am indebted to my colleague, Karl-Gustav Sandelin, for pointing this out to me.

2 Peter Winch, *Trying to Make Sense* (Oxford: Basil Blackwell, 1987), p. 166. Winch returned to the parable in his essay, 'Professor Anscombe's Moral Philosophy', which appeared posthumously in Lilli Alanen, Sara Heinamaa and Thomas Walgren (eds.), *Commonality and Particularity in Ethics* (London: Macmillan, 1997).

3 *Op. cit.*, p. 263. Emphasis added.

4 *Op. cit.*, p. 165.

5 Elsewhere, he speaks about the responses to moral modalities being 'modified or stifled *by* circumstances'. In fact, these locutions might be taken to suggest different thoughts: in one case (roughly), that a person's earlier experience has made her *insensitive* to the demands imposed by situations like this; in the other case, that the circumstances of the present case seem to her to *override* the requirements that would normally hold. However, this distinction does not have a bearing on the present discussion.

6   Reprinted in Phillips's collection of essays, *Interventions in Ethics* (London: Macmillan, 1992).
7   *Op. cit.*, pp. 229f.
8   *Op. cit.*, p. 250.
9   *Ibid.*
10 Winch, *op. cit.*, p. 159.
11 Matt. 5:44, quoted by Phillips, *op. cit.*, p. 248. For a quite different, thought-provoking perspective on the parable, see Rush Rhees, 'Christianity and Growth of Understanding', in D.Z. Phillips (ed.), *Rush Rhees on Religion and Philosophy* (Cambridge University Press, 1997), pp. 378 ff.
12 The question of how far the distinction between what is a possible way of thinking and what is a *morally* possible way of thinking can be upheld is bound up with problems that I do not have the space to go into in this context.
13 Cf., for instance, Winch's essay, 'Doing Justice or Giving the Devil his Due', in D.Z. Phillips (ed.), *Can Religion Be Explained Away?* (Basingstoke: Macmillan, 1997).
14 My use of the formulation 'difficult or impossible' is not a mark of indecision, but is connected with the point that the borderline between what is hard to imagine and what is impossible to imagine is not a sharp one.
15 *Philosophical Investigations II*, p. 178. There is a fuller discussion of this theme by Winch in an earlier essay, 'Eine Einstellung zur Seele', in *Trying to Make Sense*. For other thoughtful discussions of this theme in Wittgenstein, see David Cockburn, *Other Human Beings* (London: Macmillan, 1991), esp. Ch. 1; Raimond Gaita, *Good and Evil: An Absolute Conception* (London: Macmillan, 1991), Chs. 9–10; and Gaita's Critical Notice of Phillips, *Interventions in Ethics*, above.
16 Suppose someone suggested that we might get round the disagreement by invoking the ambiguity in the words *human being*. That is, he would argue that while the Samaritan as well as the priest and the Levite saw a human being, these words did not carry the same sense for them. However, this suggestion would not be acceptable to Winch (nor, I suspect, to Phillips). Winch might point out that it leaves no room for the possibility that the Samaritan's response might have the power of *revealing* to the priest and the Levite that they had been blind to the injured man's needs. The kinds of tension that may exist between different ways of responding to a fellow human being indicate that there is an indeterminacy in what is involved in calling someone human, and thus an indeterminacy about the question whether the word carries the same sense for two speakers. There would be no room for these tensions if it were supposed that the words *human being* are simply being used in different senses. Elsewhere Winch suggests, along these lines, that only the Samaritan sees the injured man's need, whereas the other two could perhaps be said to see *that* he needs help ('Professor Anscombe's Moral Philosophy', p. 193).
17 Peter Winch, *Eine Einstellung zur Seele*, p. 146. The Weil quotation is from 'The *Iliad*, Poem of Might', in Sian Miles (ed.), *Simone Weil: An Anthology* (London: Virago, 1986).
18 Elizabeth Wolgast, *Philosophical Investigations* 17 (1994), pp. 587–603. The quotation is from p. 596.
19 *Simone Weil: An Anthology*, p. 187.
20 A similar point is strikingly illustrated in the French film *La belle noiseuse*, by the director Jacques Rivette, in which a painter, played by Michel Piccole, makes it clear through his way of looking at and directing his model that she is for him (or

that he is determined that she should be for him) nothing but an object to be depicted.

21   I am indebted to David Cockburn for bringing the need for this qualification to my attention.

22   For another case in which moral failure consists precisely in the inability to realize how one's conduct is seen by others, consider *A Nasty Story* by Dostoevsky, discussed by Phillips in 'Some Limits to Moral Endeavor', pp. 214f.

23   Analogously, the word *pious* is rarely used today in praising someone, although it might be used ironically, as a term of criticism or derision. For all that, we may have a fairly clear idea of what it would be to use it as a term of praise. Consider, too, the way some people will use words like *glamorous, chivalrous* or *virile* as terms of praise, while others will never use them or will only use them ironically.

24   On the other hand, of course, the fact that something is a chair has consequences for what we demand *from* it.

25   Winch, 'Who is My Neighbour?', p. 161.

26   For an incisive discussion of this contrast, see Cora Diamond, 'The Dog that Gave Himself the Moral Law', in P. French, T. Uehling and H. Wettstein (eds.), *Ethical Theory: Character and Virtue* (Midwest Studies in Philosophy, vol. XII), Notre Dame, Indiana: Notre Dame University Press, 1988).

27   I discuss this point in 'On Moral Necessity', in *The Limits of Experience* (Helsinki: Societas Philosophica Fennica, 1994), p. 226. Originally in Raimond Gaita (ed.), *Value and Understanding* (London: Routledge, 1990.

28   And, of course, unless those circumstances are specified such a claim would be more or less empty. If 'the right circumstances' could be anything at all, they might include anything from behaviour therapy over a brain tumour to a psychotic episode. However, the consideration of what a person might come to think as a result of going through one of *those* processes could hardly be taken to illuminate what he knows *now*. This, of course, cuts both ways. The Croat writer Slavenka Drakulic once made the remark that each of us, given the right sort of case, might have acted just like one of the brutal torturers in the Serbian concentration camps in Bosnia. It is not quite clear what is being said here. Why, after all, should those actions that I now abhor be thought to have anything to do with *me*? If all this means is that things might be done to me, such as my having electrodes implanted in my brain, after which I would find myself behaving in a similar way, this does not reveal any deep sense in which we are all potential murderers. If, on the other hand, it means that I could *now* imagine possible circumstances in which I should find such brutality justified, this is something I could rightly deny. (On the other hand, if all she wants to express is the truism that it is not easy to predict who among us in a given set of circumstances turn into nationalist criminals, her formulation is misleading.)

29   Rhees seems to be making a similar point in saying that 'He is still capable of repentance' is a religious remark, not a remark based on empirical observation. See his 'The Sinner and the Sin', in Phillips (ed.), p. 291.

30   Versions of this essay were presented at the Peter Winch Memorial Symposium at the APA Central Division meeting in Chicago, May 1998, as well as the philosophy seminar at Åbo Academy. I wish to thank David Cockburn, Nikolai Enckell, Olli Lagerspetz, Sean Stidd and Elizabeth Wolgast for their comments on earlier versions of the essay. My special thanks are due to Joel Backstrom for his detailed and penetrating criticisms.

3
The Availability of Wisdom

John T. Edelman

When in the *Apology* Socrates assures his friends that 'nothing can harm a good man whether in life or after death',[1] this commonly strikes at least some undergraduates as plainly false. Surely Socrates is a reasonably good man, and surely he is soon to be harmed. To some, of course, this will seem to miss the point, but it is part of a fairly respectable philosophical response to Socrates' claim. Thus, many years ago Peter Winch spoke of 'a certain sort of "tough-minded" philosopher' who might say of Socrates' remark that if the words 'are being used in their ordinary sense, then they express a straightforward empirical falsehood' and that the remark can be true only by virtue of an eccentric use of the word *harm*, in which case it will be true 'by definition' and in a merely 'trivial' way.[2] This 'trivial' way might be expressed by saying that whatever happens to a good man, Socrates will not call it *harm*. But Winch suggests that perhaps we should not be too ready to join the tough-minded philosopher in thinking such a remark 'merely trivial',[3] and he sets out to try to understand what might be meant by it that would be neither obviously false nor trivially true.

What Winch attempts here is something Professor Phillips has also attempted on at least two occasions. The more recent of these is 'Necessary Rewards, Necessary Punishments and Character',[4] where in exploring the idea that a good man cannot be harmed Phillips explores differences between what he calls 'spectator judgements' about an action or a life and an agent's own judgements about his or her actions or life. (Consider, for example, a spectator's ascription of humility to an agent and what Phillips calls the 'self-refuting' claim of the agent, 'I am the humblest of men'.) But Phillips also took up Socrates' claim about a good man many years ago in an essay that Winch refers to and which became two central chapters in *Moral Practices*.[5] I mention Phillips's earlier essay now because it was that piece more than anything else that led me to Swansea in 1978 to write a doctoral dissertation under Phillips's supervision. My decision to go to Swansea is one I have never had reason to regret, not only because other members of the department – Howard Mounce, Ilham Dilman and, especially, the late Peter

Robertson – were so hospitable and encouraging to me (nor solely because Phillips himself proved to be so generous and so helpful a supervisor), but also because of the way Phillips helped me to learn from other philosophers, most especially Peter Winch, Rush Rhees and R.F. Holland, all of whom had at one time taught in the department there. It is for these autobiographical reasons that responses to Socrates' claim, and Winch's response in particular, seem to provide an especially appropriate topic for me on the present occasion.

Now the sort of project in which Phillips and Winch are engaged in their different essays is the sort of project philosophers are regularly engaged in both in Philosophy 101 classes and on countless other occasions, namely, an attempt to elucidate or to explain a remark whose meaning is not immediately evident to everyone who hears or reads it. In this particular case, however, Winch concludes that in an important sense the project cannot be completed. I think he is right in this conclusion, even if I think there is something wrong about the way he expresses it. But in fact it is the mere possibility of his being right that interests me. For this is the possibility that there exists a wisdom that is not, and perhaps cannot be made to be, available to just anyone or everyone. Taken in a variety of senses, this may seem a fairly innocuous possibility. But it can also be construed in ways that are at least puzzling, if not disturbing. I want to identify at least one of those ways of construing unavailable wisdom and to ask what might be the appropriate philosophical response to it. More precisely, I want to consider what seems to me a very inadequate response to it – one found in Martha Nussbaum's *The Fragility of Goodness* – and an alternative that I take to be one reason why Plato wrote dialogues. Finally, however, I am also interested in the way this Platonic alternative will appear to be a case of begging the question.

To speak of the possibility of a wisdom that is not available to just anyone or everyone is to involve oneself at least implicitly in some account of the nature of wisdom, and along the way it will be necessary to say something about that. But it is also to take up matters concerning the pursuit of any such wisdom. So it is to involve oneself – again at least implicitly – in a discussion of the nature of philosophy as a subject studied or taught. To get started, however, I shall return to Winch's tough-minded philosopher.

1

If I am inclined to think that Winch's tough-minded philosopher is moving too quickly; that is, if I think that he or she is missing something in what Socrates is saying, then it might seem reasonable to expect that I could say just what that is. And here the expectation is almost certain to be that in saying 'just what that is' I will do more than repeat Socrates' words. That much, it is likely to be said, will not get us very far. More accurately, it will not get the tough-minded philosopher very far, which is why it will seem natural to look for something else that will get him further. My interest in what I am calling the 'availability of wisdom' is in part an interest in what that might be.

One thing that could be done here is to try to make clear certain things that Socrates is not saying when he says that a good man cannot be harmed. Thus in the *Gorgias*, Callicles suggests that Socrates, in his unwillingness to 'flatter' the Athenians, acts as though he 'were living in another world and were not liable to be dragged into court, possibly by some scoundrel of the vilest character'.[6] But, as Professor Phillips has observed,[7] Socrates makes it clear that he is not denying this possibility: 'I should be a fool, Callicles, if I didn't realize that in this state anything may happen to anybody.'[8] On the other hand, to say something about what Socrates did not mean is not to say what he did mean. So a second strategy might be to look for other ways of saying what Socrates said. There might seem to be connections, for instance, between Socrates' remark and various religious statements. Phillips has alluded to connections between Socrates' statement and Julian of Norwich's famous 'All shall be well' and '[A]ll manner of thing shall be well.'[9] But to some, these remarks may seem no more intelligible than Socrates'. And even for those to whom they do seem intelligible, they may only increase the puzzlement over Socrates' claim. For Socrates does not say merely that all shall be well for a good man in some future life – which is what some may take Mother Julian to be saying. He seems to be saying that no harm will come to a good person even in this life. And surely it is this part of his claim that is most obviously false, or most 'trivially' true, or simply most baffling. So Mother Julian's remark, while perhaps in some respects similar to Socrates', is also quite different from it, which suggests that at least in this case this second strategy – that of identifying other ways of saying what Socrates said – collapses into the first strategy – that of identifying things that Socrates did not say. But this, I think, is what is to be expected here and it will be important to see why.

I observed above that it probably would not seem very helpful to Winch's tough-minded philosopher if one were simply to repeat Socrates' claim that a good man cannot be harmed. But if the idea here is to bring someone to understand that remark and to do so without just repeating Socrates' words, then apparently we must be thinking that it is possible to say in a way that is understandable what Socrates says here in a way that is not understandable, or at least not immediately or very readily understandable. Sometimes, of course, this sort of thing can be done. If I tell you that a concept is a formal sign and you do not understand me, then I might begin to make this clearer to you by explaining what I mean by 'formal'. What I shall be doing is giving an account of my somewhat technical use of a term. And this we might describe as a case of explaining the notation. That is to say, what I want to explain to you is my use of a term – 'formal' – in place of some other expression that you already understand. But is this the sort of problem we have in the case of Socrates' claim that a good man cannot be harmed? 'Coming to understand' here, I would suggest, may not be at all like coming to understand the words of someone speaking French when you speak very little French but a great deal of English. To the contrary, it may be more akin to coming to speak a language at all – which, I take it, Wittgenstein has shown to be quite different from coming to understand a new notation.[10] Indeed, if coming to understand what Socrates is saying were like coming to understand a new notation, then it would make perfectly good sense to wonder why Socrates talks in such paradoxical ways when, after all, he could say what he means in plain English. What I mean to be suggesting here is that the plain English version of Socrates' claim that a good man cannot be harmed may be simply 'A good man cannot be harmed'. Presently I shall consider another candidate for a 'plain English' version of what Socrates says, and try to show that it is not a version of what he says at all. But for the moment it is enough to notice that at least part of the temptation to think that Socrates' statement is something other than plain English – or plain Greek, and so can somehow be put into plain English – may be connected with a failure to appreciate the difference between learning to speak at all and learning to speak French when you already speak English.

None of this yet amounts to saying that there is no other way to say what Socrates is saying, though I think that that is very nearly the case. All I mean to do at this point is to question whether any other way should be expected to be any more understandable than Socrates' way to someone who does not already understand what Socrates is saying – as though such a person already spoke a language in which he could say what Socrates says, only not in Socrates' language. And my immediate point in raising this question is that if this expectation is somehow wrong-headed, then we should not be surprised if whatever success one does have with Winch's tough-minded philosopher turns out to be success in showing him what Socrates did not say rather than in showing him what he did say. For, of course, this tough-minded philosopher will be able to make perfectly good sense of a great many things that are not what Socrates said. Whether there is anything else one might do to enable him to understand what Socrates did say remains undetermined. But I want to notice something else before trying to address that question. For if we do set aside the expectation I am questioning, then we may also be put on our guard against another possibility: we may notice that if you do not already understand what Socrates is saying and yet I seem to explain to you what he is saying by putting what he is saying into words that you think you do understand, then the possibility we should have to consider is that we both have it wrong. Put differently, the possibility we should have to consider is that my 'explanation', my new and clearer way of 'saying the same thing', will not amount to saying the same thing at all – though you and I could hardly be expected to see this, or to see it very easily.

This I can illustrate by considering now a particular case of a philosopher offering a 'plain English' version of what Socrates is saying. Doing so will also bring to light what for my purposes is an important possibility regarding what 'understanding Socrates' may amount to.

The particular case I have in mind comes from Martha Nussbaum, though not from the *Fragility of Goodness*. It is in *Love's Knowledge: Essays in Philosophy and Literature* that Nussbaum begins a sentence thus: 'If one believes, with Socrates, that the good person cannot be harmed, that the only thing of real importance is one's own virtue . . . '[11] – apparently suggesting that to believe with Socrates that one cannot be harmed is to believe that one's own virtue is the only thing 'of real importance'. But the difficulties with this as a gloss of Socrates' statement seem to me substantial. For a start, one might expect Socrates to say that anyone who actually thought 'that the only thing of real importance is one's own virtue' had no real virtue to begin with. After all, in the *Symposium* Socrates ties virtue to the apprehension of the Beautiful,[12] and it is difficult to imagine Plato allowing anything to count as an 'apprehension of the Beautiful' that did not also involve a recognition that the Beautiful is of far greater significance – far greater importance – than one's own virtue.

But surely the more obvious difficulty with Nussbaum's gloss is that the harm may very well come to one who thinks his own virtue 'the only thing of real importance'. This is a point which Winch brings out, though without reference to Nussbaum. In the course of his essay, Winch considers a variety of remarks that he recognizes to be different from that of Socrates but that none the less 'have interesting features in common' with it.[13] Thus he explores connections between Socrates' remark and some of what Kierkegaard says about a man's 'relation to eternity'. In particular, he considers the idea that 'the characteristic expression of a person's relation to eternity is *patience*'[14] – and by 'patience' here he means 'the *voluntary* acceptance of *unavoidable* suffering'.[15] In one respect, of course, this is to connect Socrates' claim with another claim that may appear equally paradoxical. As Winch sees it, the paradoxical character of patience lies in the fact that both the voluntariness of the acceptance and the inevitability of the suffering are essential to it. So how does one voluntarily accept what is inevitable? What is important for my purposes is that any answer to this will make it clear that Kierkegaard is saying something quite different from what Socrates is saying. Winch brings out some of the difference by observing that a man who is patient in Kierkegaard's sense still thinks that *something* could harm him, namely, for him to cease to 'will the Good' – and so to cease to accept voluntarily his inevitable suffering. And this, as Winch sees it, may well befall him as a result of afflictions which he has to suffer.[16] But my point is that what Winch helps us to see here is not only a difference between Kierkegaardian patience and Socrates' idea that a good man cannot be harmed, but also a difference between Socrates' idea and what Nussbaum seems to have in mind when she talks of one's own virtue being the only thing of 'real importance'. It is not that Nussbaum captures what Kierkegaard has in mind, but that what can befall Kierkegaard's person of patience can also befall Nussbaum's moral narcissist; namely, the virtue or patience of each of them might be destroyed by affliction. Which is to say that neither Nussbaum nor Kierkegaard is talking about quite what Socrates is talking about, for Socrates says that *nothing* can harm a good man. This may be false. Or at least one may think it could be false – a point to which I shall return. But it is not the same claim as the claim that one's own virtue is all that really matters, any more than the attitude Socrates expresses with his remark is quite the same as the attitude of one with Kierkegaardian patience.

Now my initial concern in turning to Nussbaum's version of Socrates' claim was to caution against the inclination to accept as an explanation of that previously puzzling remark what in fact is a misconstrual of it, a temptation deriving from the fact that I did not understand what Socrates said in the first place. Or better: a temptation deriving from the fact that I did not understand the nature of my failure to understand, i.e. that the problem was not just one of translation, as though, again, I could already say what Socrates is saying, only not in the language in which Socrates says it. But I am primarily interested in this sort of misconstrual because it points to one thing that 'understanding Socrates' can amount to. For we might notice now that while I have introduced the possibility that Nussbaum's explanation is not an explanation but a misconstrual, I have not done so by offering any other way of saying what Socrates is saying. In fact, it seems that one can do what I have tried to do without ever claiming to understand what Socrates is saying. Put differently, my understanding that there are differences between whatever Socrates might be saying and some other things that one might say may leave me still puzzled as to what Socrates is saying. Indeed, this possibility is what makes Winch's strategy intelligible, for he expects some who do not think that they understand what Socrates is saying at least to understand a difference between whatever he is saying and what Kierkegaard is talking about. In short, 'understanding Socrates', as an understanding of the sort of logical moves Winch makes in distinguishing what Socrates says from some other things that some other people might say, need not amount to an understanding of what Socrates does say. And thus it appears that I could show you that Socrates is *not* saying what you might think he is saying when neither you nor I claim to understand what he *is* saying.

Now this is in one sense a peculiar possibility, for it raises the question of what 'really' understanding Socrates could amount to. If I understand Socrates well enough to see that he is not saying what Nussbaum thinks he is saying, nor saying what Kierkegaard is saying, then what is it I do not understand if I still do not understand what Socrates is saying? So far the only answer seems to be to repeat what Socrates said. But what has been in question all along is whether in saying this Socrates is saying anything more than the obviously false or the trivially true. Which is why it can seem so plausible to conclude that unless one can say in some plainer language what Socrates says in fairly obscure language, then Socrates is not after all saying anything more than the obviously false or the trivially true. And in a sense this is Winch's conclusion. At the end of his essay he writes:

> Can a good man be harmed? The answer to the question cannot be formulated, and this means that there is something wrong with the question. It is an attempt to get something said that can only be shown.[17]

Now if we go along with Wittgenstein's view at the time of the *Tractatus*, then what can be said is what can be true or false, which is in turn limited to what expresses how things happen to be or to go in the world. But part of what Winch brings out in his essay is that Socrates' remark is not of this sort. Socrates' claim is that nothing can harm a good man, and the absolute character of this claim lies precisely in the fact that it has no predictive content.[18] Nothing can falsify it, and if anything could, it would lose its absolute character and we should have to wait to see how things do go with the good man. This is why I will misunderstand Socrates if I take his remark to be 'obviously false'. But it is also the reason why I might describe his statement as expressing some kind of 'necessary' truth, as Winch does near the beginning of his essay.[19] And in that case, of course, the difference between understanding what Socrates is saying (where 'understanding' amounts only to knowing what other things Socrates might say in order to distinguish what he is saying from some poor 'translations' of what he is saying) and 'really' understanding what Socrates is saying will be the difference between not knowing what to make of what Socrates does say and actually accepting what he says as true. For if what he says is necessarily true, then knowing what to make of it will be inseparable from thinking it true. Again, I shall return to this.

What we need to notice now is that because Socrates' words do not express a merely contingent truth (or falsehood), on the account found in the *Tractatus* they do not express anything at all. Which takes us back to the question whether the tough-minded philosopher did after all fail to understand anything. Are we to say that he failed to understand something that Socrates understands but which cannot be put into words? This seems to be the view that Winch is taking, though I am not confident enough here to go beyond 'seems'. At any rate, if it is the view he is taking, it involves him in what Cora Diamond has argued is a questionable reading of the *Tractatus*. In her 'Throwing away the Ladder', Diamond writes:

> You can read the *Tractatus* as containing numerous doctrines which Wittgenstein holds cannot be put into words, so they do not really

count as doctrines: they do not have what counts as sense according to the doctrines in the *Tractatus* about what has sense. If you read the *Tractatus* this way, you think that, after the ladder is thrown away, you are left holding on to some truths about reality, while at the same time denying that you are actually *saying* anything about reality. Or, in contrast, you can say that the notion of something true of reality but not sayably true is to be used only with the awareness that it itself belongs to what has to be thrown away. One is not left with it at the end, after recognizing what the *Tractatus* has aimed at getting one to recognize.[20]

Diamond, then, would surely argue against a reading of the *Tractatus* according to which Socrates does understand something, but something that cannot be put into words. On the other hand, of course, one might just take this to reveal what is problematic in the *Tractatus*. For on Wittgenstein's later views it is quite possible to give a very different account of the sort of claim Socrates appears to be making, and Diamond shows how in her 'Secondary Sense'.[21] Indeed, she there offers an account of words used in 'secondary senses' according to which the sort of claim that Socrates seems to be making can be construed as neither metaphorical[22] nor obviously false nor trivially true. But it is also an account that rejects the idea that the sort of thing Socrates could say by using 'harm' in a secondary sense could be translated into words used only in their primary senses, much as I have argued that it is a mistake to think there must be some version of what Socrates says that is somehow clearer than Socrates' own version. What is important about this is that whether we say that Socrates understands something that cannot be put into words or whether we say that he uses 'harm' in a secondary sense, in both cases we shall have to recognize a limit to explanation and elucidation. For even in the case of a secondary sense, if we cannot put what is said by way of that secondary sense into words used only in their primary senses, then if you do not already understand what Socrates is saying it will be a kind of confusion – a kind of misunderstanding – to ask anyone for a 'translation' of what he is saying. And if such is the case, then one might well wonder why anyone who did not already understand what Socrates is saying would think that he was saying anything at all, or anything other than what is obviously false or trivially true. Indeed, even if I think, contrary to the *Tractatus*, that there are 'necessary truths' of the sort Socrates' statement would be, why should I think that this is one of them – when no one is able to tell me what that statement means? Put differently, why should I think that what makes no sense to me makes sense? Or that there is something to understand where I do not understand it? The obvious rejoinder might be: Why should I think there is nothing to understand except what I can already understand? But it will not be enough to acknowledge a possibility here. The difficulty is to see why I should think that in this (or any other) particular case Socrates (or anyone else) is actually saying something. Or, to put the same question in the form that interests me here: Why should I think that there is a wisdom somehow available to others but not to me? Or that any particular remark that appears to me to be obviously false, trivially true, or empty, should be an expression of that wisdom?

2

Now at least one version of the idea that there is a wisdom that is not available to just anyone or everyone has a long history. Consider the following from Albert the Great:

> ... we must say that we do not receive the things of God by means of rational principles, but experientially, in a way, by a kind of 'sympathy toward them,' as Dionysius says of Hierotheus, who learned the things of God 'by undergoing the things of God.' But if our emotions are infected by an unlawful love of things, we shall not feel the sweetness of God's inspiration, and so, because of the lack of experiential knowledge, we may be able to form syllogisms and other propositions, but we shall not have that real knowledge which is a part of beatitude.[23]

One possibility that Albert is describing here is, I think, very close to the sort of case I mentioned above, namely, the case in which 'understanding what Socrates says' amounts to understanding what other things Socrates might say and so understanding, for instance, that Nussbaum's gloss on what he says is not an accurate gloss – and all of this while still not understanding what Socrates means by what he says. Again, this may seem a very peculiar possibility. It will be natural to ask what this knowledge is supposed to be that is distinct from or additional to the ability to form syllogisms and to utter propositions? And surely in the case of Socrates' claim the answer to the analogous question would seem to be: It is the knowledge that a good man cannot be harmed – as distinct from any knowledge of what Socrates would or would not say. And while someone might ask yet again whether this actually amounts to any sort of knowledge, it is not my concern to establish that it does. My concern instead is to understand just what might be involved in doing that, if it could be done. For this would be to understand something of the availability of wisdom, if, again, there is such wisdom. After all, if Albert is correct and, consequently, if we should not expect such wisdom to be available to just anyone or everyone, then it will be a sort of confusion to ask that the reality of such wisdom be 'established' before we say anything substantive about its availability. Which takes me to the question that has been my target all along, namely: What is the appropriate philosophical response to the suggestion that Albert is making, the suggestion that there is such wisdom but that its reality is established not 'by means of rational principles' but by 'experience'?

Here it is perhaps worth noticing that Albert's claim is in fact something of a commonplace in the philosophical tradition. Consider this from Plotinus:

> It is impossible to talk about bodily beauty if one, like one born blind, has never seen and known bodily beauty. In the same way, it is impossible to talk about the 'luster' of right living and of learning and of the like if one has never cared for such things, never beheld 'the face of justice' and temperance and seen it to be 'beyond the beauty of evening or morning star.' Seeing of this sort is done only with the eye of the soul. And, seeing thus, one undergoes a joy, a wonder, and a distress more deep than any other because here one touches truth.[24]

So, apparently, if you have not experienced such wonder and such distress, then you will not understand what Plotinus has to say about the 'luster' of right living. Thus Plotinus, like Albert, suggests that certain truths are in some sense unavailable except to those who are willing to live a certain way, that is, to undergo certain experiences. This, of course, may seem exceedingly convenient. After all, it seems to put the truth of certain propositions beyond question – or at least beyond the questioning of any who do not think them true. For it suggests that individuals who do not think those propositions true are also to be identified as individuals who lack the experience by which they could be seen to be true, which, of course, is consistent with any account of them as 'necessary truths'. And yet this (to some) disconcerting consequence hardly entails that the claims themselves are false. Indeed, a more general form of these particular claims can be found in Simone Weil, in a passage in which she speaks of 'all useful knowledge concerning spiritual progress':

> Certainties of this kind are experimental. But if we do not believe in them before experiencing them, if at least we do not behave as though we believed them, we shall never have the experience that leads to such certainties. There is a kind of contradiction here. Above a certain level this is the case with all useful knowledge concerning spiritual progress. If we do not regulate our conduct by it before having proved it, if we do not hold on to it for a long time by faith alone, a faith at first stormy and without light, we shall never transform it into certainty. Faith is the indispensable condition.[25]

In each of these passages, then, there are identified certain conditions for the apprehension of what is claimed to be a kind of wisdom. But if any expression of that wisdom amounts to the sort of statement Socrates makes regarding the good man who cannot be harmed, then those of us who do not already understand that wisdom will be in the same position as one who does not already understand what Socrates is saying. That is, we may be left wondering whether the expression of such 'wisdom' really amounts to saying anything at all. So, again: What is the appropriate philosophical response to the sorts of claims these authors are making?

3

One answer to this question comes in the context of Martha Nussbaum's criticisms of the moral philosophy of many of the earlier Platonic dialogues. I mean the criticisms she offers in *The Fragility of Goodness*.[26] There are a variety of ways in which one might describe what it is that Nussbaum finds inadequate in Plato, or at least in the Plato of the *Symposium*, the *Republic* and the *Phaedo*. So, for example, she sees in the *Symposium* a rejection of love, or at least of any love for any real individual as unique and irreplaceable (see pp. 180–1). Or, perhaps better, she faults Plato for his rejection of what she calls 'the madness of personal love' (p. 201) as it is represented by Alcibiades' love for Socrates. Moreover, she believes that such love is rejected in preference for a conception of value identified from a 'standpoint of perfection' (p. 160). Indeed, this rejection of love is, she thinks, a rejection of risk and of openness (p. 339) in preference for what she calls the 'safe and eternal' (p. 420), which she in turn identifies with an ascetical ideal that involves the rejection of what she calls 'characteristic human needs' (p. 154).

Now the rhetorically loaded nature of Nussbaum's description of what she takes to be Plato's moral philosophy is, I think, evident. For surely at the heart of Plato's thought in the early and middle dialogues is the question of just what one's 'characteristically human needs' are. And this, of course, is not a sociological question to Plato, as Nussbaum recognizes. (See, for example, pp. 154 and 160.) Whatever individuals might report as their 'needs', Plato's Socrates is liable to ask whether these are their 'true'or 'real' needs. And this means that in Nussbaum's description of what she takes to be the Platonic 'perspective' there is some danger of begging the question, not only with regard to what are our 'characteristically human needs', but even with regard to what one is to take as 'the human point of view', e.g. whether that point of view is distinct from the 'standpoint of perfection' she ascribes to Plato. But Nussbaum is not unaware of this difficulty (p. 162). She recognizes that to the objection that his moral philosophy is somehow neglectful of the point of view of mere mortals, Plato might reply that the aspiration for perfection 'is actually a part of the human point of view, since the human being is by nature a being that seeks to transcend, through reason, its merely human limits' (p. 162). The point here would be that it is not Plato but his critics who misrepresent what Nussbaum calls 'the internal human viewpoint' (p. 162). But given that she does recognize this possibility, one could wish that Nussbaum had abandoned the 'internal'/'external' contrast altogether. Unfortunately, it continues to play a large role in her discussion of the contrasts between Platonic and Aristotelian moral philosophy, always to the disparagement of what she considers the 'Platonic' view. (See, for example, pp. 242, 375 and 378.) This is unfortunate because, while the contrast is rhetorically forceful, it is philosophically empty. Indeed, precisely because it is rhetorically so forceful it is important before going further to see why it is empty.

The difficulty can be brought out in this way. Either a viewpoint is intelligible to a human being or it is not. If it is, then it is a viewpoint that can be expressed in language a human being speaks and so, even if it is spoken of as 'a view from eternity' or a view *'sub specie aeternitatis'* or 'God's view', and if it is an intelligible view at all, then it is a view 'internal to a human life'. So the question can be raised – as, I think, Plato means to raise it – whether such views are appropriate to a human being. I am reminded of John Anderson objecting that the authority of any 'word of God' is still the authority of some human judgement that this or that is 'the word of God'.[27] Anderson's point is correct, but it does nothing to touch the fact that the judgement being made is a judgement that this, rather than that, is 'the word of God'. 'The word of God', like 'the eternal view' or 'the world seen *sub specie aeternitatis*', is an expression in a language human beings speak. There will be criteria for its use, if it has one; for without such criteria nothing will count as a correct use and so nothing will count as an incorrect use, at which point it will amount to nothing but noise. No doubt it is altogether a different question whether one can use any such expression oneself, which is surely part of what gives at least initial plausibility to Albert's distinction between the ability to form syllogisms and utter propositions and the 'knowledge' that is a part of beatitude. Nussbaum is critical of the 'Platonic' concept of scientific principles that 'are known to hold "themselves by themselves", entirely independently of all conceptualization and thought' (p. 255). This would seem to be a perfect illustration of what she would call an attempt to get 'beyond the human'. But even this sort of talk may play a role in a language – or, better, a life – much as the idea that God is 'beyond all experience and thought' plays a role among certain religious people.[28]

Now I am not suggesting that there is never any point to some contrast of the sort Nussbaum tries to work with here. The now infamous 'view from nowhere' is, we may say, no view at all. Moreover, a philosopher may well find him or herself slipping into such a 'viewpoint'. The *Parmenides* suggests that Plato came to think he was doing something of this sort with his own talk of 'Forms'. Aristotle seems to have been thoroughly convinced that this is precisely what Plato had done. The point here would be that Plato's talk of 'Forms' is at times incoherent. And if we want to call this 'getting beyond the human', then we may agree that 'getting beyond the human' is just talking nonsense. But not every case of talk about 'transcending the human' or 'attaining to an eternal perspective' will necessarily amount to nonsense. Cases will have to be considered one at a time, especially if it is believed that such talk will not be intelligible to just anyone at all. Indeed, Nussbaum herself points out that Plato does not expect all of what Socrates has to say to be available to just anyone and everyone (p. 157). As she recognizes, this is why education is so large a concern to him. But this just takes us back to the question of how one is to respond to a philosopher who tells us that there is an understanding – even a wisdom – that will be available to us only if we first submit to an education or take up a way of life that is not yet altogether plausible or comprehensible to us. Nussbaum's own response is this:

> I have said that it is not a strong objection to [Plato's] value-theory that it does not faithfully reflect the ordinary human's intuitive view of her practices and pursuits, since, according to Plato, no ordinary person, especially in a liberal democracy, has had the education that would sufficiently cultivate his or her potential for objective rationality. But it is, of course, still incumbent on Plato to show us, ordinary as we are, that this ideal of rational valuing and this standpoint of perfection are worthwhile goals for a human being to pursue. He must give us some reason to want to attain his ideal, or to think that it is one to whose pursuit we are already in some way committed.   (p. 160)

Now one of the strengths Nussbaum would like to claim for her discussion of Plato – and often she would be right to do so – is her appreciation of the dramatic element in his dialogues. But she is not entirely consistent on this score. In fact, my criticism of her reading of the *Symposium* in some respects amounts to saying that she does not pay enough attention to its dramatic content. For what I want to suggest is that Plato's concern with drama here is rooted in his understanding that the one thing he cannot do on behalf of the Socratic 'ideal' is to give 'us' – that is, those of us still in need of 'education' – a reason to want to attain it. Unless, of course, we will count Socrates himself as a reason. But Nussbaum speaks instead of a 'view' (p. 162) or a 'perspective' (p. 160) for which Plato is prepared to 'argue' (p. 162). And in opposition to this view she raises such objections as that 'the external god's-eye perspective is neither attractive, in that it requires the denigration of so much that we value, nor important, in that it is not relevant to the living of our *human* lives' (p. 160; the emphasis for 'human' is hers, and typically so). In fact, Nussbaum reads the *Symposium* ultimately as 'reminding us that it is as unreformed people that we must learn and judge of the value of Socratic teaching' (p. 168). My suggestion, on the other hand, is that the dialogue does not so much remind us that we must judge Socratic teaching in this way, as it recognizes that we will be inclined to do just that, and so offers us not a reason to adopt a 'view' but a kind of beauty that might lead us to withhold judgement, unfit as we are to judge. This, I think, is exactly what Diotima's speech suggests we need, which is why it should hardly be surprising that it is what Plato offers us. Put differently, the

Symposium suggests that the appropriate response to a wisdom we do not comprehend – or at least to *this* wisdom that we do not comprehend – is not to ask for reasons but to attend to a person, that is, to a life. But this should not seem a peculiar suggestion to anyone who recognizes that 'how words are understood is not told by words alone'.[29] For such a person will expect that how words are understood – and so what any wisdom actually amounts to – will not show apart from what a person does, and how he or she does it.

In suggesting that the *Symposium* calls on us to withhold judgement in the recognition that we are unfit to be judges, I do not mean to say that there are no arguments or reasons presented by Plato on behalf of what Nussbaum calls this 'Socratic ideal'. As Nussbaum brings out, the question of a motivation for pursuing this ideal 'is one to which [Plato] has devoted a great deal of consideration' (pp. 160–1). So much consideration, I might add, that he wrote dialogues with Socrates as the main character instead of treatises filled only with arguments. None the less, Nussbaum identifies both a positive and a negative strand in Plato's account of the motivation that might lead us to pursue his 'ideal'. The negative strand involves him in reminding us that 'much that is valued in the internal human viewpoint on the world is, if we reflect seriously, a source of intolerable pain for a rational being' (p. 161). The positive strand concerns, among other things, what Nussbaum, quoting Plutarch, calls 'the *joy* and *pleasure* of pure reasoning' (p. 162). But it is one thing to notice that the Platonic dialogues present 'reasons' of these sorts and another thing to ask to whom Plato thinks such reasons are available. Indeed, if I am correct, the *Symposium* expresses Plato's recognition of the point Plotinus made in the quotation from the *Enneads* above, namely, that talk of 'the "luster" of right living and of learning' will only be intelligible to those who have already 'beheld "the face of justice" and temperance and seen it to be "beyond the beauty of evening or morning star"'. What Plato recognizes is the possibility that few of his readers will have done so. What Nussbaum misses is the role Alcibiades plays in offering to those of us who still suffer from such poor vision a glimpse of just that beauty that Diotima tells us we must behold on our way to beholding 'Beauty itself' and so entering into what in the *Phaedrus* is shown to be a life 'free from harm'.[30] I mean the beauty of Socrates. If we take a moment to consider how Nussbaum misses Alcibiades' role here, I can get at some of the consequences this must have for one's understanding of the study and the teaching of philosophy.

4

Nussbaum takes the *Symposium* to present us with a choice. Alcibiades might well say the same thing. As Nussbaum sees it, the choice is between 'two kinds of value, two kinds of knowledge', where one sort 'blocks out the other' (p. 198). 'The pure light of the eternal form', as she puts it, 'eclipses, or is eclipsed by, the flickering lightning of the opened and unstably moving body.' She goes on:

> You have to refuse to see something, apparently, if you are going to act. I can choose to follow Socrates, ascending to the vision of the beautiful. But I cannot take the first step on that ladder as long as I see Alcibiades. I can follow Socrates only if, like Socrates, I am *persuaded* of the truth of Diotima's account; and Alcibiades robs me of this conviction. He makes me feel that in embarking on the ascent I am sacrificing a beauty; so I can no longer view the ascent as embracing the whole of beauty. The minute I think 'sacrifice' and 'denial', the ascent is no longer what it seemed ...
>
> (p. 198)

That the ascent speaks to her of 'sacrifice' and 'denial' says more, I think, about what Nussbaum, like Alcibiades, misses than it says about what she 'sees'. In a sense, the problem with Nussbaum's reading, according to which the *Symposium* confronts us with a choice, is that it assumes we have under-stood the options. But Plato, when he has Diotima warn Socrates that he will not be able to follow her or understand her, also warns us that we may not understand her, any more than Alcibiades understands Socrates. Alcibiades is not going to be struck by 'the beauty of temperance'. Instead, the temper-ance of Socrates is to him just an instance of remarkable self-control and self-denial.[31] Rather than being struck by Socrates' deepest beauty, Alcibiades is struck by the fact that he – Alcibiades – cannot get what he wants.

There are moments when Nussbaum appears to be blind to just the sort of thing Alcibiades is blind to. Consider what she has to say about the Lysian lover – or, rather, non-lover – in the *Phaedrus*. As Nussbaum describes it, the first two speeches of the *Phaedrus* tell Phaedrus 'that, in his search for political, social, and intellectual standing, he must above all protect himself from emotional turmoil and emotional domination' (p. 208). Thus, '[t]he madness of love is unpredictable and dangerous' (p. 208). As she reads them, the two speeches present Phaedrus with what Nussbaum calls 'two starkly defined alternatives: the beneficent detachment of Lysias, the dangerous passion of the mad lover' (p. 209). She thinks it unsurprising that a young man should find Lysias's proposal 'attractive'. After all, as Socrates puts it, 'lovers love boys – the way wolves love lambs (241a)' (p. 209). At this point, however, Nussbaum suggests that while the speech of Lysias 'may appear to have taken us rather far from the ascetic ideal of the *Phaedo*', this is not the case at all; for 'the distance between abstinence and Lysian sex is not as great as it might seem'. As she puts it, 'The crucial point is that in neither case does the person go mad' (p. 210). Or: 'The difference between this view and the ascetic view of the *Phaedo* is only a difference about means: about whether it is easier to remain intellectually calm by having sex in this non-erotic way, or by abstaining' (p. 210). But surely this is inadequate, as though it makes no difference why any sort of 'intellectual calm' was important to begin with. And is 'intellectual calm' really what matters in the *Phaedo*? To the contrary, I think, the crucial point about Socratic asceticism – certainly in the *Symposium* and, I think, in the *Phaedo*, as well – is not that one does not go mad, or that one abstains from sexual activity. It is precisely that one is drawn by love to the beautiful itself. Indeed, Nussbaum seems to miss the role of love altogether in the *Phaedo* and, I should say, in Socratic asceticism. Thus, in speaking of the *Phaedo*, she says that the Socratic *elenchos* 'teaches by appeal to intellect alone; learning takes place when the interlocutor is enmeshed in logical contradiction … The characters in the *Phaedo* do not learn about the soul by looking to their love for Socrates; they begin to learn only when they are able to put that love away and turn to thought' (p. 133). But this ignores the possibility that they are there thinking at all because this is thinking with Socrates, a point the text suggests through the opening conversation between Phaedo and Echecrates.[32] Moreoever, it ignores the possibility that what thinking is in the *Phaedo* is itself inseparable from the sort of relations that exist between Socrates and his interlocutors, the sort of relations that are not found among the characters in, say, the *Gorgias*.[33] Indeed, it ignores the fact that when the Socratic *elenchos* does seem to appeal to anything we might call 'intellect alone' – as with Polus, perhaps, or Thrasymachus – it also fails to teach much at all. Again, Nussbaum wants to be attentive to the dramatic aspect of the Platonic dialogues, but this is one place where her failure on this score seems clear. She goes so far as to claim that when Sir Richard Livingstone, editing an English version of the *Phaedo*, printed the arguments in smaller type 'so that they can be either read or omitted', this was 'an exact reversal of Plato's intentions' (p. 131). If I am correct, however, Plato's intention could be expressed by saying that he would have the dialogue printed in a single type precisely because the sense of the arguments – and the sense of arguing at all – cannot be grasped apart from the life of Socrates himself.

What Nussbaum misses in the *Phaedo*, then, is what she misses in her account of the difference between Socratic asceticism and the life of the Lysian non-lover. It is, again, what one would expect Alcibiades to miss. It is, I think, what Plato expected many of us to miss. For, again, he did not, I think, expect many of us to understand the words of Diotima, any more than Socrates understood them at first. But those words are offered as something that one could come to understand, if one would only pay attention to them. And, as with the *Phaedo*, we are given the opportunity to pay attention to the words through our attention to Socrates. Alcibiades' failure, we might say, consists in the fact that he cannot pay attention to Socrates. He can only want him, and be frustrated at not having him. Rather than offering us a choice, the *Symposium* offers us a picture of the kind of love that might – but for Alcibiades will not – serve as a beginning, though only a beginning, in an ascent to the Beautiful, the ascent that Diotima describes.[34] If we, who cannot quite understand Diotima, can none the less be moved by love for Socrates – the strange and compelling Socrates we see through the eyes of Alcibiades – then we might attend long enough to the life of Socrates to learn to pay attention to the words of Diotima. Giving reasons will not do the trick here. Indeed, on this view Plato understands what Simone Weil seemed to see so well, and surely learned herself at least in part from Plato:

> A truth can only present itself to the mind of a particular human being. How is he going to communicate it? If he tries to expound it, he won't be listened to; for other people have never heard of that particular truth, won't recognize it as such; they won't realize that what he is saying is true; they won't pay enough attention to enable them to see that it is so; for they won't have received any inducement to make the necessary effort of concentration.
>
> But friendship, admiration, sympathy, or any other sort of benevolent feeling would naturally predispose them to give a certain amount of their attention. A man who has something new to say – for as far as platitudes are concerned, no effort of attention is necessary – can only be listened to, to begin with, by those that love him.[35]

If we take this as a comment on the availability of wisdom, then we get the following: There is a wisdom that is available only to those who are willing to take up a certain kind of life. But that there is such wisdom and that such a life is worth living will not be evident to all. But neither will there be 'reasons' that can be given to just anyone for believing that there is such wisdom or that such a life is worth living. Indeed, part of this wisdom will amount to the claim that it is only love that can move a person to the pursuit of that wisdom or the living of that life. I mean, of course, the love of beauty – found first, as Diotima suggests, in bodies, then in souls, then in laws and in learning and, finally, in Beauty itself.[36]

What, then, is the appropriate philosophical response to this sort of claim? Will not one's answer to this question be determined by one's judgement as to whether or not there is such wisdom to be acquired? If you think that there is none, then you will be inclined to say regarding those on the other side of the fence not that you cannot understand what they are saying, but that what they are saying is either obviously false, trivially true or empty. On the other hand, if you think there is such wisdom, then you may be inclined to say of those who deny its reality that they suffer not from a failure to speak intelligible English, but from a failure to love. This second view, of course, will seem to the first to beg the question.[37]

Nazareth College of Rochester

Notes

1   *Apology*, 41d. This is Hugh Tredennick's translation in *The Collected Dialogues of Plato*, ed. Edith Hamilton and Huntington Cairns (Princeton, NJ: Princeton University Press, 1961).

2   'Can A Good Man Be Harmed?', in *Ethics and Action* (London: Routledge, 1972), p. 195. Originally published in the *Proceedings of the Aristotelian Society*, 1959–60. Winch, in fact, begins his essay by referring to the idea that it is worse for a man to do harm than to suffer wrong, but in the passage I refer to here he is describing what he expects would be the 'tough-minded' philosopher's response to a number of ideas, including the idea that a good man cannot be harmed.

3   *Ibid.*, p. 195.

4   Chapter 19 in *Interventions in Ethics* (Albany, NY: SUNY Press, 1992), pp. 272–281.5.

5   The essay first appeared as 'Does It Pay To Be Good?', *Proceedings of the Aristotelian Society*, Vol. LXV, 1964–65. It became Chapters 3 and 4 in *Moral Practices*, co-authored with H.O. Mounce (New York: Schocken Books, 1970).

6   521c. Quoted by Phillips in 'Necessary Rewards, Necessary Punishments and Character', p. 274.

7   *Ibid.*, p. 274.

8   521c. Also quoted by Phillips, *ibid.*, p. 274.

9   In 'Necessary Rewards, Necessary Punishments and Character', p. 274. Mother Julian's remark is to be found in Chapter 32 of her *Revelations of Divine Love*, ed. Dom Roger Huddleston, OS. B. (London: Burns Qates, 1927).

10   When I say that Wittgenstein has made this difference clear I have in mind his discussion of the possibility of a 'private' language. That this is part of what his discussion of that possibility – or, better, impossibility – shows is something Rush Rhees makes clear, I think, in his 'Can There be a Private Language?', *Discussions of Wittgenstein* (London: Routledge and Kegan Paul, 1970), pp. 55–70 and 'Wittgenstein's Builders', in the same collection, pp. 71–84. See especially pp. 79–82.

11   *Love's Knowledge: Essays in Philosophy and Literature* (New York: Oxford University Press, 1990), p. 17. The complete sentence is this: 'If one believes, with Socrates, that the good person cannot be harmed, that the only thing of real importance is one's own virtue, then one will not think that stories of reversal have deep ethical significance, and one will not want to write as if they did, or to show as worthy heroes people who believe that they do.'

12   See 212a.

13   *Op. cit.*, p. 193.

14   *Ibid.*, p. 205.

15   *Ibid.*, p. 205.

16   *Ibid.*, p. 207.

17   *Ibid.*, p. 208.

18   *Ibid.*, p. 207. In 'Necessary Rewards, Necessary Punishments and Character', Phillips observes that Winch identifies a 'predictive element in the moral patience he elucidates' (p. 275). He then takes this moral patience to be the same thing that is expressed by Socrates' remark about harm. But this, I think, is a misunderstanding. Winch does identify a predictive element in the Kierke-gaardian patience that he discusses. But that is the crucial contrast between such patience and anything that Socrates might be talking about. Phillips thinks that this same predictive element in Socrates' remark is made explicit in the *Gorgias*,

where Socrates assures Callicles that if he came to his end through a lack of flattering rhetoric he would meet his death easily (522d–e). But this specific prediction seems to me distinct from, though by no means unrelated to, the absolute claim about harm in the *Apology*.

19 *Ibid.*, p. 195.
20 See *The Realistic Spirit* (Cambridge, Mass.: MIT Press, 1995), p. 182. I think that some of what Diamond says in this essay is itself problematic, and I have argued (in 'Pointing Unknowingly: Fantasy, Nonsense and "Religious Understanding"', *Philosophical Investigations*, January 1998, pp. 86–7) that some of what has been inferred from what Diamond says is unwarranted as a reading of Wittgenstein. Happily, I can avoid entering into this debate here, for reasons that will soon be evident.
21 This essay, too, is found in *The Realistic Spirit*. My point is not that she discusses this particular remark of Socrates, which she does not, but only that Socrates' remark can be construed as employing 'harm' in a 'secondary sense'.
22 For the point about metaphor, see p. 227.
23 Commentary on Dionysius' Mystical Theology. The translation is from Simon Tugwell, *Albert and Thomas: Selected Writings* (New York: Paulist Press, 1988), p. 150.
24 *Enneads*, I, 6, 1. The translation is Elmer O'Brien's in *The Essential Plotinus* (Indianapolis: Hackett, 1986), pp. 37–8. © Elmer O'Brien 1964.
25 'Reflections on the Right Use of School Studies with a View to the Love of God', in *Waiting for God*, trans. by Emma Crawford, with an introduction by Leslie A. Fiedler (New York: G.P. Putnam's Sons, 1951), p. 107.
26 Cambridge: Cambridge University Press, 1986. I shall give all references to Nussbaum in parentheses.
27 See his 'Religion in Education', in *Education and Inquiry*, ed. D.Z. Phillips (Oxford: Basil Blackwell, 1980), p. 206.
28 I have offered some discussion of this – or at least of the idea of God as 'ineffable' – in 'Pointing Unknowingly: Fantasy, Nonsense and "Religious Understanding"', *Philosophical Investigations*, Vol. 21, No. 1, January 1998. See pp. 84–7.
29 Ludwig Wittgenstein, *Zettel*, ed. G.E.M. Anscombe and G.H. von Wright, trans. G.E.M. Anscombe (Berkeley: University of California Press, 1970), #142.
30 248c.
31 I have tried to explore some of the contrasts between temperance and both self-control and self-denial in 'Beauty and the Attainment of Temperance', *The International Philosophical Quarterly*, Vol. XXXVII, No. 1, March 1997.
32 58d.
33 On this contrast see some of what Raimond Gaita has to say in his 'The Personal in Ethics', in *Wittgenstein: Attention to Particulars*, ed. D.Z. Phillips and Peter Winch (New York: St Martin's Press, 1989), especially pp. 140–1. In particular I have in mind the following: 'It is clear that the kind of man Socrates was had as much to do with his impact as did his arguments, which is why Plato is concerned to show the difference between Socrates and Gorgias. It is not as easy to distinguish them as it might seem if one is content to say that, whereas Socrates cared for the truth and appealed to logic or to reason, the orators cared not at all for truth and appealed mainly to emotion. Socrates did care for the truth, but it is not clear what that amounts to. It is usually taken to imply that the fact that *he* said something should have no bearing on an assessment of its worth. One need only consider what the Platonic dialogues would be without Socrates to be suspicious of the easy assurance with which that is usually said.'

34   *Symposium*, 210a–21 1e.

35   *The Need for Roots*, trans. A.F. Wills (London: Routledge and Kegan Paul, 1952), p. 198.

36   *Symposium*, 210a–211e.

37   An earlier version of this essay was read at a departmental colloquium at Nazareth College of Rochester, and I am grateful to those who participated in that discussion. I am also grateful to Patty Bowen-Moore, Kip Jensen, Heidi Northwood and Dan Tkachyk, all of whom read and discussed with me a more recent version.

4
Good and Evil: Love and Egocentricity[1]

Ilham Dilman

Human nature within a multiplicity of moralities

It is a truism, at least in anthropology, that within the different cultures and ways of living which men share they have developed moralities that differ from one another in many ways. Various conditions, physical and other, obviously shape men's lives. Lives so shaped are the soil in which different values are thrown up and grow, and these in turn contribute to the shaping of men's lives. The relationship in question is a two-way one. These conditions and the way men respond and adapt to them may be spoken of as the roots of the different moralities to be found among men.

Thus in the way men adapt to them, these conditions shape people's lives, and it is in the course of this adaptation that men develop values which measure their lives and ideals. The conditions of their lives and their values are thus related in a seamless way, the values and ideals themselves contributing to the conditions to which men adapt. In the life of the individual it is difficult, if not impossible, to speak of the beginning of this two-way contribution. The individual is born into a life in which he is shaped by increasing degrees of active participation on his part. Through such participation, in turn, he contributes to the life he shares with others, shapes his own life and he himself changes in the process. What life he is born into and grows up in is, of course, in a sense, an accident, though what he makes of himself in that life is not.

Now within this multiplicity of conditions in which the lot of an individual is an accident, there are certain constants or universals which constitute what has been called *human nature*. For instance, the individual, or at any rate most individuals, show a will to survive in the way they respond and adapt to the conditions which make up their lot – such as harsh physical conditions, scarcity of food, inhospitable surroundings, hostile neighbours, etc. They have to take things for themselves, fight to keep them, confront hostility. Those who are squeamish or timorous go under: they either do not survive or fall under the dominance of others and survive in subjection to them. Others who would rather die than accept such a state fight to the bitter end.

Such aggressive energy used in surviving with at least a modicum of self-respect, with as much ingenuity, skill and knowledge as the culture in which it is exercised permits, is part of the will to survive in inhospitable conditions. It is in most of us, to some degree, and is put into motion when the need arises to struggle for our very existence. Some will say it is part of 'the struggle for existence' which Darwin highlighted in the animal kingdom. Obviously, in hospitable environments and in what one may call 'civilized social orders' the need for such a struggle is reduced. Indeed, it may go to sleep, so to speak, and only wake up – if not atrophied – when circumstances call for it. There, in normal circumstances, active aggressiveness is reduced and its energy is diverted into other uses. It is enlisted in the development of ways of increasing the kind of prosperity which will benefit others – for instance, in artistic and scientific creativity.

It thus joins forces with a capacity which we equally have in us as human beings and which can develop in propitious circumstances. I have in mind our capacity to love, feel and care for, to give ourselves to and wish to serve our family, our neighbours and even strangers whose industry or dedication to what they are engrossed in touches us, or whose misfortunes call on our compassion. The will to survive by sticking up for oneself and for one's allies which becomes active in certain circumstances, and the capacity for fellow feeling which involves the willingness to put oneself out for others, are *both* to be found in human beings in different cultures. They cut across differences of culture. It is for this reason that they are generally regarded as part of *human nature*, some would say part of our animal inheritance, transformed and *humanized*.

Obviously animals are not capable of the kind of concern and compassion that we find in human beings. Animal life cannot provide the kind and range of significances in which an individual feels threatened and has to stick up for himself. Indeed, 'sticking up for oneself' means something very different in the case of human beings, since the self for which the individual sticks up is something that develops in response to the wide range of significances that come from the language and culture which characterize human life. Thus in most cases a man has something to stick or stand up for when he stands up for himself, something that makes his life worth defending or preserving. This is very different from the struggle for existence which Darwin found in the animal kingdom.

The will to survive when one's life is threatened and the willingness to put oneself out for others can thus coexist and need not come into conflict. The energy which belongs to the one can serve the other. That is, the energy which the individual economizes when he doesn't have to fight for himself can be used in responding to and working for others. A person can fight with as much aggressiveness in defending the rights of another human being or fellow creature as he may do when someone is trying to take his food from him. Yet in his aggressiveness he may be genuinely selfless, since sticking up for oneself in the face of what one considers an injustice does not have to be putting oneself before others.

Where, however, one or the other is dominant there is the risk of its changing character if the surroundings provided by the rest of the person's personality is such as to encourage or facilitate such a change. Thus the will to survive under adverse circumstances can turn into selfishness. When it is not balanced with what makes for concern and consideration for others, it can act as a magnet for the person's egocentric impulses and emotions. There is bound to be a period in every person's early life in which he is egocentric simply because he has not yet learned, in his affective life, the separateness of those people who circle around him. He has to learn that they have a life of their own in order to grow out of this early egocentricity. The love and affection of which he is capable of developing in circumstances conducive to such development has an important role to play in the emotional learning which enables him to grow out of his egocentricity.

Few people, if any, however, succeed in outgrowing their early primitive egocentricity completely. What remains of it is then bound to contaminate what I called the will to survive, to stand up for oneself and to be counted. In its egocentric character the will to stand up for oneself is, of course, bound to conflict with a person's willingness to put himself out for others and to give of himself to them. In the way such a person resolves this conflict in particular cases he may either outgrow the remnants of his early egocentricity or allow his attachments and interests themselves to be contaminated with it.

It is thus not the will to stand up for oneself that is the problem for a person who has at heart the values of a morality of love. The problem comes from the egocentricity which threatens to contaminate his best efforts.

Egocentricity and moral alienation

By egocentricity I mean an absorption in oneself which makes one, affectively, the centre of one's world, the world which acquires a living reality in the life one lives. Everything that exists independently of one, in so far as one has any apprehension of it, is then seen in relation to this centre. It is only within the ambit of such a relation that what exists outside one has reality. In other words, the reality of everything outside oneself takes on a subordinate status, like that of a shadow. It follows, at least in extreme cases, that nothing is left for such a person to give himself to. For giving oneself to what enhances the ego, to activities which aim at redeeming its standing, is not giving oneself at all. Such a person is thus impervious to any moral concern. He may obey the commands of an authoritarian morality, but he cannot care for what it enjoins him to do.

When I say that for an egocentric person 'everything outside him', e.g. that other people, their lives, pains, joys and interests, have a subordinate, shadowy existence, I mean *affectively*. This is how he takes these things in his feelings and emotions. Egocentricity thus characterizes the perspective of his abiding emotions.

Most people have the capacity for a mixture of emotions. Different situations, given the significance which the person finds in them, call for different spontaneous affective responses from him. This significance has an objective and a subjective aspect to it. For instance, objectively, given someone's intentions, and the culture in which it takes place, his words may constitute an insult. If the recipient knows this but takes no offence, he is not touched by the insult. There is a sense in which he has been insulted and another sense in which he has not. For him to be touched by the insult and, in that sense, to be insulted, he has to be in contact, affectively, with what is going on so that he can take offence, or not do so, as the case may be.

If he is a stranger to the culture in question he will not be aware of the insult – or, at any rate, he may not be. If he is aware *and* is offended, provided he keeps a sense of proportion, the insult will have reality for him: he will see it for what it is without being overwhelmed, swamped by phantasy; he will live the insult as its recipient. But there is no one way of living it; one way of living it is to accept it, rise above it, and so take no offence. Here mere 'intellectual knowledge' would be 'second-hand', 'indirect' knowledge. Its object would not make a direct impact on his affective apprehension. It is only when its recipient is affectively open to it so that it registers in his feelings that the insult acquires or has a living reality for him.

On the other hand, his feelings can equally shield its recipient from that reality; they may amplify and exaggerate it, giving him in the eyes of the person who insulted him an importance which he does not have. The person who insulted him becomes a bearer of his phantasies and the insult, even when objectively real, becomes inflated with his phantasies and as such unreal. That which is alive for him in the insult is then a product of his imagination. Here the angry, offended sensibility through which the recipient was in touch with the person who insulted him has now degenerated into an *egocentric* oversensitiveness.

My point is that anger as such, or an offended sensibility, does not have to be egocentric or its opposite, 'other-directed'. It can take either form. This is equally true of love, except that to the extent that love becomes egocentric it ceases to be genuine and, at an extreme, it ceases to be love altogether. Pure, genuine love is that through which we come to ourselves in what it enables us to give ourselves to. It is that which enables us to open ourselves so that we can at once receive what comes from outside and appreciate it. Only thus are we affected by what exists independently of us, by what gives us both pleasure and pain. Such love, in its ideal, purified form has been central to the great spiritual religions of the world and to the moralities internal to them.

Certainly, some of the feelings with which we respond to situations that face us in our lives are egocentric. An egocentric person is someone in whom egocentric feelings preponderate; they shape his personality and through it his outlook. They, in turn, are encouraged and shaped by his personality. Such a person's contact with people in their independent existence, as having a life of their own, is precarious: they do not exist as such in his feelings. Thus their joys and sorrows do not touch or affect him. He cannot respond with compassion to their misfortunes; and if he shows any pity, it is himself that he pities in them. He cannot share their joys either. His response to the values of the morality in which he was brought up is at best conformist – that is, where he does not ignore them or use them for his own ends.

Egocentricity as such is probably recognized in most moralities, but it has a *special* significance in moralities of love. For there, where the purity of love is of prime importance, such purity ('purification of the soul' in Plato's *Phaedo*) is achieved through self-renunciation – that is, renunciation of the ego. The self renounced is the ego and not the self to which one comes through such renunciation. There is nothing paradoxical thus in the claim that 'to be genuinely selfless one has to be oneself'. What this means is that one can only be genuinely selfless if one is oneself in one's selflessness. That is, what is involved in one's being selfless must come from one. One cannot, for instance, renounce oneself out of fear for oneself. For then the self one is supposed to renounce reappears in one's fears. Thus 'self' means one thing in 'self-renunciation', 'selfless', 'selfish' and 'self-absorbed', and something quite different in 'self-knowledge', 'self-deception', 'being oneself' and 'finding oneself'.

Good and evil in moralities of love

I said that egocentricity is of special significance in moralities of love. Love is directed towards others as individuals; it is an affective form of consideration of the other. Egocentricity, on the other hand, ignores others as individuals and sees them only in relation to the ego's needs – the need of an ego for attention, the need of one hurt or slighted for the restoration of pride, of one feeling handicapped for compensation, or one drunk with power or self-importance.

Love, when it is pure, is devoid of all egocentricity. The two thus stand opposed to each other. A morality of love is one which articulates the perspective of a love thus purified and is the home of our notions of good and evil. But which ones?

There are, I think, two different ways in which we speak of *evil*. These need to be contrasted and only one is unique to moralities of love. In the one case, which interests us here, we speak of the evil that has entered a person's soul. In the second case we use this word to refer to a disgrace, to something we consider shameful, something we think the person himself ought to find shameful. In this sense, a person who considers what someone did to be dishonourable, for instance, may call it an evil, but I doubt that he would describe the agent himself as evil. He would probably characterize the man himself in terms of a specific vice. The agent, for example, if he thought of what he did as dishonourable, would feel *ashamed*. Such shame is connected primarily with one's conception of oneself and of one's worth in the light of that conception. (I put aside non-moral uses of the term 'evil' such as when certain calamities, e.g., earthquakes and pestilences, are described as 'natural evils'. They can, of course, be seen as punishments and so come to assume a moral significance.)

The same action, characterized in the same moral terms – for instance disloyalty towards or betrayal of a friend – may give rise to shame in one person and remorse in another. In the one case the person thinks of what he has done in terms of what that does to him. It is his own worth that he sees as damaged. There need be nothing egocentric in this, for it may take the form of his feeling unworthy of others with whom his relation is free of egocentricity. Here, although he is thinking of himself in relation to others, his own worth occupies a visible position in his thoughts. For that is what shame is; a damaged sense of worth, in this case by the agent's own actions, by his own mode of existence. He cares about that in the shame he feels.

In the other case the person is thinking of himself in relation to the other in a special way: as someone for whom he cares, someone whose welfare matters and is of concern to him. Concepts of welfare and harm to it vary, of course, from person to person and from culture to culture, although where a person's action springs from malice, envy, greed or hatred of the other, it is directed against the other's welfare or well-being as the agent conceives of it. That is certainly the object of his intention: to hurt the other, to damage his well-being. If he then feels remorse, it means that he has had a change of heart and thinks of his action from the perspective of his regard, care, concern or fellow feeling for the other – from the perspective of his 'good feelings' or love for him. I use the term 'love' in the broad sense to cover all this. What he feels has reference to himself only as the agent of an action which harms or ignores the well-being of the other, or at any rate as the owner of the intention to harm him. But, unlike the first case, here his own worth is not of principal concern to him; at most the damage to it is of secondary importance to him relative to the harm intended or done to the other. He is the object of his own feelings *only* as owner of the intention to harm a fellow human being or as the agent of the harm he has done. His regard for the other which finds expression in the pain he feels for what he has intended or done leaves his self-regard totally in the shade.

In this sense the evil that characterizes a person in his actions, intentions, feelings and desires, in his way of living, is connected with the horror we feel before those actions and the remorse we feel when these actions are our own. And these feelings themselves spring from what those actions are directed to, namely, to the being and welfare of something we cherish, someone special to us in a way that has nothing to do with what needs he satisfies in us (except in the case where we take the needs he satisfies in us as an expression of his goodness for which we feel gratitude, as in the case of a child's love for his parents when the child's love is pure). Obviously we cherish the things we cherish because of what we see in them, we feel concern or compassion for others in their particular plight because of the way we think of them – e.g., as sharing a common fate with us. These are two sides of the same coin: the feeling and its object stand in intelligible relation to each other, and the intelligibility of their relation comes from our moral perspective.

We may feel shame for a great variety of things – failures, humiliations, blemishes, etc. – and some of these have little or nothing to do with our conceptions of our moral worth. Vices and moral failures which may be called evils in this sense vary from one morality to another. But only those which give rise to actions and modes of existence which inspire horror in others and remorse in oneself in circumstances such as I indicated are *evil* from the perspective of a morality of love; and they are not considered 'evils' in the plural. They are seen as expressions of the evil in the person.

When one speaks of evil in *this* sense one is speaking from the perspective of a morality of love, and one has in mind such things as malice, greed unrestrained by any moral consideration, envy, lusts of various kinds which compete with a consideration of others, indifference to the fate of others, incapacity to feel remorse and gratitude, the inability to forgive others such as we find in vindictiveness. If I am asked what is evil about these things, I can tell someone only if we agree on what goodness is. It is only in its light, only from the perspective of a morality of love in which goodness has its identity, that these things are evil.

Goodness, too, like evil, in the particular sense which interests us here, is unique to moralities of love. It is true that we call 'good' those things which we approve of, morally and otherwise. This stretches even as far as to include things we simply like. But putting aside such examples as those in which we speak of 'the goodness contained in orange juice' or 'the goodness of fresh air', the noun *goodness* signifies a virtue which belongs to love and which can only be apprehended by it. Indeed, it signifies something to be found in all the virtues of moralities of love – honesty, compassion, generosity, loyalty, faith, forgiveness, trustworthiness. It signifies something that unites them. Bravery or courage may also come from goodness, and what is called 'true courage' within a morality of love perhaps is a form of goodness.[2] But what is regarded as an act of courage or bravery in a heroic morality would not be seen as an expression of goodness in a morality of love – however much it is praised. A brave man may be praised as a 'good man', of course, but here the word 'good' is no more than an adjective of commendation in the light of the values which belong to the morality in question: 'He is a good man, he has guts, you can rely on him as a fighter.' What he possesses is courage, not goodness. The latter is not something which has reality within a heroic morality. Indeed, what comes into focus for us in the use of this term may well be seen there as a form of weakness, and in an extreme case even as something to be despised – thus Callicles' *vis-à-vis* Socrates' conception of 'philosophic virtue'.

Good and evil in a diversity of cultures

I said earlier that what belongs to our nature and the conditions to which human beings adapt constitute the soil from which the values and moralities which have developed among men have grown in their *multiplicity*. Like religions, moralities can grow from different roots in us and develop in response to different conditions of life. There is *one group* of moralities, I pointed out, whose main root is the kind of love and concern for others we are capable of developing in ourselves. I called them 'moralities of love'. The love in question varies, of course, in its range from being directed to family, friends and larger groups of individuals knit together in various forms of relationships, common interests and loyalties, to outsiders in every sense except in being fellow human beings – that is directed to total strangers in need of help. When this love is pure we speak of the *goodness* of the person who has it and acts on it.

Such goodness is rare when sustained, for it is in conflict and competition with much else within and outside us. It is rarely transparent because of the impurities it contains; but, even when it is unmarked by words, it can appear in diverse cultures in rare moments of magnanimity and generosity. It is not the privilege of any one culture. Of course, moral attitudes towards it vary and some of these may work to stifle it. This claim, so far, is not controversial. For since the forms of goodness in question are moral qualities they can only appear within a moral perspective and they will be seen in their particular moral identity by those to whom the moral perspective in question is available and accessible.

My claim, however, is that we, in our culture, do not have a monopoly over it. Thus the goodness that finds expression in an act of generosity and magnanimity can strike a chord and awaken a response in its recipient, a response of gratitude which is itself an expression of its recognition. The word for gratitude in French is 'reconnaissance', which means recognition, the recognition of goodness; and the word for ungrateful in Turkish '*namkor*', means 'blind to the bread given to one', that is, to the giver's goodness, blindness to it in the recipient's feelings. Such recognition is rooted in the love that belongs to our nature and, as such, is not the exclusive property of any particular culture. Thus what we call 'goodness' can have, at least on certain occasions, a reality for individuals who have not been brought up in our culture, do not share our morality, and who may not have a word for it.

This is equally true of evil. An act of what we call treachery, even when it is motivated by the most punctilious of party loyalties, may be seen by the person so betrayed under the aspect of evil. If he is knowingly delivering the person who has put his trust in him to torture and certain death without batting an eye-lid, then he is taking part in an evil practice and is himself soiled by this evil. This is what *we* would say, certainly, but we would be articulating something to which its recipient may well himself be responsive, whatever the culture or morality to which he belongs. It is in his disregard for the bond of trust that ties him to the man he is delivering to such a fate, in the way he treats trust, that marks him as having become evil. It is being the recipient of such an act that opens one's eyes to its character.

It is because trust is something the recipient in my example is capable of and understands that he finds its betrayal so abhorrent. I suggest that trust itself is not a mere predictive belief that may be disappointed, but a form of love that can be wounded and hurt. The pain contained in such wounding is an expression of the perception or recognition of evil. I do not wish to deny that different 'moral' reactions are possible to the betrayal of trust. All I am saying is that the possibility of trust transcends the limits of any culture and that there are reactions to its betrayal which are not wholly circumscribed by the moral frameworks available in a particular culture. Forms of relationships and their obligations certainly vary from culture to culture and with the moralities belonging to these. There are, of course, in every culture, relationships of power in which fear and self-interest play an important role. This is equally true, in a modified sense, of what may be called purely 'working relationships' where the partnership is wholly pragmatic. But wherever there are relationships in which people count for each other – and they exist, I imagine, in most cultures – then trust, affection, respect and loyalty are part of these relationships. And there are certain perceptions and obligations which are internal to trust, affection and respect. They may, of course, clash on particular occasions with those obligations that are specific to a particular culture. But even if, in that culture, they are kept in the background and disregarded in the case of a clash, the fact remains that they exist and cut across the boundaries of any particular culture.

A person whose trust is betrayed, whatever the justification he is given may be, and however valid it is considered in the culture to which he belongs, will feel betrayed. Similarly, if he is the one who does the betraying, he will feel the impact of his action in the form of guilt and remorse, unless he deceives himself. It is a person's responsiveness to such things which opens 'the eyes of his feelings' to the perception of good and evil. Let me link this with what I said in the previous section by noting that the remorse that is felt for an act of evil done to others is independent of values that are specific to a culture in a way that the shame felt for a disgrace is not.

The perspective in which good and evil have reality for the individual, I submit, belongs to the way people can count for each other in personal, and then by extension in 'impersonal', relationships. The first context into which people, as children, are socially initiated is the context of the family, whatever its form in the culture to which he belongs – and if not the family then whatever else takes its place. It is here that the young child's capacity for love and affection comes into play and develops. The perspective in which good and evil have reality is a way of regarding others and oneself in relation to them, and it belongs to love in its different varieties. The kind of fellow-feeling one may feel for a total stranger in distress belongs to compassion, which is an extension of such love. The impersonal character of the relationship – e.g., attending to a perfect stranger from whom one has nothing to gain – becomes a test of the purity of such love, although even here it may be sullied by what one may receive from such an act in the form of self-congratulation.

I am suggesting that the source of such actions is love, just as it is the source of trust and forgiveness too. I further suggest that what I called initiation to love, for which human beings have an innate capacity, a capacity which belongs to our nature as human beings, is an initiation to a particular perspective, one in which others are seen as counting as individuals. The initiation is the bringing out and development of that for which we have a capacity. This capacity to love develops through experiences which provide it with the opportunity for its exercise and by the individual's surmounting of obstacles which threaten to impede such development. These obstacles are provided by situations which rouse the individual's egocentric impulses – such as greed and hatred – or call up defensive measures meant to protect the individual in his egocentric identity, such as when he responds to a slight or humiliation with an angry impulse to redress the balance, tit-for-tat, tilted unfavourably relative towards the ego.

Let me note here that what belongs to the loving, caring side of man's nature gives him the capacity to tolerate pain, fear, privation and frustration, to bear abuse without feeling demeaned and so wanting to retaliate. It is the source of his ability to give, forgive and to be grateful for the good he receives. It is through what belongs to this side of his nature that a child or adult grows out of what is egocentric in him. Indeed, it has a great deal to contribute to a child's coming to a 'normal' sense of self – i.e. to a lack of doubt in his own existence for others. For such a sense of self is built in the formation of relationships of trust and affection. A person comes to it in feeling that there are others, originally his parents, for whom he counts and on whom he can depend, and in wanting to be worthy of their trust in him. One who lacks such a sense of self doubts whether he has anything to give to others. It is often in a person who has a weak sense of self that egocentricity thrives.

Phillips raises the following difficulty for what I say. I claim, as I did in an earlier paper, that we find the responses which are expressions of regard for the values of a morality of love in cultures where there is no explicit recognition and acknowledgement of these values. But how can we speak of these responses – for instance, the horror that stays the hand of someone engaged in a ritual which involves taking someone's life – as expressions of regard for values which do not exist in the culture in question? How can we take the response in question as an acknowledgement of values which are not available in the culture?[3]

I do not wish to go back on what I said in my earlier paper about moral frameworks which give people particular moral perspectives. But I still wish to say that what the person I have imagined finds out when he cannot take the life of someone he is expected to take is comparable to a soldier at war when he finds he cannot bring himself to kill an enemy soldier. There is a difference, of course, and it lies in the way that in our culture such responses can be integrated with various others. Indeed, we can compare the person in my example with someone within our culture in whom such spontaneous responses remain unintegrated – for instance, Raskolnikov in Dostoevsky's *Crime and Punishment* who gives his last twenty copecks to save a young girl from sexual molestation and then calls after the policeman he asked to take her home and tells him to let them be.[4] The difference lies in what it would take for such an integration to come about. Raskolnikov, Dostoevsky tells us, was brought up in his mother's religion, namely Christianity. He has to go through the fire of remorse for the crime he has committed before he can make his own the beliefs in which he was brought up. Only then does the goodness in him which finds expression in sporadic impulses become part of his settled personality. The person in my example, on the other hand, needs to be *converted* to a framework of beliefs which is alien to his culture before this can be true of him.

Phillips chides me for seeking an explanation for 'this universal phenomenon', as I called it, meaning that it is not confined to any particular culture.[5] I accept this criticism and withdraw the one sentence in my earlier paper[6] where I lay myself open to it: 'It seems to me that this [universal] phenomenon must have something to do with the "humanity" in us human beings.' I agree that this is circular and is, therefore, no explanation. What I should have said – and I now say it – is that the humanity in us, that is our capacity for compassion, forgiveness and gratitude, is not the product of a specific culture, although the possibility of its existence presupposes some form of culture or other.

I also accept Phillips's criticism for what I say in another sentence he quotes from my paper: 'Most people have it in them, though often buried in a mixture of rubble.'[7] I will not now explain what made me say it, but

I withdraw this claim. All I should like to say is that the *potential* for goodness exists in most people at the start of their lives. There are, however, cultures in which it is not nurtured and developed, but is instead stunted so that mostly it perishes. That is what makes its survival in particular cases so remarkable. In our culture it mostly reaches an average height in personalities which don't give it much head room, and coexists with what, given its head, would make for evil – much of this under a blanket of moral conformity and finding expression in terms of such conformity.

Phillips also asks whether what I claim in speaking of the 'universality' of goodness is not in flagrant conflict with Simone Weil's claim that the kind of love which she speaks of – 'selfless and impersonal' – is something very rare. Have I forgotten this? No, I have not. What is not confined to a particular culture and is thus 'universal' in its appearance may still be something very rare. There is therefore no conflict between what I say and Simone Weil's claim to which I subscribe. Obviously there is a great distance to be covered by anyone if he is to move from the capacity for love with which most people are born to the kind of love which, in Simone Weil's language, constitutes a 'supernatural virtue'. Very few people travel that distance; the obstacles to it in the soul, which she points out, prove insurmountable for most people. It is one thing to risk one's life to save the life of another, for instance, another thing to be a saint. One is a spontaneously generous action, a genuine expression of goodness, the other takes the consolidation of such actions in a life of self-denial.

Egocentric pursuit of evil: self-stultifying?

Now evil, which is a notion specific to moralities of love, is egocentric. It attacks or ignores what other people cherish. It is destructive of what others hold dear and at the same time it impoverishes the life in which it thrives. It desiccates it of the kind of sense in which only a person can come to himself. Phillips finds ambiguities in these claims and is critical of them.[8] He argues that particular vices alienate people from *particular* moralities, and that the evil and the good man stand in symmetrical relation to what each is alienated from in his life: what the evil man is alienated from is what the good man engages with, and similarly the other way around; what the evil man engages with is what the good man is alienated from. Therefore, if the evil man is limited in his life, then so is the good man. What is called a limitation or impoverishment is relative to the speaker's perspective, and there is nothing self-stultifying about what is a limitation from a perspective which a person does not share. For it to be self-stultifying he must *himself* consider the life he wants to live to be limiting and so feel deprived of something he wants or cares for while living it. So if there is anything self-stultifying about such a life its source must lie in particular features of the personality of the person who lives it: he must stand in his own way, live a life which excludes what he himself needs or values. There is nothing self-stultifying about mere indifference or non-engagement. Such a man has, therefore, to be contrasted with the man with an insatiable ego-hunger whom Socrates likened to someone who tries to fill a leaky vessel with a sieve. In *his* case there is a tension between his self-importance which reduces others to mere shadows in his feelings and the way he needs them to be real so that he can have his own importance confirmed in their eyes.

I agree with Phillips that the egocentric desire to put oneself first is primitive.[9] It has its roots in the egocentricity which belongs to early life which, as I pointed out, most people outgrow to various degrees as they engage in relationships in which their capacity to care and put themselves out for others comes into play. Thus it need not be a desire for compensation for the lack of importance one feels in oneself. Yet if someone who has been unable to outgrow his early egocentricity puts himself first to a degree where others take on a shadowy existence in his affective life, his engagements with them will be very tenuous. So these others will not be able to sustain his conviction of existing in his own right. This may then give rise to a *secondary* need for compensation so that he seeks to acquire status and be somebody in their eyes. That is, he comes to seek to make up for what he has been deprived of in his primary or primitive egocentricity. But this dependence on others may, in turn, further undermine his inner confidence in himself and lead to a reaction-formation; 'I need nobody; I am self-sufficient.' This further reinforces his egocentricity. Both the need for compensation and the reaction-formation against it, his egocentric self-sufficiency, are thus secondary formations. They have their source in the person's primitive or primary egocentricity and its consequences. These constitute a vicious circle in which the person is further anchored in his egocentricity.

Still, an egocentric person's self-sufficiency may not be a secondary formation in this way; it does not have to be. A person who has been badly spoiled in his early childhood may gain the conviction that he can have anything he wants and that others are there to provide it for him. He will then come to expect it as his due, feel no gratitude for what he gets and consider that nothing that constitutes a frustration is to be tolerated. If such a person continues to be successful in having his own way in life his conviction that he owes nothing to anyone and that he is the source of his success and good fortune will be reinforced. This is a perfectly genuine conviction in him and such a person will not find his egocentric self sufficiently stultifying. Can *we* nevertheless still say that it is 'self-stultifying'?

Yes we can; and I believe Socrates does. When he used the simile of the leaky vessel and the sieve he was thinking of egocentricity as such; not a particular form of it. What he had in mind, as I understand it, may be expressed as follows: the more the ego is fed the more it expands and the more it expands the more it needs. The egocentric person thus cannot catch up with his needs. As for the sieve: what the ego grabs to feed its needs is automatically devalued; its sustenance is lost in the way the egocentric person appropriates it. It is devalued because he is incapable of any genuine regard or appreciation. What looks desirable, when appropriated loses its value. What I am referring to is well known in the case of envy: the grass is always greener on the other side of the fence.

I am suggesting that the ego's way of feeding itself, namely by appropriation, is itself destructive of the value of what it wants. It expands the ego but leaves the person forever unfed and hungry, without sustenance and dependent on the ego. There is a big difference between the arrogant self-satisfaction of the ego and the self-fulfilment a person finds in forgetting himself and getting on with something outside that interests him, something to which he gives himself. To so forget himself and be open and responsive to the call of things and people on him, a person has to have accepted himself. It is only then that the ego leaves him alone and shrinks. The inner peace and freedom that come from this belong to self-acceptance, and in the give-and-take which this allows the person finds enrichment.

If a person, successful in his egocentric pursuits, in the sense of attaining his immediate goals, says that he doesn't care for any of this, it is because he has no conception of it. He cannot compare what he has with what he misses. He cannot have a conception of it while he is driven by the needs of the ego. So, yes, there need be no tension in him, no conflict between what he craves for and what his pursuits exclude, since he does not know what he thus misses and, therefore, cannot want it. It remains true that in feeding his ego he starves himself and that this increases the hunger he feels in the ego. He is a person *driven* by the ego with which he is at one in his egocentricity. He is driven by the ultimate unattainability of what he craves for and the way this increases his craving. In the words Alcibiades uses in the *Symposium* we could say that the egocentric person 'neglects his own true interests' in pursuing the goals set for him by the ego. Socrates would say that he thus neglects his soul. In doing so, I am arguing, he neglects himself – the self from which he has strayed. His pursuits stand in the way of its growth and flourishing. It is in this sense that what is pursued egocentrically is self-stultifying.

The self, its growth and flourishing, are of course invisible from the ego's perspective and so to the person who has adopted an egocentric perspective. When, therefore, I speak of what such a person *needs* to come to himself, I am not speaking of what he, in his egocentricity, wants. The need belongs to a self from which he has strayed and so to which he has not come. The 'self-sufficient' egocentric person lives a life that is stultifying to the self in this sense. In his identification with the ego he cannot, of course, find that life stultifying. It is, therefore, true, as Phillips says, that what I claim is meant to be a comment on how *others* see.[10]

But was not Phillips himself happy to make a similar claim about Tolstoy's Ivan Ilytch when he said that Ilytch is self-deceived, that his life is a life of self-deception? Did he not, quite rightly, point out that this is a judgement Ilytch could not himself have made without changing in himself and coming to a perspective from which the deception can be appreciated – a perspective which belongs to a new self?[11] Did he not go along with Socrates' judgement that Archelaus is an unhappy man, even though Archelaus himself had no reservation about the pursuits that characterized his life and could not acknowledge Socrates' judgement without departing from the life judged?

My judgement that the egocentric thug's life is self-stultifying is a similar judgement, one made from the same perspective as the two other judgements, Tolstoy's and Socrates'. The self that is stultified here is the same self as the one deceived in Tolstoy's story and the one Socrates pities in Archelaus. Ilytch had strayed from the self he finds just before his death. In thus straying from it he was deceived *in* the self from which he had strayed. Similarly, the 'self-sufficient' egocentric person lives a life which stands in the way of his coming to a self in which he would be disgusted or horrified by the life he lives. The self stultified is outside his conception; he is 'all ego'. He is thus alienated from *himself* in being alienated from a life in which other people's separate or independent existence is acknowledged and respected, a life of give-and-take with them as such. For my claim is that it is only in such a life, whatever form it takes in the culture to which it belongs, that a person finds himself.

Egocentric pursuit of evil: Self-alienating?

Phillips expresses scepticism about this notion of the self in which a person is said not to have come to himself even though, in full identification with his ego, he is behind his actions – as in the case of Archelaus. For Phillips, if Archelaus is behind his evil actions, then he is himself: he is the evil person that he really is. To say that even then he is not himself, that evil alienates a person from himself, is simply to court confusion. He doubts that there is any benefit in speaking this way.[12]

I am not applying to Archelaus a way of speaking I have invented. In Ibsen's play Peer Gynt is represented as having strayed from his 'true self'. When this finally catches up with him, he is terrified that he is going to be melted down in the casting ladle of the button moulder who has come to claim his soul. In other words, his fear is that he is going to be cast into the nonentity that he has become in the life he has lived and that he will never be able to redeem himself.[13] Yet Peer Gynt's self-alienation does not consist of wanting one thing and doing another, and consequently living a life which involves inner tension. It consists of living a life of dissipation and rootlessness in which he fails to come together. He pursues his desires and follows impulses of the moment, but he cannot be said to know what he wants. It is not so much that he is not behind his actions as that he has not come to a self with which to be behind what he does.

There are many forms of character or modes of being which represent what a person is really like, that is, in which he is what he is, and not false or insincere, but in which, nevertheless, he is said not to have come to himself. Rootlessness is one; an impulsiveness which fragments a person's life into a series of disconnected moments is another. Egocentricity is yet another. There are many different forms of self-alienation. What Archelaus has not found is the kind of unity of self that belongs to moral integrity of one kind or another. He is alienated from any kind of moral concern in what, from the perspective of a morality of love, is seen as the evil which has entered his soul. He pursues what he wants for himself without considering himself accountable to anything or anyone for what he does. The only consider- ations that weigh with him are instrumental: under the present circum- stances what is the best, the most efficient, way of getting what I want? When those circumstances change, some other line of action becomes the best way to what he wants. He has nothing to be loyal to and no one, therefore, can trust *him* or depend on *him*. Others can assess his character and depend on *that* for their judgement of what he would do, how he would act in certain circumstances. But that is very different from trusting or depending on *him* – counting on his word, for instance.

He has not thus come to a self which has anything dependable about it; there is nothing in him to make him trustworthy. Such a person may, as I said, be behind his actions moment by moment; he does what he wants at the time. But he has not come to a self to which to be true. Rather, it is what he wants that calls the tune in his life and the question of being true to any conviction does not arise for him. In thus having nothing to be loyal to he has no self to be true to. It is in this sense that he has not come to himself.

The maturity of goodness and the kind of contact which evil excludes: some further criticisms considered

Phillips finds a systematic ambiguity in the concepts crucial to my claims and elucidations: development, arrest, authenticity, maturity, contact.[14] Their meaning varies with the moral perspective from which we view things. He quotes the words in which I summarize Erich Fromm's view, which I say contains some truth: 'maturity, autonomy, being oneself and moral good- ness in the humanistic sense coincide'. He then writes: 'But when we look to see what authenticity, autonomy, and maturity amount to, on Dilman's view, we are told that they are arrested in someone who simply conforms to a morality which has been imposed on him. But that would apply to *any* seriously held moral viewpoint, not simply to humanistic ethics. One cer- tainly could not maintain that "the mature" individual is at the same time someone whose morality is humanistic, since what "maturity" comes to may vary with the moral perspective.'[15] 'A similar ambiguity can be found in Dilman's discussion of moral development. Sometimes he is speaking of factors which would make moral development impossible within any moral perspective... At other times he has a specific *kind of* moral development in mind.'[16] He then quotes my words: 'When we speak of a person having to become an individual we are inevitably referring to his *moral* development.' He asks: 'But in what context is Dilman speaking? Is he elucidating *one* kind of moral development, or discussing what he thinks *any* moral development involves?'[17]

Let me begin by answering this last question: 'we are referring to his *moral* development'. What I am saying here is that the notion of individual development, which has played such an important role in psychoanalysis, is a *moral* notion; it cannot be understood in terms of a biological model or in purely psychological terms. Thus maturity, which is a developmental concept, cannot be understood in morally neutral terms. It follows that there is not one concept of maturity.[18] What Fromm calls 'humanistic ethics' represents his attempt to spell out the moral ethos that belongs to psychoanalysis. It is from its perspective, which is the perspective of psycho-analysis, that Fromm argues (i) that evil is a form of *immaturity*, the kind that analysts focus on in psychoanalytic therapy, that *it* comes from an immature part of the self, and (ii) that to come to goodness, in the humanistic sense, a person has to grow in maturity and move towards authenticity: find himself and in doing so put greater honesty into his relationships.

As I said, I believe there is truth in this claim and I try to spell it out. But, as I make clear, I dissent from Fromm on at least two points: (i) While Fromm's humanistic ethics may give an accurate representation of the morality im-plicit in the psychoanalytic outlook, it is not to be identified with the moral perspective in which Christianity, in the broad sense, is continuous with Platonic morality, and where good and evil have their unique reality. It differs, for instance, in so far at least as it is partly an 'ethics of self-realiza-tion'. Thus I contrast Fromm and Plato's Socrates in this respect – Socrates, whose notion of the 'care and cure of the soul' has sometimes been misun-derstood in just this way. (ii) I am critical of Fromm's attempts to elevate 'humanistic ethics' to the objective status of the only true or authentic morality.

Phillips seems to ignore all this in his criticism. So let me answer his question: what *kind* of maturity does it take to come to goodness in the Christian-*cum*-Platonic sense in one's life and actions? My short answer is: the kind in which a person outgrows the egocentricity that belongs to his early life so that the love and care with which he is able to respond to others is freed from any trace of egocentricity it had contained. What is *distinctive* about such a morality, which I characterize as a 'morality of love', is the distinction it makes between the ego and the self, and the way coming to goodness is conceived in it as a turning away from the ego. The kind of maturity that is in focus here involves emotional independence from others which permits one to respond to them in their 'separate' existence[19] – an independence which is not a reaction-formation to a dependency which survives unconsciously, in which one remains closed to others in wanting to hide one's vulnerabilities. It has sometimes been called 'mature dependence' (Fairbairn) because it takes the kind of inner security which belongs to the maturity in question to accept one's dependence on others, not to try to deny it. Moving towards such maturity is thus moving towards greater openness towards others and so greater honesty with them as well as with oneself. This makes for greater contact with the life around one and so for increased opportunities for emotional learning in one's interactions with others.

Here Phillips wants me to remember that both 'contact' and 'learning' mean different things in different moral perspectives. This is certainly true of what counts as *learning* – as it is of what counts as development. What I am saying, then, is that when a person is open with others in his personal relationships, while this may initially awaken greater resistance in the other person, it will in many instances change the character of the relationship towards greater honesty. One will thus learn greater honesty, modesty and patience in such a relationship and develop the ability for greater warmth and sympathy.

I find, however, what Phillips says about the relativity of what *contact* may mean in different moralities unconvincing. He rightly focuses on the notion of *reciprocity* on which I laid stress in my account and considered the form it takes between enemies.[20] My enemy, I argued, must be 'there for me to respond to him' and trust is only one way in which a person can be 'there' for me. For my adversary to be 'there' for me in our conflict I must respect him – I must find something in him that calls for my respect. More than this, *he* must recognize and acknowledge my respect, must see *me*. Otherwise, 'though I come in contact with a side of him that is real, I do not make contact with *him* since he does not see me. Hence although I do see him, and not simply as a witness through a one-way screen, *I do not see him seeing me*: our eyes do not meet so to speak.'[21] If I am right, then this rules out (i) contact with an evil man, and (ii) the evil man making contact with his victims as well as his allies.

Of course, we can make contact with people belonging to different cultures. But to do so we have to find something common between us – for instance the exchange of gifts and the good feelings that go with such an exchange. As for the respect that we may feel for our enemy (for the way, for instance, he remains true to his convictions) this respect will vary with what inspires such respect and hence with the moral perspective we take on our enemy. I have never suggested that contact with others is the privilege of those belonging to a morality of love. However, I think that while that in which people make contact with one another varies from people to people, from culture to culture, all the same 'contact' means the same thing in these different cases.

So what about the example Phillips gives, which is supposed to illustrate a Cossack making contact with his enemy even while deliberately trampling him to death?[22] On Phillips's reading, 'the soul, faced with certain death, is afforded a terrible opportunity to show itself as exhibiting grace under extreme pressure, or as broken'.[23] Phillips is taking the trampling to show some kind of 'respect' for the person trampled on in considering him worthy of being given such an opportunity. Even if one could go along with such a reading, the person trampled on, in his extreme condition, must see his enemy as giving him a chance to redeem his soul and respond to this. It would take a very great deal for this to be the case.

Anyway, it seems to me that 'to trample an enemy for over an hour' is to indulge in an orgy of destructiveness, irrespective of what morality the person belongs to. As such it must exclude any form of respect for one's enemy. I doubt that such an orgy could constitute giving one's enemy a chance to redeem his soul. What could happen, however, is this: a man thus being trampled on may refuse to crawl and this may stop the man trampling on him in his tracks, arrest the orgy, and a look of recognition may pass between them. Now that would be an instance of contact between two human beings, however short-lived. We must remember that in such a waking up from his orgy the man trampling on his enemy distances himself from the evil that has got hold of his soul at the moment of his triumph. Such an awakening is a further instance of the 'universality' of the love and 'humanity', as *we* would call it, that I spoke of earlier.

I repeat. A man immersed in a life of evil cannot make contact with either the allies he uses or with the enemies he is intent on harming or plundering. He sees neither as individuals; they do not have a reality for him in their own right. The evil which 'limits' his affective perspective and determines what he can see with the eyes of his feelings in this way comes from the egocentricity which he has not outgrown and which has taken root in his personality. As such it prevents the kind of interaction with others which involves give and take and the learning and growth which that makes possible.

Asymmetry between good and evil

In my description of the poverty of the evil person's life, which Phillips quotes, I have in mind the thug who cares for no one and nothing except himself. At any rate he cares for things only in so far as they are of use to him in enhancing his ego and satisfying its cravings. Hence his greed for material things and craving for power, his determination to get his own back and 'punish' those who cross him, to get the better of his rivals by one means or another, his meanness towards those in need, his contempt for the weak, his need to make an impression on those who speak his language. I pointed out that the majority of people have in common with him something of what emanates from the ego. It is reflected in different cultures in different ways – in ways that can be characterized as 'culture syntonic'. It thus pervades the world we all live in as human beings, the human world – not surprisingly, since egocentric reactions form part of human nature and few people outgrow them completely.

I argued that the thug who has no morality understands the moral language of those around him, though it means little to him in the sense that it does not speak to him personally, does not engage him affectively. He thus lives in a limited world and has shallow relationships. But that does not mean that he is cut off from human life altogether. He engages with those aspects of the life and culture to which he belongs. They take up what is egocentric in human beings, legitimize and institutionalize it in forms of relationships and activities, in the common interests and identities they promote, in the types of jokes they tell and even in their rituals.

Phillips, we have seen, takes issue with what I said about the limiting and impoverishing character of evil. He argues for the relativity of this limitation to the point of view or perspective from which we describe a form of life. Thus, he says, from the point of view of the thug the good man's life will be seen as equally limiting. To make this point he puts my words in the mouth of the thug substituting 'vice' or 'immorality' for 'morality':

> one who is alienated from vice is not cut off from human life altogether – immorality is internal to human life . . . our vices are an articulation of what belongs to our relationships and makes them what they are . . . The significance which our vices enable us to attribute to the various things to which we respond in living our lives characterise those things for us in themselves . . . our immorality enters into the very constitution of the world in which we live. It is in this world that we find ourselves: the very self which we succeed or fail to come to has reality in our interactions in this world.[24]

I agree with much of this, but for one big reservation to which I shall come presently. Evil is, of course, part of human life and, therefore, belongs to the human world; it is part of the human scene. What emanates from it, as I said, is taken into and made part of human cultures and so characterizes the meanings of many of our words and the identity and significance of the things we describe in terms of these words – for instance, many slang expressions for sexual intercourse and other human acts and for types of human character. Indeed, evil has a way of seeping into many of our moral attitudes to things and into the meanings of the words in which we express such attitudes.

The expression obtained by substituting 'vice' for 'morality', namely, 'one who is alienated from vice', has to mean something like 'one who has not been corrupted by vice', 'one who has remained innocent' – that is, if it is to mean anything. Such a person is, of course, not cut off from human life altogether. But there is much in the life to which he belongs from which he may be cut off, as there is in the case of the immoral, egocentric thug – though they are cut off from different aspects of that life. I said *may* because innocence may be a form of naivety. However, one who has not been corrupted by vice may not be someone who is innocent in this sense. He may be someone who has experienced the temptations of vice and has overcome them in himself. Such a person will not be cut off from the way evil marks human life everywhere. He may even be someone who has been the victim of such evil, or someone who has felt and even suffered for those who have been hurt by it. The mere fact of having loved ones and caring enough about the injustices in one's immediate surroundings is enough to keep a person in touch with the ways in which evil works in human life.

The symmetry which Phillips claims is to be found between what good and evil exclude from the lives of individuals does not go all the way as he suggests. Indeed, I doubt that it goes very far. Imagine a good man who comes to be corrupted by some vice. He may well remember what he once knew. But that doesn't mean that he still knows it, that he is in touch with goodness as he once was. He no longer has the feelings he had. Things that horrified or disgusted him no longer do so; he no longer sees what horrified or disgusted him in them as horrifying or disgusting. He no longer understands what goodness means to those who are pure at heart. He has lost sight of what they see in it, what makes it attractive to those who find it attractive.

In contrast, the man who overcomes actual vices in which he indulged or, at any rate, their temptations, does not lose touch with them. He would have to become smug for this to be so. But then he would not really have come to goodness; he would have succumbed to a different vice. He knows from experience what makes them tempting. Indeed, the vices he has overcome do not lose their reality for him in the attraction they once held for him. Rather, they become repugnant to him in that very attraction. It is to this that the goodness he finds opens his eyes, the eyes of his feelings.

It is true that in the case of the man who loses his innocence, succumbs to vice and is corrupted, there is a corresponding opening of the eyes to a world of pleasure, to a world of swaggering, a world of power and its ruthlessness, but one to which the man who overcomes these vices and comes to be repulsed by them does not become blind. Indeed, the very repugnance the latter feels for them now contains an acknowledgement of the attractiveness which people are susceptible to in them. This attractiveness is part of what makes them repugnant to him now.

The asymmetry between them lies in this. The man who overcomes vice is not blind to the pleasure he once found in it. He retains his understanding of the pleasure he once found in, or at least expected from, it and which others do. Whereas the man who succumbs to vice becomes blinded to the repugnance which the very idea of such pleasures once inspired in him. He loses his understanding of what once made them repugnant to him and still makes them so to others. To put it succinctly, one can be innocent of moral knowledge, as Adam and Eve are portrayed as being in their original state, but one cannot know goodness or even have a conception of it without knowledge of evil. Whereas, in contrast, as Plato says, those who are evil do not know they are. They do not know evil and are not aware of it in their own actions and pursuits, for they are cut off from goodness and are, therefore, deprived of its illumination.

There is another side to this asymmetry. The man who is corrupted is one who succumbs, gives in to something in himself, whatever its source. He may struggle against it, but he is corrupted in that he lets go. There is complicity, but it takes the form of giving in. Furthermore, the response to what corrupts comes from within, it contains what lies within one. That is why I speak of complicity. This is often represented as entering into a pact with the Devil. In contrast, the man who comes to goodness is someone who overcomes something in himself and what he comes to is something he attains, even though he is thankful and doesn't take any credit for it. The pride which taking credit for it and thinking of it as an achievement represents is, of course, incompatible with what he comes to understand as goodness. Still the fact remains that there is a radical difference between the way a person is corrupted and the way he comes to goodness. As Simone Weil puts it: one doesn't fall into goodness ('on ne tombe pas dans le bien').[25] To come to goodness one has to 'rise' against what she calls the force of 'moral gravity' in the soul, exercised by our egocentricity. The person who comes to goodness comes to something he is not; for he has to be awakened to the love to which the goodness he comes to belongs. And even if that love is already in him, it has to be purified so that in the process he changes in himself and finds a new mode of being. In the goodness towards which he thus moves he finds the inspiration to work and make it his. Such inspiration thus comes from without. That is what is contrasted with 'a fall into evil'.

It is true that the man of whom we say that he has been corrupted may himself say that he has freed himself from the hold which what he once called 'goodness' had on him. He may even say that he had to fight for such freedom; he may say that it took guts and that it was not an easy thing. He may describe where he has got to as an attainment. He may also speak of the life it has opened up for him as being a richer and more rewarding life than the one from which he has thus been liberated. He may even say that in it at last he has found himself.

He may, of course, not have been himself in his previous life. His earlier morality may have been something external to him and, as such, a constraint. This would justify him in speaking the way he does: he has thrown away a shackle. But in that case it was not goodness that moved him in his former life; it was the fear of others – the fear of losing their approbation and all that hung on it, or the fear of gaining their disapprobation.

However, this need not have been the case: what he describes as 'bondage' may be the genuine hold which what we call goodness had on him. Such a person was torn between the pull of the good and the temptation of evil. He identified himself with the temptation and so now speaks of the attraction of the good as a snare. He has rejected it and turned to evil. He now uses the language I have used and says that he has made the evil he has embraced his own and in doing so he has risen to it. He denies that this is a fall. In doing so he is using moral language, not the language of moral alienation; he is saying, 'evil, be my good'. If these are not mere empty words, then he is trying to put evil in the place which previously goodness occupied in his soul.

Looking at him in a slightly different way, *we* could say that he has given himself to a form of evil which houses itself in a morality and which, as such, engages something of the good in him. Such a person is not simply taken over by evil; the good in him is tricked into making this possible. It is made to work for the devil until it ends up by being taken over. He is thus deceived in the way that a person who falls in love with someone worthless, who is out to exploit him, is deceived.

I have argued that the good man's life is not limited and impoverished in the way the egocentric thug's life is. For he is not cut off from evil in the way that the egocentric thug is cut off from goodness. But does this asymmetry hold in the case of the good man who is converted to evil in the way I have imagined? I have argued, in his case, that not being totally egocentric he has the capacity to give himself to something outside himself – at any rate to begin with. It is this capacity that he puts into action when he is tricked to give his love to something that appeals to his egocentricity. While he uses moral language to express his relation to it – a language he uses misguidedly but not vacuously – he has not lost touch completely with his earlier life. That language still contains echoes of what he was in touch with earlier. There is in him still, even if tricked, that with which he is in touch in what that language echoes. If the evil which he is tricked into embracing gets hold of him totally – and that is the direction in which he is changing – then he will lose touch with his earlier life and will turn into someone egocentric in his affective orientation. All that will remain of his past life then will be the memory of something from which he is totally dissociated. In this transformation he will lose touch with everything which the goodness he had in him illuminated.

So my claim that the good man is in touch with what is evil in human life, whereas a man whose life is steeped in evil has no contact with and no understanding of what the good man sees and is moved by, stands. It is, of course, true that 'one who is alienated from vice is not cut off from human life altogether' – although 'alienated' is the wrong word to use in connection with vice, since 'alienation' is a phenomenon of passivity. What we have in the case of a good man is a person who has *outgrown* his egocentricity. But although he has turned away from vice or has grown strong against the temptation to it, he is not cut off from the reality of evil in the life he shares with others – in the way that those who are naive or smug are. In contrast the evil person is cut off from the reality of goodness where it exists; he sees it as stupidity or weakness, as anything but goodness, and will have nothing to do with it.

Summing up

I have argued that though we find our individuality as *human beings* in the culture in which we grow up and to which we belong, it nevertheless makes sense to talk of a *human nature* which cuts across cultural boundaries. Since, however, our nature as human beings is not something that exists independently of one form of culture or another, what belongs to it cannot be distinguished in any simple way from what comes to us from the particular culture to which we belong.

Moralities, I have argued, grow from human responses to the particular conditions of life to which human beings have to adapt in their struggle to make a life for themselves. They have their roots in both human nature and the particular culture in which these conditions have their significance for those who have to adapt to them. I then tried to make clear what is meant by good and evil and the way the reality of these is unique to a morality of love – that is a morality that has its source in the love, in the broad sense, which belongs to our nature as human beings in its primitive form. Within the framework of such a morality this love is purified of all traces of egocentricity and developed and, as such, made into an ideal in which those who give themselves to it find inspiration. I have argued that in the primitive reactions of such love we find expressions of a recognition of good and evil, so that in this sense such recognition is not confined to any particular culture. It is in this sense that there is something *universal* about moralities of love.

In such moralities human nature is seen as having two poles: one in which human beings have the capacity to come out of themselves and respond to others in their separateness and individual identity, and the other in which they are egocentric in their primitive reactions. Such a morality enjoins those who give themselves to it to purify their love from all egocentricity. The notion of *coming to oneself* presupposes the contrast between the self and the ego which is specific to moralities of love, and it is what such purification makes possible that enables a person to come to himself in his interest in and concern for what exists independently of him.

The notions of self-alienation and self-stultification employed go with this. I have tried to make clear why I say that 'there is something self-stultifying about making oneself the centre of one's concern' and this is equally true about the self-satisfied person. In his egocentricity such a person has no idea that his pursuits are self-stultifying. He has no conception of a self distinct from the ego. The fact that such a person is really egocentric, egocentric in his very mode of being, does not in any way preclude his not having found himself, and so his not being himself in that egocentricity. Phillips may say that this means no more than that the egocentric person is egocentric and dismiss my claim as tautological. But that is to make light of the profound differences which egocentricity makes in the life of a person. It is these that the notions of 'being oneself' and 'failing to find oneself' bring into focus.

Part of the reason for saying that the egocentric person is someone who has not found himself is that in his egocentricity such a person remains rooted in something that belongs to his early life and which he has failed to outgrow. In his failure to do so his life remains impoverished. He is deprived of what relationships of genuine give and take, and an interest in things outside him for their own sake, can bring into a person's life. He is deprived of the wisdom and understanding that a person can come to through this.

Finally, I have argued that Phillips is wrong about the symmetry which he claims holds between what the life of a good man and what that of an evil man excludes. Evil is not alien to the life a good man participates in and this is something he appreciates. Goodness, on the other hand, is alien to a life shaped by evil. The good and the evil man lead different lives, of course, but in its horizons the life of the good man is not limited in the way that the life of the evil man is. The good man does not participate in practices which he sees to contain evil, but he sees those practices to be a part of the life to which he belongs. The evil man does not, in the same way, see the practices and restraints in which the good man's regard for and loyalty to goodness find expression as part of the life to which he belongs, except as aberrations rooted in men's foolishness. He cannot understand how any man can have regard for goodness itself. For goodness means nothing to him. The good man, on the other hand, is not in this way alienated from evil; he understands it and knows only too well the reality of the attraction it exercises on men.

University of Wales, Swansea

Notes

1   This essay is a continuation of the discussion in an earlier paper, in *Ethics and Understanding*, ed. Lilli Alanen, Thomas Walgren and Sara Heinamaa (London: Macmillan and St Martin's Press, 1977), of good and evil and what can be said about the life of those who give themselves to one or the other. In it I take up some of the criticisms made of what I said by Professor Phillips in the same volume, pp. 153–76.

2   See Socrates' discussion of courage and philosophical virtue in the *Phaedo*.
3   Phillips, 'Ethics and Humanistic Ethics: A Reply to Dilman', in *Ethics and Understanding*, ed. Alanen et al., p. 165.
4   Dostoevsky, Fyodor, *Crime and Punishment*, trans. by David Magarshack (London: Penguin Classics, 1956), p. 68.
5   Phillips, in *Ethics and Understanding*, pp. 164–5.
6   Dilman, in *Ethics and Understanding*, p. 151.
7   *Ibid.*, p. 136.
8   Phillips, in *Ethics and Understanding*, sec. 3, pp. 155–9.
9   *Ibid.*, p. 158.
10 *Ibid.*
11 See Dilman and Phillips, *Sense and Delusion* (Routledge and Kegan Paul, 1971), chs. 2 and 4.
12 Phillips, in *Ethics and Understanding*, p. 173.
13 Compare with Ivan Ilytch's terror when he realizes that he is going to die. Leo Tolstoy, trans. and ed. Leo Weiner, *The Complete Works of Count Tolstoy* (AMS Press, 1968), vol. 13, pp. 45ff. *passim*.
14 Phillips, in *Ethics and Understanding*, sections 6–9.
15 *Ibid.*, p. 167.
16 *Ibid.*
17 *Ibid.*, p. 168.
18 I have argued this in Dilman, *Morality and the Inner Life, A Study in Plato's Gorgias* (London: Macmillan, 1979); see chapters 7, 'Development and Character', and 8, 'Character and Morality'.
19 I have discussed this question in Dilman, *Love and Human Separateness* (London: Macmillan, 1987), chapter 7.
20 Dilman, *Philosophy and Life, Essays on John Wisdom* (The Hague: Martinus Nijhoff, 1984), chapter 8.
21 *Ibid.*, p. 158, emphasis added.
22 Phillips, in *Ethics and Understanding*, pp. 170–1.
23 *Ibid.*
24 *Ibid.*, pp. 161–2.
25 Simone Weil, *La Pesanteur et la Grâce* (Paris: Librarie Plon, 1948), p. 82.

5
On Going the Bloody *Hard* Way in Philosophy

James Conant

Rush Rhees tells us: 'Wittgenstein used to say to me, "Go the bloody *hard* way".' And, Rhees adds: 'I remember this more often, perhaps, than any other single remark of his.'[1] This essay is about what Wittgenstein meant when he spoke of going the bloody *hard* way in philosophy.

Ethics?

> *'Nothing is hidden' is, for Wittgenstein, an ethical as well as a logical remark.*
>
> Ray Monk[2]

Rhees connects what Wittgenstein means by going the bloody hard way with the manner in which Wittgenstein himself sought to practise philosophy:

> Unless one understands this, then I do not think one can understand Wittgenstein's conviction that philosophy is important.... Philosophy, as he practised it, was 'the bloody hard way'.... And it was not only a way of thinking and working, but a way of living as well. And the *'hardness'* was really a criterion of the sort of life that was worthwhile. Perhaps I should add 'for him'.[3]

This suggests that the injunction to go the bloody hard way is an injunction to *lead a certain sort of life*. (And that, as far as it goes, is surely right.) That might suggest, in turn, that, in so far as 'going the bloody hard way' is the description of a demand that one ought to place on oneself in philosophizing, it primarily has to do with those 'areas of philosophy' that are most intimately connected with – or somehow bear most directly on – 'the task of living'. It is a short step from here to the conclusion that – alongside logic, epistemology, metaphysics, philosophy of language, philosophy of mind, etc. – Wittgenstein has interesting 'views' on ethics. And if one starts looking

85

through Wittgenstein's corpus for his remarks that seem to touch on 'ethical' topics, they may appear to be scattered all over the place.[4] And, in particular, if one looks for remarks that touch on the topic of going the bloody hard way, one won't have far to look.

Consider the following five passages from Wittgenstein:

1. You cannot write anything about yourself that is more truthful than you yourself are.[5]
2. Nothing is so difficult as not deceiving oneself.[6]
3. If anyone is *unwilling* to descend into himself . . . he will remain superficial in his writing.[7]
4. Working in philosophy . . . is really more a working on oneself.[8]
5. That man will be revolutionary who can revolutionize himself.[9]

Numerous remarks similar to these can be found scattered throughout Wittgenstein's writings.[10] Such a remark – when one comes upon it, in the middle of an extended Wittgensteinian philosophical investigation (on, e.g., whether it is possible for me to give myself a private ostensive definition, or for another person to have my pains, or for there to be only one occasion on which someone obeys a rule, etc.) – is apt to strike one as a *non sequitur*. Why do such remarks crop up in the midst of Wittgenstein's philosophical investigations, apparently changing the topic and interrupting the course of the investigation?

Having read thus far, the reader may have formed the impression that the topic of this essay is one that could be summarized under the heading 'Wittgenstein on Ethics', or at least 'Wittgenstein's Remarks about Ethics'. Is that my topic? Are these remarks about ethics? It depends upon what you think 'ethics' is. Stanley Cavell remarks upon the 'pervasiveness of something that may express itself as a moral or religious demand in the *Investigations*', and goes on to observe that 'the demand is not the subject of a *separate* study within it, call it Ethics'.[11] I take the five remarks from Wittgenstein quoted above to be attempts to articulate (aspects of) that demand. But what sort of a *demand* – or '*something*' (that 'may express itself as a moral or religious demand') – is this? *In what way* is it present in a work such as Wittgenstein's *Philosophical Investigations*? And how can it be the case that it is *pervasively* present in that work? After all, isn't most (if not all) of that work concerned with 'topics' that have nothing to do with (what we usually call) 'ethics'?

In a previous paper, in which I touch very briefly on questions such as these, I had occasion to quote these same five remarks from Wittgenstein; and D.Z. Phillips, in a reply to my paper, observed that Wittgenstein, in each of these five passages, should be understood as 'referring to difficulties in *doing philosophy*, difficulties in giving the problems the kind of attention philosophy asks of us'.[12] I agree with this.[13] If this is right, it helps to explain

why these remarks are not *non sequiturs*, and how it is that they touch on a
dimension of difficulty which is pervasively, if often only tacitly, in play in
Wittgenstein's investigations. We can put Phillips's point this way: when
such a remark occurs in the midst of one of Wittgenstein's investigations, it
does not introduce an abrupt change of topic; it interrupts the investigation
in order to step back for a moment and comment on a difficulty in doing
philosophy which one runs up against in such investigations. Thus one will
not understand what such remarks are about, unless one understands why
they occur in the contexts they do.[14]

Rhees makes it clear that he takes Wittgenstein's injunction (to go the
bloody hard way) neither to be a mere idiosyncrasy of Wittgenstein's 'style'
of philosophy, nor to bear on one particular 'area of philosophy' (say,
'ethics') to the exclusion of others. In support of this, he draws on a variety
of related remarks of Wittgenstein's:

> 'Go the bloody *hard* way.' I have said that for him philosophy was this.
> And this was not just a personal matter: it was not just the spirit in which
> he happened to pursue philosophy. In the manuscript books on which I
> am working he makes remarks like, 'In logic one cannot by-pass any
> difficulty.' (... [H]e often spoke of 'logic' when he took it to cover the
> whole of philosophy.) Or again he said: 'In logic there is no substi-
> tute.'... Put it another way: If you see the kind of difficulty that is raised
> in philosophy, you will see why there cannot be a simplified way of
> meeting it.... And this means: take the *difficulties* seriously: 'unless you
> recognise that they *are* difficulties; unless you recognise that they are
> difficult – unless they make things difficult.'[15]

The sorts of difficulties that are at issue here are evidently not tied to some
particular subject matter. (Indeed, the term 'ethics' in Wittgenstein's vocabulary no more names an independent subject matter or separable area
of philosophy than does the term 'logic'.[16] For Wittgenstein, logic and
ethics are each, and each differently, concerned with a pervasive dimension
of human thought and action.[17]) For Wittgenstein, it is an integral aspect of
what it is to confront a philosophical difficulty that one 'see why there
cannot be a simplified way of meeting it'. Progress in philosophy, on such
a conception, always depends in part on overcoming one's own powerful
inclination to evade seeing the difficulties as the kind of difficulties they are
– overcoming one's reluctance to face up to the genuine hopelessness of a
philosophical difficulty, given the terms in which one, all but inevitably,
seeks to frame it.[18] The reluctance is tied to the fact that it often seems as if
one can cease to frame the difficulty in the terms in question only at
tremendous cost. Doing what Wittgenstein's investigations ask of us –
loosening our determination to represent the difficulty in the terms in
which it initially presents itself to us – 'seems only to destroy everything

interesting, that is, all that is great and important'.[19] It thus is essential to an appreciation of Wittgenstein's conception of philosophy that one appreciate (not only that he sees our philosophical perplexities as arising from certain forms of confusion and their dissolution as calling for the attainment of certain forms of clarity, but) that he sees us as deeply attached to our confusions, resistant to giving up the ways of looking at things upon which they rest.

Phillips goes on to remark that the sort of difficulties that are at issue in the five passages from Wittgenstein quoted above will be 'missed if one equates the difficulties with *personal* difficulties'.[20] This is surely right if by '*personal* difficulties' Phillips means *merely* personal (as opposed to philosophical) difficulties. But it is equally wrong if by this Phillips means 'philosophical, and therefore *in no way* personal, difficulties'.[21] Erecting an opposition here between mutually exclusive categories of 'the personal' and 'the philosophical' will block the way to understanding why Wittgenstein thinks that work in philosophy (properly conducted) is a kind of working on oneself, and why he thinks that one cannot be any more honest in one's philosophical thinking than one can be with oneself, and why he thinks that the greatness of a philosophical work is expressive of the greatness of the particular human being that is its author. Phillips is certainly right that the wrong sort of insistence on the (idea that the sorts of *difficulty* with which Wittgenstein, in his philosophical work, is concerned are) 'personal' can lead to disastrous misinterpretations of Wittgenstein's work.[22] But too sharp a recoil from such misinterpretations – with its complementary insistence upon too sharp a separation between ethical and philosophical difficulty – is equally obstructive of an understanding of Wittgenstein's conception of the nature of the difficulty of philosophy.

Wittgenstein's remark that 'nothing is so difficult as not deceiving oneself' is neither more nor less a remark about a particular difficulty which arises in philosophy than it is a remark about a general ethical difficulty. For Wittgenstein's thought here is that one's ability to avoid self-deception in philosophy can be neither more nor less than one's ability to avoid it outside philosophy. (Wittgenstein concludes a meditation on the effects of the all but inevitable tendency to 'lie to oneself' on one's writing with the remark: 'If you are unwilling to know what you are, your writing is a form of deceit.'[23]) If you are unwilling to descend into yourself, then you will remain superficial in your thinking and writing generally, and *a fortiori* you will remain superficial in your efforts to write philosophy. Hence Wittgenstein writes to Malcolm: 'You can't think decently if you don't want to hurt yourself.'[24] The issue here – as in each of the five remarks from Wittgenstein quoted above – is at once personal and philosophical.

'If anyone is *unwilling* to descend into himself . . . he will remain superficial in his writing.' Wittgenstein is equally committed to the converse of this remark: if someone remains superficial in his thinking or writing this can (where it is not a function of immaturity or ineptitude) be a reflection of the character of the person whose thinking and writing it is. It is, for Wittgenstein, not only possible to discern aspects of a person's character in the character of their philosophizing, but essential to the formation of any true estimate of their philosophy that one be able to do so. The exercise of such discernment is never far below the surface in the judgements Wittgenstein himself offers of the value of the philosophical work of others.[25] But this means that the line between 'the personal' and 'the philosophical' cannot be as sharp, for Wittgenstein, as Phillips imagines it to be. To put the point more positively and in a more Wittgensteinian idiom: the spirit of a person shows itself in the spirit of his philosophy, which in turn shows itself in the way he philosophizes.

The numerous remarks about other thinkers sprinkled throughout Wittgenstein's notebooks and recorded conversations furnish vivid documentation of the manifold sorts of ways in which Wittgenstein himself exercises such discernment. When Wittgenstein says about Frank Ramsey: 'Ramsey's incapacity for genuine enthusiasm or (what is really the same thing) reverence came to disgust me more and more',[26] he is commenting on something about Ramsey's sensibility that reflects itself in, but certainly not only in, the character of his response to philosophical ideas. What is at issue here is a kind of limitation of sensibility that is neither merely personal nor merely philosophical, but rather equally – and, in Wittgenstein's eyes, equally fatefully – both. When Maurice Drury tells Wittgenstein: 'I always enjoy reading William James. He is such a human person,' Wittgenstein responds: 'Yes, that is what makes him a good philosopher; he was a real human being.'[27] That James is 'a real human being' is something Wittgenstein takes himself to be able to discern as a reader of James's philosophical writings. And the estimate he forms in this regard of James *qua* person is not – and, for Wittgenstein, cannot be – utterly independent of his estimate of James *qua* philosopher. When Wittgenstein remarks about A.J. Ayer: 'He has something to say but he is incredibly shallow',[28] this is, in the first instance, of course, a remark about the shallowness of Ayer's philosophizing. But it is not *merely* a remark about the quality of Ayer's efforts at philosophizing, and as such wholly without bearing on an estimate of the shallowness or depth of the sensibility of the person whose philosophizing it is.[29] Similarly, when Wittgenstein says about James Frazer: 'Frazer is much more savage than most of these savages',[30] this is a comment on both the man and his thought. It is a comment on something that shows itself in Frazer's writing about the forms of life and modes of thought of the primitive peoples he studies – where part of what shows itself is something about what sorts of possibilities of thought and life are (and are not) closed to Frazer himself.

'You cannot write anything about yourself that is more truthful than you yourself are.' That is simultaneously a remark about a personal and a philosophical difficulty. (If you cannot write anything that is more truthful than you yourself are, then you cannot write anything *in philosophy* that is more truthful than you yourself are.) For Wittgenstein, the two difficulties are inseparable – they are aspects of a single difficulty.[31] One can, if one will, take the words 'perspicuity' and 'clarity' to stand for things Wittgenstein struggles to attain in philosophy. And one can, with equal justification, take the words 'honesty' and '*Anständigkeit*' to stand for things Wittgenstein thinks everyone should struggle to attain in life. If you do not think of yourself as ever practising philosophy, then you may take yourself only to have reason to think of yourself as caught up in the second of these two kinds of struggle.[32] If you evidently do practise philosophy, but most decidedly not in the spirit of Wittgenstein, then these two struggles may strike you as utterly independent of one another. (Though, it is worth remembering, they did not seem so to philosophers as different from one another as Socrates, Augustine and Nietzsche.) But if you wish to think of yourself as practising philosophy in anything like the spirit of Wittgenstein, then these two struggles must become for you – as they did for Wittgenstein – twin aspects of a single struggle, each partially constitutive of the other.

When Wittgenstein writes '*Call me a truth-seeker and I will be satisfied*', he specifies the character of his striving in terms of something which is for him equally a philosophical and an ethical ideal.[33] All philosophical thinking and writing accordingly has, for Wittgenstein, its ethical aspect. Wittgenstein thought that what (and more importantly *how*) we think is revelatory of who we are (and how we live), and that learning to think better (and, above all, to *change* the ways in which one thinks) is an important means to becoming a better – i.e. to becoming (what Wittgenstein calls) 'a real' – 'human being'.[34] So, even though Wittgenstein, in one sense, 'has no ethics' (if 'ethics' names a branch of philosophy with its own proprietary subject matter), in another sense, his thinking and writing – on every page of his work – takes place under the pressure of an ethical demand. Any writing answerable to Wittgenstein's conception of the nature of the difficulty of philosophy – of what it means to acknowledge a philosophical difficulty to be the kind of difficulty it is – necessarily has *ein Ethischer Sinn*.[35]

But the question still remains: what sort of 'difficulties in doing philosophy' are these (that require that one go the bloody hard way)? In what way can 'working in philosophy', as Wittgenstein seeks to practise it, really be said to be a case of 'working on oneself'? Or to put the same question differently: when and how can failure in philosophy be a function of failure of character, or of will, or of soul – rather than mere failure of acumen, or of wit, or of intellectual penetration? Or conversely: how can success in philosophy depend upon the formation of character, the cultivation of will, or (as Socrates likes to put it) 'the state of one's soul'?

Schopenhauer's cab

> *Wittgenstein's writing is deeply practical . . . the way Freud's is. And like Freud's therapy, it wishes to prevent understanding which is unaccompanied by inner change.*
>
> Stanley Cavell[36]

> *I must quickly make a short digression, to avoid the risk of your imagining that this therapeutic work is accomplished too easily. From what I have said so far . . . [the problem] would seem to be the result of ignorance – a not knowing about mental events that one ought to know of. . . . So it ought not to be very difficult [for the therapist] . . . to restore the patient by communicating his knowledge to him thus remedying his ignorance. . . . If only that was how things happened! . . . Knowledge is not always the same as knowledge: there are different sorts of knowledge, which are far from equivalent psychologically. . . . The knowledge [the patient requires] must rest on an internal change in the patient.*
>
> Sigmund Freud[37]

I want to start with a comparatively straightforward example of one philosopher charging another philosopher with a deficiency in his philosophy of a sort which is inseparable from a moral criticism of the philosopher himself. For it to be an example of the relevant sort, the charge must be directed in the first instance at the character of the philosophy – at the *thought* itself – and not merely at the character of the man. Yet it must not be directed at the character of the thought to the exclusion of that of the man. Rather it must be directed at the character of the thinker as revealed in and through the character of his thought. Thus what is uncovered through an examination of the thought is a deficiency of virtue in the thinker, not merely a deficit in his intellectual candlepower.

Consider the following criticism which Schopenhauer makes of Spinoza:

> Spinoza, who always boasts of proceeding *more geometrico*, has actually done so more than he himself knew. For what to him was certain and settled from an immediate perceptive apprehension of the nature of the world, he tries to demonstrate logically and independently of this knowledge. But of course he arrives at the intended result predetermined by him, only by taking as the starting-point concepts arbitrarily made by him . . . and allowing himself in the demonstration all the freedom of choice for which the nature of those wide-ranging concepts afforded convenient opportunity.[38]

The first sentence of this passage presupposes a familiarity with Schopenhauer's theory of geometry – in particular, with his doctrine that 'geometry…always proves only that of which we are already convinced through another kind of knowledge'.[39] In the case of geometry, Schopenhauer thinks, no self-deception need be involved in the activity of furnishing ourselves with proofs of conclusions of whose truth we are already convinced by other means. The discipline of offering proofs can play an important role in articulating and systemizing our knowledge of geometrical truths, without pretence to being the sole foundation upon which such knowledge rests. And, in principle, it ought to be possible for proof to play a similar role in philosophy. But Schopenhauer's complaint about Spinoza is that he doesn't offer his proofs merely as a means of systemizing truths to which he has legitimately helped himself by other means. Rather, he represents his conviction in his conclusions as if it derived solely from his demonstrations. Yet his demonstrations appear to succeed only because they have been carefully tailored by him to vindicate their 'predetermined' results. The assumption implicit in Schopenhauer's charge against Spinoza here is that anyone with an equal talent for constructing 'demonstrations', but with a predilection for a divergent set of predetermined results, could have succeeded equally well in 'proving' the opposite of what Spinoza alleged to have succeeded in proving. The implicit charge is one of *intellectual dishonesty*: of pretending to explore the logic of our concepts, while actually curbing and bending them to one's own ends – of pretending to follow the lead of reason, while herding it in the direction one antecedently wants it to go.

My interest, for present purposes, is not in the broader questions of philosophical methodology which this passage might be taken to raise (e.g., what is the proper role of argument or proof in philosophy?) nor in any questions of Spinoza exegesis (e.g., is this passage fair in its criticism of Spinoza?). I want rather to attend only to the character of the criticism and, in particular, to the ethical demand which Schopenhauer takes Spinoza to have failed to have respected. The implicit demand might be formulated as follows: it is our obligation, in philosophy (and not only philosophy), to *think things through* – and not (in the guise of thinking things through) to tailor our arguments so as to predetermine the outcome of our investigations. Schopenhauer makes no secret of the fact that he sees his fellow-philosophers (with the notable exception of Kant) as everywhere failing to accede to this demand.

Schopenhauer's criticisms of his fellow philosophers serve as particularly vivid examples of the sort I said I wanted to begin with – of a philosopher criticizing other philosophers for failings that go beyond the merely intellectual. Schopenhauer offers a clear case of this because when he seeks to expose a failing in his contemporaries of the relevant sort, it is generally hard to miss the acerbic moralizing note (the note of accusation, contempt and dismay) sounded in his descriptions of their work. His remarks take on a bitingly ironic, witheringly disapproving edge, leaving no doubt that in his view the species of failure he seeks to expose is not merely due to a lack of intellectual acuity.[40] Let us take a look at one example of such a passage:

> What have our own worthy honest German professors of philosophy done on their part for their dear cosmological proof... – they who value intellect and truth above all else?... They know that a first cause is just as inconceivable as is the point where space has an end.... For every cause is a *change*, and here we are necessarily bound to ask about the change which preceded it, and by which it had been brought about, and so on ad infinitum, ad infinitum! Not even a first state of matter is conceivable from which... all subsequent states could have proceeded. For if in itself it had been their cause, they too would have had to exist from all eternity, and hence the present state would not be only at this moment. But if that first state began to be causal only at a certain time, then something must have *changed* it at that time for its inactivity to have ceased. But then something came about, a change occurred, and we must ask at once about its cause, in other words, about a change which preceded *it*, and again we find ourselves on the ladder of causes up which we are whipped by the inexorable law of causality higher and higher, ad infinitum, ad infinitum.... The law of causality is therefore not so obliging as to allow itself to be used like a cab which we dismiss after we reach our destination.... And so what did they do, these noble and sincere friends of truth?... What did they do for their old friend, the hard-pressed and prostrate cosmological proof? They thought of a clever ruse.... They said:... [Y]our theme will now have the name of 'the Absolute'; this has a foreign, decent, and aristocratic ring; and we know best what can be done by Germans by assuming an air of superiority. Everyone, of course, understands what is meant and thus thinks he is a sage.... You shout (and we accompany you): 'The Absolute, confound it, *this must exist*, otherwise there would be nothing at all!' (With this you bang on the table.) But where does this come from? 'Silly question! Haven't I said that it was the Absolute?'[41]

Schopenhauer's ire is directed at those who employ a principle for as long as it suits their purposes, and then conveniently abandon it as soon as its consequences fail to lead in the direction which suits them. The specific target in the above passage is those 'worthy honest German professors of philosophy' who seek to argue for a *causa sui* of the universe by first employing the principle of causality ('Every event has a cause') in order to trace the chain of causes back to an earlier and still earlier stage and, then, refrain from applying the principle as they (allegedly coming upon that most exalted of causes: 'the Absolute') reach the point at which their 'demonstration' arrives at its 'intended and predetermined result'.

Schopenhauer characterizes the principle in question as refusing to allow itself to be *dismissed like a cab* ('The law of causality is . . . not so obliging as to allow itself to be used like a cab which we dismiss after we reach our destination'), thus implying that, once the principle no longer suits their purposes, the parties in question actively seek to dismiss it. The subtextual allegation here is that, in suddenly at a certain point actively seeking to dismiss it, these parties betray an awareness that if they want to be able to be rid of the principle at just the right moment, they will need to get rid of it themselves – as if they knew that, apart from such an active effort on their part to rid themselves of it, the principle would inconveniently remain in effect, hindering their purposes. This bit of hyperbole, sounding the note of purposive agency, highlights the sort of case with which Schopenhauer is concerned. It is not one in which someone merely *happens* to fail to do something – merely happens, say, to fail to draw the requisite inference (due to a deficit of, say, attentiveness, or intelligence, or nourishment). The sort of failure with which Schopenhauer is concerned, whenever he adopts his characteristic ironically moralizing tone, is a *motivated* one. It is a failure that is alleged to be at some level *wilful*. Hence Schopenhauer's sense of entitlement to his tone of moral condemnation.

I say 'at some level wilful' in order to register a question about how one should characterize the degree of consciousness which accompanies such failure. How, after all, can such a form of failure – one of the will, and not merely of the intellect – be operative here, if it is true, as it generally seems to be (and, as Schopenhauer himself seems to think), that the guilty parties in such cases are also in some sense 'unaware' of their misdeed. They didn't ever *decide* to bring their train of thought to a halt at some point short of thinking things through. Indeed, they are of the belief that they have gone as far as they can go (all the way to the Absolute!): they need to be brought to see that their thinking is characterized by a failure to think things through; and it may be quite difficult to convince them that this is so. If to dismiss something like a cab involves full-blooded agency, then how is one able to pull the trick off *unknowingly*? More puzzling still: how can one not only will oneself to be blind to something one thus in some sense *does* (such as dismissing an argument like a cab once it has ceased to serve one's purposes), but also will oneself to be blind to the fact that one so wills? How can one be in a state in which one both knows and yet does not know that one is cheating (both oneself and others) in one's thinking? To ask such questions is to enter into a consideration of certain very puzzling kinds of self-blindness and self-knowledge. As Freud says, one will need to distinguish different kinds of 'knowing' in order to make sense of such operations of the will; and one will need to find ways to make the subject herself aware that that which she (in one sense) does not know she nevertheless (in another sense) does know. Hence Schopenhauer's devices of irony and hyperbole. The aim of these devices is to bring to a person's consciousness that which she cannot help but, and yet simultaneously is somehow able not to, know – to make vivid a sort of rupture between will and understanding that is peculiarly invisible to the person who suffers from it. Such failures of self-transparency are matters that belong to something one might call the ethical dimension of intellectual confusion.[42] A preoccupation with this dimension, on the part of authors such as Schopenhauer, Nietzsche and Kierkegaard, is part of what is responsible for the jarringly ethical note in the midst of discussions of an otherwise apparently purely metaphysical or narrowly philosophical nature (such as whether there can be such a thing as a first cause). What such authors share with Wittgenstein is the belief that philosophical criticism when pushed to its deepest level – when it seeks to identify the most fundamental forms of confusion and dishonesty in our thinking – operates at a level at which it is necessarily no longer possible neatly to distinguish between criticism of the thought of a person and criticism of the person whose thought it is. And this is one of the (many) reasons why the works of such authors will always fit at best uncomfortably into the curriculum of a university.

Wittgenstein's relative estimate of Frege and Russell

> *The style of my sentences is extraordinarily strongly influenced by Frege. And if I wanted to, I could establish this influence where at first sight no one would see it.*
>
> Wittgenstein[43]

> *A man's style is a picture of him.*
>
> Wittgenstein[44]

In order to see further how 'nothing is hidden' could be, for Wittgenstein, an ethical as well as a logical remark, it might help to consider Wittgenstein's relative estimate of Frege and Russell. But first, a word regarding what I mean – or rather do not merely mean – by 'Frege' and by 'Russell' when I speak of 'Wittgenstein's relative estimate of Frege and Russell': what will be at issue, in what follows, is neither *merely* Wittgenstein's relative estimate of two individual persons named Frege and Russell (if such an estimate is taken to be something distinct from his estimate of their philosophies), nor *merely* his relative estimate of their writings (if such an estimate is taken to be something that has no bearing on an estimate of the persons who are the authors of those writings). 'Frege' and 'Russell' will refer, in what follows, to the whole of the respective sensibilities expressed through – i.e. which *show themselves* in – the writings of Frege and Russell.

Elizabeth Anscombe writes:

> Wittgenstein's *Tractatus* has captured the interest and excited the admiration of many, yet almost all that has been published about it has been

wildly irrelevant. If this has had any one cause, that cause has been the neglect of Frege. . . . In the *Tractatus* Wittgenstein assumes, and does not try to stimulate, an interest in the kind of questions that Frege wrote about.[45]

How can the neglect of Frege be the reason why much of the commentary on Wittgenstein's *Tractatus* is wildly irrelevant to a proper understanding of that work? What more widely accepted platitude about that book could there be than that it develops and responds to ideas put forward by Frege and Russell? But Anscombe's point presumably is not that Frege is seldom mentioned in discussions of Wittgenstein's *Tractatus*. Her point must rather be that we do not know who Frege is for the author of the *Tractatus*.[46] One part of what this means is: an appreciation of Wittgenstein's early work presupposes an immersion in a particular philosophical background ('an interest in the kind of questions that Frege wrote about') which most of the commentary on that work has lost sight of. It is not that we are unfamiliar with Frege's or Wittgenstein's texts, but that we have failed to see what it is that is at issue in them. We fail to get hold of the questions that figure most centrally in these texts and of *the kind of questions* these questions are for Frege and for Wittgenstein. But another part of what it means is: we fail to appreciate how Wittgenstein's conception of what it is to *engage* a philosophical problem is indebted to the example Frege afforded of what such engagement, at its bloody hardest, involves.

In the opening section of this essay, following the lead of Rhees, I suggested that the sorts of failures to think things through in philosophy that most exercised Wittgenstein are by no means limited to cases where the failure to carry through on the part of a philosopher can easily be traced to overtly moral or religious evasions or predilections on his part. Now, following the lead of Anscombe, I want to suggest that apart from an appreciation of what honesty in thinking (or the exposure of dishonesty in thinking) comes to for Wittgenstein – how an effort to accede to such a demand ought to pervade every page of one's writing – it is impossible to understand why Wittgenstein, throughout his life, holds *Frege* (whose work is taken up almost exclusively with problems in the philosophy of logic and mathematics) in the sort of esteem which he otherwise reserves for thinkers such as Søren Kierkegaard and Karl Kraus. Frege's critiques of philosophical 'positions' – such as 'formalism', 'empiricism', 'idealism', 'psychologism', etc. – represent, for early and later Wittgenstein, guiding paradigms of the manner in which philosophical elucidation, at its most penetrating, is able to reveal how a philosophical 'ism', fully thought through, can be shown 'in the end to coincide' with the very 'ism' which is its alleged opposite. In particular, Frege's attempt to demonstrate how psychologism, when thought through *bei grösster Folgerichtigkeit* – 'with the utmost consequentiality' – can be seen 'to flow into' solipsism[47] serves as perhaps the example *par excellence* for Wittgenstein, throughout his life, of what it means to think a 'position' through in philosophy all the way to the point where it collapses in on itself.[48] Such a mode of critique, Wittgenstein believes, inevitably lays bare the degree to which unclarity in one's philosophizing is a function of forms of residual dishonesty in one's thinking *überhaupt*. Apart from an understanding of what it means in such cases to think the matter through *bei grösster Folgerichtigkeit* – and thus why Wittgenstein is able to regard Frege's critiques of philosophical 'positions' as paradigmatic demonstrations of what it is to do this – there will be no understanding Wittgenstein's own descriptions of the peculiar sort of ground he seeks to traverse (and calls upon his reader to traverse) in philosophy. To take one example: there will be no understanding what Wittgenstein means when he talks about 'strictly thinking something through' or 'strictly following something through' in philosophy – as, for example, when he says: 'idealism, strictly thought out [*streng durchgedacht*], leads to realism';[49] or: 'solipsism, strictly followed through [*streng durchgeführt*], collapses into pure realism'.[50] And apart from an appreciation of what is involved in thus strictly thinking or following matters through in philosophy, there is no understanding Wittgenstein's work. For in his philosophical work, early and late, Wittgenstein, in a sense, attempts nothing more nor less than to furnish the reader with examples of what it is strictly to think through what it is that we (his readers) imagine we mean when we say the sorts of things that we find ourselves, in taking the pressure of philosophical thought, wanting to say.

One frequently finds commentators on Wittgenstein's work either implicitly or explicitly committing themselves to a thought along the following lines: 'If, on the one hand, we wish to understand Wittgenstein's views on the nature of facts, propositions, or logical necessity, then we should begin by reading the writings of Frege and Russell; if, on the other hand, we wish to understand his views on "ethical" topics [as touched on in remarks such as the five quoted above], then we should begin by looking at the writings of figures such as Schopenhauer, Tolstoy and Kierkegaard.' Surely, there is much that is sound in this advice. But there is a possible implication in such advice (exacerbated by the presence of the words 'on the one hand' and 'on the other hand' in the above wording of the advice) that is worth making explicit. It might be taken to imply: 'If you seek illumination on the topic of seemingly "ethical" remarks, such as the five quoted above, then exploring Wittgenstein's admiration for a thinker such as Frege (or his dissatisfaction with aspects of Russell's work regarding the nature of facts, propositions, logical necessity, etc.) will be of no avail; you must turn instead to what Wittgenstein admired in the writings of thinkers such as Schopenhauer, Kierkegaard and Tolstoy – only then will you understand the import of remarks such as the five quoted above.' This is (at least with respect to the five remarks quoted above), in one sense, exactly wrong.[51] For it implies that the high esteem in which Wittgenstein holds, e.g., Frege throughout his life is in no way tied to the topic of what it is to go the bloody hard way in philosophy, and thus obscures from view how the character of Frege's attention to philosophical problems is able to represent for Wittgenstein a touchstone of what honesty and resoluteness in philosophical thinking ought to come to.

It is, Wittgenstein writes in his Preface to the *Tractatus*, 'to the great works of Frege and the writings of my friend Bertrand Russell that I owe in large measure the stimulation of my thoughts'.[52] Anscombe comments: 'Wittgenstein's relative estimate of Frege and Russell comes out in the acknowledgment he makes in the Preface to the *Tractatus*.'[53] This is surely right. This is not to deny that if one wants to know what Wittgenstein's philosophical problems were, during the period that led up to the writing of the *Tractatus*, then one should look, above all, to various writings of Russell's. For it is undeniable that Wittgenstein's thinking about the questions which centrally preoccupy the *Tractatus* originates in his struggles with problems that arise in Russell's philosophy. But to concede this does not require that one deny that if one wants to know what the author of the *Tractatus* thinks *great* philosophy is then one should look, above all, to 'the great works of Frege'.

Now, if Rhees is right (if 'going the bloody *hard* way' is what philosophy was for Wittgenstein, because 'in logic one cannot by-pass any difficulty' and seeing the kind of difficulty that is raised in logic requires seeing 'why there cannot be a simplified way of meeting it') and if Anscombe is right (that 'Wittgenstein's relative estimate of Frege and Russell comes out in the acknowledgment he makes in the Preface to the *Tractatus*'), then it should be possible, by trying to see the work of Frege and Russell through Wittgenstein's eyes, to shed some light on Wittgenstein's conception of what going the bloody hard way with respect to a philosophical difficulty ought and ought not to involve. So, in what follows, I will attempt briefly to explore wherein Wittgenstein took the greatness of 'the great works of Frege' to lie and why he took 'the writings of [his] friend Bertrand Russell' to fall short of such greatness – and, more particularly, how the contrast that he discerned in this regard (at least at the time of writing the *Tractatus*) between the work of his two philosophical mentors helped to shape his own conception of what he sought to accomplish in philosophy. I hope thereby to shed some light on what it means, for Wittgenstein, 'to take the *difficulties* [we encounter in philosophy] seriously', 'to recognise that they *are* difficulties', and to allow them to '*make things difficult*'.[54]

Russell and the problem of the unity of the proposition

> *I have an uneasiness about philosophy altogether; what remains for me to do in philosophy (I mean in* technical *philosophy) does not seem of first-rate importance.*
>
> Russell, 13 December 1911[55]

> *I have developed a certain nausea for the subtleties and distinctions that make up good philosophy; I should like to write things of human interest, like bad philosophers, only without being bad. But perhaps it is the badness that is interesting.*
>
> Russell, 27 December 1911[56]

One way of summarizing a recurring dissatisfaction that Wittgenstein had with the work of his friend and mentor Bertrand Russell during their years of close collaboration would be to say that he believed that Russell did not take the difficulties that kept recurring in his philosophical work seriously enough; rather than seeking a way *through* the difficulties – allowing them to 'make things difficult' – Russell was inclined to seek a way *around* them.

The shape of a central problem in Wittgenstein's early notebooks and other writings, which Wittgenstein inherits from Russell, can be put as follows: '[T]he point . . . is to say how propositions hang together internally. How the *propositional bond* comes into existence.'[57] Wittgenstein's thinking about these questions has its overt source in troubles inherent in Russell's notion of *logical form*. However, the guise in which the problem first arises in Russell's philosophy is as a problem about *the unity of the proposition*; and this problem, in turn, first arises as a problem about *the difference between verbal nouns and verbs as verbs*. (These problems, as we shall see, closely parallel problems Frege encounters in his philosophy.) Here is Russell, in 1903, on the problem of the difference between verbal nouns and verbs as verbs:

> It is plain . . . that the concept which occurs in the verbal noun is the very same as that which occurs as verb. . . . [E]very constituent of every proposition must, on pain of self-contradiction, be capable of being made a logical subject. . . . Thus the very verb which occurs as verb can occur also as subject. The question is: What logical difference is expressed by this difference of grammatical form? . . . And it is plain that the difference must be one in external relations. But in regard to verbs, there is a further point. . . . 'Caesar died' and 'the death of Caesar' will illustrate this point. If we ask: What is asserted in the proposition 'Caesar died'? the answer must be 'the death of Caesar is asserted'. In that case, it would seem, it is the death of Caesar which is true or false; and yet neither truth nor falsity belongs to a mere logical subject. . . . [I]t is quite plain that ['the death of Caesar'] . . . is never equivalent to 'Caesar died'. There appears to be an ultimate notion of assertion, given by the verb, which is lost as soon as we substitute a verbal noun. . . . Thus the contradiction which was to have been avoided, of an entity which cannot be made a logical subject, appears to have become inevitable. This difficulty, which seems to be inherent in the very nature of truth and falsehood, is one with which I do not know how to deal satisfactorily.[58]

We have here the general shape of a problem that continues to haunt Russell's thinking for the next decade and a half – until, that is, he quite explicitly cedes the problem (and with it 'the fundamental problems of logic') to Wittgenstein. Russell here, in 1903, wants to maintain both: (1) that 'every constituent of every proposition must...be capable of being made a logical subject' (to deny this he thinks would be self-contradictory and, moreover, would strike at the root of his entire atomist metaphysics and its correlative conception of analysis), and (2) that there are cases of 'entities' which apparently cannot be made into logical subjects (the case which here gives Russell pause being that which is expressed by *the verb functioning* qua *verb in a proposition*). Taking advantage of his conclusion above that 'this difficulty...seems to be inherent in the very nature of truth and falsehood', Russell goes on, in the remainder of *The Principles of Mathematics*, §52, to give a very weird reason for why he can afford to leave the issue unresolved:

> The nature of truth...belongs no more to the principles of mathematics than to the principles of everything else. I therefore leave this question to the logicians with the above brief indication of a difficulty.[59]

Russell seeks to excuse himself here from further exploring the problem by consigning it to a different 'area' of philosophy. Since the difficulty is not peculiar to the philosophy of mathematics, which is the official topic of Russell's book, it can be postponed for a more suitable occasion. That he should allow himself to rest content with thus leaving the question (to the logicians!) becomes all the more puzzling, two sections later, when it emerges that this problem (concerning the elusiveness of that which is expressed by the verb as verb) is really a version of a more general problem (concerning the nature of the unity of the proposition):

> The twofold nature of the verb, as actual verb and as verbal noun, may be expressed, if all verbs are held to be relations, as the difference between a relation in itself and a relation actually relating. Consider, for example, the proposition 'A differs from B'. The constituents of this proposition, if we analyze it, appear to be only A, difference, B. Yet these constituents, thus placed side by side, do not reconstitute the proposition. The differ-ence which occurs in the proposition actually relates A and B, whereas the difference after analysis is a notion which has no connection with A and B....A proposition...is essentially a unity, and when analysis has destroyed the unity, no enumeration of the constituents will restore the proposition. The verb, when used as verb, embodies the unity of the proposition, and is thus distinguishable from the verb considered as term, though I do not know how to give a clear account of the precise nature of the distinction.[60]

Given the generality the problem here assumes, it becomes all the more remarkable that Russell takes the difficulty in question to be one that can be postponed for a later occasion. This deferral takes on an even more puzzling aspect when, later in the same work,[61] Russell gives Frege credit for 'recognizing the unity of the proposition' only, two sections later, to refuse Frege the pinch of salt that Russell himself seemingly required in his own earlier discussion of the verb as verb. Russell here vehemently rejects Fregean *Begriffe* on what he is here prepared to represent as decisive grounds: if *Begriffe* cannot 'be made into logical subjects without change of meaning' any attempt to talk about them will reduce one to stammering, thus any theory that purports to say something about them contradicts itself.

The problem that Russell faces in the above passage is that of saying what the difference is between a proposition and a mere list (e.g. the difference between the proposition 'A differs from B' and the list consisting of the constituents of that proposition – 'A', 'the relation of *differing from*', and 'B' – placed side by side). Versions of this problem continue to haunt Russell's work, and become vividly manifest to him, nine years later, while trying to write an essay entitled 'What is Logic?'. In that essay, he attempts to introduce a notion that explains how the constituents of a proposition are *united*: the notion of *logical form*. As Russell later formulates it: the logical form of a proposition is the way in which the constituents of the proposition are put together. The difference between a proposition and a list is that in the latter the constituents merely co-occur in a single sequence whereas in the former they figure in a complex united by a logical form. Russell thus defines logic as 'the study of the forms of complexes'. This naturally raises the question: what exactly are these forms? The purpose of the essay was to have been to answer this question. But after declaring 'We *must* take *form* as a primitive', Russell is able to furnish only negative answers to this question (and hence to the question posed by the title of his essay): 'A *form* is . . . not a constituent of complexes having this form. A *form* is not a mere symbol: a symbol composed entirely of variables symbolises a form, but is not a form';[62] and so on. Every answer Russell canvasses in this essay (purporting to furnish a positive characterization of the nature of logical form) he rejects on the grounds that it threatens to transform logical form into something which itself 'is not a form' but rather only a constituent or symbolic counterpart of a form. In his attempts to offer a theoretical characterization of logical form, Russell here finds himself on the verge of the very sort of stammering that he previously castigated Frege for having acknowledged as an inevitable consequence of any attempt to convert *Begriffe* into logical subjects. The closest thing to a positive statement on the subject of the nature of logical form Russell ever manages to offer anywhere in his unfinished essay 'What is Logic?' is the following: 'A *form* is something.'[63] This leaves him with nothing more, by way of answer to his title question, than roughly: 'Logic is the study of something.' Russell wants to have something *positive* to say (about what kind of a 'something' a logical form is), but every positive characterization he tries out is manifestly flawed.[64] He again feels a strong inclination to sidestep the topic and leave it to someone else – this time someone in particular. Announcing his decision to leave the essay unfinished, he writes Ottoline Morrell: 'I can't get on with "What is Logic?", the subject is hopelessly difficult, and for the present I am stuck. I feel very much inclined to leave it to Wittgenstein.'[65]

Wittgenstein, in the years that follow, in both discussion and correspondence, continues to try to force Russell's attention on the question of 'the nature of the form of complexes', thus making Russell increasingly aware of problems such as the following:

> The proposition 'if Socrates is human, and whatever is human is mortal, then Socrates is mortal' might be thought, at first, to be a proposition of logic. But it is obvious that its truth is in no way dependent on any peculiarity of Socrates or humanity or mortality, but only on the *form* of the proposition. . . . Thus we arrive at the pure logical proposition: 'Whatever x and α and β may be, if x is α and whatever is α is β, then x is β'. Here there is no longer any constituent corresponding to Socrates and humanity and mortality: the only thing that has been preserved is the pure *form* of the proposition, and the form is not a 'thing', not another constituent along with the objects that were previously related in that form. . . . [It] represents merely the way in which the constituents are put together. This cannot be a new constituent, for if it were, there would have to be a new way in which it and the other constituents are put together, and if we take this way again as a constituent, we find ourselves embarked on an endless regress.[66]

This is from a never-finished book entitled *Theory of Knowledge*. Here, in 1913, Russell forthrightly concludes that logical forms cannot occur as constituents of propositions, thus violating the principle he enunciated ten years earlier (that any theory which purports to treat of entities which cannot 'be made into logical subjects without change of meaning' contradicts itself). This reopens the very problem which generated Russell's resistance to such a conclusion in 1903: Russell himself talks about logical forms at length in *Theory of Knowledge* and discusses particular examples of logical forms. A dilemma looms: either the logical forms he there discusses figure as constituents of the propositions in which they occur or they do not – if they do, they are not examples of logical forms; if they do not, he has failed to talk about them. Consider, for example, Russell's series of declarations, with regard to the nature of 'Whatever x and α and β may be, if x is α and whatever is α is β, then x is β', such as that 'here there is no longer any constituent corresponding to Socrates and humanity and mortality', and that 'here . . . the only thing that has been preserved is the pure *form* of the proposition', and that this form 'is not a "thing", not another constituent along with the objects that were previously related in that form'. Now with regard to each of these statements, we can ask: does the aforementioned logical form occur as the logical subject – and thus as a logical constituent – of the statement in question or not? If it does so occur: then it looks as if, by Russell's own lights, that which so occurs is not an example of a logical form after all (for a logical form is, by definition, something which cannot occur as a constituent of a proposition). If it doesn't so occur: then the following question becomes urgent: what is the logical subject of these statements? And if it is not a logical form, then it would seem to follow that nothing about any logical form is actually 'said' in any of these remarks, thus forcing the reader to the conclusion that none of these remarks (successfully) engages the topic that they purport to engage. It looks as if, if what Russell himself says about the nature of logical forms is true, then, by his own lights, many of the sentences in his manuscript (from which the above quotation is drawn) are nonsense (including much of that quotation itself). Russell – unlike Frege – never faces up to this problem.

When Russell (re-)encounters this version of his old problem, his inclination is to react much the same way as ten years earlier, essentially leaving it to others; and indeed he concludes his discussion of the topic in his manuscript with the remark: 'In the present chaotic state of our knowledge concerning the primitive ideas of logic, it is impossible to pursue this topic further.'[67] Russell, however, here in 1913, is no longer able to get around the problem by confining his attention to the topic officially announced in the title of the book (in this case the theory of knowledge, rather than the principles of mathematics) – by, as it were, leaving it to the logicians – because Russell is convinced in 1913, and constructs the design of the entire manuscript around the principle, that 'it is impossible to assign to the theory of knowledge a province distinct from that of logic'.[68] That the problem is an urgent one is repeatedly borne in on him by Wittgenstein in both correspondence and conversation. Wittgenstein, at the same time, makes things worse by suggesting that Russell's 1913 manuscript runs into an additional, related problem – a problem that arises in the theory of judgement.

Judgement, according to Russell, is the mental act by means of which objects are united so as to form propositions. But once he introduces the notion of logical form into his theory of the nature of logical complexes, difficulties creep into his theory of judgement. As we saw before: any collection of objects for which there is no corresponding logical form cannot be united into a proposition – it can be arranged at most into (a constellation that has 'the form' of) a mere list. Thus, for Russell, logical form becomes the source of the constraints on what can (and cannot) be judged: the totality of possible logical forms determines the range of possible judgeable contents. Russell, however, has no account of why certain collections of objects can and others cannot be combined into logically unified complexes, and thus no account of why we can only judge of some things and not others – that is, of why we cannot judge a nonsense. In his conversations with Russell at the time, Wittgenstein hammers away at this point. He formulates the dimension of this problem that touches on the theory of judgement in the *Tractatus* as follows: 'The correct explanation of the form of the proposition "A judges that *p*" must show that it is impossible to judge a nonsense. (Russell's theory does not satisfy this condition.)'[69]

The details of this objection (and why it is that Russell should find *this* objection – of the several fundamental objections Wittgenstein urges against Russell's doctrines in 1913 – to be particularly troubling) do not matter for our present purpose. What does matter is Russell's initial reaction to Wittgenstein's initial (apparently rather inept) attempt to formulate his objection to Russell's theory:

> He said it was all wrong, not realizing the difficulties – that he had tried my view and knew it wouldn't work. I couldn't understand his objection – in fact he was very inarticulate – but I feel in my bones that he must be right, and that he has seen something I have missed. If I could see it too I shouldn't mind, but as it is, it is worrying, and has rather destroyed the pleasure in my writing – I can only go on with what I see and yet I feel it is probably all wrong, and that Wittgenstein will think me a dishonest scoundrel for going on with it.[70]

The thought that Wittgenstein will think him 'a dishonest scoundrel for going on with it' doesn't of itself deter Russell from going on with it. For Russell has been trying to convince Wittgenstein for some time that he really ought to relax his own unreasonably exacting standards with regard to the writing of philosophy (and the evaluation of the writing of others) – at least enough to allow himself actually to finish writing something (and to allow Russell to publish what he has finished writing without drawing his student's anger and contempt). Russell sums up his own view of Wittgenstein's tormented relation to philosophical writing in a letter to Ottoline Morrell in the following terms: Wittgenstein's 'artistic conscience gets in the way' so that if he can't 'do it perfectly' then he would rather not do it at all.[71]

Ray Monk has suggested that Russell continues to 'go on with it' – 'appealing to the results of a theory of logic in the absence of a theory' – in part because he was assuming: (1) that, even if it turned out he himself wouldn't ever be able to figure out what to do about the difficulty, Wittgenstein surely would, and (2) that whatever Wittgenstein came up with in his concurrent work on 'the problem of logical complexes' would fit perfectly into Russell's own plans for the book.[72] But the direction in which Wittgenstein's own thinking was moving proved increasingly less serviceable to

Russell's purposes. Whereas Russell wanted a *theory* of the nature of logical forms (and the nature of our acquaintance with them) to serve as a foundation for his epistemology, Wittgenstein was slowly moving in the direction of becoming more and more convinced not only that no such theory was possible but that the goal should be to show why all such theories are superfluous. Even if one thinks Monk's suggestion uncharitable, it is incontrovertible (as evidenced, for example, by numerous remarks in Russell's correspondence with Ottoline Morrell, F.H. Bradley, and others during this period) that the person Russell looks to for a solution to this problem is his student Wittgenstein – naturally enough, since this student keeps insisting, from a very early point on, that the problem is 'a very fundamental one', that Russell himself has failed to grasp what is required in the way of a solution, and that he (Wittgenstein) himself is on the verge of seeing his way clear to a (dis)solution of it.

As with his earlier essay 'What is Logic?', rather than leaving his discussion of these fundamental ideas in their 'present chaotic state', Russell decides to leave the entire manuscript unpublished. He decides it is the only intellectually honest thing to do, since the rest of his manuscript quite explicitly presupposes and builds on the very theory of logical forms which he never successfully works out. But he achieves this realization only after continuing to work on the manuscript for a period while trying to believe that the problem 'wasn't so bad'. Eventually, however, the worry that Wittgenstein will think him 'a dishonest scoundrel for going on with it' is eclipsed by the worry that Wittgenstein might be right in so thinking. Russell later describes his behaviour during this period as a 'failure of honesty' with regard to his work:

> All that has gone wrong with me lately came from Wittgenstein's attack on my work – I have only just realised this. It was very difficult to be honest about it, as it makes a large part of the book I meant to write impossible for years to come probably. I tried to believe it wasn't so bad as that.... And the failure of honesty over my work – which was very slight and subtle, more an attitude than anything definite – spread like a poison in every direction.[73]

As the epigraphs to this section indicate, as early as 1911, Russell (in the immediate aftermath of the completion of *Principia Mathematica*) begins to be beset with doubts about his ability to continue to do important work in technical philosophy; Russell's inability to bring his manuscript on *Theory of Knowledge* to completion, however, vastly exacerbates these doubts. Three years later, he writes to Ottoline: 'His [Wittgenstein's] criticism...was an event of first-rate importance in my life, and affected everything I have done since. I saw he was right, and I saw that I could not hope ever again to do fundamental work in philosophy.'[74]

In at least one sense of 'facing up to the problem', Russell, as signalled by his decision to abandon the 1913 manuscript, faces up to the problem in the following by no means trivial (but, from Wittgenstein's point of view, none the less minimal) sense: he acknowledges that he has no solution to the problem, that he needs one, and that he ought to look for one. (In response to criticisms from F.H. Bradley not all that dissimilar to ones Wittgenstein had already raised, Russell writes to Bradley, in 1914: 'I fully recognise the vital importance of the questions you raise.... I recognise that it is my duty to answer if I can, and if I cannot, to look for an answer as long as I live.'[75]) And it is equally evident, despite the persistent recurrence of a problem of this sort in his work (be it in the guise of the problem of the unity of the proposition, the verbal noun, the Fregean *Begriffe*, the violation of logical type or the nature of logical form), that Russell remains uncomfortable with the problem, and is, accordingly, reluctant to face it head on. As soon as he identifies a problem as being one of this general shape, he begins either to run from it or to search for a technical fix – thus leaving himself always in the position of having to treat the symptoms of the problem without ever confronting their source.[76] Although he increasingly comes to suspect that there might not be any 'simplified way of meeting the difficulty', Russell never sees why there cannot be one and never ceases to hanker after one – which means that, by Wittgenstein's lights, Russell never genuinely *encounters* (what Wittgenstein takes to be) the difficulty. Or to put it more precisely: Russell never sees the difficulty as bearing the features of that peculiar species of difficulty that Wittgenstein calls 'philosophical' – that is, he never sees it as an instance of the kind of difficulty which Rhees has in mind (in explicating what Wittgenstein means by the need to 'go the bloody *hard* way' in philosophy) when he quotes Wittgenstein as saying that the sorts of difficulties that most concern him are ones of the sort that one cannot by-pass.

What could Russell have done which, by Wittgenstein's lights, would have counted as his having taken a first step towards going the bloody hard way here? A first step would have been for him to *acknowledge* the difficulty as the kind of difficulty that (Wittgenstein thought) it was. This would have required him to affirm a pervasive and apparently irremediable inadequacy in his mode of expression in his discussions of the topic. Indeed, in the eyes of the author of the *Tractatus*, the courageous (and ultimately philosophically fruitful) way with this difficulty would have been for Russell forthrightly to highlight that which was logically defective in his own formulations, thereby flagging that in order for his reader to understand what Russell wanted to – but was unable to – say (about the nature of logical forms), the reader would first need to come to appreciate that which was defective in Russell's avowedly unsuccessful efforts to try to say it. Thus Russell, if he had wished to retain the notion of logical form he develops in his 1913 manuscript, might, for example, have acknowledged that he had reached an impasse in his thought which required him to make something along the lines of the following (Fregean) sort of admission concerning the status of his own talk about logical forms:

> I admit that there is a peculiar obstacle in the way of an understanding with the reader. By a kind of necessity of language, my expressions, taken literally, miss my thought; I mention a constituent of a proposition when what I intend is a logical form. I fully realise that I am relying upon a reader who is ready to meet me half-way – who does not begrudge a pinch of salt.

This (fictitious) admission – in regard to logical forms – resembles in certain ways the (actual) admission – in regard to *verbs* qua *verbs* – made in *The Principles of Mathematics*, ten years earlier; but the latter admission tends in the direction of treating the problem as a merely 'technical' one which further efforts at analysis will eventually clear up, whereas the former (fictitious) admission is sensitive to the depth of the problem and forthright about the implications the problem has for the status of any philosophical prose which purports to engage it. As we shall see, Frege makes just this former sort of admission (when he confronts a version of Russell's problem) in his own attempts to shed light on the nature of concepts. It is perhaps, above all, this moment in Frege's work which comes to epitomise for early Wittgenstein the difference in the character of Russell's and Frege's respective responses to a fundamental philosophical difficulty.

As Wittgenstein comes to appreciate the *depth* of this difference, it becomes increasingly clear to him that his own and Russell's ways in philosophy must permanently diverge. Seven years after the original publication of the *Tractatus*, and hence at a time when he was already a world-famous philosopher, Wittgenstein found himself (in order to satisfy certain bureaucratic requirements of Oxford University) in the humorous position of needing a *PhD*. As a way around the problem, the *Tractatus* was declared his 'thesis' and, in accordance with university regulations, an oral examination took place, with Moore and Russell serving as Wittgenstein's examiners. Monk recounts the episode as follows:

> Russell advanced his view that Wittgenstein was inconsistent in claiming to have expressed unassailable truths by means of meaningless propositions. He was, of course, unable to convince Wittgenstein, who brought the proceeding to an end by clapping each of his examiners on the shoulder and remarking consolingly: 'Don't worry, I know you'll never understand it.'[77]

Wittgenstein's confidence that Russell would never understand his book is not a function of his estimate of Russell's logical acumen (which he held in high esteem), but of his *sensibility*.[78] Nine years earlier, in 1920, Wittgenstein

had vehemently refused to allow a German translation of Russell's 'Introduction' to the *Tractatus* to be published as an introduction to the then
planned German-language edition of the book (which refusal at the time
cost Wittgenstein what appeared to be the only chance of ever getting the
book published). He refused on the grounds that, once 'all the refinement
of ... [Russell's] English style was lost in the translation ... what remained
was superficiality and misunderstanding' – not only where Russell is critical
but even where he was 'simply trying to make clear [*klarlegen*] the point of
view' of Wittgenstein's book.[79] What Wittgenstein had become confident
of, by 1929, was that Russell would never be willing to do what that book
asks of its reader – namely, 'strictly follow through' on the very difficulties
which Russell, in Wittgenstein's eyes, had always sought a way around.

Russell not infrequently made remarks regarding Wittgenstein's *Tractatus*
of the following sort: 'I think (though he wouldn't agree) that what he likes
best in mysticism is its power to make him stop thinking.'[80] There is considerable irony in this. For Wittgenstein (who, as Russell says, certainly
wouldn't have acceded to this description of himself) did come to think
something quite analogous to be true of Russell – and, moreover, thought
that, with each passing year, it came to be increasingly true: namely, that
what *he*, Russell (though he wouldn't agree), liked best about certain (putatively 'scientific') ways of approaching philosophical problems is that they
held out the promise of relieving him of the obligation to have to think the
problems through all the way.[81]

Frege on the elucidation of that which is logically primitive

> *There is no more light in a genius than in any other honest man – but he has
> a particular kind of lens to concentrate this light into a burning point. ...*
> One might say: '*Genius is* talent exercised with courage'.
>
> Wittgenstein[82]

> *Frege's courage as a philosopher clearly inspired Wittgenstein; his own
> conception of what philosophy might demand of one reflects his view of
> Frege's response to those demands.*
>
> Cora Diamond[83]

A version of the problem which Russell first explicitly stumbles over in 1903
(when he asks about the difference between using an expression to signify a
verbal noun and using it to signify a verb as verb) also occurs in Frege's work
– most famously, as a question about what the difference is between using an
expression to signify a concept and using it to signify an object. And Frege's
most famous discussion of that question is to be found in his article 'On
Concept and Object' – an article which is structured round his reply to an
objection put forward by Benno Kerry.

Kerry objects to Frege's claim that concepts cannot be objects and objects cannot be concepts. Kerry proposes, as a counter-example to Frege's claim, the statement 'the concept *horse* is a concept easily attained'. This statement seems to assert that something – the concept *horse* – falls under a concept (namely, that of being a concept easily attained). Now anything that falls under a (first-level) concept must – on Frege's conception of an object – be an object. That *is* what it is to be an object for Frege – to be the kind of a thing of which concepts can be predicated. So, for Frege, the grammatical subject of Kerry's statement – the concept *horse* – (since it falls under a concept) must be an object. But, if what the statement says is true, then it is a concept easily attained; and if it is a concept easily attained then it is a kind of a concept. The two prongs of Kerry's argument, based on his putative counter-example, can thus be summarized as follows: (a) given Frege's conception of what it is to be an object, we have reason (by virtue of its logical role in the statement) to conclude that 'the concept *horse*' is an object; and (b) given the (apparent) truth of what the statement itself asserts, we have reason to conclude that it is a concept. So Kerry concludes that his statement furnishes us with an example of something – the concept *horse* – that is both an object and a concept.

Frege's article responding to Kerry begins with the following remark:

> The word 'concept' is used in various ways; its sense is sometimes psychological, sometimes logical, and perhaps sometimes a confused mixture of both. Since this license exists, it is natural to restrict it by requiring that when once a usage is adopted it shall be maintained. What I decided was to keep to the strictly logical use.... It seems to me that Kerry's misunderstanding results from his unintentionally confusing his own usage of the word 'concept' with mine. This readily gives rise to contradictions, for which my usage is not to blame.[84]

Frege insists here that he uses the word 'concept' in 'a strictly logical sense' and that Kerry's misunderstanding of his view is due to his failure to appreciate this. In particular, Frege will charge that Kerry's apparent counter-example is generated by equivocating between 'a strictly logical' and (what Frege will call) a 'psychological' sense of the term 'concept'.[85] But what is it to use the word 'concept' in a strictly logical sense? This question is best approached through a consideration of Frege's three principles:

> In the enquiry that follows, I have kept to three fundamental principles:
>   [1] always to separate sharply the psychological from the logical, the subjective from the objective;
>   [2] never to ask for the meaning of a word in isolation, but only in the context of a proposition;
>   [3] never to lose sight of the distinction between concept and object.[86]

These three principles are closely linked: to deny any one of them is to deny each of the other two. Frege himself immediately goes on to explicate how a denial of the first principle leads to a denial of the second:

> In compliance with the first principle, I have used the word 'idea' always in the psychological sense, and have distinguished ideas from concepts and from objects. If the second principle is not observed, one is almost forced to take as the meanings of words mental pictures or acts of the individual mind, and so to offend against the first principle as well.[87]

If we disobey the second principle and ask for the meaning of a word in isolation, we shall look for an answer in the realm of the psychological – we shall explain what it is for a term to have a meaning in terms of mental accompaniments (such as the psychological associations the word carries with it), or in terms of mental acts (such as the linguistic intention with which we utter it); and *that* will constitute a violation of the first principle. Underlying these principles is a doctrine of the primacy of judgement. Frege writes: 'I do not begin with concepts and put them together to form a thought or judgement; I come by the parts of a thought by analyzing the thought.'[88] Frege here opposes the intuitive view of how we come by a thought which Russell takes for granted: we grasp a thought by taking hold of its independently thinkable components and putting them together so as to form a coherent whole.[89] The sort of 'parts'[90] which are at issue when we speak of the 'parts of a thought', according to Frege, are only to be identified by comparing and contrasting the logical structure of whole propositions and seeing how the respective 'parts' resemble and differ from one another in the contributions they make to the respective wholes.[91] In order to determine the meaning of a word, according to Frege, we need to know what logical role it plays in the context of a judgement. What we want to discover is thus not to be seen at all, if we look at the mere isolated word rather than at the working parts of the proposition in action. When Frege insists that he is going to keep to a strictly logical use of the word 'concept', he is declaring his interest in how a certain kind of working part of a judgement contributes to the sense of a judgement as a whole.

But Frege finds that he runs into a peculiar sort of trouble when he tries to say in a straightforward fashion just what it is that he wants to mean by (his 'strictly logical use' of) the word 'concept' or (by 'his strictly logical use' of) any of the other words – such as 'object' – he employs to denote something logically primitive. There are no symbols for terms such as 'concept' (or 'object') in Frege's *Begriffsschrift* – his logical symbolism. Nevertheless, these terms play an ineliminable role in his explanations of his symbolism. He thinks that an understanding of such terms is required if one is to master the notation of the symbolism and properly understand its significance. Yet he also insists that what he thus wishes to draw our attention to – when he employs, for example, the word 'concept' in its strictly logical sense – is not something that can be properly defined. It can only be exhibited through an activity (which Frege calls that) of *Erläuterung* – (which I will henceforth translate as) elucidation.[92] Elucidations, in turn, play only a transitional role: once they have successfully conveyed the logical distinctions which form the basis of Frege's *Begriffsschrift*,[93] we are to see that there is no way to express the thoughts which they (appear to be attempting to) convey in a *Begriffsschrift*.[94] Yet if we appreciate the logically fundamental character of the distinctions upon which Frege's *Begriffsschrift* is based, then we will see that anything which can be thought can be expressed in *Begriffsschrift*. In grasping the distinction between that which can and that which cannot be expressed in a *Begriffsschrift*, we furnish ourselves with a logically precise articulation of the distinction between that which ('in a strictly logical sense') is, and that which is not, a *thought*. Thus Frege's elucidations are meant to play the role of a ladder which we are to climb up and then throw away.[95] Frege might have said about his own elucidatory remarks, echoing §6.54 of the *Tractatus*: 'My propositions serve as elucidations in the following way: he who understands me recognises that my propositions cannot be expressed in my *Begriffsschrift*, once he has used them – as steps – to climb up beyond them. He must, so to speak, throw away the ladder after he has used it to climb up to my *Begriffsschrift*.'

The distinction between elucidation and definition in Frege rests upon a prior distinction between what is primitive and what is defined in a theory. Any theoretical term which is not susceptible of a formal definition requires elucidation. Every science must employ some primitive terms whose meanings must be presupposed from the outset. Even in a logically perfect language there will be some terms which are not (and cannot be) introduced by definition and which must remain indefinable. The purpose of elucidations is to convey the meanings of such terms. In 'On Concept and Object', Frege is concerned with only one species of the genus elucidation, namely the activity of elucidating what is *logically* primitive. When one is engaged in this particular species of elucidation, Frege thinks one is compelled to come out with sentences which cannot be translated into a proper *Begriffsschrift*. For something to count as a definition, for Frege, it must be possible to invoke it in proofs. Wherever the *definiendum* occurs in a sentence, it must be possible to replace it with the *definiens*. Nothing of the sort is possible, Frege maintains, for those terms occurring in his elucidatory remarks which refer to logically primitive categories.[96] Their meaning must be presupposed from the outset. The most one can do is to lead the reader to what is meant by such terms – what it is one's words are trying to gesture at – by means of a series of *hints*.[97] Early on in his reply to Kerry, Frege insists upon the ineliminable role of hints in offering an elucidation of that which is logically fundamental and hence indefinable:

On the introduction of a name for what is logically simple, a definition is not possible; there is nothing for it but to lead the reader or hearer, by means of hints, to understand the word as it is intended.[98]

The term 'elucidation', in this context, stands for the activity of leading the reader by means of hints to what is intended by a term which denotes something logically primitive. This requires not only that we count on the patience and goodwill of our audience while we encourage them to guess at our intended meaning, but also that – here in the antechamber to that most precise of all sciences: the science of logic – we resort to figurative modes of expression. Worse still, Frege thinks that in the elucidation of logically primitive notions (such as that of *concept* or *object*) there is an ineliminable role to be played by (the artful employment of) nonsense. Thus, from the point of view of the author of the *Tractatus*, Frege here encounters the fundamental difficulty – common to Frege's and Russell's philosophies, and which each of these philosophies, in its own way, renders unavoidable – but Frege, unlike Russell, recognises it *as a difficulty* (in the sense of that phrase which Rhees attempts to elucidate in the service of explicating Wittgenstein's conception of philosophy).

Frege frankly concedes that such a process of offering hints and relying on guesswork might, in principle, never culminate in the desired meeting of minds between the elucidator and the audience of an elucidation. He hastens to reassure us, however, that it turns out that, in practice, we are quite good at guessing what another person means even when all we are offered is a series of such hints. It is, moreover, of crucial importance when offering an elucidation, Frege says, that the originator of the elucidation himself understand the transitional character of the talk that he engages in:

Theoretically, one might never achieve one's goal this way. In practice, however, we do manage to come to an understanding about the meanings of words. Of course we have to be able to count on a meeting of minds, on others guessing what we have in mind. But all this precedes the construction of a system and does not belong within a system.[99]

Once the elucidation is successful the recourse to figurative modes of speech and bits of nonsense can be dispensed with; the elucidations will have served their transitional pragmatic purpose and are to be thrown away. The activity of elucidation 'has no place in the system of a science'. Its role is entirely that of a propaedeutic.[100] Thus Frege, that most precise of modern philosophers and logicians, frankly acknowledges that the sort of discourse one most resort to in order to elucidate the meaning of that which is logically primitive has no place in a logically well-regimented system of discourse.

The elucidatory strategy of the essay 'On Concept and Object' can be seen as proceeding in five steps: (1) to make explicit a logical distinction implicit in our everyday linguistic practices, (2) to demonstrate that Kerry's employment of the terminology of 'object' and 'concept' fails to track the distinction in question, (3) to furnish statements (employing the terminology of 'object' and 'concept') that aim to track the distinction in question, (4) to elicit an appreciation of what is defective about such statements, and (5) to indicate how a recognition of the defective character of such statements enables one to attain an insight (into, e.g., what a concept is) which could not have been communicated in any other way. Thus Frege might have said: He who *recognizes* my elucidatory remarks in 'On Concept and Object' as *defective* understands me. Frege thus makes the very acknowledgement that Russell awkwardly tries to evade: he acknowledges that the modes of expression he employs are, by his own 'strictly logical' lights, irremediably defective; and, without flinching from the consequences, he tries resolutely to *think through* what this entails about the status of his own philosophical procedures.

One example of Fregean elucidation occurs in a letter to Russell:

> In the proposition 'Something is an object', the word 'something'... stands for a proper name. Thus whatever we put in place of 'something', we always get a true proposition; for a function name cannot take the place of 'something'. Here we find ourselves in a situation where the nature of language forces us to make use of imprecise expressions. The proposition 'A is a function' is such an expression: it is always imprecise; for A stands for a proper name.... While I am writing this, I am well aware of having again expressed myself imprecisely. Sometimes this is just unavoidable. *All that matters is that we know we are doing it and how it happens.*[101]

When Russell uses the term 'function' to make statements like 'A is a function', he wants to be saying something informative: he wants to be telling us something about the nature of A. Frege wants to show Russell that attempts to say what one wants to say misfire when one attempts to say something about functions by some means other than by using functions as functions. The proposition 'A is a function' is here invoked by Frege as an example of the paradoxical character inevitably attaching to the sort of utterances one comes out with when one attempts to elucidate what a function is. To see why Frege thinks that the endeavour in question necessarily leads to paradoxical assertions, consider the following four propositions:

(1) 'A is an object.'
(2) 'Everything is an object.'
(3) 'A is a function.'
(4) 'Nothing is a function.'

In (1), the word 'A' stands for a proper name; and so, by Frege's lights, whatever we plug in for 'A' will occupy the argument place for an object, and thus (according to Frege's second principle) will be an object. Thus it would appear that no matter what we plug in for 'A', (1) will be true. But if (1) is true no matter what we plug in for 'A', it would seem to follow that (2) is true! Similarly, in (3), as in (1), the word 'A' stands for a proper name; and so, once again, whatever occupies this argument place will be an object. Thus it would appear in this case that no matter what we plug in for 'A', (3) will be false. But if (3) is false no matter what we plug in for 'A', it would seem to follow that (4) is true! The point of this elucidation is not to secure the truth of the paradoxical claim that 'Nothing is a function' (or 'There are no functions'). On the contrary: it is to offer a *reductio ad absurdum* of the idea that the proposition 'A is a function' can just straightforwardly *say* what Russell (for the sake of his argument with Frege) wants it to. The point is to show that sentences in which the expression 'function' occurs misfire, and to show that – as long as we know what we are doing with such sentences – such self-defeating sentences can none the less be put to use to communicate an insight into what a function is. What matters when we employ such sentences, as Frege's final sentence (in the passage quoted above) indicates, is that we know what we are doing (i.e. uttering nonsense) when we come out with them, and that we know how it has come to pass that we find ourselves doing it.

The point of the paradoxical assertions that comprise the preceding elucidation is to show us (i) that we end up speaking nonsense when we try to say what a function is, (ii) that we here 'find ourselves in a situation where the nature of language itself' makes it impossible for us to say that which we want to say, (iii) that to grasp how it is that the nature of language itself thus stands in the way of saying what we want to say (when we want to say what a function is) *is* to grasp what a function is. The point is thus not merely *to expose* what we end up saying (when we employ such a term) as nonsense – in order, say, to debar us from engaging in such ways of speaking – but, rather, to teach us how *self-consciously* to cultivate such ways of speaking (in order to allow us to attain insight into the nature of functions). The point of cultivating such ways of speaking is to enable us to recognize *why* it is that we end up with nonsense when we try to say such things. The attainment of such a recognition constitutes the sign that we have grasped an elucidation of the meaning of a term (such as 'function') which denotes something logically primitive.

Frege repeatedly says, when offering such elucidatory examples, that he is *forced* or *compelled* to express himself in an infelicitous manner: he is attempting to struggle against 'an imprecision forced on us by the nature of language', one which 'compels' him 'to use an inappropriate expression which obscures – falsifies – the thought'. Frege (1) takes himself in such cases to be trying to say something which, properly speaking, *cannot* be said, and (2) speaks in such cases of there being a *thought* which his words struggle but fail adequately to express. In a famous passage in 'On Concept and Object', Frege makes the admission I alluded to earlier in order to prepare the contrast between the character of Frege's admission and the sorts of admission one characteristically finds in Russell's writings (with regard to the parallel problem in Russell's philosophy). Here is Frege:

> I admit that there is a quite peculiar obstacle in the way of an understanding with the reader. By a kind of necessity of language, my expressions, taken literally, sometimes miss my thought; I mention an object when what I intend is a concept. I fully realise that in such cases I was relying upon a reader who would be ready to meet me half-way – who does not begrudge a pinch of salt.[102]

His words miss his thought (and end up being nonsense); so there is a thought they are aiming at: an understanding of what his words intend to say depends upon his reader latching onto the thought his words fail properly to express. This failure is due, according to Frege, to 'a kind of necessity of language'. If the author is to convey the thought he here seeks to convey he has no alternative but to have recourse to (elucidatory) nonsense. Frege's reader is therefore left with the task of doing something with the words that the author here provides. It does not suffice here for the reader to do what one ordinarily does with an author's words: to shape up to agreeing (or disagreeing) with that which the words themselves (appear to) say. The point of the exercise which, by a kind of necessity of language, Frege is forced to bequeath to the reader is: first to come to see why the author's words necessarily fail to say what they (at least at first) appear to say and, secondly, to grasp the point behind the author's availing himself of such an intentionally self-defeating form of expression.

This passage represents the very moment in Frege's work which is perhaps most frequently adduced as an example of how the feet of even the great Frege were made of clay. Yet this moment in Frege's work is, arguably, inseparable from those aspects of his work that constitute the essence of what *for Wittgenstein* was great about 'the great works of Frege'. The very moments in Frege, such as the one represented in the passage above, which are bound to appear most embarrassingly disastrous (when viewed from the vantage point of a certain species of professionalized philosophical common sense) epitomize, for Wittgenstein, that which is most exemplary in Frege: his refusal to accept a technical or makeshift fix – one which would allow him to by-pass the difficulty – and his correlative willingness to take the *difficulty* seriously, think it through to the point where he can begin to see why there cannot be a simplified way of meeting it, and then, having thought it through, to allow the difficulty itself to make things difficult and see where it leads him. The author of the *Tractatus* does not think that

Frege manages, by any means, to come to the end of the philosophical task of seeing where this particular difficulty leads.[103] But he does think that Frege has an appreciation of the *kind* of task this is and why it is bloody *hard*, thus furnishing Wittgenstein with an example (of what it means to try to think things through in philosophy) that he strives to emulate in all of his own subsequent philosophical work.

   To understand the sense in which Wittgenstein strives, in his philosophical work, to emulate Frege's example (and thus the sense in which Wittgenstein's early book is rightly said to be indebted, above all, to the great works of Frege) it is crucial to understand wherein Wittgenstein thinks the greatness of Frege's work lies. It is not that Frege, in Wittgenstein's estimation, possesses a greater degree of sheer philosophical candlepower than, say, a Ramsey or a Russell. It is rather that, when faced with certain fundamental difficulties, Frege exhibits honesty and courage of a sort which furnishes him with 'a particular kind of lens to concentrate the light into a burning point'. When, in an effort further to concentrate the light, Wittgenstein himself emulates (what he takes to be most important in) Frege's example, directing his own particular kind of lens at the same burning point, the difficulties in question – those which Wittgenstein inherits from Frege and Russell – are consumed in that burst of philosophical flame now known to us as the *Tractatus Logico-Philosophicus*.

Going against the grain

> *You are inclined to put our difference in one way, as a difference of* opinion. *But I am not trying to persuade you to change your opinion. I am only trying to recommend a certain sort of investigation. If there is an opinion involved, my only opinion is that this sort of investigation is immensely important and very much* against the grain.
>
> Wittgenstein[104]

The *Tractatus* represents the first of many steps in a lifelong effort on Wittgenstein's part to apply – and, in the process of applying, increasingly radicalize – what he learned from Frege's exemplary effort to engage in that peculiar form of philosophical activity that Frege calls 'elucidation'. In §4.1212 of the *Tractatus*, we are told that a work of philosophy 'consists essentially of elucidations' – where the term 'elucidation' is a rendering of the same German word, *Erläuterung*, which, as we have seen, figures prominently in Frege's writings. 'Philosophy' here means: philosophy as practised by the author of the *Tractatus*. The notion of elucidation is tied in §4.1212 to the idea of philosophy being a certain kind of *activity*: 'Philosophy is not a theory [*Lehre*] but an activity. A philosophical work consists essentially of elucidations.' Wittgenstein here declares that the work of philosophy, as he pursues it, does not consist in putting forward a theory or a doctrine but rather in *doing* something – namely, in engaging in the activity of elucidation. *How* do such 'elucidations' elucidate? The answer to this question comes in the notorious penultimate section of the *Tractatus*, where we again come upon the term 'elucidation' [*Erläuterung*]:

> My propositions serve as *elucidations* in the following way: anyone who understands me eventually recognizes them as nonsensical, when he has used them – as steps – to climb out through them, on them, over them.[105]

This passage tells a reader of the work what he must 'eventually recognize' in order to understand its author. The author's 'propositions' serve as elucidations by *our* – that is, the reader's – coming to *recognize* them as nonsensical. That is, everything depends on the reader doing something – attaining a certain kind of recognition – on his own. Wittgenstein does not ask his reader here to 'grasp' the 'thoughts' which his nonsensical propositions seek to convey. He does not call upon the reader to understand his sentences, but rather to understand *him*: namely the author and the kind of activity in which he is engaged. An understanding of this activity can be achieved only by the reader who engages in this activity himself, that is, who practises elucidation on himself, as Wittgenstein practises it – as the author of the *Tractatus* exhibits the practice of it – on himself. In not asking the reader to understand (and thus be in a position to 'agree with') his propositions, Wittgenstein therefore is not asking of him what most authors ask: to believe something – perhaps something the reader, prior to reading the book, does not (yet) believe. Wittgenstein is rather asking the reader to do something here which he anticipates will 'go against the grain'. (Thus Wittgenstein anticipates no one will understand his book.[106]) It goes against the grain both because the form the 'solution' to the problems takes ('the problems are dissolved in the actual sense of the word – like a lump of sugar in water'[107]) is one which the reader takes himself to know in advance cannot satisfy him and because the reader can only discover it does satisfy him (indeed 'complete satisfaction comes, since *no* question remains'[108]) if he is first willing to move in a direction in which it is bloody hard to go (because 'what has to be overcome is not a difficulty of the intellect, but one of the will'[109]).

This essay began with a quotation from Wittgenstein as reported by Rhees; it is fitting that it should end the same way. Wittgenstein, Rhees tells us, summed up what he does *not* want (but anticipates the reader will think he must want) and what he *does* want (but anticipates he will not get) from his reader in the following proposition: 'I don't try to make you *believe* something you don't believe, but to make you *do* something you won't do.'[110] Wittgenstein's eventual disappointment with Russell's and correlative esteem for Frege's philosophical work can each be understood in relation to what Wittgenstein here asks of his reader. Russell keeps trying to hit upon a thing to *believe* – a doctrine ('the right theory of logic') – that would make the philosophical problem go away; so that all that would then be required of a reader of a work that 'contained' its 'solution' would be to familiarize himself with the doctrine in question and thereby convince himself that someone else (namely Russell) had said everything which needed to be said in order to dispense with the problem. Whereas Frege asks his reader to *do* something – participate in an activity in which he must struggle to meet the author half-way – where the culmination of the activity lies in the reader's eventually coming to recognize that there is nothing (of the sort he originally imagines) to be said and hence nothing (of the originally imagined sort) to be believed either. Thus Frege, in the practical demonstration he furnishes of what it means strictly to think a problem all the way through, helps to bring into focus the possibility of a certain conception of what it means genuinely to make progress – a conception which Wittgenstein makes his own – with regard to the problems of philosophy and the problems of life: '[W]hen there is no question left ... just this is the answer. The solution of the problem ... is seen in the vanishing of the problem.'[111]

Whatever else one thinks of this conception, one has only to look around in order to convince oneself of the following: it goes – both inside and outside of (those circles that now fly the banner of) philosophy – very much against the grain.[112]

University of Chicago

Notes

1   Rush Rhees, 'The Study of Philosophy', in *Without Answers* (New York: Schocken, 1969), p. 169. For an example, see Wittgenstein's letter to Rhees of 28 November 1944; quoted in Ray Monk, *Ludwig Wittgenstein: The Duty of Genius* (New York: Free Press, 1990), p. 476.
2   Ray Monk, 'Philosophical Biography – The Very Idea', in *Wittgenstein: Biography and Philosophy*, ed. James Klagge (forthcoming).
3   Rhees, 'The Study of Philosophy', pp. 169–70.
4   'They may appear to be scattered all over the place' both in the sense that there may appear to be hardly any *consecutive* discussion of 'ethics' and in the sense that there may appear to be remarks on 'ethics' making odd appearances in unlikely locations all over Wittgenstein's corpus.
5   *Culture and Value*, ed. G.H. von Wright, tr. Peter Winch (Chicago: University of Chicago Press, 1980), p. 33.
6   *Ibid.*, p. 34.
7   Rush Rhees, ed., *Ludwig Wittgenstein: Personal Recollections*, p. 193.
8   *Culture and Value*, p. 16.
9   *Ibid.*, p. 45.
10 'But these passages', someone might complain, 'are mostly taken from a single work: *Culture and Value* – the work which Wittgenstein devotes exclusively to topics in ethics, aesthetics and religion!' This is not true. Wittgenstein never

wrote (nor ever planned to write) such a work. The passages in *Culture and Value* are drawn from all over Wittgenstein's *Nachlass*. The passages from *Culture and Value* which are quoted here (like many such passages) occur, in their original home in Wittgenstein's manuscripts, in the midst of investigations of questions such as what is it to follow a rule?, or name an object?, or understand the meaning of a word?, etc. In the opening sentence of his editor's preface to the volume, G.H. von Wright suggests that the remarks he has chosen to bring together in *Culture and Value* are remarks of Wittgenstein's 'which *do not belong directly with his philosophical works* although they are scattered amongst the philosophical texts' [my emphasis] (*ibid.*, p. i). One aim of the present essay is to cast doubt on (the italicised portion of) this description of these remarks.

11 Stanley Cavell, *This New yet Unapproachable America* (Albuquerque: Living Batch Press, 1989), p. 40.

12 D.Z. Phillips, *Philosophy's Cool Place* (Ithaca, NY: Cornell University Press, 1999), p. 46.

13 Phillips seems to assume that I would disagree with this. (I presume this is because he – mostly rightly – takes himself to disagree with so much of what I say elsewhere in my paper.)

14 To put a somewhat more polemical edge on the point: one cannot understand many of the remarks that occur in a text such as *Culture and Value* by engaging in a close reading of that 'work' alone and neglecting Wittgenstein's investigations of the sorts of questions with which the bulk of his work is concerned (questions such as is it possible for me to give myself a private ostensive definition?, or for another person to have my pains?, or for there to be only one occasion on which someone obeys a rule?, etc.) – neglecting, that is, what he thought philosophy is.

15 Rhees, *op. cit.*, pp. 170–1.

16 The entire conception of philosophy as a subject that can be divided into 'areas', which comes so naturally to us, is utterly alien to Wittgenstein.

17 See Cora Diamond's 'Ethics, Imagination, and the Method of the Tractatus' in R. Heinrich and H. Vetter, eds., *Bilder der Philosophie* (Vienna: Oldenbourg, 1991), pp. 55–90; and her 'Wittgenstein, Mathematics, and Ethics: Resisting the Attractions of Realism', in H. Sluga and D. Stern, eds., *The Cambridge Companion to Wittgenstein* (Cambridge: Cambridge University Press, 1996).

18 Hence the frequency of similes such as the following in Wittgenstein's writings: 'A human being is *imprisoned* in a room, if the door is unlocked but opens inwards; he, however, never gets the idea of *pulling* instead of pushing against it'; *Remarks on the Foundations of Mathematics*, tr. G.E.M. Anscombe (Oxford: Basil Blackwell, 1956), p. 125.

19 *Philosophical Investigations*; eds. G.E.M. Anscombe and R. Rhees, tr. G.E.M. Anscombe (Oxford: Basil Blackwell, 1953), §118.

20 Phillips, *Philosophy's Cool Place*, p. 46.

21 And this does appear to be what Phillips means. The most he seems to be prepared to concede by way of a connection between 'the personal' and 'the philosophical' is an *analogy* 'between working on philosophical problems and working on moral problems' (*ibid.*, p. 46). Phillips is unwilling to allow for any connection more intimate than this because it seems important to him to be able to maintain that 'Wittgenstein... is not saying, as Conant thinks, that a shoddiness in how we speak is, at the same time, a shoddiness in how we live' (*ibid.*).

22 Many of these misinterpretations have been occasioned by picking up Wittgenstein's oft-repeated analogy between philosophy and therapy from the wrong end.

23   Quoted by Rush Rhees in *Recollections of Wittgenstein*, ed. Rush Rhees (Oxford: Oxford University Press, 1984), p. 174.
24   Letter to Norman Malcolm, 16 November 1944; quoted in Norman Malcolm, *Ludwig Wittgenstein: A Memoir* (Oxford: Oxford University Press, 1984).
25   Such discernment is essential to the capacity for distinguishing (genuine) *philosophy* from, what Wittgenstein was fond of calling, (mere) *cleverness* – a distinction which underlies a great many of Wittgenstein's judgements of the work of other 'philosophers'.
26   *Ludwig Wittgenstein: Denkbewegungen, Tagebücher 1930–1932/1936–1937*; ed. Ilse Sommavilla (Innsbruck: Haymon-Verlag, 1997), p. 21.
27   'Conversations with Drury', in *Recollections of Wittgenstein*, p. 106.
28   *Ibid.*, p. 159.
29   See, in this regard, Ray Monk's review of Ben Rogers's *A.J. Ayer: A Life*; in *The Sunday Times*, 13 June 1999, Book Section, p. 12.
30   *Remarks on Frazer's Golden Bough*, ed. Rush Rhees; reprinted in *Ludwig Wittgenstein: Philosophical Occasions, 1912–1951* (Indianapolis: Hackett, 1993), p. 131.
31   A related double-faced 'difficulty' that surfaces repeatedly in Wittgenstein's notebooks as an urgent topic for him is the danger of *pride* (or *vanity*). Consider the following remark: 'The edifice of your pride has to be dismantled. And that is terribly hard work' (*Culture and Value*, p. 26). Phillips's mutually exclusive opposition between the personal and the philosophical gets in the way of an understanding of this remark. The question 'Is "dismantling the edifice of one's pride" a personal or a philosophical difficulty?' is, by Wittgenstein's lights, misconceived from the start. In one of the possible prefaces he drafts for a possible book, Wittgenstein writes:

> I would like to say 'This book is written to the glory of God', but nowadays that would be chicanery, that is, it would not be rightly understood. It means the book is written in good will, and in so far as it is not so written, but out of vanity, etc., the author would wish to see it condemned. *He cannot free it of these impurities further than he himself is free of them.* [my emphasis] (*Philosophical Remarks* (ed. R. Rhees, trs. R. Hargreaves and R. White; Oxford: Basil Blackwell, 1975), Preface)

32   Though it is a mistake to assume, as some commentators do, that Wittgenstein thinks that there can be a kind of person – call him an 'ordinary' person or a 'non-philosopher' – who is in full possession of his intellectual faculties and yet utterly free from philosophical perplexity and hence the need for philosophy and the forms of perspicuity and clarity which it aims to confer.
33   The remark occurs in a letter to his sister; Letter to Helene Salzer (*née* Wittgenstein), quoted in M. Nedo and M. Ranchetti, eds., *Ludwig Wittgenstein, Sein Leben in Bildern und Texten* (Frankfurt am Main: Suhrkamp, 1983), p. 292.
34   Wittgenstein therefore does not only think that the limitations of a person *qua* person limit his possibilities of imagination and reflection *qua* philosopher; he also thinks that the activity of philosophy itself represents a possible means of overcoming such limitation in oneself. Hence both the promise and the danger of philosophy. Throughout Wittgenstein's life, an important ground of his motivation to philosophy (to, that is, what he hopes philosophy, at its best, can be) – and of his fear of philosophy (of, that is, what he knows philosophy, at its worst, can do to a person) – is the thought that in developing her philosophical sensibility a person is thereby (for better or worse) profoundly shaping herself as a person.

35 Wittgenstein, Letter to Ludwig von Ficker: '*In Wirklichkeit is [der Stoff meines Buches] Ihnen nicht fremd, denn der Sinn des Buches ist ein Ethischer*' (reprinted in *Prototractatus*, eds. B.F. McGuinness, T. Nyberg, and G.H. von Wright, trs. D.F. Pears and B.F. McGuinness; Ithaca: Cornell University Press), p. 15.

36 Stanley Cavell, 'The Availability of Wittgenstein's Later Philosophy', in *Must We Mean What We Say?* (New York: Charles Scribner's Sons, 1969), p. 72.

37 Sigmund Freud, *Introductory Lectures on Psychoanalysis* (New York: W.W. Norton, 1969), pp. 280–1.

38 Arthur Schopenhauer, *The World as Will and Representation*, *Vol. I*, tr. E.F.J. Payne (New York: Dover, 1969), p. 76n. (I have amended the translation.)

39 *Ibid.*, p. 76. (I have amended the translation.) I, of course, do not mean here to be endorsing Schopenhauer's theory of geometry.

40 The strident moralism of Schopenhauer's tone marks an important difference between Schopenhauer's work, on the one hand, and that of Kierkegaard and Wittgenstein, on the other. Neither Kierkegaard nor Wittgenstein are as anxious as Schopenhauer (at least often appears to be) to make it clear that they themselves are free of the sorts of intellectual failings they seek to make their reader aware of in herself.

41 Schopenhauer, *The Fourfold Root of the Principle of Sufficient Reason*, tr. E.F.J. Payne (La Salle: Open Court, 1974), pp. 58–60.

42 But these are not matters that are generally taken up – or at present could easily be taken up – under the heading of (what analytic philosophers call) 'Ethics'. (They are more likely to come up under some heading such as 'paradoxes of irrationality'.) Yet they are integral to the category of the ethical as marked off in the writings of Kierkegaard. Here, as elsewhere, Wittgenstein's ways of thinking and talking about philosophical problems bear the trace of Kierkegaard's influence. I discuss the parallels here between Kierkegaard and Wittgenstein in my 'On Putting Two and Two Together: Kierkegaard, Wittgenstein and the Point of View for Their Work as Authors', in *The Grammar of Religious Belief*, edited by D.Z. Phillips (New York: St Martin's Press, 1996), pp. 248–331; and my 'Kierkegaard, Wittgenstein and Nonsense', in *Pursuits of Reason*, edited by Ted Cohen, Paul Guyer and Hilary Putnam (Lubbock: Texas Tech University Press, 1992), pp. 195–224. For a critique of my way of aligning Kierkegaard and Wittgenstein, see Phillips's *Philosophy's Cool Place*, pp. 13–64.

43 *Zettel*; eds. G.H. von Wright and G.E.M. Anscombe, tr. G.E.M. Anscombe (Oxford: Basil Blackwell, 1967), §712.

44 *Culture and Value*, p. 78.

45 G.E.M. Anscombe, *An Introduction to Wittgenstein's Tractatus* (Philadelphia: University of Pennsylvania Press, 1971), p. 12.

46 Anscombe's point might also be put as follows: we are not able to appreciate what Wittgenstein means (when he writes in the preface of the *Tractatus*) about the 'greatness' of Frege's work or (when he writes Frege himself) about how the *Tractatus* owes 'a great debt' [*eine grosse Dankesschuld*] to Frege's work. ('Gottlob Frege: Briefe an Ludwig Wittgenstein aus den Jahren 1914–1920', in *Wittgenstein im Brennpunkt*, ed. Brian McGuinness and Rudolf Haller (Amsterdam: Rodopi, 1989), p. 16.)

47 '*So wird schliesslich Alles in das Bereich der Psychologie einbezogen. . . . So mündet denn Alles in den Idealismus und bei grösster Folgerichtigkeit in den Solipsismus ein*' (*Grundgesetze der Arithmetik* (Hildesheim: Georg Olms, 1962), p. xix). Montgomery Furth translates the passage as follows: 'In the end everything is drawn [by the

psychologistic theorist of logic] into the sphere of psychology. . . . Thus everything drifts into idealism and from that point with perfect consistency into
solipsism' (*The Basic Laws of Arithmetic*, tr. M. Furth (Berkeley: University of
California Press, 1967), p. 17). What this translation slightly obscures is that
thinking the matter through *bei grösster Folgerichtigkeit* and seeing what it flows
into [*einmündet in*] requires that *we* think it through – i.e., that we follow through
and draw the *richtige Folgen* ourselves.

48   For further elaboration and defence of this claim, see my 'The Search for Logically
Alien Thought: Descartes, Kant, Frege and the *Tractatus*', in *Philosophical Topics*,
Vol. 20, No. 1, 115–80.

49   *Notebooks: 1914–1916*, eds. G.H. von Wright and G.E.M. Anscombe, tr. G.E.M.
Anscombe (Chicago: University of Chicago Press, 1979), p. 85. I have emended
the translation.

50   *Tractatus Logico-Philosophicus*; trs. David Pears and Brian McGuinness (London:
Routledge & Kegan Paul, 1963), §5.64. I have emended the translation.

51   Wittgenstein's sense of the urgency of achieving honesty in one's thinking may
well have been sharpened or otherwise refined by his reading of Tolstoy, Schopenhauer and/or Kierkegaard. I have no wish to deny that by studying these three
authors, and seeking to understand what Wittgenstein admired in their works, we
can deepen our understanding of wherein Wittgenstein took such honesty to
consist. But to attain such understanding requires not merely canvassing what it
is that these authors have to say about ethical and religious matters, but rather
being struck by the character of the attention they give to any matter to which
they give thought (regardless of whether the matter be of an overtly 'ethical'
nature or not).

52   *Tractatus Logico-Philosophicus*, p. 29.

53   Anscombe, *op. cit.*, p. 12.

54   Before turning to Russell and Frege, a cautionary note should be sounded: what
follows will be an unabashedly partial and unbalanced selection of moments
from Russell's and Frege's philosophies respectively. The only justification for
the cursory and partisan character of the selection lies in its capacity to shed
light on the respects in which Wittgenstein was able to view Frege as an example
of a philosopher who went the bloody hard way and Russell as an example of one
who tended to shrink from doing so. Thus the exercise will, by design, leave out
of account numerous estimable things about Russell and some inestimable things
about Frege. The aim is not to deny either the former or the latter, but simply to
try to illuminate the grounds for the relative estimate of Frege and Russell implicit
in Wittgenstein's prefatory acknowledgement in the *Tractatus* and in many of his
other remarks about each of them.

55   Letter to Ottoline Morrell, 13 December 1911; in *The Selected Letters of Bertrand
Russell, Vol. I*, ed. N. Griffin (Boston: Houghton Mifflin, 1992), p. 403.

56   Letter to Lucy Donnelly, 21 January 1912; quoted by Ray Monk in *Bertrand Russell:
The Spirit of Solitude* (London: Jonathan Cape, 1996), p. 296.

57   Wittgenstein, *Notebooks: 1914–1916*, eds. G.H. von Wright and G.E.M.
Anscombe, tr. G.E.M. Anscombe (Chicago: University of Chicago Press, 1979),
p. 5.

58   Bertrand Russell, *The Principles of Mathematics* (New York: Norton, 1903), §52.

59   *Ibid.*

60   *Ibid.*, §54.

61   In his appendix on Frege; *ibid.*, §481.

62   Russell, *The Collected Paper of Bertrand Russell, Vol. 6*, ed. by John G. Slater (London: Routledge, 1983), pp. 55–56.
63   *Ibid.*, p. 56.
64   Indeed, the author of the *Tractatus* would reject 'Logic is the study of something' as an equally flawed characterization.
65   Letter to Ottoline Morrell, 27 September 1912; quoted by John G. Slater in a prefatory note in *The Collected Paper of Bertrand Russell, Vol. 6*, p. 54.
66   Russell, *Theory of Knowledge: The 1913 Manuscript* (London: Routledge, 1992), p. 98.
67   *Theory of Knowledge*, p. 99.
68   *Ibid.*, p. 46.
69   *Tractatus Logico-Philosophicus*, §5.422. The point is formulated in *Notebooks: 1914–1916* as follows: 'Every right theory of judgement must make it impossible for me to judge that this table penholders the book. Russell's theory does not satisfy this requirement' (p. 103).
70   Letter to Ottoline Morrell, 27 May 1913; *The Selected Letters of Bertrand Russell, Vol. I*, p. 459.
71   Letter to Ottoline Morrell, 9 October 1913; *The Selected Letters of Bertrand Russell, Vol. I*, p. 479.
72   Ray Monk, *Bertrand Russell: The Spirit of Solitude*, p. 296.
73   Letter to Ottoline Morrell, 19 June 1913; *The Selected Letters of Bertrand Russell, Vol. I*, ed. N. Griffin, p. 462.
74   Letter to Ottoline Morrell, 1916 (exact date unknown), quoted in *The Autobiography of Bertrand Russell, Vol. II* (London: George Allen & Unwin), p. 57.
75   The letter to Bradley continues: 'Chiefly through the work of an Austrian pupil of mine, I seem now to see answers about unities; but the subject is so difficult and fundamental that I still hesitate' (Letter to Bradley, 30 January 1914; *The Selected Letters of Bertrand Russell, Vol. I, op. cit.*).
76   The discomfort is perhaps connected with the fact that, throughout his life, Russell takes the very idea that there are inexpressible yet significant truths – i.e., that there are 'entities' that are (1) incapable of becoming the logical subjects of propositions, and none the less (2) possible and important objects of contemplation – to be constitutive of *mysticism*. Moreover, he identifies logic as a branch of 'scientific philosophy', and he insists that mysticism and scientific philosophy are 'fundamentally irreconcilable tendencies of the human spirit'. As Ray Monk's *Bertrand Russell: The Spirit of Solitude* vividly depicts, Russell was, throughout this same period, alternately attracted to and repelled by (what he regarded as) the mystical mode of thought – the one constant in his attitude during this period being that, whatever the merits of mysticism might be, it was necessarily fundamentally opposed to the scientific mode of thought. That early Wittgenstein 'detested' what Russell himself wrote about mysticism is well known; and that Russell viewed the *Tractatus* as evidence that Wittgenstein had capitulated to mystical modes of thought (of a sort putatively to be found in authors Wittgenstein happily admitted to admiring such as Kierkegaard, Tolstoy and William James) is equally well known. What is less well known is that the *Tractatus* aims to turn the tables on Russell by showing that Russell's own conception of logic entails a doctrine which is (by Russell's own lights) a species of mysticism: for Russell's logical theory presupposes a conception of logical form which requires both that (1) logical forms are the proper objects of contemplation for logical theory and that (2) they are not possible subjects of discourse!
77   *Ludwig Wittgenstein: The Duty of Genius*, p. 271.

78   Phillips might wish to protest at this point: 'But Wittgenstein's confidence here
would rest on his assessment of (the limitations of) Russell's *philosophical* sensibility.' Yes, of course. But this returns us to the topic of the first section of this
paper. Wittgenstein's estimate of Russell's philosophical sensibility cannot be
divorced from his estimate of Russell as a person – of his estimate of Russell's
capacities for imagination, reflection, and response generally. One's philosophical sensibility is not independent of one's sensibility *tout court*.

79   Letter to Russell, 6 May 1920 and the previous undated letter; both in *Ludwig
Wittgenstein: Cambridge Letters*, eds. B. McGuinness and G.H. von Wright (Oxford:
Basil Blackwell, 1995), pp. 152, 154. It should be an urgent question for contemporary commentary on the *Tractatus* why Wittgenstein thought that even Russell's
attempts merely to expound the teaching of the book were full of 'superficiality
and misunderstanding', since – at least in broad outline – Russell's exposition does
not differ substantially from that offered by most contemporary commentators.

80   Letter to Ottoline Morrell, 20 December 1919; quoted by G.H. von Wright in an
editor's note in *Ludwig Wittgenstein: Letters to Russell, Keynes and Moore* (Oxford:
Basil Blackwell, 1974), p. 82.

81   Wittgenstein would have found a similar irony in the parallel sorts of remark
about his later philosophy that Russell, in his later years, was equally fond of
making – such as the following:

> The earlier Wittgenstein was a man addicted to passionately intense thinking,
> profoundly aware of difficult problems of which I, like him, felt the importance,
> and possessed (or at least so I thought) of true philosophical genius . . . . The later
> Wittgenstein, on the contrary, seems to have grown tired of serious thinking and
> to have invented a doctrine which would make such an activity unnecessary.
> (*My Philosophical Development* (London: Unwin, 1959), p. 161)

82   *Culture and Value*, pp. 35, 38.

83   The sentence in Diamond's essay which immediately precedes the one quoted
here is equally pertinent: 'Frege's writings shaped, to a great extent, the problems
Wittgenstein confronted in his own thought – and not just the problems, but also
methods of approach, and ideas about what could count as a satisfactory solution.' (Cora Diamond, 'Inheriting from Frege', in *The Cambridge Companion to
Frege*, ed. Thomas Ricketts (Cambridge: Cambridge University Press, 2002).)

84   *Collected Papers on Mathematics, Logic, and Philosophy*, ed. Brian McGuinness (London: Blackwell, 1984) [henceforth referred to as *CP*], p. 182.

85   This charge is expressed more emphatically in the unpublished version of 'On
Concept and Object':

> In my view the reason for the sorry state of affairs we find in Kerry, where the
> distinctions between concept and object, characteristic mark and property, are
> effaced is that logical and psychological questions and viewpoints are
> scrambled together. . . . He will speak now of a concept, then of the idea of a
> concept, now of an object, then of the idea of it, without its even being wholly
> clear whether it is one or the other that is in question, whether we are engaged
> in a logical or psychological inquiry. . . . [H]ere Kerry has simply succumbed to a
> widespread sickness. (*Posthumous Writings*, ed. H. Hermes, F. Kambartel, and F.
> Kaulbach (Chicago, IL: University of Chicago Press, 1979) [henceforth *PW*],
> pp. 104–5)

86   *The Foundations of Arithmetic*, trans. J.L. Austin (Evanston, IL: Northwestern University Press, 1980) [henceforth FA], p. x.
87   *FA*, p. x.
88   *PW*, p. 253.
89   In conformity with this doctrine of the primacy of judgement, Frege's concept-script forbids the isolated occurrence of designations for the various possible components of a judgement:

> [I]nstead of putting a judgement together out of an individual as subject and an already previously formed concept as predicate, we do the opposite and arrive at a concept by splitting up the content of possible judgement. . . . But it doesn't follow from this that the ideas of these properties and relations are formed apart from their objects: on the contrary they arise simultaneously with the first judgement in which they are ascribed to things. Hence in the concept-script their designations never occur on their own, but always in combinations which express contents of possible judgement. . . . A sign for a property never appears without a thing to which it might belong being at least indicated, a designation of a relation never without indication of the things which might stand in it. (*PW*, pp. 15–17)

90   Frege does sometimes speak of a thought's having 'parts' out of which it is 'built up' (see, e.g., *PW*, p. 225), and of how we can 'distinguish parts in the thought corresponding to parts of a sentence, so that the structure of the sentence can serve as a picture of the structure of the thought' (*CP*, p. 390). But Frege immediately follows this latter remark with the observation:

> To be sure, we really talk figuratively when we transfer the relation of whole and part to thoughts; yet the analogy is so ready to hand and so generally appropriate that we are hardly bothered by the hitches that occur from time to time. (*CP*, p. 390)

What kind of hitches? Hitches, for example, of the sort Kerry fails to notice when he imagines that he can get hold of a concept merely by employing an expression which elsewhere, in its usual employment, is able to symbolize a concept. Frege thus worries that the all but unavoidable (and in itself potentially innocent) locution of a thought's having 'parts' or 'components' will mislead one into attributing a false independence to the parts of a thought – so that we imagine that the parts could retain their identity apart from their participation in a whole of the appropriate structure:

> But the words 'made up of', 'consist of', 'component', 'part' may lead to our looking at it the wrong way. If we choose to speak of parts in this connection, all the same these parts are not mutually independent in the way that we are elsewhere used to find when we have parts of a whole. (*CP*, p. 386)

Frege's context principle – and the correlative doctrine of the primacy of judgement (which refuses to allow that the parts of the whole are 'mutually independent in the way that we are elsewhere used to find when we have parts of a whole') – in thus insisting upon the *unity* of a thought or a proposition, in no way denies the compositionality of either thought or language. It insists only upon the mutual interdependence of compositionality and contextuality.

91   Gilbert Ryle attempted to summarize this 'difficult but crucial point' of Frege's by saying that the meanings of words 'are not proposition components but propositional differences':

> Frege's difficult but crucial point . . . [is] that the unitary something that is *said* in a sentence or the unitary sense that it expresses is not an assemblage of detachable sense atoms, of, that is, parts enjoying separate existence and separate thinkability, and yet that one truth or falsehood may have discernible, countable, and classifiable similarities to and dissimilarities from other truths and falsehoods. Word meanings or concepts are not proposition components but propositional differences. They are distinguishables, not detachables; abstractables, not extractables. (Gilbert Ryle, *Collected Papers, Volume 1* (London: Hutchinson, 1971), p. 58)

92   The ensuing discussion is indebted to Joan Weiner's *Frege in Perspective* (Ithaca: Cornell University Press, 1990), chapter 6 and to her 'Theory and Elucidation: The End of the Age of Innocence' (in *Future Pasts: Reflections on the History of Analytic Philosophy*, eds. J. Floyd and S. Shieh (Oxford: Oxford University Press, 2001)).

93   The sign that such a Fregean elucidation has been successful – that the desired 'meeting of minds' between the elucidator and his audience has been achieved – is that the other person is able to go on as a user of *Begriffsschrift* on his or her own in the right way. Frege therefore has an answer to an obvious objection (voiced by some commentators on the *Tractatus*) with regard to the doctrine that there are fundamental logical distinctions which underlie but cannot be expressed in language. The objection goes as follows: there is no way to adjudicate the success of an attempt to communicate such distinctions – for there is no way for someone who has grasped such a distinction to exhibit his mastery of the distinction. But Frege furnishes a touchstone of success: the sign that we have grasped his elucidations is that we emerge masters of his symbolism. A reader can be said to have grasped one of Frege's elucidations (for example, his elucidation of the distinction between concept and object) if he is able to employ the appropriate elements of the symbolism (the symbol for an object only if an object is denoted, etc.) when segmenting judgements and translating them from ordinary language into *Begriffsschrift*. His segmentation of the judgement can, in turn, be checked by making sure that the translation of the judgement into *Begriffsschrift* preserves the appropriate inference and substitution licences between the judgement in question and other judgements.

94   This and related aspects of Frege's conception of elucidation are discussed in illuminating detail in the final chapter of Joan Weiner's book *Frege in Perspective* (Ithaca: Cornell University Press, 1990).

95   Peter Geach is one of the few commentators who sees a connection between this moment in Frege's work and the concerns of both the *Tractatus* and Wittgenstein's later work:

> One thing I learned from Wittgenstein, in part from the *Tractatus* but still more from personal contact, is that philosophical mistakes are often not refutable falsehoods but confusions; similarly the contrary insights cannot be conveyed in proper propositions with a truth-value. I offer as [an] instance . . . of such [an] insight . . . Frege's distinction between concept and object ('No concept is an

object' has no translation into a well-constructed symbolism)...Such insights cannot be demonstrated as theses, but only conveyed dialectically; the dialectic process largely consists in the art, whose practice I have perhaps learned in some measure from Wittgenstein, of reducing to patent nonsense the buried nonsense that is found in attempts to reject these insights. We cannot refute nonsense by a straightforward process; as Frege said, logic cannot deal with nonsense, but only characterise it as being nonsense.

Having come to Frege by way of the *Tractatus*, I could see that his difficulties in expressing himself about function, concept, and object were not from a muddled self-bemusement but from the nature of the case. (Peter Geach, 'Philosophical Autobiography', in *Peter Geach: Philosophical Encounters*, ed. Harry A. Lewis (Dordrecht: Kluwer, 1991), pp. 13–14, 16)

It is remarkable how little of the secondary literature on the *Tractatus* has interested itself in this moment in Frege's thought. The contrast Max Black draws in the following passage between Frege (who has no use for the idea that nonsense can be illuminating) and Wittgenstein (who does have a use for the idea) is typical of the sort of contrast between Frege and Wittgenstein one finds throughout the secondary literature on the *Tractatus*:

> Is the *Tractatus* self-defeating? Nothing in the book has aroused more interest or provoked more scandal than its concluding remarks....[T]he very words in which our predecessors' errors were castigated have to be acknowledged as nonsensical....With what relish Frege would have assaulted this position. One can imagine him smacking his lips over the deliciously absurd notion that 'nonsense' can be understood. 'If we understand the conclusion', he might well have said, 'then it *cannot* be nonsensical. Since it implies its own lack of sense it must at best be false. For, if it were true, it would have to be nonsensical, and hence without truth-value, which is a contradiction. So, the supposed conclusion is at best *necessarily* false. But all this is unnecessary – we can't begin to take seriously a statement that claims to imply its own absurdity.' (Max Black, *A Companion to Wittgenstein's* Tractatus (Ithaca: Cornell University Press, 1982), pp. 378–9)

This stock contrast of Frege and Wittgenstein renders invisible how Wittgenstein's notion of elucidation (in, e.g., *Ttractatus Logico-Philosophicus*, §§4.112, 6.53) inherits and reshapes Frege's notion of elucidation.

96   The word 'categories' won't really do here. Russell happily speaks of 'entities', whenever he runs up against this problem, emphasizing how extraordinarily inclusive this 'category' is. (Russell's willingness to lapse into such an idiom is itself a symptom of his having failed, by Wittgenstein's lights, to have faced up to the difficulty here.) There is, according to Frege, no word that will do. I finesse this problem here by pretending that talk of 'logical categories' is able to possess greater referential powers than Frege thinks it can. For both Frege and early Wittgenstein such talk is permissible only if it is self-consciously employed as a ladder which the listener/reader is to climb up and then throw away.

97   Here are some representative passages:

> [T]he question arises what it is that we are here calling an object....It is only possible to gesture towards [*hinzudeuten*] what is meant. (*CP*, p. 147)

> If ... the meaning to be assigned is logically simple, then one ... must confine oneself to warding off the unwanted meanings among those that occur in linguistic usage and to pointing to the wanted one, and here one must always rely on being met half-way by an intelligent guess. (*Philosophical and Mathematical Correspondence*, ed. B. McGuinness, tr. H. Kaal, Oxford: Basil Blackwell [henceforth *Corr*], p. 37)

> *It is not possible to give a definition of what a function is.* ... It is only possible to hint at what is meant and to make it clearer by relating it to what is known. Instead of a definition we must provide elucidations [*Erläuterungen*]; here of course we must count on a meeting of minds. [Frege's emphasis] (*PW*, p. 235)

> I must confine myself [in attempting to explain the 'unsaturatedness' of functional signs] to hinting at what I have in mind by means of a metaphorical expression, and here I must rely on my reader's meeting me half-way. (*CP*, p. 292)

98   *CP*, pp. 182–3.
99   *PW*, p. 207 [I have emended the translation].
100   Here are two representative passages:

> We must admit logically primitive elements that are indefinable. Even here there seems to be a need to make sure that we designate the same thing by the same sign (word). ... Since definitions are not possible for primitive elements, something else must enter in. I call it elucidation [*Erläuterung*]. It is this, therefore, that serves the purpose of mutual understanding among investigators. ... We may relegate it to a propaedeutic. It has no place in the system of a science; in the latter, no conclusions are based on it. [I have emended the translation] (*CP*, pp. 300–1)

> I should like to divide up the totality of mathematical propositions into definitions and all the remaining propositions (axioms, fundamental laws, theorems). ... One can also recognize a third kind of proposition, elucidatory propositions, but I would not want to count them as part of mathematics itself but refer them to the antechamber, the propaedeutics. (*Corr*, p. 37)

101   My emphasis; *Corr*, p. 136. The conclusion of this passage – the idea that what matters in such cases (where we are forced to make use of such inappropriate forms of expression) is that 'we know we are doing it and how it happens' – parallels the conclusion of 'On Concept and Object':

> [O]ver the question of what it is that is called a function in Analysis, we come up against the same obstacle; and on thorough investigation it will be found that the obstacle is essential, and founded on the nature of language; that we cannot avoid a certain inappropriateness of linguistic expression; and that there is nothing for it but to realise this and always take it into account. (*CP*, p. 194)

102   *CP*, p. 193.
103   Why the author of the *Tractatus* did not think that Frege had come to the end of the philosophical task of seeing where this difficulty leads (and where this

difficulty does lead, once 'strictly thought through' by the author of the *Tractatus*) is a tale I try to tell in my 'The Method of the *Tractatus*', in *From Frege to Wittgenstein: Perspectives on Early Analytic Philosophy*, edited by Erich H. Reck (Oxford: Oxford University Press, 2001).

104 *Wittgenstein's Lectures on Foundations of Mathematics, Cambridge, 1939*, ed. Cora Diamond (Ithaca: Cornell University Press, 1976), p. 103.

105 *Tractatus Logico-Philosophicus*, §6.54 [my translation].

106 'I've written a book called *Logisch-Philosophische Abhandlung*....Nobody will understand it'; Letter to Russell, 13 March 1919; in *Ludwig Wittgenstein: Cambridge Letters*.

107 *Ludwig Wittgenstein: Philosophical Occasions, 1912–1951*, p. 183.

108 *Ibid*., p. 183.

109 *Ibid*., p. 161.

110 Quoted by Rush Rhees in *Discussions of Wittgenstein* (London: Routledge and Kegan Paul, 1970), p. 43.

111 *Tractatus Logico-Philosophicus*, §§6.52–6.521.

112 This paper is indebted to conversations with Stanley Cavell, Cora Diamond, Michael Kremer, Ray Monk and Joan Weiner, and to comments on a previous draft by Arnold Davidson and Lisa Van Alstyne.

Part II
Philosophy of Religion

6
'At the End of Reason Comes Persuasion'[1]

John H. Whittaker

One of the more remarkable things about D.Z. Phillips's treatment of the philosophy of religion, particularly from the standpoint of traditional philosophy, is that he regards the search for religion's rational grounds as hopeless – and yet, he doesn't reject religious belief on that account. What he sees more clearly than most is that religious claims have a peculiar logic, and that we, in trying to assess them, lose sight of what good judgement in religion involves. Typically, we extend to them overly generalized and presumptuous standards of what being reasonable means, only to become confused when we cannot find the sorts of reasons our model leads us to expect.

A favourite example that Phillips uses to illustrate this confusion comes from Wittgenstein, who asks us to imagine the difference between believing that a certain aeroplane overhead is German and believing that there will be a Last Judgement.[2] If people had doubts about the identity of the plane, we would still say that they are very near in their judgements because they share the understanding of what it would take to pursue the matter. They know what would count as evidence, what would improve the case for saying the plane is or is not German, and so on. But we don't find this kind of closeness between the religious sceptic and the religious believer. Non-believers generally do not know what sort of evidence the belief in a Last Judgement could be based on, or indeed, whether it is based on any evidence at all. They often do not understand the point of the doctrine, as I would say, and thus they do not know how to frame the issue in their reflection. It comes as no surprise, therefore, that they have trouble finding its basis in what they call 'reason'. The difficulty here, as Wittgenstein suggests, is that the belief in a Last Judgement is not a hypothesis whose truth can be represented as a function of evidence, but is an expression that 'regulates for all in [the believer's] life'.[3]

Unfortunately, many philosophers fail to appreciate this last point. The way they see it, religious claims have a cognitive content, and whatever role these claims might or might not play in the life of believers is secondary to this. Their content is what counts because that is what stands to be judged as a truth claim, and therefore it is the content of religious claims that calls for the application of universal standards of reason, evidence, rational grounds, etc. Yet by setting aside the regulative role of a belief in order to concentrate on the belief's content, we abstract our attention from everything that makes the belief a *religious* belief. We fail to see that a belief's religious distinctiveness affects the logic of its judgement – that it is in fact a different kind of belief. Believing in something like a Last Judgement arises out of a different species of reflection; and the evidence that the sceptic demands, and generally does not receive, fails to convince because it is entered in the wrong arena. What is needed is not evidence that would support an opinion – something that would leave the basic framework of one's judgements unchanged – but something that would persuade the non-believer to embrace an altered *perspective* in the way in which issues of religious truth are considered. This kind of change takes more than evidence to supply.

Phillips elaborates on this point in one of his essays ('On Really Believing') by showing that the meaning of a belief cannot be divorced from the role that it plays in people's thoughts and lives.[4] This role both gives a belief its point and governs how the belief is to be understood and handled in judgement. Without attending to this role, one presumes to know, as if by some previous intuition, how to think critically about the belief in question. One tends to think, for example, that anyone who understands the words of a belief is thereby qualified to consider it critically. Yet without having a life that *affords* religious ideas their characteristic roles, one never catches sight of their *real* meaning, and therefore never fits them into the *kind* of reflection that suits them. Then everything that highlights the appeal of religious ideas is simply lost from view.

The needful thing is to stop looking for rational grounds (scientific or historical evidence, the application of abstract criteria such as comprehensiveness, etc.), as if this were the key to critical religious judgement. Not every issue is fully *intelligible* from this rationalistic perspective, let alone *resolvable*, and the typical disagreements between believers and non-believers are prime examples. Still, it is hard to give up the expectation that the truth or falsity of every meaningful assertion must be objectively determinable, and that 'logic' or 'reason' must provide us (in principle) with the means of making these determinations. That is the very thing that leads us to separate out the cognitive content of religious teachings in the first place. We want something to judge *with the methods that we use for other objective claims*, and so we ignore the distinctive features of religious belief, such as the necessity that one cannot affirm religious teachings without abiding in them, as if this were something inessential and unrelated to the essence of what is at stake in believing. Phillips, on the other hand, tries to show us that the differences that show up in such practical surroundings of belief reflect differences in the way the issues themselves are understood, so that the effort to separate the cognitive content of religious claims from the roles that these beliefs play in the thinking and living of believers might be recognized as the philosophical crudity that it is. That is why his work consists in large part of contrasts drawn between *examples* of religious believing and other kinds of believing; he wants us to accept religious belief for what it is, without trying to pass judgement on it by forcing it into the procrustean bed of rationalistic ideals.

Unfortunately, the more examples Phillips cites in making this point the more he seems to be misunderstood. In what follows, I want to take one of these misunderstandings and trace its development. The misunderstanding that I have in mind is the view that religious beliefs, being rationally ungrounded, are *logically arbitrary judgements*, formed to satisfy the needs of believers rather than the demands of truth. Phillips leaves himself open to being read in this way (as a relativist, as I will call it) because of what seems like a negative approach to religious belief. Religious beliefs, he says, do not have the logic of hypotheses, their meaning cannot be read off the face of the words used to formulate them, they are not descriptive judgements of fact, their credibility is not to be found in the objective support offered by evidence, they are not to be treated as if their truth were a function of their grounds, etc. Such remarks tell us more about what religious belief is not than about what it is, though in fairness to him, Phillips does sometimes accompany these efforts with positive characterizations of belief. He says repeatedly, for example, that religious beliefs *are* truth claims and that they *do* refer to reality; it is just that the truths that they represent and the realities that they depict are *different* from those assumed in the usual models of what a true belief is.

Nevertheless, given the hold that these rationalistic models have had on us, it is understandable that we should want to know what these realities are, and about how the existence of such things is responsibly to be determined. For how can theistic belief depend on the reality of God if this is not what the belief in God advances as its 'cognitive content'? Here it will not do simply to say, 'yes, if such a belief has cognitive content, it must refer to the reality of God', since the crucial point at issue depends on what one means by 'the reality of God'. That is what Phillips tries to explain in showing what it means for believers *in practice* to speak of God's reality.[5] In other words, the *kind* of reality at issue only comes out in seeing how believers react to the impenetrable facts of human life, such as the arbitrariness of fate or the inexplicability of suffering. Believers might speak as if they were cognitively aware of a force that stands invisibly behind life's events and causes them to occur, and the language that they use might even suggest that they have evidence for such a claim. 'God wills that our nation prosper, that some shall live and some shall die, etc. etc.' And yet in the actual use of this language we might find none of the surrounding concerns that usually accompany causal explanations. Thus, believers may say 'God exists as the cause of our lives'; but in conforming themselves to this belief they show no interest in testing it, no interest in tracking various cases, no openness to the possibility of there being other causes – in short, no interest whatsoever in *any* of the things that *would* be appropriate if it were a causal claim. By looking at this belief closely, one can see that it has nothing to do with drawing inferences from the visible to the invisible, or with the rationalistic attitude that wants to refine theories under the pressure of critical scrutiny. Instead, believers who express such judgements use them to deal with the weight of events that they *cannot explain*, naturalistically or in any other way. They conform themselves *to* the belief by *bearing up* under the weight of the inexplicable, refusing to be dispirited; and this bearing up belongs to the grammar of god-talk, as it reveals the wider roles that are responsible for the meaningfulness of religious language – in this case, the language of God as the source or 'cause' of all that is.

Here the sense of believing in God depends on the sense that there is *reality* in this altered *mode* of thinking. One believes by affirming the *verdict* that life in general, and one's own life in particular, is acceptable *apart from any of the means we use to establish its worth.* And the reality of God is the reality of *this mode of thinking.* Thus, just as one might say that the 'world' of the religious believer is different from the world of the secular person, one might also say that the reality that the believer inhabits is different from that of the non-believer. Or just as one might say that an ethical person lives in a world of moral realities, one might as easily say that the believer inhabits a world of divine realities. The way to understand the meaning of the word 'reality' in these senses is not by measuring it against what we mean by empirical or physical realities. The reality of God is obviously *not* the reality of the physical world, but the concept of divine reality does have a meaning. It is just that this meaning can be appreciated only by exploring the fundamentally transformative perspectives which believing brings into view.

I want to come back to this point later, but for now it is enough to note that Phillips tries to explain the grammar of religious ideas, not by grounding them in a metaphysical sense of 'reality', given prior to all forms of discourse (science, religion, ethics, etc.), but by relocating these concepts in the manner of thinking and living in which they have their sense.

Meanwhile we need to ask why so many philosophers insist on the possibility of giving grounds for religious belief – especially the sort of grounds that might show God, for example, to be the sort of reality presumed by purely descriptive or naturalistic claims. I have already suggested that the reason why they see religious belief as standing in need of objective justification is that they see it from an *untransformed* perspective, a perspective in which religious claims remain comparable to other descriptive (scientific or metaphysical) assertions. From this viewpoint, if there are no independent rational grounds for belief (that is, grounds that can be understood without presuming the truth of the belief in question), then there can be no epistemological warrant for believing in religious realities. Nor can there be any means of rescuing religious belief from the charge of being subjective, logically arbitrary or irrational in the pejorative sense.

I would like to offer another approach. We can reframe these issues from an appropriately transformed perspective if we begin with Wittgenstein's suggestion that we consider 'what happens when missionaries convert natives'. That should help us to understand the possibility of commending one's beliefs in a way that does not depend on the accumulation of evidence or on the application of clear criteria of judgement. It should help us not merely to recognize the existence of alternative means of commending beliefs and the realities that go with them, but to acknowledge a certain form of persuasion as a logically appropriate substitute for justifying beliefs on rational grounds. And if the logical relevance of such an alternative can be brought to light, it should quieten the fears that religious belief, in being divorced from the usual means of rational justification, must be surrendered to subjective relativism. It need not be.

1

All this, of course, needs an explanation, so let us start with some of the things that Phillips says on the subject. In Part II of *Faith after Foundationalism* he criticizes several writers for depicting our situation as one in which we are faced with options about fundamental matters (epistemologically 'basic beliefs') but given no grounds for choosing among them. All that we can do, suggests Richard Rorty, is to keep the search going for common grounds of judgement, since the hope of finding such grounds is all that unites us as rational believers. Sadly, we know of no grounds *now* on which one moral or religious position might be justified over and against all others; so we must acknowledge the unconvincing nature of our own commitments while seeking a better understanding of other options. Yet a greater sense of common judgement might emerge if we only keep conversation going.[6]

Peter Berger comes to a similar point of view as a sociologist of knowledge.[7] Having realized the groundlessness of what he calls our 'nomological orderings' – i.e., the systems by which we interpret life's meaning – Berger describes them as 'human inventions'. His point is that we invent these systems and then impose them on the blank and insignificant world that is objectively given to us. To realize the groundlessness of our nomological systems is to realize that we have imposed a 'fictitious inexorability upon the humanly constructed world'.[8] Simple honesty requires us to admit the audacity of portraying the world according to these systems, and so we need to draw back from the illusion of trying to show that meaning is objectively real. Still, Berger thinks that human beings might recover some dignity in daring to choose none the less, knowing the illusory character of the constructions that they impose on the world.[9]

These are just two of the many writers who tell us that we are adrift in subjectivity, abandoned by the illusory ideal of objective assurances and facing forlornly the prospect of criterionless choices. Phillips will have none of this – and *this despite the fact that he too acknowledges the groundlessness of rudimentary convictions*. The problem with Berger and Rorty's view is that it gives priority to what is objectively or empirically given. Only the observable and testable is said to be objectively real. Indeed, that is the problem with foundationalism in general: it sets up scientific or naturalistic conceptions of reality as the paradigmatically real, and forces all other truth claims to justify themselves according to the logical methods that are appropriate to this model. How many thinkers, for example, suppose that *all* claims are or ought to be objectively resolvable on evidentiary grounds? And how many of these forget the innumerable other seriously held beliefs that are not hypotheses at all, and cannot be judged as if they were. Some of these beliefs – e.g., that the future will be like the past, or that the laboratory I locked up today existed the day before – are (in normal circumstances) as certain as anything on which they might be based. Yet beliefs like this, even though they belong to the range of thought in which we considered hypothetical claims, are not the logical products of evidence. Rather, their truth is written into the very *way* that we think. Instead of being ventured as possibilities that we might think about *within* our customary means of adjudicating hypotheses, their truth seems somehow *prior* to all that. We do not say, 'physical objects might or might not exist; let us run some tests and let the facts decide'. Rather, as we go about the testing of other claims, we simply show no doubt at all about the fact that physical objects exist. That is somehow too obvious to doubt; it lies too deep to be framed as an issue.

The truth of the matter is that the truth of every reasonable belief *does not* rest on factual evidence – that is, on information having the character of the given. There are many other beliefs, including not only commonsensical beliefs but scientific assumptions, whose truth is not determinable as a function of prior facts that can be unproblematically observed. This means that we cannot rest the truth or falsity of such certainties on what the world gives us in the way of evidence. For the evidence itself and the manner in which it is understood is, at bottom, either too basic to allow its *own* testing (in which case it does not rest on prior evidence), or it is impossibly ambiguous in its interpretation. All of this suggests that the contrast that Berger draws between what is objectively given and what is subjectively determined is crudely presented. We cannot justify every scientific belief as an objectively adjudicable hypothesis, nor can we justify all those beliefs that involve other conceptions of the real. This does not mean that all such beliefs are subjective in the sense of being arbitrary or unreasonable; it simply means that their credibility depends on other factors.

Thus, we need to be reminded that the lack of objective grounds does not make every belief logically suspect. To see this in the case of beliefs other than the working assumptions of science, consider moral claims. When we see someone resisting the temptations of professional advancement in order to spend time taking care of her handicapped child, we might say that she realizes the reality of her moral obligation to her child. We might not say this with utter confidence, especially if we do not know the details of her situation. But we do not doubt that her behaviour is circumscribed by moral considerations. That we do not doubt. She must choose her course amidst the temptations and the *moral realities* of life. That is something that we take for granted. It is true, of course, that we can doubt the moral character of a person's behaviour in a great many cases, but that does not mean that we must be doubtful about *morality itself*. Even when we realize that there are moral alternatives that are unthinkable for us, but which are fully embraced by others, this need not lead us to doubt that we live in a world where moral considerations *weigh on us*. Yet that, in effect, is what Berger suggests that we should do. We should choose even our most basic moral beliefs knowing full well that our choices are unconstrained by reality in any sense. There will always be alternatives to our choices, and they will always be as arbitrary as our own convictions, since neither can be established on objective grounds.

This mistake is pernicious. It suggests that there is a kind of nobility in choosing to follow one standard when one knows very well that one's choice is arbitrary. Far from being commendable, such behaviour is morally bankrupt. It implies that we live in a world which is without genuine moral constraints and that genuine moral obligation is a myth. Here we have to be honest with ourselves. We know that moral considerations are not to be taken this lightly. That is why we treat adults who show no moral sense as being somehow *arrested* in their development. Perhaps they have had no moral education at all, or perhaps their moral experience has been drastically distorted. Perhaps they are simply mentally ill. One way or the other we struggle to explain people who know nothing at all of the moral world. And yet we do not expect them to think morally *as the result of rationally coming to moral conclusions on objective grounds*.

Moral arguments obviously are possible, even unavoidable; but people must learn to make them, and they learn this by learning to think morally *by means other than inference from non-moral grounds*. Thus, they do not acquire their moral capacities by first establishing their intuitions and moral premises argumentatively – but they do acquire a moral framework of understanding. And it is important to give this fact its due. At the foundation of our moral judgements there are always rough notions of right and wrong, and if we are to move in the world of moral judgement at all, we cannot suspend this basic moral sense for the pluralism of the intellectual marketplace. We would simply not know what to make of a person who treated such fundamental intuitions as optional convictions, as if they were fictions forced over the blind facts of life. Rather than saying that the world was blind to him, we would say that he was blind to the world of moral reality.

And here we have every right to use the word 'reality'. The rudimentary conceptions through which we gain access to a moral life disclose the moral constraints in the midst of which our humanity unfolds. The fact that their existence cannot be demonstrated on non-moral, objective grounds doesn't change this. It simply shows us that we acquire our sense of moral realities in ways other than those in which we judge hypothetical matters of descriptive fact.

If I am right about this and objectively confirmable beliefs (descriptions) must be distinguished from unconfirmable and yet *sensible* beliefs, how does it happen that these sensible beliefs are acquired? What if someone knows nothing of the moral obligations that we take for granted, so that the differences between us cannot be submitted to common grounds and argument loses its purchase? Then what do we do? Do we give up the sense that moral realities are at stake? It was at a point like this that Wittgenstein asked us to think about what happens 'when missionaries convert natives'. I take this remark as suggesting that there is more to be said about the appeal of certain sensible but unprovable beliefs.

2

Having brought us to the brink of such thoughts, *however*, Wittgenstein does not offer us any help in pressing on. And neither does Phillips. Phillips occasionally comes close to recognizing the possibility of persuasive appeals, but he never explains the *sense* or the *logic* that might be involved in them. Indeed, as I eventually want to show, his grammatical studies *often make this kind of appeal*. He admits as much when he says, especially of his grammatical studies of religion, that his remarks can often be read by asking oneself if one can get along with the conceptual understanding that they elucidate. Often it is hard *not* to read his remarks in this way. But trying to convince readers that they should 'get along' with the understanding that he uncovers is not his intention. He wants only to sort out various religious and non-religious concepts so as to avoid their confusion, and this, as he never tires of saying, can be done without recommending or condemning any of the possible religious ways of thinking that are involved. Nevertheless, his philosophical interest in clarification need not be the only motivation *of his readers*, for they might also want to see what they can make of these ideas in their own judgement. Again, he writes in *Belief, Change, and Forms of Life*:

> The philosopher wants to be clear about character of [religious] language. He may not want to speak it ... [But] the philosopher's search for clarity is [also] to see what kind of language is involved here, whether or not he, personally, can get along with it or not.[10]

We are not told what is involved in seeing 'whether or not [one], personally, can get along with [religious ideas]'; but he clearly suggests that above and beyond the philosophical purpose of sorting out confusions a philosopher might want to examine religious concepts – and oneself – to see what force these concepts exert. Are they personally persuasive? Are they convincing, even though nothing but their clarification has been involved in the efforts to recover their sense? And what, after all, could it mean to be convinced by a concept?

In the last section of this essay, I shall come back to these questions. A number of points, however, need to be made first about the general subject of persuasion, to which these last questions belong. For one thing, the concept of persuasion conceals an important ambiguity. According to one sense, persuasion encompasses a variety of techniques, rhetorical and other-wise, that are designed to elicit belief as a form of behaviour. According to another sense, persuasion refers to a certain kind of non-evidential support that strengthens the credibility of the beliefs in question. This distinction is crucial. Persuasion of the first sort involves techniques that are used to secure a certain causal result; namely, that people who do not believe in certain teachings come to accept them. They change their minds. They *do* something. The event of their believing presumably is the result of certain causal events that occur prior to conversion, and it makes perfectly good sense to wonder what these events are. How is their mental behaviour changed? As a question about human behaviour, this query anticipates the search for those causal factors that have the greatest efficacy in producing the behaviours in question. But notice – and this is the important point – persuasive factors of this sort say nothing directly about the truth or falsity of the beliefs at issue; they only concern what *causes* people to adopt them, and people can be caused to hold beliefs irrespective of the truth of those beliefs. Reasons for believing of *this* sort (causes), in other words, are not reasons of the sort that logically support or sustain the judgement that a belief is true.

Normally, of course, we assume that people act in accepting a belief because they recognize *logical grounds* for accepting its truth. The fact remains, however, that beliefs can be viewed either as logical entities, like numbers or propositions, or they can be viewed as behaviour patterns; and there is a world of difference between the two. Rhetoric, so far as I understand it, usually takes the latter approach to beliefs by concentrating on the causal efficacy of those situations that are relevant to public speaking – the power of a speaker's delivery, the extent to which the speaker accentu-ates the interests of the audience, etc. From this perspective, then, the question is, 'are such factors causally effective in promoting the favourable reactions associated with belief?' I am not interested in this rhetorical con-cept of persuasion. I want to concentrate on the possibility of there being forms of persuasion that are *logically* relevant to the adoption of concepts, and not simply to the concepts alone, but to the associated forms of belief that go with the conceptual reordering of one's understanding.

How, though, can there be logical persuasive factors involved in believing that are not *grounds* for believing in the cognitive content of the relevant claim? Is there some kind of support for propositions that does not consist of evidence for their truth? Precisely because we think so readily of propositions as being dependent on grounds for their support – empirical evidence, abstract considerations of coherence, consistency, etc. – we think that any form of persuasion that is directly relevant to the truth of a proposition must involve similar kinds of propositional justification. 'There must be a means for determining truth,' we say. 'Somehow, we must be able to invoke criteria whose application will yield evidence.' In a word, we think that we must be able to *rest* the truth or falsity of propositions on something other than sheer intuition. That, after all, is what makes a proposition 'objective': its judgement does not depend on the indeterminate notion of personal intuition but on evidence or other justificatory grounds. This means that if persuasion is to have any role in supporting propositions in a logical sense, this support must come from standards of judgement that enable us to say, not on our own authority but on the objective matter of their assessment, that these propositions are true. Because we assimilate *rational* persuasion to this *ideal of objective justification*, we can hardly find room for it at all as a category of judgement. We think of it as if it were simply a weaker form of this same *pattern* of justification – i.e., as if it were a matter of making the most of weak evidence. Perhaps a persuasive speaker (in this sense of the word) exaggerates the power of the evidence by suppressing counter-evidence. Perhaps she hides the questionableness of the assumptions on which her conclusions rest. I have no reason to deny that such forms of persuasion exist; they obviously do. But they are not the *kind* of persuasion that I have in mind. The kind that I am after is neither a matter of using rhetorical or psychological techniques to sustain belief, nor is it a matter of making the most out of weak arguments. It is something altogether different.

The sort of persuasion that I am thinking of applies only to propositions whose truth or falsity cannot be treated objectively on the basis of rational criteria. It applies, in other words, only to *groundless* beliefs such as those that Phillips sees at the heart of morality and religion. These, in the language of Berger, are subjective beliefs that make up the 'nomological order' through which we construe the meaning of our lives in a variety of ways. They are not groundless simply because we *now* lack the evidence or the experience on which they might ideally be judged; their groundlessness belongs to their logical nature as fundamental beliefs that play a formative role in shaping our thought. They are similar to what other philosophers have called basic propositions or intuitive assumptions or first principles, but they have an indissoluble relation to our practical disposition because of their *regulative* role. They are essentially transformative beliefs, in other words, because their adoption entails a corresponding adjustment in one's mental life and its outward manifestations. For that reason, one can believe in them only by following them, by abiding in them, by converting to them, like one adheres to a set of principles that founds an entirely new way of looking at things. Since such ideas regulate a whole new framework of judgement, coming to believe in them is not an outgrowth of a way of thinking that one *already* understands, as would be the case if the beliefs at issue were hypotheses to be judged on familiar historical or scientific grounds. No; in this case believing requires reconfiguring one's thinking, as the regulative beliefs at issue represent the gateway to a whole new manner of seeing.

Such transformative beliefs have no independently assessable content as bare propositions, stripped of their regulative implications. What they say 'about the world' is inseparable from the form of thinking that they underwrite. Thus, one might say that believing in the good is believing that an evaluative life is called for, or that believing in the uniformity of nature is believing that knowledge is to be found in temporally and spatially unrestricted natural laws. One implication of this is that we cannot possibly justify such truly basic or regulative beliefs on independent argumentative grounds, as if they followed *by inference* from evidence of some kind. The 'evidence' that supports them is evidence that they themselves are used to define. And that means that if there is some form of persuasion that might enhance their credibility, this persuasion *cannot* be a function of evidence.

I think that there is such a form of persuasion. We have to remember, however, that this form of persuasion applies only to those convictions that lie too deep in our ways of thinking to be justified in any other way. For them the alternative of justifying them objectively, through the application of critical criteria, is not possible. Søren Kierkegaard made this point by saying, rather bluntly, 'There is only one relation to revealed truth – believing it.'[11] That is not a dogmatic remark but a logical observation. It means that revealed truths differ in their logic from ordinary truths; and the difference here can be seen in the fact that it makes no sense to wait on revealed truths to be established *for us*, by the evidence, whereas it does make sense to wait on the truth of most ordinary claims to be determined in this way. We cannot wait on revealed truths to be settled for us by the facts, not because it is impractical to accumulate the evidence that we need, but because judging them to be true demands another kind of reception entirely. As Kierkegaard said, they demand subjective commitment, something that is *not* dependent on any process of objective confirmation or independent ratiocination. That, after all, is one of the things that it means to say that they are *revealed*. Their status as revealed claims distinguishes them logically – that is, *in kind* – from claims that are to be treated as the function of objective information.

The point that we need to hang on to here is that some of our beliefs are personal in the sense that they cannot be handled logically as objective questions (whose truth is made to *rest* on facts) without distorting their meaning. A good portion of Phillips's work in the philosophy of religion is a testimony to this insight. Yet again, it is one thing to distinguish such claims from objective issues; it is another to illuminate the kind of judgement which *does* go into them. Sometimes, Phillips is so concerned to deny that religious beliefs can be handled as if they were the products of evidence that he says nothing about any alternative means of enlivening their acceptance. 'Some people believe; others don't. Life is like that.'

There is more to be said, though. Where conviction cannot be communicated *via* the means of objective mediation, it might develop by way of a growing appreciation of the depth of the thinking that affirmation entails. For when one does not understand the kind of thinking that hinges on a moral or religious belief – or on any transformative belief – one is in no position to adopt it. To attempt to adopt it under those circumstances is to force assent to an idea whose essential point one fails to understand, which is why adducing rational grounds for religious beliefs *irrespective of their regulative role* is so deeply wrongheaded. It fosters the illusion that a belief can be understood and affirmed while setting aside the whole *point* of the belief in underwriting a new form of thinking. And because this is so deeply wrongheaded, there is no alternative to approaching the question of belief along the lines of an increased appreciation for *this very aspect of their sense*. Understanding the point of a belief in this sense is understanding its regulative force, and this is a logical prerequisite to judging it.

In short, there is no way of coming to accept such beliefs other than by growing in appreciation for them and their roles. One appreciates a belief in this sense when one comes to understand not only the words of a belief but the forcefulness it has in encapsulating a distinctive manner of thinking, something that is not always evident in the words used to formulate the belief. The point or the force of a belief in this sense (there are several different ways in which beliefs can be said to have a point[12]) concerns the role that it plays as a foundation or principle of judgement. It has this kind of force if the role it plays in shaping our manner of understanding is constitutive of its meaning, so that the sharing of this understanding belongs to the very essence of believing. That is what we embrace when we affirm a *moral claim*, for example. We know the prescriptive sort of judgement that it expresses, and the prescriptive or evaluative form of other judgements that would be in keeping with its acceptance. The point that moral claims have in this sense is almost too obvious to notice, and yet it is of crucial importance to stand back from the discussion for a minute to think about what I am saying. Before we can make any moral judgements in a 'rational' way, we must already know what it means to think morally. We have to locate ourselves in a moral world, so to speak. We have to understand what it means to accept the reality of our obligations. Being able to locate ourselves in this way is what understanding the point of moral claims involves. Yet something must have led us to locate ourselves in such a world. Something must have led us to enter the whole realm of moral deliberation, and this can only be an appreciation for the *point* of moral discourse. If we have not learned to understand that, then it is impossible for us to approach them in a logically relevant way.

Suppose that we stay with moral examples to illustrate the points that I have been making. We subject our children to a process of moral education that depends on the very possibility of the kind of persuasion that I have been talking about. Our children begin without any moral sense and yet, if all goes well in their education, they wind up with moral concepts that are of a piece with moral sensibilities which find expression in moral convictions. How does this happen? We obviously do not convince our children who have yet to understand anything of morality by objectively compelling arguments. We train them. We teach by example, our own example and the examples of others that we set before them. We show them how to behave *as if* they respected the rights of others, and we ask them to put themselves in the shoes of others whose feelings or welfare their behaviour affects. Sometimes we express our moral disapproval for what they do, saying that it is 'not nice' or 'not right', while at other times we praise them for taking the needs and desires of others into consideration. In this whole process, it is difficult to find anything that one would call an argument that objectively supports the truth of the fundamental beliefs that we ought to respect the feelings of other people, that we ought not to harm them simply in order to get what we want, that we should be thankful for the consideration they extend to us, etc. Some people, I suppose, might say that the reason why we do not try to give our children an argumentative justification on rational grounds is that children are too young to understand such arguments. But what could these arguments possibly be? How does one convince someone to be moral if he or she is altogether *lacking in a moral sense* to begin with? The only way in which one could convince such a person would be by invoking arguments that get their purchase from things that the child *does* understand, such as prudential considerations. But then one has to represent morality as if it were simply a matter of prudence, which is to say that those who are convinced by such arguments would not be *morally* persuaded at all. They would never *get the point* of genuinely moral deliberation.

The only plausible answer to the question of how people come to appreciate moral ideas is by admitting that there is an alternative avenue by which they come to understand moral concepts and to appreciate moral principles. When we travel on this path, we forswear inferential arguments and rely on training, time and experience to engender the moral sensitivity that is needed to participate in a moral life. To admit this is to admit that some of our most basic beliefs are dependent for their credibility on some form of preliminary training which is *necessary to their affirmation*. To ask what this training involves, or how it works, is to ask how the kind of persuasion that I am talking about works.

Since this kind of persuasive training runs before a full understanding of concepts, it is difficult to describe. But one thing that we can say is that moral or religious persuasion's power depends on showing our beliefs off to good effect by helping others to appreciate their point. So far I have been suggesting, following Phillips, that many critically minded philosophers attempt to judge moral and religious ideas, especially the latter, before a fully ripened understanding of this aspect of their sense is in place. But now I am suggesting that there are perfectly appropriate means to trying to develop this understanding, so that the force of the transformative beliefs becomes clear. There is a difference, of course, between appreciating a belief and accepting it, and this is reflected in our knowledge that the best of training and the best of persuasive efforts do not always take with people. That, in fact, is one of the factors that distinguishes appropriate forms of persuasion from rational justification: persuasion cannot guarantee a belief's truth simply because it lacks the relationship between grounds and conclusion that is characteristic of argument. It offers a means of appreciation instead. And so it might be objected that this account of belief-formation in religion or in morality fails, since persuasion is not enough to fully underwrite the claims of religious or ethical beliefs to rationality. But as I have already tried to show, and as Phillips has laboured at length to show, to expect this kind of conclusive justification is to expect too much. Forcing that conception of rationality over moral and religious belief does not fit the logic of the issues. Once this last point is fully realized, one should be more willing to accept the fact that a growing appreciation for regulative beliefs can ripen into acceptance unless there are other, more persuasive ideas that stand in the way.

In the end, I think that we have to say that the hold that such beliefs gain over us is finally a primitive notion. At some point in the process whereby we come to understand and appreciate moral teachings, we submit to them. Generally, we do not adopt them simply because we find them suitable to our taste; we become believers because we are taken by the form of thinking and living that they open up to us. They call forth appreciation in us, and if we sense that our thinking is expanded by conforming to the pattern which they suggest, we yield to them. This does not happen in every case, of course; it is perfectly possible, again, to appreciate the force of certain moral ideas (the absolute value of human life, the obligatory compassion for all that lives, etc.) but not to share these beliefs. Yet as long as the judgements of non-believers have been subjected to the same sort of persuasive influences that generally produce moral or religious conviction, we cannot complain by saying that the non-believers are being illogical or irrational. Or, if we *do* say this, we cannot mean by it that they have made any formal mistakes in the process of forming inferences – that they have *miscalculated*, as it were. Instead, the claim that such people are unreasonable because they do not accept ways of thinking that have long since become natural for us expresses a normative condemnation of them for what they fail to believe. They do not accept something to which we feel entitled, *even though we cannot justify our convictions on logical grounds*. What gives us this right? *Not* an objective argument, but the force of all that which leads us to appreciate the point of believing.

3

I want to look at Phillips's work more closely now, but before I do, let me review the points I have tried to make so far. (1) There is a difference between persuasion which is logically relevant to the beliefs at issue and persuasion which is not. One way of noting this difference is to distinguish between persuasion that is relevant to the content of propositions and persuasion that is concerned only with the act of believing. (2) Logical persuasion applies to those beliefs for which no other means of judgement, such as objective testing or rational grounding, is logically possible. (3) Because such persuasion is taken for granted as we educate children and cultural outsiders to commonplace certainties and to moral realities, we tend to overlook its importance. (4) The effectiveness of this persuasion is not the result of an increase in *evidential* support that it brings to the propositions in question, but the result of the enhancement of our understanding of and appreciation for a belief's point. (5) Such persuasion is never conclusive in the sense that it allows us to shift the burden of proof to external grounds of assessment. In that sense, the judgements that we are persuaded to make remain personal judgements. (6) Yet persuasion none the less belongs to good judgement because it includes an appropriate means of conditioning the affirmation of objectively irresolvable, regulatively significant, ideas. Without it, good judgement in such matters would be impossible.

My reason for turning to Phillips at this point is not that he articulates such a case for persuasion but that his own grammatical studies *illustrate* persuasion of the sort that I have been trying to define. In his various discussions of the problem of evil, for example, we can get some idea of what this kind of persuasion amounts to by seeing how his grammatical remarks might increase one's appreciation for religious claims.[13] In those discussions he is not trying to convince people to accept a Christian view of suffering; he is merely trying to make the character of a Christian response clear. Nevertheless, much of what he says can have an edifying and potentially persuasive relation to belief.

His intent is to show that the meaning of referring unjust suffering to God is not what it appears to be. One would think that belief in God provides an answer for human suffering by assuring us that it serves a divine purpose, thereby putting our trials into a perspective that shows that they have a divine rationale. For many people that is what the belief in God *is*; it is believing in a kind of cosmic order in which evil is never absurdly out of line but always integrated into a meaningful system. Believers certainly *appear* to say as much when they tell us that God has an answer to our suffering, that God's plan for the world is always just, that the accidents that come our way are not as absurd as they appear, and so forth. The reality, though, is that believing in God does not provide these kinds of answers to the problem of unjust suffering. Believers *do*, of course, understand their suffering in religious terms; but in referring their suffering to God, they do not discover the intellectual solution to the problem that the outward form of Christian discourse leads us to expect.[14]

Yet to appreciate the hidden meaning that lies beneath the outward form in which the belief is expressed (which here makes the existence of God into an explanatory postulate), one must look to lives in which the grammar (that is, the *sense*) of the relevant concepts is illustrated. There one can see that the belief in God and in God's will enables people to respond to life's injustices with a kind of hope that has nothing to do with the vision of divine plans or the expectations of future rewards. Here there is an element of resignation that many philosophers and theologians have missed. So instead of locating faith in the *quality* of this resignation, they assume that we need not accept the inexplicability of our suffering at all. For God might balance our current sufferings by goods to come, whether these be found in the enhancement of present virtues (suffering builds character) or in heavenly joys (a happiness so great that it dwarfs all worldly misery). Or perhaps, some suggest, God so desires our voluntary allegiance that he creates us as free beings, and thereafter either cannot or will not revoke the harmful consequences of our misuse of that freedom. If only such compensations are available, or if only we might see the reasons which God might have for allowing us to misuse our freedom, then suffering might be made meaningful. Yet Phillips finds in the depth grammar or religious language another spirit, one that survives the *giving up* of all such hopes for an explanation, a giving up that finds a substitute for explanation in *religious* hope.

> Belief in God, [some philosophers] would say demands such an order. I do not think that it makes sense to look for such an order and that the belief in God is connected with a recognition of this fact.
> ...I have already suggested, in discussing what might be meant by someone who said the outcome was in the hands of God, that the force of the belief depends on the *absence* of the kind of higher level planning so essential to...theodicy. (italics mine)[15]

No doubt there are believers who do not understand how belief can be preserved at all in the absence of a divine explanation for suffering. Phillips does not deny this but suggests that there is a deeper response that we can recognize in the lives of other believers, if only we learn to listen for it. Such believers cry out to God to bewail their suffering, just as every believer does;

and yet in turning to God they are acknowledging the utter senselessness of tragic events, no longer searching for any explanation and no longer pretending that any might be found. In turning to God they come to accept this. They make their peace with the *utter* inexplicability of their fate, something that, as Leo Tolstoy says, 'remains necessarily incomprehensible'.[16] Thus, they find in God a way of living *with* that absurdity without despair. And the recognition of this absurdity is a precondition for attributing one's life to God.[17]

As Simone Weil says, 'The extreme greatness of Christianity lies in the fact that it does not seek a supernatural remedy for suffering but a supernatural use for it.' This 'use' consists of withdrawing one's claims to compensation, including the feeling that one is entitled to an explanation. Such claims and feelings are equivalent to the special interest that we take in ourselves, and the renunciation of them is humility. Those who possess this humility surrender the belief that anything is theirs by right and accept all things as gifts of grace. They give up the idea that the future owes them something for what they have suffered in the past, and they deny the self with all of its centred demands and expectations, replacing selfishness with a form of contemplation that is in fact love. There is a religious sense to be found in this, and yet it has nothing to do with figuring out a divine plan that justifies all suffering. Phillips writes:

> The instinct for self-preservation makes men ask, 'Why is this happening to *me*?' But suffering can also be used to teach one that one is nothing just because it does tempt one to put oneself at the center of one's concern. Simone Weil expressed this point well: 'If I thought that God sent me suffering by an act of his will and for my good, I should think that I was something, and I should miss the chief use of suffering which is to teach me that I am nothing. It is therefore necessary to avoid all such thoughts and to love God through the suffering'.[18]

If one were to ask how Weil loved God through her suffering, the answer would not be because she found in the concept of God a plausible answer for it, but because she found a use for it in overcoming her feelings of entitlement. Instead of insisting on her right to have an explanation, she used her own sufferings to learn humility, to accept her fate without reproach and to yield all of her self-concerns in exchange for Christian love.

The understanding to which Weil finds her way here is part of Christianity's depth, which lies hidden beneath superficial similarities between religious and other forms of expression. The fact that we speak of the belief in God as *answering* the problem of evil, or the fact that we speak of God's will in the same way as we speak of the will of other people, suggests that believing in God or in God's will answers the problem of evil. But the unexpected form of understanding (the 'hint of grammar') that we find in

Weil's remarks shows us that there is an alternative. And because there is something of a strain in the old theodicies, this alternative *has an appeal*. After all, we struggle to imagine benefits of such glory that they might make up for the utter senselessness of what human beings suffer. But too often these imaginings simply blunt the true horror of what happens. Sometimes the only adequate expression for the depth of this suffering is an unstinting acknowledgement of its absurdity. Then it becomes clear that it is simply self-deception 'to embark on a speculation [about the justifying causes of evil] that we should not even contemplate'.[19]

To drive this last point home Phillips quotes not only Simone Weil but a number of other literary figures – Somerset Maugham, Thomas Mann, Fyodor Dostoevsky, Billie Holliday, etc. The words from Ivan Karamazov in Dostoevsky's *The Brothers Karamazov* are representative. Ivan asks his brother Alyosha,

> 'Imagine that you are creating a fabric of human destiny with the object of making men happy in the end, giving them peace and rest at last, but that it was essential and inevitable to torture to death only one tiny creature – that baby beating its breast with its fist, for instance – and to found that edifice on unavenged tears, would you consent to be the architect on those conditions? Tell me, and tell me the truth.'
> 'No, I wouldn't consent,' said Alyosha softly.[20]

'There are screams and screams,' as Phillips says, and some are to be understood by a silence that refuses to be consoled.

In all these writers, the strain of imagining how God could pay us back for our sufferings is 'not even contemplated'. But along with this despair over ever finding an answer, there is another means of contemplation, which is both religiously deep and humanely honest. And simply coming to realize that there *is* sense in this alternative can be profoundly moving. This is exactly the kind of realization that a study of religion's depth grammar often promotes.

Indeed, there are really two kinds of depth in religion's grammar. Revealing the hidden sense behind the superficial grammar of religious claims is only the first kind of depth. In this sense, the grammar of religious concepts is deep only because it is hard to recognize behind the misleading forms of expression with which its logic is so easily confused. But there is another kind of depth, consisting of the profundity that religious conceptions acquire by virtue of being the products of deeply human experience. The grammar of a religion like Christianity (and surely others as well) exhibits a depth in both of these senses, not only because it is easily confused by misleading analogies in the outward forms of its expression, but also because it is formed in the lives of people who have suffered much. That is why Wittgenstein spoke of life experiences leading one to belief,[21] and why he spoke of there being a kind of torment that opens the heart to faith.[22]

This second kind of depth is a logically primitive notion. It cannot be communicated in the usual way by words alone. It can be elucidated, however, *by being shown forth* – and therein lies much of the importance that Phillips finds in literature. In the examples which I have quoted, we see two human responses to suffering, one that seeks compensation through a divine agent that encompasses it in a purposive plan, and another that *uses* the inexplicability of suffering as a means of personal transformation. This transformation has a depth which the untransformed, explanatory way of looking at suffering lacks. Given the transformed perspective, in fact, the earlier attempt to explain suffering seems naive, possibly dishonest or self-deceptive, as if those who are caught up in it were yet to realize the full enormity of life. This is a contrast which helps to show us *what is meant by depth*.

Since persuasion finds the ring of truth, in any presentation that deepens our appreciation for that which we once only barely understood, grammatical studies can be persuasive. Their persuasiveness is a function of their power to illuminate the sense of concepts and beliefs, in this case the transformation point of affirming religious ideas. There is obviously nothing compelling about this, as people invariably differ on how they react on this deeply human level. Yet mature believers often feel as if the conceptual remarks that open to them this second kind of depth represent a way of understanding in which their thoughts were meant to settle, as if believers who had lost their way in obscurity had come home after years of travelling. Perhaps we can generalize by saying that in cases like this, where deeply existential issues are involved, we respond to perspectives that yield not only radically new ways of understanding, but ways that bring us into a more honest engagement with ourselves. This gives religious belief a passive aspect, making it akin to *acknowledgement* or *resignation*, something quite different from believing in the sense of selecting opinions on the basis of rational criteria. For believers who are persuaded in the way that I have been describing do not pick and choose what suits their standards; they are drawn into belief, often against the better judgement that their narrow-minded conception of 'reason' would suggest.

Before any of this can happen, though, one's understanding needs to be opened to a new understanding of the point of religious beliefs. To take one last example of how a literary portrayal might help to bring such understanding to light, consider that case of the priest and the doctor in Albert Camus' *The Plague*. The doctor, Rieux, refuses 'to embark on the speculation' of what reasons a God might have for allowing the suffering of his people. But though Rieux has given up the hope for such explanations, he works tirelessly to alleviate the illness that has suddenly and senselessly struck his town.[23] In this Rieux emerges as the character who is ironically much closer to the spirit of religion than the priest who tries to explain the plague as divine punishment. Here Camus helps us to see that there is nobility and depth in a man like Rieux, indeed, that his reactions to suffering are more honest and inspiring than those that are commonly advanced by superficial forms of religion. And because we feel this depth, we are prepared for Phillips's arguments that the priest's understanding *is indeed superficial*. For the priest's reactions accord neither with the depth of Rieux's feeling *nor* with the depth available in the grammar of genuine Christianity.

Again, none of this means that there is anything logically compelling about the recognition of a religion's depth. One person might submit to it, much as a child submits to moral principles in learning how to think morally; then again, others might not. Often there is no clear way of explaining the difference – which means that one can acknowledge the power of persuasion without being persuaded. Phillips is right about that.

My point, therefore, is not to explain how persuasion as a logical concept might function as a means of resolving all objectively intractable differences. It does not do that. It provides no criteria that make the determination of religious truth logically possible. Depth is not a criterion like that, and nor is saliency or nobility or any other aspect of religious persuasion, such as the power of examples of the forcefulness of transformative ideas. Even if such notions could be specified clearly enough to serve as criteria (and I doubt that they can), there would be no contradiction in admitting the nobility or depth of a conception while refusing to accept it. To admit this is simply to admit that persuasion is *not* a variety of objective adjudication.

Because there is no way to illuminate such transformative judgements except by uncovering their depth, there is no way for writers like Phillips to avoid the possibility that the accounts that do reveal this depth will have potentially persuasive aspects. So despite the fact he prefers to stress the fact that our arguments cannot settle our religious disputes, and despite the fact that he typically wants to leave the intractability of religious disputes where it is, we can see in his work the outlines of another possibility. His own grammatical studies help us to see that there is indeed a form of persuasion that comes after reason, one that might help philosophers, personally, decide whether they can get along with religious ideas.

Louisiana State University

Notes

1 'I would say that I "combat" the other man [who disagrees with me about principles], – but wouldn't I give him reasons? At the end of reason comes *persuasion*. (Think of "what happens when missionaries convert natives.")' Ludwig Wittgenstein, *On Certainty*, ed. G.E.M. Anscombe and G.H. von Wright (New York: Harper and Row, 1969), para. number 612.

At the End of Reason Comes Persuasion' 153

2 Wittgenstein, *Lectures and Conversations on Aesthetics, Psychology, and Religious Belief*, ed. Cyril Barrett (Berkeley: University of California Press, 1967), pp. 53ff.

3 'On Really Believing', in *Wittgenstein and Religion* (New York: St Martin's Press, 1993), pp. 33–55.

4 I tried to make a similar point in 'Religious Beliefs: Their Point and Their Reference', in *Is God Real*, ed. Joseph Runzo (New York: Macmillan, 1992).

5 Phillips discusses the contextually bound differences in the concept of reality in several essays in *Wittgenstein and Religion*, not only in 'On Really Believing', but in 'Philosophy, Theology, and the Reality of God' and 'Sublime Existence'.

6 Phillips discusses Rorty in *Faith after Foundationalism* (London: Routledge, 1988), pp. 132–6, 143–66.

7 See *Faith after Foundationalism*, pp. 167–91.

8 *Ibid.*, p. 176.

9 In *A Rumor of Angels* Berger recoils from the view that our life views are utterly arbitrary. He claims that our unquenchable need to impose orders of meaning on the world implies a kind of *a priori* trust in life's meaningfulness. Thus we can think of life as having some kind of resonance with this need, despite the fact that this knowledge can never be empirically verified. See pp. 52–3 *passim*.

10 *Belief, Change and Forms of Life* (London: Macmillan, 1986), p. 113.

11 Søren Kierkegaard, *The Attack on Christendom*, trans. Walter Lowrie (Princeton: Princeton University Press, 1968), p. 271.

12 See Whittaker, 'The Point of a Belief', in *Metaphor and Religion: Theolinguistics 2*, ed. J.P. van Noppen (Brussels: University of Brussels, 1983), pp. 91–109.

13 Phillips discusses the problem of evil in *The Concept of Prayer*, pp. 86–95, 102–3; in *Belief, Change and Forms of Life*, ch. 4; and in several other places in his work.

14 For example, in *The Concept of Prayer*, pp. 86–95, 102–3.

15 *Belief, Change and Forms of Life*, p. 75.

16 Leo Tolstoy, *A Confession*, trans. David Patterson (New York: W.W. Norton, 1983), pp. 90–1.

17 *The Concept of Prayer*, p. 62.

18 *Ibid.*, p. 102.

19 *Belief, Change and Forms of Life*, p. 68.

20 Quoted in *The Concept of Prayer*, p. 94.

21 Wittgenstein, *Culture and Value*, ed. G.H. von Wright, trans. Peter Winch (Chicago: University of Chicago Press, 1977), p. 86.

22 *Culture and Value*, p. 46.

23 Phillips discusses Camus and *The Plague* in *From Fantasy to Faith* (London: Macmillan, 1991), pp. 158–67.

7
Phillips: An Inheritance Reconsidered

M. Jamie Ferreira

> *There is a way of asking us for our reasons that leads us not only to forget our best reasons but also to conceive a stubborn aversion to all reasons. This way of asking makes people very stupid and is a trick used by tyrannical people.*
>
> Nietzsche[1]

One of the persistent themes in Phillips's writings on religion, a theme highlighted in *Religion without Explanation*, is that the 'terms of Hume's legacy are inadequate for understanding religious belief', yet 'philosophers of religion still think their enquiries are limited by Hume's terms of reference'.[2] In what follows I propose to reconsider how much Phillips himself inherits of Hume's legacy. The chapter in which Phillips explicitly addresses Hume's legacy examines three levels of argument found in Hume's *Dialogues* and concludes that the effect of these 'three levels of argument which go to make up Hume's legacy is to make any attempt to infer the existence of God from the world in which we live logically problematic' (22). Such an account of Hume's legacy, however, limited as it is to Hume's epistemological criticisms, is not a comprehensive account. I propose, on the contrary, to take a broader view of Hume's legacy by taking his *Natural History of Religion* more seriously. The *Natural History* suggests, first, the need of a refinement of Phillips's view of Hume with respect to explanatory accounts of religion. It reveals, second, and more importantly, a Humean legacy which includes moral criticisms. I shall indicate a significant locus of agreement between Phillips and Hume suggested by their views of what constitutes 'superstition', and I shall be arguing that their common motivation is a moral critique which is as important a Humean legacy as the one Phillips explicitly rejects.

Religion without explanation

In so far as Phillips is proposing 'religion without explanation', he is construing Hume's legacy as the source of a variety of accounts of 'religion *with* explanation'. Phillips formulates Hume's legacy in terms of a stipulative standard of verification; on this view, the only alternative to direct verification is 'inference' from the evidence of this world. Constrained by these terms, Hume's legacy is to 'treat nature naturally', to render logically problematical 'any attempt to infer the existence of God from the world in which we live'; it is, 'in the main, to put explanation within this world' (22, 25). Humean explanation and its descendants are thus the focus of Phillips's critique of the adequacy of Hume's 'terms of reference'.[3]

In order to assess Phillips's disagreement with Hume, it is important to admit at the outset that some of his explicit descriptions of Hume's terms of reference would seem to make Phillips very Humean. In so far as Hume's project of putting explanation within this world is seen by Phillips as the legacy which renders problematical any attempt to infer the existence of God from the world in which we live, Hume's legacy centrally involves a proscription which we could as easily hear coming from Phillips's own mouth. If it is Hume's legacy that there are 'insuperable difficulties in talking about the world as a great big object', then surely Phillips is a dutiful son of Hume, having internalized Hume's lesson that not all questions which can be appropriately asked of particulars can be extrapolated to other categories (19–20). Moreover, Hume's criticisms issue in an anti-theoretical position with which Phillips agrees wholeheartedly, one that he calls Hume's critical rejection of an argumentative basis for religion.

Their attack on theory and justification is similar in so far as both construe religion 'without argument' – in that sense, without explanation. But this minimal sense of congeniality, in which the enemy of my enemy is my friend, would make every critic of religion an ancestor of even the deepest religious mystic. On Phillips's view, something which he wants to accept lies at the heart of what Hume wants to reject; any agreement with Hume with respect to justification of religious belief is fatally undermined by what Phillips sees as Hume's reductive explanation. That reduction is characterized as follows:

> Hume's criticisms constitute a powerful attack on the notion of two worlds, an earthly one and a heavenly one, the latter being the explanation of the former. He is, I believe, an advocate of belief in one world, the world we know; a world in which we find no evidence of the existence of God, and from which we have neither reason nor need to infer a divine reality. (22)

What is at stake for Phillips is the rejection of any explanation which reduces religious reactions to non-religious ones, any explanation which does not 'make room for faith' in any way in which specifically religious (as contrasted with moral) direction could be given to life. Phillips's construal of religion 'without explanation' is thus an attempted construal of religion *without reduction* as well as *without argument*.

It is worth noting that Hume's attacks on the standard 'proofs' for God's existence could be seen as an attack on an imperialistic view of *the* grammar of belief, implying that the standard grammar is irrelevant in this case. In this sense it would be Hume's legacy that religious belief is not subject to the grammar of empirical propositions; Hume would be rejecting an alien grammar rather than imposing one on religion. Presumably the reason Phillips reads Hume's attacks as imposing on religious belief an alien grammar of belief and truth (143) is that he reads into Hume's legacy the additional claim that there can be no other grammar than the one which is suited to empirical propositions and prediction of future events. Phillips connects such exclusivity with the reduction of religious reactions to non-religious ones. However, I suggest that we can hear echoes of such exclusivity when Phillips himself says of religious beliefs that 'what they want to say cannot be said' (109), since this implies that there is indeed only one grammar for 'saying'; moreover, he explicitly concedes that there is only one grammar for 'inferring' (see pp. 148ff.). It thus begins to become unclear just how the elimination of reference as a function for religious language differs from the commitment to 'one world, the world we know', which Phillips attributes to Hume and characterizes as reductive. One way of providing sense to Phillips's critique of Hume's reductionism is to distinguish the contrast between natural and supernatural from the contrast between non-religious and religious. Presumably, if there can be no meaningful reference to a world other than the one 'we know', Phillips cannot be committed to the notion of 'two worlds' – natural and supernatural – any more than is Hume. But this world, this natural one, can, for Phillips, reveal both nature and God, both non-religious and religious dimensions.

In any case, the phrase 'religion without explanation' is, I have been suggesting, richly ambiguous. It is ambiguous first with respect to the kind of explanation religion is supposed to do without. On the one hand, Phillips wants to assess Hume's legacy as revealed in the variety of reactions which have uncritically accepted Hume's terms of reference and consequently avoided any problematical 'inference' by resorting to reductive 'explanations' of religion. On the other hand, he also wants to reject another kind of explanation – one which tries to preclude reduction by attempting to provide an argumentative basis for religious belief. In other words, when Phillips calls the former 'conscious' reduction and the latter 'unconscious' reduction, he is not simply referring to a difference in degree of explicitness, but rather to a difference in what constitutes reduction.

To be more specific, one result of holding Hume's legacy as a necessary context for reflection on religious belief is found, for Phillips, in the work of Tylor, Marrett, Freud and Braithwaite: there we find that the response to Hume's charge 'that there are logically insuperable barriers to talking of a God beyond the world we know' has been to 'offer explanations of religion as a human product' (98). These thinkers provide examples of the reductive explanatory accounts of religion (religion-with-non-religious causal explanation) which Phillips rejects. The reductive explanation at issue here is the *alternative* to claiming that religious beliefs are inferential beliefs. But by the end of the book it is clear that Phillips also has in view another kind of explanatory account of religion, one that accepts the terms of Hume's challenge while holding that religion is more than a human product. That is, Phillips addresses and also rejects attempts to counter Humean reduction by supporting the referentiality of religious language. His discussion of the question 'Does God exist?' implies that attempts like those made by Wittgenstein's Father O'Hara to justify religion as more than a human product are also a kind of reductive explanation – because being 'justified' amounts to being rendered conditional, relative to non-religious reasons. Here the explanation at issue is precisely the result of claiming that religious beliefs are inferential beliefs. Phillips's Wittgensteinian proposal of 'religion without a rational (causal) explanation' is at the same time a proposal of 'religion without rational (justifying) explanation'. More significantly, the phrase 'religion without explanation' (like the phrase 'explanatory account of religion') is also ambiguous because it fails to distinguish between first-order explanation and meta-level explanation. The attempt to explain (vs. describe) the phenomenon of religion is different from the attempt to offer an account of religion as itself an explanatory enterprise (which can issue in hypotheses). This distinction is relevant to determining more precisely the character of Hume's legacy and Phillips's relation to it.

The view of Hume's legacy which focuses on his critique of the theistic inference is misleading in so far as it suggests that Hume thought religious beliefs were attempts to make such inferences. Phillips makes this suggestion explicit when he concedes that if religious beliefs are 'as Hume describes them' – that is, if they are supposed to be inferences from this world to another – then Hume's challenge is 'unanswerable' (25). This turns religion into an explanatory enterprise for Hume, even if an unsuccessful or illegitimate explanatory enterprise. But such a view ignores the *Natural History of Religion*'s insistent claim that religious beliefs, whether or not they can be rationalized after the fact, are not the product of reasoning (faulty or otherwise). In other words, Phillips assumes what I have argued elsewhere is a common but mistaken view of Hume's project.[4]

Indeed, Hume makes quite clear in the *Natural History* that our imaginative personifications are an 'expedient' (and this is Hume's own word for it) for *coping* with the world, not an attempt to explain or understand it.[5] In the situation of barbarism, necessity and ignorance, in which religious belief originates, people were not, according to Hume, motivated by a desire to explain things. But this is a situation we share, since according to Hume *we* are placed in this world, 'as in a great theatre, where the true springs and causes of every event are entirely concealed from us ... *we* hang in perpetual suspense between life and death, health and sickness, plenty and want'

(*NHR*, 28–9; emphasis added). Although Hume's claim is initially addressed to the origin of religious beliefs 'at the first origin of society', his easy alternation between 'them' and 'us'[6] suggests that the situation which issues in such reactive, non-reasoned beliefs is common to us, even now. Indeed, it is the fate of the vulgar, 'even at this day and in EUROPE' that they, 'in nations which have embraced the doctrine of theism, still build it upon irrational and superstitious principles' (*NHR*, 41–2).

Hume insists that 'the common people were never likely to push their researches so far [into ultimate or first causes], or derive from reasoning their systems of religion' (*NHR*, 37). He explicitly denies the concern with any but the most immediate concerns, the instrumental knowledge necessary for survival.[7] When one is alarmed by novelty, one is immediately set to 'trembling, and sacrificing, and praying' – not explaining; in the face of an 'ordinary spectacle . . . a few removes satisfy his curiosity'. In sum, 'Imagine not that he will so much as start the question, whence the first animal; much less, whence the whole system, or united fabric of the universe arose. Or, if you start such a question to him, expect not that he will employ his mind with any anxiety about a subject, so remote, so uninteresting, and which so much exceeds the bounds of his capacity' (*NHR*, 25). The 'propensity in human nature, which leads into a system' (*NHR*, 29) is only the propensity to form determinate ideas on which one can focus as an 'expedient' for gaining some control.

Hume insists that it is 'not speculative curiosity, surely, or the pure love of truth' that motivates them/us (*NHR*, 28); it is not even the impure love of *truth* as a god. Hume's account appeals fundamentally to 'propensities', and the propensity to which he refers more than to any other is the propensity to 'adulation' – this is a far cry from any propensity to make things intelligible.[8] The view that either early societies or 'the common people' now *reason* to belief in gods or God with the goal of intelligibility is not Hume's. Such an interpretation treats Hume as if he were Auguste Comte; it identifies Hume's view with a common view of the intellectualized origin of religious belief which Hume himself argued is implausible (*NHR*, 25, 35). On Hume's view religious beliefs are not, as Comte would have it, the first fruits of our 'budding intelligence'; they neither were nor are our naive and immature attempts to theorize, to determine ultimate causes.

This misleading implication of Phillips's account of Hume is carried on in his chapter on 'mistaken hypotheses'. Phillips explicitly attributes to Tylor the view that religious beliefs are mistaken assumptions or hypotheses generated by fear and ignorance; he describes Tylor's view as follows: 'in order to make these strange events less frightening, primitive man *reasoned* that if no human could control such things they must be controlled by spirits more powerful than himself. In this way primitive man tried to make events in the animal and inanimate world *intelligible* by interpreting them in terms of his own experience' (27–8; emphasis added). He associates this with Hume's view by citing Tylor's quotation of Hume's *Natural History* (and this is the only reference Phillips makes to the *Natural History* in his entire analysis in *Religion Without Explanation*).[9] But, as I suggested earlier, the view that primitive man 'reasoned' and tried to make events 'intelligible' is more Comtean than Humean. Thus, Hume may offer an explanation of the phenomenon of religious belief, but it is an explanation of a religion with no explanatory intent, a religion without explanation. Phillips's alignment of Hume with the view that religious beliefs are mistaken hypotheses (first-order explanation) obscures the differences between them which lie, if anywhere, at the meta-level. Hume's legacy should not be seen as the source of that type of intellectualized account of religion which Phillips treats as one form of the attempt to explain religion.

Phillips and Wittgenstein reject the attempt to explain religion as well as the attempt to see the origin of religious belief in attempts at explanation. One might conclude that Hume rejects only the latter, comfortably engaging in the former kind of meta-explanation. One might conclude that the difference between Phillips and Hume in this respect is located in the contrast between the method of description and the method of explanation. Was Hume attempting the meta-level explanation of the phenomenon of a religion not directed to explanation? For a Wittgensteinian it seems confused to ask *why* religious people say what they do or find what they do impressive. Hume does ask why – but it should be noted that his questions are answered by reference to instinctive reactions, and for these (as with Phillips and Wittgenstein) there is no why. The answer to both 'Why are you so impressed?' and 'Why do you cope in this way?' is the same – we just do. Hume's appeals to tendencies in us – like tendencies to adulation and personification – do not even attempt to explain anything in a way which differs from description.

Phillips emphasizes the expressive dimension of religious belief. The *coping* which Hume opposes to reasoning as the actual source of religious belief may seem instrumental or means/end oriented in a way that *expressing* does not. But we are talking about instinctive unreasoned reactions in both cases. Phillips illustrates his Wittgensteinian alternative to Hume with Wittgenstein's insight in the 'Remarks on Frazer's *Golden Bough*':

> How could fire or fire's resemblance to the sun have failed to make an impression on the awakening mind of man? But not 'because he can't explain it (the stupid superstition of our time) – for does an 'explanation make it less impressive'. (114)

Explanations solve confusions, but they/we are not confused. Phillips continues: '*That a* man says that God cares for him in all things is the expression of the terms in which he meets and makes sense of the contingencies of life' (114). But there is nothing in all this that Hume could not have said or agreed with. Expressing the terms in which one meets the contingencies of life sounds quite like what Hume suggested in the *Natural History*. The appeal to 'this is how people cope' is not so different from the appeal to 'this is how people come to terms with life's contingencies'. If in light of the above we now ask again whether the methodologies of Phillips and Hume are the appropriate locus of contrast, the answer is not so clear. In other words, if one looks outside the *Dialogues* for Hume's legacy, one finds less distance between Hume and Phillips.

This is not to deny that there may well be important differences between a Wittgensteinian account of religion and the Humean account in the *Natural History*, but they need to be located more precisely than has been done. If I am right, the charge that Hume makes the 'mistake' of seeing religious belief as 'based on a primitive act of explanatory hypothesizing'[10] (any more than Wittgenstein or Phillips do) is off the mark. Moreover, although it is true that Wittgenstein calls attention to a wider range of instinctual responses (including responses to humans as well as to the natural world, and responses which issue in more diverse feelings than hope and fear), it is not clear that Hume's account of the 'natural history' of religion is the sort of attempt at explanation which Wittgenstein and Phillips reject. Finally, the charge that Hume makes the 'mistake' of believing that 'the provision of a *causal* explanation for a practice (as opposed to a reasoned one) is dispositive' (that is, that such a causal account is a discrediting account) also seems off the mark.[11] It is, after all, an intriguing fact about the *Natural History* that at least as many chapters are devoted to a moral critique of religion, as to a genetic account of it. Hume was fully aware of the distinction between a belief's origin, its truth value and its moral value, and one could argue that his lengthy attention to a moral critique of religion revealed an appreciation of the Wittgensteinian insight that an explanation would not make religion less impressive. Hume, fully aware of the genetic fallacy and the limits of a genetic critique, may have wisely put his stake in another way of showing that religion was not impressive. One could argue, that is, that he sought to come to terms with religion by a moral critique rather than to explain it. And it is in this arena – the arena of moral criticism – that I would venture to find more of Hume's legacy than might normally be acknowledged in Phillips's work.

Superstition

Superstition is a category to which Hume appeals, at least in passing, in the *Natural History of Religion*: 'In proportion as any man's course of life is governed by accident, we always find, that he encreases in superstition'; the vulgar 'still build [theism] upon irrational and superstitious principles'; religious faith and 'species of superstition' are effectively equated (*NHR*, 30, 42, 62).[12] Although such references might be read as identifying superstition with intellectual error, a case can be made that Hume generally construes religion's corrupting influence in moral terms. The fact that he exemplifies superstition with 'devotion and supplications, and the observance of religious days' (*NHR*, 32) hints at the kind of problem he is attacking. Let me indicate briefly some of the reasons for seeing a moral animus, rather than an intellectual one, at the heart of his critique of religion.[13]

Early in his career, in the essay 'Of Superstition and Enthusiasm', Hume had contrasted these as two 'corruptions of true religion'.[14] Enthusiasm, he suggests, 'produces the most cruel disorders in human society' and tends to lead to the rejection of 'reason, and even morality', while superstition only leads to 'absurd or frivolous behavior'. But in the end superstition is seen as the more threatening corruption of human well-being because of its congeniality with authoritarian structures which promote 'persecutions and religious wars'. Enthusiasm's unfriendliness to external forms and authority (based on its commitment to inwardness and passion) was a redeeming feature, while superstition was 'an enemy to civil liberty', fitting people for slavery.[15] These are moral objections, and this orientation is reinforced by his later charge in the *Treatise* that 'Generally speaking, the errors in religion are dangerous; those in philosophy only ridiculous'.[16] Other essays, like 'Of Suicide' and 'Of the Immortality of the Soul', constitute diatribes against the 'pernicious' effects of popular religion; moreover, his *History of England* gave examples of those pernicious effects and resulted in a barrage of hostile attacks on superstitious forms of religion.[17] Part XII of the *Dialogues* calls our attention to religion's 'pernicious' weakening of our 'attachment to the natural motives of justice and humanity', and complements the general conclusion at the end of the *Natural History* that religious principles have 'in fact' been pathological (*NHR*, 75).

Indeed, Hume's moral critique of religion in the *Natural History* comprises over half the book[18] and is elaborated in terms of two significantly different sources of criticism. On the one hand, Hume details, chapter by chapter, a variety of specific consequences of religion which he suggests are uncontroversially immoral – e.g., intolerance, hypocrisy. But more importantly, he highlights the more encompassing conceptual challenge that where religion does not simply redundantly repeat moral prescriptions, it can undermine the authority of moral injunctions. Unlike Kant, for whom 'morality leads ineluctably to religion' and for whom morality is clearly the hermeneutical principle for interpreting religious commands,[19] Hume assumes that religion is committed to the view that the 'gods have maxims of justice peculiar to themselves' (*NHR*, 69). He assumes that religion necessarily places the maxims of the gods above, and hence potentially in conflict with, morality; and one can speculate that the reason he dismisses the alternative option, developed in the Kantian tradition, is because of the theological price it pays.

We clearly do not have in Hume's critique the same kind of venomous attack on the intrinsic immorality of religion which we find in other more colourful or more angry writers (like Nietzsche), but it is a harsh attack none the less. It is as conceptually strong as it is simple. I suggest that for Phillips too a moral impulse is at the base of his charges of superstition.

By way of background to Phillips's use of the term, it is interesting to note that Wittgenstein's earliest usages of the term 'superstition' were applied to philosophy and our general tendencies, rather than to forms of religion. In the *Tractatus* he seems to give a generic definition of superstition – 'Superstition is nothing but belief in the causal nexus' (5.1361). It is not religion that is superstitious, but rather our philosophical illusions about physical causality. He also attributes to us the 'primitive superstition' concerning the religious responses of 'primitive peoples'.[20]

Phillips, more than Wittgenstein, concentrates on superstitious construals of religious belief, but here he is still following Wittgenstein's lead. In 1948 Wittgenstein had explicitly contrasted religion with superstition: 'Religious faith and superstition [*Aberglaube*] are quite different. One of them results from *fear* and is a son of false science. The other is a trusting.'[21] Earlier in his lectures on religious belief, Wittgenstein had chastised Father O'Hara for putting forth inferential reasoning as justification of religious belief, and he explicitly termed this 'superstition':

> if this is religious belief, then it's all superstition. But I would ridicule it, not by saying it is based on insufficient evidence. I would say: here is a man who is cheating himself. You can say: this man is ridiculous because he believes, and bases it on weak reasons.[22]

But what is it that characterizes superstition? Although both remarks could be subsumed under the rubric of 'false science', something more is suggested. In the first case Wittgenstein's criticism highlights superstition's basis in fear. In the case of Father O'Hara, superstition is the failure to appreciate the grammar of absoluteness appropriate to religious belief – that is, providing justification demeans religious belief. It is arguable that in both cases what is at issue is not an intellectual error (as in Enlightenment attributions of superstition), but a moral failing. This may come out a little more clearly in Phillips's own discussions of superstition.

I will focus here on an older essay, namely, 'Religious Beliefs and Language Games', because in that essay Phillips explicitly intends to show that 'The distinction between religious belief and superstition is extremely important.'[23] I want to suggest that his essay reveals what is at heart a moral critique of superstitious beliefs. For Phillips, the superstitious, or illegitimate, response to 'why believe?' is couched in terms of power and consequentialism; such a means/end orientation is obsessed with the extrinsic ('external') justification of power and reward. These examples of 'reasons' which Phillips criticizes at the outset of the essay are tinged with insinuations of moral unworthiness; such 'reasons' are not appeals to evidence or rational justification. This does not mean that the appropriate response would be one which did appeal to evidence or rational justification, since Phillips insists that the imperialistic standard of 'common criteria of rationality' falsifies religious belief's grammar of absoluteness. Here, however, even when he turns to the question of the purported rationality of religious belief, the moral motivation remains. There are, he reminds us, 'common criteria not in dispute' and these are standards for taking the world 'seriously'. This, I suggest, refers to moral seriousness.

Phillips considers the following examples: 'a boxer crosses himself before the fight – a mother places a garland on a statue of the Virgin Mary – parents pray for their child lost in a wreck' (137). These examples show ways in which religious beliefs *can* be turned into testable hypotheses, employing causal connections, bringing the subject under 'a system where theory, repeatability, explanatory force, etc. are important features' (137). If the boxer thinks 'that anyone who crosses himself before a fight will not come to serious harm', if the mother thinks 'that the garland's value is prudential', if the parents think 'that all true prayers for the recovery of children lead to that recovery', then these are superstitious activities motivated by superstitious beliefs. Neither Wittgenstein nor Phillips share the Enlightenment critique of religion as superstition because it is not scientific enough – i.e., because it goes against known causal laws. What is superstitious emerges when religion tries to be scientific at all.[24]

For Phillips religious beliefs are not testable hypotheses but rather 'experiences of faith and trust' (138). He equates 'superstitious' responses with 'fantastic' responses (141) – that is, those which fail to 'take the world seriously' (135). Such a failure distorts or ignores 'what we already know' (137). Religious difficulties, Phillips suggests, 'cannot be understood unless serious account is taken of what pride, envy, and lust involve' (136); here we can make a parallel with Hume's assumption of an unproblematical world of virtue/vice on which there is a consensus. Moreover, what we know about pride and lust is on a par with what we know about taking birth, suffering and death seriously (135). Although at times Phillips implies that what is objectionable in superstition is a dependence on 'non-existent quasi-causal connections' (138), connections which we should know are not valid, that is not a sufficient account of superstition. The moral edge of the criticism is apparent in the tone of his description of the means/end instrumentalism involved, in which, e.g., the Virgin is 'reduced to the status of a lucky charm' (139).

It seems to me that his objections to the boxer, mother and parents who rely on quasi-causal connections or instrumentalism are objections to what one could call moral unworthiness, perhaps specifically moral cowardice. If so, he follows a Kierkegaardian lead, recalling the kind of objection Johannes Climacus has to attempts at rational justification of religious beliefs. Climacus writes provocatively that 'the point is rather to do away with introductory observations, reliabilities, demonstrations from effects, and the whole mob of pawnbrokers and guarantors, in order to get the absurd clear – so that one can believe if one will – I merely say that this must be extremely strenuous'.[25] The opposite of such strenuousness is moral cowardice, not insufficient intellectual insight.

Climacus makes clear that it is not a question of intellectual error, but a moral inadequacy. He explicitly associates cowardice with 'superstition' when he observes:

> Whether it is a word, a sentence, a book, a man, a society, whatever it is, as soon as it is supposed to be a boundary, so that the boundary itself is not dialectical, it is superstition and narrow-mindedness. In a human being there is always a desire, at once comfortable and concerned, to have something really firm and fixed that can exclude the dialectical, but this is cowardliness and fraudulence toward the divine.[26]

In other words, superstitious instrumentalism is a version of superstitious justification – it is an unworthy attempt to pose the issue in terms which allow some guarantees. One can see it in moral terms as the attempt to hedge one's bets.

Trusting in causal connections should not be confused with the trust of which both Wittgenstein and Phillips speak approvingly; rather, such justifications are superstitious because they are not trusting, but rather are expressions of attempts to manipulate outcomes. The qualifier 'Not as I will, but Thy will be done', which is inherent in the absoluteness to which the believer is, at least at one level, committed, is ignored when someone relies on quasi-causal connections which have only an extrinsic relation between the religious and the 'good' consequence. Phillips echoes the proposal Kierkegaard makes in his journals: namely, that 'the true prayer-relationship does not exist when God hears what is being *prayed* about, but when the *pray-er* continues to pray until he is the *one who hears*, who hears what God wills'. 'The immediate spontaneous person uses a lot of words and therefore is actually demanding when he prays', but 'the true pray-er is simply obedient'.[27]

This qualifier, 'Not as I will...', is taken seriously by those who relegate such instrumentalism to the realm of superstition; this qualifier, however, must not be taken to mean 'not taking the world seriously'. The grammar of absoluteness is not an excuse for ignoring 'what we already know'. 'Not as I will...' is a metaphor for the unconditionedness, the absoluteness, of religious belief – describing this element of religious practice is the corrective to the other expressions of religious practice which attempt to belie it. The superstitious character of instrumental construals of religious beliefs can be determined, and only determined, by reference to the other commitments held by religious believers. It is the undermining of such absoluteness to which Nietzsche, like Phillips, calls our attention when he writes angrily:

Even the slightest trace of piety in us ought to make us feel that a God who cures a headcold at just the right moment or tells us to get into a coach just as a downpour is about to start is so absurd a God he would have to be abolished even if he existed. A God as a domestic servant, as a postman, as an almanac-maker – at bottom a word for the stupidest kind of accidental occurrence.[28]

Nietzsche insists that 'Error (faith in the ideal) is not blindness, error is *cowardice*'.[29] I have been suggesting that with respect to his moral critique, as with explanation, Phillips is closer to Hume than might at first sight appear.

University of Virginia

Notes

1 *The Gay Science*, trans. Walter Kaufman (New York, 1974), §209.
2 *RWE* (Oxford, 1976), pp. 140 and 142. Further parenthetical page references in the text will be to *RWE* unless otherwise indicated.
3 In this work Phillips limits his critique by saying that not all religious belief fits Hume's model; elsewhere, though, he seems committed to the view that there is one grammar of *normative* religious belief – i.e. that the instrumental construal of religious belief, prayer and ritual is, at best, superstitious religion.
4 More detail can be found in my 'Hume's *Natural History*: Religion and "Explanation"', *Journal of the History of Philosophy* 33 (October 1995).
5 *The Natural History of Religion*, ed. H.E. Root (Stanford, 1956), p. 40.
6 The chapters either alternate or include examples of both. This, by the way, belies John Churchill's charge that it is a 'shortcoming' in Hume's account that he does not appreciate the continuities between the sensibilities of 'them' and 'us' ('The Squirrel Does Not Infer By Induction: Wittgenstein and the Natural History of Religion', *Philosophy and the Grammar of Religious Belief*, Claremont Studies in the Philosophy of Religion, eds. T. Tessin and M. von der Ruhr (London, 1995), p. 75).
7 In so far as the word 'explanation' is meant to include mediate and instrumental explanation my criticism does not apply, but Hume clearly distinguishes between two kinds of explanation and felt pressed to argue against what he took to be the common assumption that explanation means 'ultimate explanation'. Thus, commentary which refers simply to explanation, without qualification, is, at the very least, misleading.
8 He refers to adulation five times (*NHR*, pp. 43–5, 66). The point of explanation seems lost if the relevant propensities are like the propensity to have perceptual beliefs or experiences of sensation.
9 Although Phillips at times suggests that Tylor's view is an attempt to sidestep Hume's epistemological challenge, shifting to a causal theory of religion, the view of religious beliefs as 'mistaken hypotheses' might better be seen as a development of Hume's challenge since the view of 'mistaken hypotheses' presupposes explanatory inferences.
10 Churchill, 'The Squirrel Does Not Infer By Induction...', p. 66.
11 Churchill, pp. 66 and 69.

12   He refers to it at least eight times in the *Natural History*. It refers to a variety of things ranging from practices of supplication and other attempts at manipulation to polytheism in general.

13   More detail can be found in my 'Hume's *Natural History*: Religion and "Explanation"' (note 4 above).

14   Hume contrasts 'Two species of false religion' – 'Weakness, fear, melancholy, together with ignorance, are, therefore, the true sources of SUPERSTITION… Hope, pride, presumption, a warm imagination, together with ignorance, are, therefore, the true sources of ENTHUSIASM' (*Essays: Moral, Political and Literary*, ed. Eugene Miller [Indianapolis, 1985], p. 74).

15   Even his later negative assessment of enthusiasm's tendency to displace social concern by encouraging a privatized inner life supports this moral criticism (see *The Moral Animus of David Hume*, Donald T. Seibert [Newark, 1990], pp. 106–11).

16   *A Treatise of Human Nature*, ed. L.A. Selby-Bigge (Oxford, 1978), p. 272.

17   Siebert, *The Moral Animus of David Hume*.

18   Of the entire 53 pages of the book, 28 pages (6 chapters) elaborate a moral critique; 25 pages (8 chapters) detail the genetic account.

19   *Religion Within the Limits of Reason Alone* (New York, 1960), pp. 5, 82, 101.

20   *Culture and Value*, ed. G.H. von Wright, trans. Peter Winch (Oxford, 1980), p. 5e.

21   *Culture and Value*, p. 72e.

22   *Lectures and Conversations on Aesthetics, Psychology, and Religious Belief*, ed. C. Barrett (Oxford, 1972), p. 59.

23   In *The Philosophy of Religion*, ed. Basil Mitchell (Oxford, 1971), p. 138; initially in *Ratio* 12 (1970). Further parenthetical page references in this section will be to this essay.

24   Initially Phillips contrasted superstition and religion; on such a view one can see why philosophy cannot correct religion, although it can show that what purports to be religion is not. Later he claims that religion and superstition are not mutually exclusive: there are 'superstitious' forms of religion, as well as 'ugly', 'banal' and 'vulgar' forms of religion ('Religion in Wittgenstein's Mirror', *Wittgenstein: Centenary Essays*, ed. A. Phillips Griffiths [Cambridge, 1990], p. 147). Here, as in his early references to 'genuine prayer' (*Concept of Prayer* [Routledge, 1965], p. 158), he has a normative picture in mind; that normativity is not imposed from outside, but is rather a function of observable religious commitments in relation to our moral commitments to 'what we already know'.

25   *Concluding Unscientific Postscript*, ed. Howard V. Hong and Edna H. Hong (Princeton, 1992), p. 212.

26   *Ibid.*, p. 35n.

27   *Journals and Papers*, Vol. 3, eds. Howard V. Hong and Edna H. Hong (Bloomington, 1975), #3403, p. 558. Kierkegaard also writes: 'was it not a victory that instead of receiving an explanation from God he was transfigured in God, and his transfiguration is this: to reflect the image of God' (*Eighteen Upbuilding Discourses*, eds. Howard V. Hong and Edna H. Hong [Princeton, 1990], p. 400).

28   *The Anti-Christ*, trans. R.J. Hollingdale (New York, 1968), p. 170.

29   *Ecce Homo*, trans. Walter Kaufman (New York, 1989), §3, p. 218.

8
Free Will Defences and Foundationalism[1]

Ben Tilghman

There is a spectrum of responses to the problem of evil in the philosophy of religion that can be called generically the free will defence. Although the free will defence has been widely discussed, I want to show that there are aspects of the issue that lead to difficulties those discussions have not considered and that, when brought to light, suggest that the entire project of constructing a free will defence may be a questionable one. I shall try to show that there are three such difficulties. In the first place a free will defence demands a 'global' or transcendent judgement on the value of the world and the human condition that turns out to be a piece of unacceptable metaphysics. Second, it demands that we entertain the possibility of a world that contains only moral good and no moral evil, a possibility that no one has given a coherent account of, if they have tried to at all. Finally, it involves a questionable search for philosophical foundations to explain why the world is like it is. In addition, an examination of these difficulties can lead to a better understanding of just what the problem of evil is.

1

The problem of evil as philosophers have traditionally understood it arises out of the question of whether or not the following four propositions are logically inconsistent: (1) God is omnipotent; (2) God is omniscient; (3) God is infinitely benevolent; (4) There is evil. Hume's presentation of the problem through his character Philo is well known.

> Epicurus's old questions are yet unanswered. Is he willing to prevent evil, but not able? then he is impotent. Is he able, but not willing? then he is malevolent. Is he both able and willing? whence then is evil?[2]

When Philo suggests that God may be unable to prevent evil, we must suppose this to question his knowledge of how to do it as well as his power to do it. What Philo says is, of course, but one part of his general challenge to Cleanthes to make sense out of the whole business of natural theology, an enterprise that Philo clearly believes is misbegotten from the beginning.

St Augustine raises the same difficulties in several places. He argues that since God is good, everything he creates must be good. If, as one hypothesis has it, there was something evil in the matter from which the world was created, then surely God's omnipotence could have overcome it. In his *Confessions* he asks, 'Where then does evil come from, if God made all things and, because he is good, made them good too?'[3]

There is a tension in the treatment of the problem of evil between a purely intellectual or logical motivation on the one hand, and a religious motivation on the other. The spirit in which Augustine struggles with the problem, for example, is very different from either the 'careless scepticism' with which Philo approaches the issue or the 'accurate philosophical turn' with which Cleanthes tries to explain things. What we might call an accurate scepticism in approaching the problem is presented by J.L. Mackie when he said that the problem of evil is

> a logical problem, the problem of clarifying and reconciling a number of beliefs: it is not a scientific problem that might be solved by further observations, or a practical problem that might be solved by a decision or an action.[4]

John Hick, by contrast, makes clear that the religious motivation is uppermost in his discussion of evil. He says that 'The setting within which the subject is to be treated is, quite explicitly, that of Christian faith.'[5] In the same passage he adds that to the non-believer the problem is a major obstacle to religious commitment while to the believer 'it sets up an acute internal tension to disturb his faith and to lay upon it a perpetual burden of doubt'.

Augustine's work manifests both motivations. In the first place there are the struggles with his own sins which he described in *Confessions* that provide a religious background to his thought, struggles that ran much more deeply into his life than anything that is apparent in the conversation between Hume's characters, where there is little if any reflection of a religious life underlying the arguments. In the second place there is his ongoing project of refuting the theories of Manichaeism by means of the philosophical theory he adapted from neo-Platonism and it comes to dominate his writing on evil and free will. While Augustine no doubt begins from genuine religious concerns the end-result is metaphysical theorizing.

Some philosophers – Hume's Philo, for example – have wanted to use the apparent inconsistencies that get the traditional problem going to show either that God is not what he is usually thought to be or that he does not exist at all. Others have claimed that the propositions are not inconsistent and then have sought to give an account of evil that does not put the blame for it on God's doorstep. Augustine, of course, is one of these latter.

2

It is traditional to distinguish moral evil from natural evil. While the free will defence is concerned altogether with the former, the questions it raises run over into the latter. Moral evil is the result of human choice, but since God created human beings with the ability to make choices – too often, unfortunately, the wrong ones – it can be argued that God is indeed responsible for evil. Mackie has put this charge most forcefully:

> if God has made men such that in their free choices they sometimes prefer what is good and sometimes what is evil, why could he not have made men such that they always choose the good? If there is no logical impossibility in man's freely choosing the good on one, or on several, occasions, there cannot be a logical impossibility in his freely choosing the good on every occasion. There was open to him the obviously better possibility of making beings who would act freely but always go right.[6]

In its narrowest form the free will defence undertakes to show that there is no logical inconsistency between the propositions describing the traditional attributes of God and the proposition that evil exists.[7] More broadly, it is a defence of God intended to relieve him of culpability for creating evil in general.

Augustine sets out to defend God in this way. In the first place he says that evil is not a substance, that is, it is not a thing that God created. If God had created it, it would, by definition, be good and not evil. Evil is the result of man's free choice. God gave men free will, but too often men misuse what God has given them. Evil resulting from sin is a perversion of the will. The obvious question to raise about this solution is put to Augustine by Evodius in his dialogue on free will. Evodius agrees with him that evil comes from the free choice of the will:

> But now I am asking whether He who created us should have given us that very freedom of choice by which it has been shown we have the power to sin. For, without this power, we apparently would not have been capable of sinning, and there is reason to fear that God will be adjudged the cause even of our evil deeds.[8]

Augustine's task is now to explain why God created men with free will prone to perversion rather than creating creatures that could never sin. Augustine's strategy is to show free will is a good thing and that it is better for men to have it than not to have it. He argues in terms of an analogy. Just as men can use their free will to do bad things, people can use their hands and feet to do bad things. It is obvious, however, that someone who lacked hands or feet would most unfortunately be deprived of good things. In like manner, one who lacked free will would be lacking a good thing. The fact that free will can be misused is no more objection to its goodness than is the fact that hands and feet can be misused.[9]

We can certainly agree that anyone who lacks hands or feet is to be pitied. By contrast with the ordinary person there are so many things that he or she cannot do or do only with the greatest difficulty. Our judgement that such a person suffers from physical defects or handicaps is made from the point of view of the normal human physical condition and its location in the context of the usual activities of life. What then is the nature of the defect or handicap suffered by the person lacking free will? What is the point of comparison from which a judgement about it is to be made?

We may think we can begin with the example of someone who is brain-damaged or mad to the extent that he is incapable of looking after himself. He must be kept in an institution and constantly attended. Alternatively, we may imagine a prisoner who is not permitted to exercise choice in so many of the affairs of daily life as the rest of us do, with respect, say, when to come and go, what clothes to wear, what to have for dinner, when to have it, and so on. We can all agree that it is a bad thing to be mentally incompetent or locked up behind bars and that it is much better to be able to lead a normal life.

Augustine's analogy, however, may not do the job for him that he wishes. We understand physical deformity, mental deficiency and confinement – these more or less exceptional cases – to be bad by contrast with what we think of as the normal human condition. Augustine, let us note, does not want to judge the lack of free will bad by contrast with the normal human condition. He does not say that it is bad that this or that individual cannot exercise choice like the rest of us; he wants to ask whether it is good or bad that there is such a thing as free will at all. That is why the examples just mentioned are not to Augustine's point. His concern is, rather, with the entire human condition itself. The analogy with physical deformity is thus misleading. We agree that it is bad for an individual not to have hands or feet and then are invited to agree that it would be bad for the entire human race not to have free will. If we do respond to the invitation it is because we have not seen that the question has changed materially and is no longer a matter of 'in this or that case', but has taken on the kind of 'global' aspect that is characteristic of metaphysical theory and that change in the question wants examining.

Would Augustine also want to say that it would be bad for the entire human race not to have hands or feet? If this were our natural condition, as it is the natural condition of the snake or the fish, then obviously the race would not be the *human* race and we would all be some other kind of creature. (Could we then even speak of *we*?) John Hick makes a similar point with respect to free will with his remark that 'to say that God should not have created beings who might sin amounts to saying that God should not have created people'.[10] This point will be discussed in a later section.

There is an interesting similarity between the logic of Augustine's move and one of the ways that Cleanthes argues. This can be illuminating. Cleanthes claims that this world is a most excellent world and he wants to use that contention as evidence for God's existence and perfection: the creator of such an excellent product, he argues, must be the most excellent of craftsmen. Philo questions this contention by means of an analogy with a peasant who is asked to pass judgement on the excellence of the *Aeneid*. He makes it clear that a necessary condition for judging the value of a literary work is a reasonably wide acquaintance with other works of literature. The peasant, whom we assume to be altogether unlettered, has no such acquaintance and consequently has no basis whatsoever for assessing the value of Virgil or any other work of literature for that matter. In like manner, then, Philo urges, if we are to pronounce upon the value of this world (universe), we must have knowledge of other worlds and their possibilities. We have no such knowledge, of course, and thus can say nothing about the excellence, or lack of it, of this world.

Philo's objection is devastating for Cleanthes' position, but it leaves a question unanswered and is by no means the last word. Let us note that although the peasant cannot practise literary criticism, there are others who can. That the *Aeneid* is a good work is a perfectly intelligible proposition. Does Philo's position suggest that although *we* cannot practise world criticism, there may be *someone* who can? If that is so, then that this is a most excellent world is also an intelligible proposition. I would like to think that what Philo really ought to say is that the question about the excellence of the world has been given no sense and that what Cleanthes wants to say about it is not just beyond our reach, but is not even intelligible.

Here is the striking logical similarity between Augustine's thesis that free will is a good thing and Cleanthes' thesis that this is an excellent world. Augustine's thesis demands that we look at human life as a whole and from the outside, but that demand forces us to try to understand it in independence of any human context that could make such a judgement intelligible. Cleanthes' thesis demands that we do the same, only this time with respect to the world as a whole rather than just the human condition. Here again there is no context to make the thesis intelligible. What has happened in both instances is that the form of a question, in this case 'Is x good?', that has perfectly ordinary and intelligible instantiations in the stream of life, has been taken out of any context in which it can be understood and hence answered. What is left is language on holiday which exudes only the illusion of sense.

3

Alvin Plantinga has offered a version of the free will defence that begins with a contention remarkably similar to Augustine's. The position of the free will defender, he says, is that

> A world containing creatures who are sometimes significantly free (and freely perform more good than evil actions) is more valuable, all else being equal, than a world containing no free creatures at all.[11]

Once again we have what is essentially a metaphysical judgement about the world as a whole, only this time one that relies on the contemporary post-Leibnizian logical apparatus of possible worlds. Plantinga does not argue for the contention that a world containing freedom is more valuable than one that does not. What he does argue for, however, is the proposition that God can create a world containing creatures capable of moral good only if they are also capable of moral evil. In order to show that the existence of evil is compatible with God's goodness he must counter objections such as J.L. Mackie's that it is logically possible for God to have created a world in which men are free to choose, but always choose the good and never evil.[12] If this is possible and God did not create that world, then God is responsible for evil. His strategy for this counter is to employ the contemporary logician's mechanism of the logic of possible worlds and possible world semantics.

He constructs arguments to the conclusion that it is logically impossible for God to create (he prefers 'actualize') a possible world that contains only moral good and no moral evil. The arguments begin from particular examples that we all can understand, e.g. the mayor accepting a bribe, which are then generalized and expressed in terms of quantified variables. The difficulty with this procedure is that the language with which we describe a familiar situation is by the quantification made abstract and so removed from any context in which we understand how to apply it. What constitutes an instantiation of the variables remains obscure and, perforce, it remains obscure what application, if any, it has to our lives. All this play with possible worlds has a certain plausibility only as long as we think of our words merely as counters to be shuffled about in a logician's game. When we remind ourselves of the actual *use* of words in the stream of life, however, we must scratch our heads over just what the possible situations are to which Plantinga's logic is supposed to apply.

Although the logical mechanisms of possible worlds may simply pass by the problems about evil that have concerned so many, there remains an issue that we can engage armed only with our common moral understanding. Plantinga's aim is to prove that God could not create a world containing only moral good and no moral evil. In order to follow Plantinga we must be able to give an account of such a world, otherwise we would have no idea what he is denying. Such a world is Mackie's world in which everyone always goes right. What is this world like? We understand what it is like for particular people in particular situations to go right. Examples are not wanting. A woman goes right when she pays her debts; an industrialist goes right when he ensures safe working conditions for his workers; a government official goes right when he refuses to accept a bribe. Whether we understand what it is for *everyone always* to go right is, however, quite a different question.[13]

An interesting feature of the examples just mentioned is that each presupposes a background of social and economic practices and institutions. Debts can be paid where money can be borrowed, goods put in pledge to be redeemed or forfeited, and so on. Fair working practices presuppose systems of industrial production and market economies, but such systems seem to have inherent injustices which one does not need to be a Marxist to recognize. Even the most honest of government officials are in the service of institutions which are by their nature coercive. The temptation may be to think of the best of all possible worlds as comprised of a large number of essentially isolated deeds, each of which is right or good in itself. This, however, cannot be right. All our actions take place against the context of complex networks of human relations. We can praise this or that good deed, but can we praise the social institution which makes it possible? While it was fitting and proper for the factory owner to install clean washroom facilities in the plant, there is still the factory system.

These considerations strongly suggest that a world in which everyone always goes right would have to be a world in which the complex web of human relations that underlie our particular actions is very different from the world we know. Would there be industrial production, governments, money and finance? Augustine would have it that this world is the world before the fall when humankind dwelt in the Earthly Paradise undisrupted by temptation. In *The City of God* he makes an essay at providing a description of this world. Our first parents 'were agitated by no mental perturbations, and annoyed by no bodily discomforts'. There was neither heat nor cold. It was a paradise that provided both spiritual and physical enjoyment. 'No languor made their leisure wearisome'; procreation occurred without passion and apparently without defloration and childbirth was painless, 'For though he could not do all things in Paradise before he sinned, yet he wished to do what he could do, and therefore he could do all things he wished'.[14] It is significant that we are given no hint in any of this of what he wished to do. What was daily life like then? Was there any economic basis for life there? Was it all leisure and no work? Did fish jump from the lake into the frying pan? Was no one ever bored or frustrated by not getting anything done? There is still no description of the situation that does the job that needs to be done.

Some further hints about that world may be gleaned from a curious ancient document, although it is one that puts rather a different slant on things and may not help Augustine's cause. A part of it is excerpted below.

He said that Adam and Eve weren't real names at all and that they preferred to call themselves Morris and Rosalie. Morris said that in those days the lion did indeed lie down with the lamb. He knew that the lamb ate grass, but he was never sure what the lion ate. Whenever Rosalie made blintzes she always gave one to the lion, but he didn't think he really liked it and only ate it out of politeness. From time to time the lion tried to talk to them about it, but they couldn't understand him.

Morris reported that the fruit of the tree of knowledge was a real eye opener. He was aware that he never had what you would call an upbringing and it was the fruit that gave him values, including family values. He was skeptical about the tree of life business and suspected it may have been simply an excuse to get rid of them. At any rate, Morris believed that getting run out of that place was the best thing that ever happened to him. He had to find a job and make something of himself, not to mention the fact that evenings with Rosalie became much more fun. When asked if he would ever like to go back he said maybe for a few days of vacation, but that he soon gets bored with that kind of lotus eating and would be eager to get back to work.[15]

Augustine's incomplete sketch of Prelapsaria is hardly one we can take seriously and it is curious that recent thinkers have never seen the necessity of asking the question about that better world. Until some details are forthcoming, however, we have no idea what the possibility is that Mackie thinks God should have created – if the Author of Nature is to live up to his reputation – nor have we any idea of what the possibility is that Plantinga argues God could not have created.

Plantinga believes that he has solved the problem of evil to the extent that he has shown that there is no logical inconsistency between the propositions describing the traditional attributes of God and the proposition that evil exists. So far he is one with Mackie in thinking of the problem as a logical problem of clarifying and reconciling a number of beliefs. He does add, however, that a person may find a *religious* problem in evil:

Faced with great personal suffering or misfortune, he may be tempted to rebel against God, to shake his fist in God's face, to curse God. He may despair of God's goodness, or even give up belief in God altogether. But this is a problem of a different dimension. Such a problem calls for pastoral rather than philosophical counsel.[16]

We may well ask whether Plantinga's logical excursions have given us any philosophical counsel. I would like to think that the true philosophical question may lie in getting clear about the nature of the problem of evil itself rather than in the details of some proposed solution. Is it indeed a problem that can be solved by a proof in one or another logical system or is it rather a religious question that arises out of the experiences of one's life? The tension in the understanding of the problem is still there.

4

A philosophically more interesting approach to the problem of evil is taken by John Hick. Hick's aim is to construct a theodicy developed out of the Irenaean tradition which he contrasts with the tradition stemming from Augustine. The Augustinian tradition understands the perfection of man to lie in the prelapsarian past. It was, of course, the exercise of man's God-given free will that allowed sin to enter the world and the original state of perfection to be lost. The Irenaean tradition, on the other hand, understands perfection to lie in the future. In answer to the question why men should have free will, the Augustinian says that a world with free will is better than one without it. The Irenaean argues that the exercise of free will is necessary for us to develop into more perfect human beings.

Hick defends the very idea of a theodicy against those who suppose it 'to represent a foolish pretension of the human creature, under the illusion that he can judge God's acts by human standards'.[17] He suggests that if it is thought impious to try to *justify* God's ways, that does not entail that we should understand God's ways. He poses the rhetorical question, 'Is it impious to try to understand God's dealing with mankind?'[18] At this point we must pause to ask what form this understanding is to take. Is it the kind of understanding we seek of someone's actions as when we want to know why he trumped his partner's ace? Is it some kind of theoretical understanding that seeks to map logical connections between the relevant concepts of God, evil, suffering, and so on? Or is it some kind of religious understanding that is available only to a knight of faith? We shall return to this question.

Hick describes his position as a 'soul-making' theodicy. If people are to reach a stage of perfection, it must be through life in the world and its consequent struggle with evil. He puts it this way:

> and so man, created as a personal being in the image of God, is only the raw material for a further and more difficult stage of God's creative work. It is the leading of men as relatively free and autonomous persons, through their own dealings with life in the world in which he has placed them, towards that quality of personal existence that is the finite likeness of God. The features of this likeness are revealed in the person of Christ....[19]

Although Hick's Christian conception of the completion of the soul-making process and the achievement of perfection requires an afterlife, that aspect of his view shall not concern us. It is this life that is in question. God, it is claimed, wishes us to achieve the finite likeness of himself and since this likeness is defined for us by Christ, our lives should presumably be led in the imitation of Christ. Here is a problem.

What is it to imitate Christ? At the very least it surely involves compassion and loving one's neighbour as oneself. Thomas à Kempis, for one, makes much of the role of humility in the imitation of Christ. But what else? It more than likely does not involve withering fig trees, and most of us would assume it unprofitable to try the water into wine trick or the loaves and fishes *shtick*. At one point Jesus told us to render unto Caesar what is Caesar's. I suppose he meant that we should pay our taxes and obey the laws in general. Are we to do this despite our knowledge that the taxes are unjust and the enforcement of the law corrupt? We also want to know what he would have said to Caesar himself had the opportunity been presented. Would he have told Caesar to be rendered unto? To reform the tax laws? To do away with the entire governmental structure? Thomas à Kempis says that in patterning one's life after Christ it is more beneficial to live in subjection than in authority and that to obey is safer than to command.[20] Such a remark suggests that Christians are to leave power structures unchanged and even avoid positions of responsibility that could effect reforms. Such advice does not sit well today. There is here a problem analogous to the one about Mackie's and Plantinga's possible world containing only moral goodness. So many of the necessary details are lacking. Jesus did not address all the contingencies of life and there still remain all those issues about the institutional backgrounds to our actions that the remarks about Caesar are intended to call attention to. If ultimate perfection is to be achieved only in an afterlife, then, whatever that condition is, that life must be radically different from anything we know and more than likely will not include governmental or economic arrangements, even kinder and gentler ones. The afterlife aside, we are still in the dark about what it would be to achieve that degree of perfection possible in this world.

I do not want to leave the impression that the imitation of Christ is a useless or unintelligible notion for it has an essential role to play in the life of Christians. When faced with difficult choices Christians are frequently enjoined to consider what Jesus would have done in similar circumstances and the result can be that compassion is shown in this case, righteous indignation in this other and humility in a third. The important thing to notice is that it is usually some particular aspect of the life and teachings of Christ that is appealed to in some particular circumstance. In its general form the injunction to imitate Christ is empty until cashed in terms of particulars and for this reason I do not think that Hick's reference to Christ can play a role in a solution to any theoretical problem including any philosophical version of the problem of evil.

In the passage quoted above in which Hick describes his theodicy of soul-making, one sentence begins, 'It is the leading of men as relatively free and autonomous persons, *through their own dealings with life in the world* in which he has placed them . . . ' That is, God has given men free will and put them to dealing with the vicissitudes of life in the world that he has created. The phrase I have emphasized suggests very strongly that the notion of free will carries with it the entirety of human life, the full gamut of our moral, social and personal life. We might put this by saying that the expression 'free will' is the general heading under which is subsumed the entire catalogue of the language we use to describe human beings and their thoughts, feelings and doings. The existence of free will is then presumably the ground that makes intelligible the description of actions as right or wrong, of people as good or bad, that makes intelligible praise and remonstration, and, in a word, the application of all the concepts that we use to describe ourselves and our doings, whether of the greatest moral import or trivially mundane. The force of the remark is one with his comment quoted earlier that if God had created beings incapable of sinning, that is, without free will, they would not be people.

The problem of evil starts with the question of why there should be evil. The answer to that question is because there is free will. We have just seen, however, that talk of free will is equivalent to talk of people. So it seems that the question why there should be evil turns out to be the question why there should be people. This latter is clearly not a scientific question about the biological and evolutionary development of a particular species. One way of taking it, I think, is as a question about both concepts and the form of life that underlies the concepts. Why should there be concepts of action, reasons, responsibility, feelings and all the rest? Why should there be the form of life in which people laugh, cry and react in all the ways that give these concepts application? The free will defence does not recognize the conceptual aspect of the question, but treats it as if it is a factual question about what God wants.

The appeal to how God wants things cannot offer a theoretical answer to the question, for no matter how the world is the believer has to say that is how God wanted it to be. Theoretically, that is empty. Furthermore, the appeal to God seems to be only another version of foundationalism that seeks to explain a form of life and justify the language games that rest upon it. That such a search for foundations is misbegotten does not need to be argued for here. That we are God's creatures is, nevertheless, at the centre of any religious view of the question. To that religious aspect we shall now turn.

5

We have seen that there is a tension in the way the problem of evil is understood between those who take it as essentially a logical or theoretical one and those for whom it is a pressing problem in their religious lives. The problem of evil presupposes a religious perspective. For the non-religious person the problem does not exist. For him the pain and suffering resulting from the wrongdoing of people and the natural ills visited upon life are just part of how the world is. There is no God for anything to be reconciled with. If there is a problem for such people it is simply how to live with and make the best of what are often bad situations.

Peter De Vries, in his novel *The Blood of the Lamb*, provides an example of doing what one can in a bad situation. The narrator is the product of a strict Dutch Calvinist upbringing who early in life had begun to question his family's beliefs. The death of his wife and his daughter's leukaemia, which would claim her life at the age of twelve, led to some revival of religious inclinations. These inclinations, however, did not outlast the hope of a cure, and the death of his daughter produced a final rejection of all religious belief. He reflected on something he had written earlier in his life when he said that we must learn to live without religious consolations. His eventual realization of what that kind of living is comes out in the concluding lines of the book:

> Time heals nothing – which should make us the better able to minister. There may be griefs beyond the reach of solace, but none worthy of the name that does not set free the springs of sympathy. Blessed are they that comfort, for they too have mourned, may be more likely the human truth. . . . Again the throb of compassion rather than the breath of consolation: the recognition of how long, how long is the mourner's bench upon which we sit, arms linked in undeluded friendship, all of us, brief links, ourselves, in the eternal pity.

I will assert it without argument that one's religion is shown more in how one lives one's life than in how one constructs theoretically consistent accounts of God and his relation to the world. If the problem of evil is a serious one, it is because it arises out of one's religious life. It is Job who instructs us in this. Why should I suffer, cries Job, when I have been righteous and God has promised that the righteous will prosper? Job never poses his problem in terms of the consistency of a set of propositions. The problem arises out of his afflictions. Plantinga can offer no help to Job – nor, we might add, can pastoral counselling.

Hick's theodicy seeks not to *justify* the ways of God to men, but to *understand* God in his relation to the world. We are now in a position to say something about the nature of that understanding. The theodicy would appear to offer us something like a theory about God and his purposes, but that appearance, I suggest, is misleading. Hick writes movingly of the problem of evil and how it arises out of the tension between the facts of human suffering and religious faith. He says that the task of theodicy is one of 'faith seeking understanding', seeking in this case an understanding of the grounds of its own practical victory in the face of the harsh facts of evil. . . . It cannot profess to create faith, but only preserve an already existing faith from being overcome by this dark mystery.[21]

If the problem of evil is, indeed, one that arises out of a religious life, an already existing faith, then the only relevant solution to it must be a religious one, and Hick is offering a religious solution. His position, that it is through the experience of evil and suffering that souls are made, should not be confused with the familiar view that one is sometimes made a better and stronger person by suffering. That is no doubt true, but it can remind us of Mark Twain's account of the chap who was run out of town on a rail. That unfortunate fellow was reported to have remarked that had it not been for the honour of the thing he had rather walked. A man who has been falsely imprisoned and tortured may indeed have learned something about suffering and fortitude and may even emerge from his ordeal a stronger person. Should he be reminded at the end of it all of what he has learned and how he is a better person for it, we can imagine him being quite willing to have traded the improvement for the tuition.

This person need not recognize anything of religious significance in what he went through. Hick's position, by contrast, is that the point of the suffering is not to make one a 'better person' in some secular sense, but to bring one closer to God. It follows that Hick's solution to the problem of evil cannot be a philosophical or in any way a theoretical solution whose merits could be understood and debated by any intelligent educated person. It is a 'solution' that can operate only in the course of the lives of individuals. It demands a view of the world and a way of living in the light of that view that can be held only by Christians. Whether all Christians would find it compelling is another question. If Plantinga could give no solace to Job, neither could Hick, but for a different reason.

Mackie has denied that the problem of evil is a practical one that might be solved by a decision or an action, but I have represented it to be a practical problem, that is, a problem that arises in the lives of many religious people. Mackie's denial may be the result of holding far too narrow a view of decisions and actions. What he says suggests that one might suppose the problem of evil could be solved by a single decision or action unconnected with anything else. Actions, as insisted all along, must be understood against the contexts of appropriate backgrounds. In the case of religious decisions and actions, that background is one's entire life as lived in accordance with a religious view of the world.

We find an example of this in C.S. Lewis's account of a crucial episode in his life.[22] Lewis's wife died of cancer and, like De Vries's narrator, he had to face the loss and the resulting grief that was to be his for the rest of his life. Unlike De Vries's character Lewis was, and continued to be, a deeply religious person. His grief occasioned all the familiar questions about God and his goodness and there is a temptation to say with Hick that it set up 'an acute internal tension to disturb his faith and to lay upon it a perpetual burden of doubt'. There is no question about its disturbing his faith, but it laid upon it no *perpetual* burden of doubt. And, also in contrast to Hick, there is no theodicy, not even an incipient one, to provide an understanding of what God is up to. Lewis says:

> When I lay these questions before God I get no answer. But a rather special sort of 'No answer'. It is not the locked door. It is more like a silent, certainly not uncompassionate, gaze. As though He shook his head not in refusal but waiving the question. Like, 'Peace, child; you don't understand.'[23]

He adds this:

> Heaven will solve our problems, but not, I think, by showing us subtle reconciliations between all our apparently contradictory notions. The notions will all be knocked from under our feet. We shall see that there never was any problem.[24]

There is no logical problem of evil to be solved by some kind of theory. It is, however, surprising to find him saying, 'And now that I come to think of it, there's no practical problem before me at all' for I have all along been representing the problem as a practical one. What he has in mind, I think, comes out in the next sentence: 'I know the two great commandments, and I better get on with them . . .'[25] There is no practical problem in the sense of some particular thing that one can do or some course of action that can be followed that will make things come out right or at least improve the situation. It is rather a matter of looking on the world and of getting on with one's life in the way that the religious person would describe as loving God with all one's heart and keeping his commandments.

I have argued that free will defence entails three difficulties: it demands that we entertain an idea of an ideal world free of evil, but of which no description is ever forthcoming; it demands a judgement about the value of the world as a whole in the absence of any context or criteria that could make the judgement intelligible; and, finally, it involves an unacceptable demand for foundations. If the responses to suffering that I have reviewed, whether the deeply Christian response of C.S. Lewis or the response of a Christianity rejected, exhibited by Peter De Vries's character, are taken seriously, then we are prompted to believe that there is something amiss in the traditional and familiar formulations of the problem of evil. The problem with the problem of evil goes quite beyond the adequacy of any of its proposed solutions. The problem arises out of religious belief and religious life, but the philosopher misrepresents the problem by making it a theoretical one rather than one about how life is to be lived. The philosopher's language has here gone on holiday and his problem is simply irrelevant to what really matters.

Kansas State University

Notes

1 I am indebted to Robert T. Herbert for a number of criticisms and helpful suggestions.
2 David Hume, *Dialogues Concerning Natural Religion* (New York: Bobbs-Merrill, 1947), Part X.
3 Saint Augustine, *Confessions*, trans. R.S. Pine-Coffin (Harmondsworth: Penguin Books, 1961), VII, 5.
4 J.L. Mackie, 'Evil and Omnipotence', *Mind* (April 1955), p. 200.
5 John Hick, *Evil and the God of Love* (New York: Harper and Row, 1966), p. 3.
6 *Op. cit.*, p. 209.
7 This is the way it is understood by Alvin Plantinga, *The Nature of Necessity* (Oxford: Clarendon Press, 1974), p. 165.
8 Saint Augustine, *De libero arbitrio* (Free Choice of the Will), trans. Robert R. Russell (Washington: Catholic University of America Press, 1968), Bk I, ch. 16.
9 *Ibid.*, II, ch. 18.
10 *Philosophy of Religion*, third edition (Englewood Cliffs: Prentice-Hall, 1983), p. 41.
11 *The Nature of Necessity*, p. 168.
12 'Evil and Omnipotence', p. 209.
13 Anthony Kenny seems to have acknowledged something of this difficulty when he says: 'A material world of precarious competition is the only world of which we have experience, and our imaginations are too feeble for us to be sure whether other forms of world are genuinely conceivable.' In 'The Argument from Design and the Problem of Evil', in *What is Faith?* (Oxford: Oxford University Press, 1992), p. 82.
14 *City of God*, trans. Marcus Dods (New York: Random House, 1950). These remarks are scattered through XIV, 10–26.
15 The provenance of this document is obscure and its whereabouts is now unknown.
16 *The Nature of Necessity*, p. 195.
17 *Op. cit.*, p. 6.
18 *Ibid.*, p. 7.
19 *Ibid.*, p. 290.
20 Thomas à Kempis, *The Imitation of Christ*, trans. Leo Sherley-Price (Harmondsworth: Penguin Books, 1952), I, p. ix.
21 *Evil and the God of Love*, p. 280.
22 C.S. Lewis, *A Grief Observed* (Greenwich, Conn.: The Seabury Press, 1963), pp. 54–5. The book was published under the pseudonym, N.W. Clerk.
23 *Ibid.*
24 *Ibid.*, pp. 55–6.
25 *Ibid.*

9
Lessing and the Resurrection

Peter Winch

> *Der ehrliche religiöse Denker ist wie em Seiltänzer. Er geht, dem Anscheine nach, beinahe nur auf der Luft. Sein Boden ist der schmalste, der sich denken läßt. Und doch läßt sich auf ihm wirklich gehen.*
>
> [An honest religious thinker is like a tightrope walker. He almost looks as though he were walking on nothing but air. His support is the slenderest imaginable. And yet it really is possible to walk on it.[1]]

Heinrich Heine, in a wonderful image that James Conant drew to my attention, says of Lessing's opponents (or should I say victims) in the celebrated Wolfenbuttel controversy, that they would have been lost to history but for Lessing's polemics against them, and have been preserved in Lessing's own contributions to the controversy, *like insects trapped in a piece of amber.*[2] The chief of these transfigured 'insects' is Hauptpastor Goeze of Hamburg, who had argued passionately against Lessing that the Bible, and more particularly the Gospels, are the sole authoritative source of Christianity. Just about the only thesis of Lessing's that Goeze correctly identified was a denial of this claim. He had developed this denial in a number of independent writings, for instance *Die Erziehung des Menschengeschlechts* (The Education of the Human Race) and *Axiomata*, but the issue was brought to a head in the following way. In his capacity as ducal librarian at Wolfenbuttel Lessing published a number of fragments of an extensive manuscript written by Hermann Samuel Reimarus (whom Lessing did not name, but referred to as '*der Ungenannte*' [Anonymous]). These fragments vigorously attack the historical authenticity of the Gospels largely on the grounds of the inconsistencies between the narrations of the Resurrection offered, respectively, by the four Evangelists. On the basis of this *historical* point Reimarus had argued against the truth of the Christian religion, which he took to be founded on these narrations. Goeze took vigorous exception to practically everything in the fragments and his attack initiated a long and bitter polemical duel between him and Lessing who, in his capacity as publisher of the fragments, expressed substantial agreement with Reimarus' account of the inconsistencies between the Gospels, but disagreed both with his contention that these inconsistencies invalidated the claim of the Gospels to historical authenticity and also with his claim that to undermine this historical authenticity is effectively to refute Christianity's claim to religious truth.

In '*Eine Duplik*' Lessing points out that when we are dealing with secular history we would never think of concluding from the fact that different accounts of the same event were inconsistent, that the event never took place. He notes too that independent accounts of major events of such detail are nearly *always* inconsistent with each other at various points. Goeze's very different attitude to the Gospels is based on the belief that they were directly inspired by the Holy Ghost but, Lessing notes, this inference is justified only given a certain theory of what it *means* to speak of a text as being inspired by the Holy Ghost, and therefore betrays that what is at issue is not the credibility of the Resurrection but Goeze's own concept of '*Theopneustie*': 'Not the Gospel but his own dogmas'.[3]

This last point comes closer to the major philosophical issues that I want to identify and is, I think, also closely connected with the feature of Lessing's attitude to Reimarus's fragments that I have left till last, because it seems to me the most important. Both Reimarus and Goeze take it for granted that to question the historical authenticity of the New Testament is necessarily to question the *religious truth* of Christianity. Lessing denies this. This is a fact that Goeze never properly comes to terms with argumentatively.

In '*Eine Duplik*' Lessing reminds us that the new religion of Christianity, with faith in Christ's Resurrection as one of its main features, was founded on just such (inconsistent) accounts. How, he asks, should *our* conviction have a better foundation? His answer is that we have available the edifice that was subsequently built on that original conviction as the earliest Christians obviously could not have:

> What fool rummages inquisitively round the foundation of his house simply to assure himself of its soundness? . . . I know now that the foundation is sound with greater conviction than those who saw it being laid could have had.[4]

Lessing was a subtle man and it behoves us not unthinkingly to attribute to him here a crude pragmatism that was very much *not* his style. He is certainly not arguing that the subsequent historical success of Christianity is evidence for the historical truth of the Resurrection; nor even that the immense value of Christianity for humankind (which Lessing is here not questioning)[5] is evidence for this. His point is rather that there is a certain incommensurability between the question of Christianity's religious truth and any question about the historical accuracy of the Gospels. We can hope to answer the question about Christianity's religious truth only by *looking at the Christian religion itself*. Of course, an important part of what we shall need to look at will be the role of belief in the Resurrection within Christianity. How far, or in what ways, the methods of critical historiography throw light on that role must at this stage be an open question; it is one to which I shall be returning.

One central feature of Lessing's contention that the Bible is not the sole authoritative source of Christianity, besides being important in itself, is relevant to some of the matters I want to discuss. This is his emphasis on the *oral* tradition of religious teaching and preaching into which Jesus and his disciples were born, which formed the background of his teaching and of their reception of that teaching and which continues. Lessing speaks of the *regulae fidei* in this connection,[6] orally transmitted standards which, for instance, determined which writings became canonical, and the authenticity of which was and presumably is much more firmly established than that of the scriptures themselves. There is an underlying conceptual point here, not explicitly stated so much as implied – but quite clearly implied – namely, that only in the context of this oral tradition does it even make sense to speak of these writings as we do, to understand them as we do, for them to have the kind of religious authority that they do. The *regulae fidei* do not merely apply externally to what we do with the Gospels; they help to constitute the sense of the texts themselves. Hence, one might perhaps say, the *regulae fidei* bind together Christian readers of the Gospels with the Church Fathers who determined the canonical status of these writings, with the writers of the Gospels, with the participants in the events described therein, with the prophets whose words are 'fulfilled' in the happenings described, and with the religious communities which, historically, responded to and kept alive those prophecies. We are, as it were, bound together in a common community of understanding.

To the extent that Lessing is making points like these when he contends that the Bible, and in particular the New Testament, is not the sole foundation for Christianity, he seems to me quite right. However, he sometimes uses imagery that seems to me misleading and which *perhaps* at times misleads him. In *Axiomata* (II), for example, rejecting Goeze's contention that the 'historical' parts of the Gospels carry the same religious authority as do the 'prophetic' parts, he writes:

> Where is the proof that the prophetic message must be understood as containing all the historical message as well? Where is it? The historical message is the vehicle of the prophetic message. But a vehicle does not have to have, and is not permitted to have, the power and the nature belonging to the medication.[7]

This will deal with *some* issues: e.g. the inconsistencies between the various evangelists. But in other cases, which I shall be discussing, the historical and the prophetic are inextricably mixed up together and the image will not help.

Lessing calls the scriptural writings themselves a mere '*Schachtel*'[8] (packaging), whereas religious significance attaches only to the contents of the package. He does not speak in the same way of the preaching to which he (perhaps rightly) attaches such importance as a bearer of the Christian message. Perhaps this is because the same question has not been raised concerning the special authoritative status of a preacher's words. And perhaps because in talking, vaguely, about 'preaching' we are not making the sort of precise reference to a text as when we talk about 'the Gospels'. Hence we are less likely to think of the preaching which is being spoken of as consisting just of these and these words – a wider context is more explicitly presupposed.

But I think there is a good deal more to Lessing's position on this point. I will approach it by looking at an important exchange between him and Goeze concerning Axiom IX, which reads:

> Religion[9] is not true because the evangelists and apostles taught it; they taught it because it is true.[10]

To this Lessing quotes Goeze as objecting:

> For if the evangelists and apostles were men who were driven by the Holy Ghost in what they said and wrote, then the Christian religion is true, because the evangelists and apostles, or really God himself has taught it. The second sentence is just idle.

He replies:

> Well then! I must just heap one sin on the others and support one antithesis with another. What God teaches too is not true because God *wills* to teach it, but rather God teaches it because it is true.
>   Is the second sentence idle here too? – Well, as if we didn't know what a fancy conception of God's will these gentlemen construct! As if we didn't know that according to them God can will something simply because he wills it. And even that, understood in a certain way, could be said, so that I hardly know how I am to capture their nonsense in words.[11]

It may well be true that a good deal of nonsense about the will of God lies in the background to Goeze's remarks, but even so Lessing's concluding sentence betrays some embarrassment and, if we take the above exchange simply as it stands, it seems to me that Goeze's position has much to be said for it. To take – seriously to take – the Gospels as the word of God is to accept them as the truth. To cast doubt on their truth would be to cast doubt on their divine origin. This is *not* to say that the expressions 'the truth' and 'the word of God' mean the same, since a non-believer might take much of what is written in the Gospels as the truth without having any use for the expression 'the word of God': seriously using *this* expression involves, amongst much else, seriously using it in a lot of other contexts as well which would be alien to the non-believer.

It is evident that expressions like 'true' or 'the truth' are used very differently here from the way they are used, for example, in geometry. Lessing himself uses this analogy and, I think, is led astray by it. In Axiom X he speaks of the 'inner truth' of religion:

> The scriptures must be explained by reference to its (sc. religion's) inner truth and if it has no inner truth all the scriptures cannot give it any.

Where then are we to find the bearer of this inner truth? Lessing constructs a curious imaginary dialogue consisting of quotations from Goeze, devoted to this question, to which he replies; here is an extract:

> But where is he to get his knowledge of the inner truth of the Christian religion?
> I. Where is he to get it? From religion itself. That after all is why it is called *inner* truth; truth which needs no guarantee from outside.
> He. – 'except from the writings of the evangelists and apostles'
> I. What are we to take from them? The inner truth? or our historically first knowledge of this truth? The former would be as strange as if I had to regard a geometrical theorem as true not on account of its demonstration, but because it is in Euclid. That it is in Euclid can justifiably prejudice you in favour of its truth; to what extent you please. But it is one thing to believe it is the truth out of prejudice; and another thing to believe it on its own account. Perhaps both can in practice have the same result, but does that make them the same? – So is it just the historical knowledge of the inner truth that we draw simply and solely from the writings of the evangelists and apostles? But most Christians claim that there is another source of this historical knowledge: namely the oral tradition of the church. And it is anyway undeniable that the oral tradition was once its only source and that absolutely no time can be named when it has not just become the secondary source but has ceased altogether to be a source ... [12]

There is a subtle shifting to and fro between two different positions here. On the one hand, there is Lessing's conception of religion as consisting of 'universal truths of reason', which finds expression in the Euclid analogy; on the other hand, there is the emphasis on the oral traditions of the church. Where the analogy with Euclid goes wrong is inadvertently hinted at by

Lessing himself when he refers to the *demonstration* on the basis of which we accept a theorem. There is nothing plausibly corresponding to this in the case of a 'religious truth', such as 'Christ came into the world to save us from our sins'.[13] What we *do* have in this case are in the first instance the Gospels and beyond that the Messianic tradition and the writings of the prophets, as well as the teaching of the church and the various possibilities of *application* of the doctrine in the life of a believer. For a believer located in the centre of this context, the doctrine of the Atonement may indeed have the force of necessity in the sense that it is unthinkable for him or her to give it up. But here 'necessity' is not being used in the same way as it is when we speak of a geometrical theorem as necessarily true.[14]

Let me now return to the point that gave rise to this phase of the discussion: namely, Lessing's calling the scriptural writings a mere 'vehicle' or 'packaging' for the religion whose truth is in question. My question was, where are we to find this bearer of truth? – and I identified two suggestions Lessing gives in answer: one is that it is simply a product of pure reason; the other, that it is conveyed in the oral traditions of the Christian church. I have rejected (necessarily rather cursorily) the first alternative and I now want to examine the second.

A natural question to ask is: why should Lessing think that Christianity's *oral* traditions are in any different a logical position from its *written* traditions? We have already considered a partial answer to this: the oral traditions have a much broader temporal span than do the written traditions and the latter are not the *sole* source of Christianity. That having been said, though, and its importance recognized, it still remains problematic why, if writings are a mere packaging (*Schachtel*) for their content, the same should not be true of *spoken* words. That we have here much more extensive and more ancient packaging would not make it any the less packaging.

It is true that there are, in certain contexts, important differences in the impact made by the spoken and by the written word respectively. That the former involves a direct relation between human beings in a way lacking in the latter case with the influence of appearance, tone of voice, gesture, etc. may give it a much greater power to influence the listener. I say it *may*. But we must not forget that people differ enormously in what they respond to; and writing can have power too.

It may be objected with some justice that when Lessing speaks of the church's oral traditions he is not speaking merely of particular words uttered on particular occasions, but of a whole way of thinking and acting conveyed in these words. This seems particularly evident, for instance, in what he says about the *regulae fidei* in '*Nötige Antwort zu einer unnötigen Frage*'. However, the point is not developed and in any case would still hardly justify a radical distinction between the religious significance of spoken as against written words, since a written text has its existence and sense in the context of such *regulae fidei* no less than does, say, a particular sermon.

I believe that there *is* some obscurity concerning Lessing's position on this point and one which may be a sign of serious confusion. I want to pursue the point by looking more closely at his argument in *'Über den Beweis des Geistes und der Kraft'*.[15] The issue to which most of that article is devoted is the relation between historical and religious truths which, as we have already seen, Lessing thinks of in terms of a distinction between contingent statements about what happened in the past and necessary truths of reason. But the question with which Lessing approaches this issue here seems to me rather curious. Why is it that miracles and fulfilments of prophecies which we know of only by historical report do not have the same power over us as miracles and fulfilled prophecies that we experience ourselves? (Assuming that we do.) His answer to the question is not that which many would give, namely scepticism about the accuracy of the reports, doubts about whether what is reported really happened. Rather:

> What accounts for it is that this proof of spirit and power no longer possesses either spirit or power, but has declined into human testimony concerning spirit and power.

I call this a 'curious' way to approach the issue because, as far as getting from a merely contingent matter of fact to a religious truth is concerned, it seems to me that the same difficulties are involved whether one's starting point be an historical report or a personally witnessed event. It seems clear that the 'spirit and power' of which Lessing writes cannot be identified with the extraordinariness of a miraculous event or a fulfilled prophecy. Where one observer may be filled with religious awe, another may murmur 'Trickery!' or 'Black magic!'[16] Jesus himself, it may be remembered, warned his disciples against being taken in by such things.[17] Furthermore, a miracle need have nothing in that sense extraordinary about it. In 'The Enduring Chill', a story by Flannery O'Connor, the Holy Ghost appears to a sick man in the form of a creeping damp stain on the bedroom wall.[18] I may well myself be in doubt how to interpret something inexplicable that I have seen: what, if anything, is significant about it, what conclusions can be drawn, what built on it; and these are precisely the kinds of consideration which Lessing regards as ruling out mere historical accounts as having spirit and power.

Looking at the matter from the other side, it is not necessarily or even normally true that 'this proof of spirit and power' in *scriptural* form 'no longer possesses either spirit or power, but has declined into human testimony of spirit and power'. Words can have their own spirit and power, as Lessing himself almost concedes with regard to the spoken word, when he speaks of the importance of the oral traditions of preaching, etc., which lie behind Christianity and keep it alive. This is certainly not true only of the spoken word either: if, for instance, we complain about the spiritual aridity of modern translations of the Bible, we are complaining that they lack the spirit and the power that belongs, say, to the King James Version.

It seems to me that here Lessing is looking in the wrong direction. He says of historical accounts of miracles that they 'have to operate through a *medium* which robs them of all their power'. He is looking to the relation between the written text and the event reported (something like the packaging theory again!), when he would do better to look at the relation between the text and its readers. If we *do* now look in this latter direction, we may see that an account of an event may quite well make a greater impression on the reader or hearer than did the event itself. (The old joke about the elderly man who always turned to the obituary page of *The Times* first thing every morning to see if he was still alive trades on this point.) Felicitously, one of the notable gifts of the versatile honorary recipient of this volume, Dewi Phillips, also illustrates my point. Anyone who knows him even slightly has to be aware of his wonderful skill as a *raconteur*. I have myself more than once had the experience of hearing him tell a marvellously funny story of an incident we had taken part in together, which, at the time, had not struck me as especially funny at all. I do not mean that he falsified the incident: his words had the power to illuminate an aspect of it which had gone unnoticed by me (not in the sense that I had failed to notice any part of what had happened, of course). There seems no reason at all why something similar should not often be the case with the *religious* significance of an observed incident or fact, which is brought out only by a subsequent description or characterization.[19]

A very closely connected point of great importance is that for an observer too the way in which an event is *perceived* may depend heavily on the terms in which he or she *thinks* of it. To see an event as miraculous, or as the fulfilment of a prophecy, is to react to it in a certain way, a way that is expressive of the concepts in terms of which one confronts the event. These concepts are available to one in large part by virtue of what one has heard said, or has read (which may have possessed its own spirit and power), and the extent to which one has made it one's own.

More than this, the actions of active participants in an event themselves have the character they do by virtue of the agents' concepts they express:

> For even if it is true that moral acts considered in themselves, no matter how different the times at which, or the peoples among whom, they occur, always remain the same: still, the same acts do not always have the same designations, and it is unjust to give to any of them a designation other than that which it customarily had in its own times and amongst its own people.

Lessing makes this important point in relation to the accusation that Christ's Resurrection was engineered by the Apostles who robbed the grave and spirited away the body. I want to try to say a bit more about this. In the main it seems to me that Lessing's treatment of the issue is masterly, but there are also problems, problems which spring from the way he tries to distinguish between the 'prophetic' and the 'historical' in the Gospel stories, a distinction closely connected with his view that the scriptures are merely the 'packaging' of a religious, or prophetic, message (his idea being that the prophetic message is, as it were, embedded in, but cannot be identified with, the historical account). The following remark is from *Der Beweis des Geistes und der Kraft*:

> I willingly accept that Christ, against whose Resurrection I can make no historical objection of any importance, was on that account proclaimed to be the Son of God, and that his disciples regarded him as such on that account. For these truths, *being truths of one and the same class*, followed quite naturally the one from the other.[20]

But, he goes on, it is quite another matter for him to be asked on his own account to accept this religious doctrine, which is in conflict with all his 'metaphysical and moral' concepts concerning the divine.

What interests me here is the untroubled acceptance of the account of the Resurrection as *historical*. My problem lies not with accepting it as an historically *true* account, but with accepting it as an account which can be evaluated in the dimension of straightforward historical truth and falsity at all. As Lessing himself makes clear in the course of the same essay, treating a narrative as history involves making certain kinds of inference from it, asking certain kinds of questions concerning the evidence for it and concerning the details of what is supposed to have happened, being ready to try to deal with certain kinds of criticism of it, etc.

Now, after the end of the war in Europe in 1945, there were stories that Hitler had not died in the Berlin bunker, but escaped. Such stories, I imagine, were believed by few. Suppose the stories had taken a different form. Suppose that various members of Hitler's entourage circulated stories claiming that Hitler had indeed died in the bunker, but that some days later had come to life again and escaped to South America from which place he would eventually return and reinstate the Thousand-Year Reich. I will not be so rash as to claim that *no one* would have believed such a story since it is hard to set a limit to human lunacies, but still, I feel quite safe in saying that no serious historian would have regarded it as even worth investigating, and this not so much because of the story's improbability, as because of its unintelligibility. We may set on one side as uninteresting the possibility that Hitler was not really dead at all, but in a state of suspended animation from which he subsequently revived. If someone is dead then, as we all know, processes of decay set in almost immediately and many of these processes, after a few days, will certainly have gone so far that to speak of them as being 'reversed' would just make no physiological sense, etc. I need not go on. My point is that to accept a narrative as a (true or false) *historical* narrative is to accept certain constraints on what can and what cannot intelligibly go into it and the kinds of question which must, or which cannot, be asked about it.

It may be objected that we, living at the time and in the culture we do, will, partly because we know so much more,[21] want to ask questions which could not have occurred to those involved in these events two thousand years ago. To this I answer first that, be that as it may, *we now* have to discuss the matter according to our *own* notions of historicity if we want to be clear about what we think. Second, I answer that, as a corollary, those involved with the events at the time they occurred, if they were not in a position to ask such questions, clearly cannot be regarded as having been making historical claims in the sense in which *we* speak of such claims. If it is said further that, after all, many people living at that time *did* accept the claims that Jesus had risen from the dead, I reply that I am not denying this; nor of course am I denying that many – even more – people accept those claims today. The point is that these claims and this acceptance cannot be thought of as unproblematically *historical* in character. This is not of course to say that what it is claimed happened 'didn't *really* happen'; it is to say that the concept of what it is claimed really happened has, not an historical, but a religious, or what Lessing called a 'prophetic', character. A corollary of this is that any investigation of the *veracity* of such a claim will be different in kind.[22]

To pursue this further let us look at a curious incident related by Luke[23] as happening on the day of the Resurrection. Two of the disciples were travelling to a village called Emmaus, a few miles from Jerusalem, discussing the events of the last few days, when they were joined by Jesus; but 'their eyes were closed and they did not recognize him'. Jesus asked them to explain what they were talking about and they recounted the story of the crucifixion and of the stories that had been told that day by the women who had visited the tomb and found it empty, etc. In response Jesus upbraided them for their lack of understanding and expounded the passages in the prophets relating to the Messiah. When they reached Emmaus, Jesus made as if to leave them, but they persuaded him to stay. At supper, when Jesus blessed the bread, 'their eyes were opened' and they recognized who he was. At this point he vanished from their sight.

Let us try to look at this story with a cold, historical eye. Two men who had been taught by, had studied and prayed and worked with, Jesus over a period of many months, *did not recognize him* when he joined them and engaged them in deep and animated conversation. We are not even told that they were struck by any resemblance between the 'stranger' and Jesus. There seems to be no suggestion that he was in disguise; we cannot think of the incident as analogous to one of those stories in which Dr Watson fails to recognize his friend, that master of disguises, Sherlock Holmes. How can we harmonize such a story with what we understand human relationships to be like, with what is involved in being on intimate terms with someone, with recognizing, and failing to recognize, someone we know? The circumstance that Jesus had been crucified and had incontrovertibly died three days previously of course makes a difference; but what sort of difference does it make? One interpretation that – if the other surrounding circumstances had been different – might have had some plausibility would be that the two disciples' knowledge of Jesus' death and burial made them incapable of countenancing the possibility that he might be this fellow traveller. This however is ruled out by the fact that the disciples had already heard, and were indeed discussing, what the women who had visited the tomb earlier that day had reported. One might rather think that this would have made them more receptive to recognizing Jesus when he appeared to them on the road.

I repeat what I said earlier. The point of raising all these difficulties is not to cast doubt on the Gospel story, but to throw light on what kind of story it is. To ask these kinds of question, which would cry out to be asked if the context were a straightforwardly historical one, is precisely to miss the point of the story. To the question: what then is the point of the story? I could only point to what in fact is done with it in the religious context to which it belongs: to the Christian practice of commemorating the meeting on the road to Emmaus by asking a stranger into one's home to share a meal, to the kinds of sermon preached on this particular text, to the ways in which the scene has been variously represented in religious art, and so on.

Of course, to look on the story in this way is to reject the way Lessing distinguishes the 'prophetic' from the 'historical'. The narrative of what happened at Emmaus is not an historical 'vehicle' which carries a religious message; *it is itself the religious message*. As I have myself insisted, it is so only when considered in the wider religious context. But there is nothing suspect about this as it stands, since it is true of any kind of message that it is what it is only in so far as it is seen in the context to which it belongs.

What I have been saying about the Emmaus incident can be said about the story of the Resurrection as a whole. Consider Paul's First Epistle to the Corinthians 15, a passage frequently pointed to as a paradigm case of basing a religious doctrine on an alleged historical fact. Most of the time in this passage, however, he does not talk as though he is basing his preaching on an established fact: rather he insists that the Resurrection is an essential part of his (and the other Apostles') preaching, that this preaching is 'according to the scriptures', and that acceptance of it is essential to salvation.

1. Moreover brethren, I declare unto you the gospel which I preached unto you, which also ye have received, and wherein ye stand;
2. By which also ye are saved, if ye keep in memory what I preached unto you, unless ye have believed in vain.

3. For I delivered unto you first of all that which I also received, how that Christ died for our sins according to the scriptures:

4. And that he was buried, and that he rose again the third day according to the scriptures ...

There follows a passage which *might* be taken as an appeal to 'historical fact', in which Paul writes of the various occasions on which the risen Christ manifested himself to the Apostles and others. The passage is remarkable for its lack of harmony with the Gospel accounts in, amongst other things, including the statement that Christ appeared 'to more than five hundred brethren at once'.[24] It also includes, in the same breath as it were, Paul's own vision of Christ on the road to Damascus, which surely cannot be included in the same category, if only because it happened after Christ's ascension into heaven. Here too, the stress is not on historicity so much as on the fact that all this belongs to the preaching and acceptance of Christianity:

11. Therefore whether it were I or they, so we preach, and so ye believed.

12. Now if Christ be preached that he rose from the dead, how say some among you that there is no resurrection of the dead?

13. But if there be no resurrection of the dead, then is Christ not risen:

14. And if Christ be not risen, then is our preaching vain, and your faith is also vain.

15. Yea, and we are found false witnesses of God; because we have testified of God that he raised up Christ: whom he raised not up, if so be that the dead rise not.

16. For if the dead rise not, then is not Christ raised:

17. And if Christ be not raised, your faith is vain; ye are yet in your sins.

18. Then they also which are fallen asleep in Christ are perished.

19. If in this life only we have hope in Christ, we are of all men most miserable.

The argument here is not: 'You say there is no such thing as resurrection of the dead, but, since we know that Christ rose from the dead, you are wrong', but rather: 'You say there is no such thing as resurrection of the dead, but our religion requires belief in Christ's resurrection, and it is only through that belief that you can be saved from sin; so, since believing there is no resurrection of the dead entails not believing in Christ's resurrection, such a belief stands in the way of your being saved from sin.' The appeal to the Corinthians is not that they should accept the clear historical evidence but that they should do what is necessary to be saved from sin, viz., believe in Christ's resurrection. But, it seems to me, if this is to make sense, then the *concept* of Christ's resurrection cannot be an historical one and it *cannot make sense* to ask whether or not it is historically true that Christ rose from the dead. I say this because it really would not make sense to use an historical concept in the way Paul uses this one. It would make no sense to say to a despairing Nazi: 'Go on, believe that Hitler did not die in the bunker, but escaped to South America; you will feel much better for it' (as opposed to trying to cure him of his despair by convincing him by – good or bad – historical arguments that Hitler survived).

Furthermore, when Paul tries to explain how we should think of the resurrection of the dead, he responds to the likelihood that

> 35. Some man will say, How are the dead raised up? and with what body do they come?

When he asks this he does not speak in terms of reconstitution of bodily particles, etc., but in terms of a distinction between 'celestial bodies, and bodies terrestrial' which differ in 'glory'. The terrestrial body is characterized through its relationship with *sin*, whereas the celestial, or 'spiritual', body is purged of sin. I need hardly say that these are *religious* distinctions.

Pace Lessing, then, when we are speaking of the Resurrection of Christ, talk of not having any *historical* objections to accepting its occurrence is entirely out of place. As I put it before, the story of the Resurrection is not an historical vehicle for the religious message. It *is* the religious message. However, there is the possibility here of a serious misunderstanding of what I am saying. I am *not* saying that the Gospel story should not be taken as an account of what happened in Palestine two thousand or so years ago. Of course it is. But it is a *religious* account, not what we nowadays, with our understanding of historiography, would call an *historical* account.[25] With this point I come now to one of the most important *cruces* in the argument between Lessing and Goeze.

Goeze had accused Reimarus of claiming that the disciples had stolen the body of Jesus and hidden it and had said that critics of Christianity must not be allowed the freedom to calumniate those holy men of God, who were inspired by the Holy Spirit, '*als Dummkopfe, als Bösewichter, als Leichenräuber*' ('as fools, as villains, as grave robbers'). Lessing's initial response to this, though couched in passionately polemical terms, seems perhaps at first somewhat muted. 'Der Ungenannte' (i.e. Reimarus) did *not* say: 'Christ did not rise, but his disciples stole his corpse':

> It is not true that my anonymous writer says without qualification: 'Christ did not rise, but his disciples stole his body'. He did not accuse the apostles of this robbery, nor did he *want* to accuse them of it. He understood too well that he *could* not accuse them of it. For a suspicion, even a highly probable suspicion, is still a long way from being a proof.
> My anonymous writer simply says: this suspicion, which is not a product of his own brain, which comes out of the New Testament itself,[26] this suspicion is not so completely allayed or refuted by Matthew's narra-

tion of the guarding of the tomb that it does not continue to be *probable* and *plausible*;[27] in so far as said narration is not merely highly suspect in its own terms, but is also an *apax legomenon*, of a kind which in general deserves little historical credence and all the less so in this case, because even those who have the greatest interest in its being true have never had the confidence to appeal to it.[28]

I call this a 'muted' response since it does after all express considerable doubt about the credibility of the Gospel story, which is surely what Goeze was mainly objecting to in Reimarus. It is true that Lessing's response was hardly calculated to allay Goeze's indignation, but nevertheless it makes an extremely important, if obvious, logical point. I cannot intelligibly say: 'The Gospel story of the Resurrection was based on a conspiracy to deceive and is a tissue of lies as far as its basic claims are concerned, but I believe the story nevertheless.' This would look like a version of Moore's paradox: 'p is false, but I believe that p'. However, I *can* intelligibly say: 'The Gospel story is improbable and implausible, but nevertheless I believe it.' No doubt from the point of view of a 'pure' historian, such a response might be deemed unprofessional, but of course there are other interests than those of the pure historian and in the context of those other interests, there may be quite compelling considerations for accepting a particular story even when there are strong reasons for disbelieving it. Religious interests may quite well provide one such context. Moreover, a religious attitude is precisely characterized, not exactly by one's being willing to accept implausible stories, but by one's not in the first place asking the kinds of question which raise issues of plausibility.[29] I have pointed out earlier that Lessing himself emphasizes how the value someone attaches to Christianity may quite legitimately be taken as a reason for not raising sceptical questions about the scriptural accounts with which it is interwoven, but which are not its sole authoritative foundation. No doubt the use of the word 'true' in such a context differs in important respects from its use by a secular critical historian, but that does not make it any the less legitimate.

I think we have here a case of what Wittgenstein was referring to in the passage that stands as epigraph to this essay. Whereas Goeze's reading of Reimarus' charge would indeed leave no support for a 'serious religious thinker' to walk on, Lessing's *does* leave such support and, even if it is the slenderest imaginable, one can nevertheless walk on it. I use Wittgenstein's image of the tightrope walker here for the following reason. Speculations like those of Reimarus are an attempt to look behind the scriptural accounts with a view to discovering 'what really happened'. To think like this involves assuming, or at least suspecting, that the accounts in the Gospels do *not* recount what really happened; and this means that one is placing the two statements 'Christ rose from the dead on the third day' and 'Certain disciples removed Jesus' body from the tomb on the third day' on the same conceptual level, so that one must choose between them. It is pretty clear, I think, that this is how both Reimarus and Goeze saw the situation and that this is in large part the source of Goeze's indignation.

One apparently attractive way of putting the point that the two above statements are not on the same conceptual level is to say that the first, 'Christ rose from the dead on the third day', should not be taken as referring at all to anything that actually took place, but as having a figurative, purely spiritual significance, as a graphic way of teaching a religious lesson. This is a favourite route taken by contemporary liberal theologians. It excites hardly less indignation than Reimarus excited in Goeze amongst the less liberal religious opponents of such theologians.[30] I think there is some justification for this, since it seems to me that such a path involves a descent from the tightrope walked by the serious religious thinker. Wittgenstein himself seems to me, if not to descend from, at least to teeter dangerously on, the tightrope in the following remark (probably similar to one that seems to have upset Drury in a conversation with Wittgenstein):

> Queer as it sounds: The historical accounts of the Gospels might, historically speaking, be demonstrably false and yet belief would lose nothing by this: *not*, however, because it concerns 'universal truths of reason'! Rather because historical proof (the historical proof-game) is irrelevant to belief. This message (the Gospels) is seized on by men believingly (i.e. lovingly). *That* is the certainty characterizing this particular acceptance-as-true, not something else.
>
> A believer's relation to these messages is *neither* the relation to historical truth (probability), *nor yet* that to a theory consisting of 'truths of reason'. There is such a thing. – (We have quite different attitudes even to different species of what we call fiction!)[31]

While Wittgenstein is perfectly right to claim that a religious 'acceptance-as-true' is not the same as the acceptance of a historical truth, still, in the case of Christianity (perhaps) especially, a believer does typically believe *these things happened*. It is important, too, I think, that what is believed to have happened is located in 'historical' time and is not wildly at odds with what is accepted, on the basis of normal historical evidence, to have been happening at the time in question. However, the religious acceptance of, say, the life and passion of Christ, does not depend on the same sort of historical testing as does the acceptance of other occurrences. Furthermore, it *cannot* so depend, since it eventually involves events conceived in such a way that it is senseless to speak of 'historical testing' in the ordinary sense in their case, just because these concepts involve ignoring the constraints which have to be observed in such testing: constraints such as those involved in the idea of birth and death, to take two highly relevant examples. It is worth remembering here too that, religion apart, subjecting our beliefs about the past to rigorous historical testing is far from being the rule; most people, I imagine, have only a quite hazy idea of what is involved in such testing and cannot be said for that reason to be ignorant of the past. And even within the realm of what is recognized as history, there are wide variations between the kind of relation that exists between the historian's account and 'what happened'. Consider, for instance, Thucydides' imaginative reconstruction of the speech of Pericles. No one supposes this, or requires this, to have the same sort of relation to what Pericles actually said on the occasion, as would be the case with an official court reporter's transcript of the proceedings of a trial. Yet to say on that account that Thucydides' report is simply made up, a piece of fiction, would clearly be to miss the point. The way to assess *how much truth* there is in it lies in a different direction – which I will not try to specify further here. This means that if we want to understand what is being said, even here, there are *certain questions we must not ask*.

Something similar applies to the Gospel accounts of the Resurrection, although here there are difficulties of a different sort. While in the case of Pericles both what we accept and what we reject lie clearly in the realm of the historical, we cannot say the same in the case of the Resurrection. It makes sense to ask whether Pericles actually uttered those words, even though it is fruitless and even misleading for us to ask whether or not he did *if* we really want to evaluate Thucydides' story. But, I have suggested, it does not in the same way make sense to ask whether, 'as a matter of historical fact', Jesus of Nazareth died and then came to life again after three days. We just do not have the same sort of use for that latter expression as we have for the statement that someone remained in a coma for three days and then regained consciousness. In this sense, what is being rejected may be said 'not to lie in the realm of the historical'.

There is still considerable danger in putting the matter like this, since it sounds close to saying it has nothing to do with anything that really happened in the past. This would be quite wrong. What we have to understand is just that there is more than one way in which a text can relate to the past; and the concept of *what really happened* changes according to the kind of relation that is in question. Thus I cannot bring myself to say, with Lessing, that 'I have no historical objections' to the Resurrection. I have reservations concerning what is to be understood by the word 'historical' in this context – not doubts about 'whether it really happened'.

But perhaps more important than this loose fit, as it were, between a Christian's belief in the events described in the Gospels and what actually happened in the Middle East two millennia ago is this. What would damage the integrity of such a belief is not so much a demonstration of its historical falsity as the asking of such technical historical questions concerning it in the first place. It is a belief of a sort which *precludes* the asking of such questions. This suggests another way of looking at Goeze's indignation, which was perhaps directed less at Reimarus' actual claims as at his impiety in asking such questions in the first place. At least, if he had phrased his attack in such terms, I think he could have made a stronger case.

This having been said, let me return to Lessing. He argues[32] that even if Reimarus had gone further than he actually did and argued that it is not a merely plausible hypothesis that the Apostles removed the body of Jesus from the tomb, but that this is actually what happened:

> I am all the same still sure that he would have refrained from calling these men, through whom nevertheless so much untold good has come into the world, a judgement with which he himself does not disagree, that he, I say, would have refrained from calling these so cherished men, by the disgraceful names of deceivers, villains, grave-robbers, which come so easily to the chief pastor's lips.

Not for the first time there is considerably more to what Lessing is saying here than first meets the inattentive eye. His point is not that consideration of the good brought about by the Apostles should make us charitably blind to their villainies, but that to describe them thus would actually be to go too far (*ihnen zu viel damit geschahe*), would be a sort of mistake. Then comes the following remarkable pronouncement (already cited):

> For even if it is true that moral acts considered in themselves, no matter how different the times at which, or the peoples among whom, they occur, always remain the same still, the same acts do not always have the same designations, and it is unjust to give to any of them a designation other than that which it customarily had in its own times and among its own people.

Lessing's ironical economy of expression again makes it easy to miss his point, which we have to *work* for. It might be thought, for instance, that he is making no more than *a verbal* point here, a distinction between what actions are 'in themselves' and the different ways in which they are described in different cultural contexts. But at this point it is important to remember, first, that 'what an action is in itself' is not independent of how the agent understands it; and how the agent understands it, is conditioned by the ways of describing actions current in the contemporary culture. It is important to remember, second, how imbued is the New Testament with the idea of fulfilment of the words of the prophets.[33] This idea goes naturally with the duty of acting in accordance with, or in fulfilment of, the Law and with a strong sense of the ritualistic element in human life. (Some of the most important events in the New Testament are associated with ritual occasions: e.g. the Last Supper and Passover, the descent of the Holy Spirit and Whitsun.) It also seems entirely natural to suppose that there were occasions when Jesus' disciples would have acted *in order that* a prophecy might be fulfilled. One clear instance of this is the election of Matthew in fulfilment of a passage in the Psalms to fill the place left vacant by Judas's defection and suicide.[34]

Jesus prophesied his own resurrection on the third day. Can one not imagine some Apostles regarding themselves as having a divine mission to ensure that this prophecy should be fulfilled? Perhaps by removing the body from the tomb? (This could almost be regarded as part of a solemn religious ritual.) But not of course *only* by this means; it would have been a prelude to, even a necessary condition of, their fulfilling the duty to continue preaching what Jesus had taught them – which he had specifically commanded them to do. As to the stories of Jesus' various appearances subsequent to the Resurrection: must not these, according to my imaginative reconstruction of a possibility (which is of course all it is – not a hypothesis) be clear cases of lying or attempts to deceive? Not necessarily. I have already noted how Paul, in insisting on the importance of the Resurrection, laid most emphasis on showing how central to Christian preaching about the possibility of being saved from sin is the story of the Resurrection and how necessary to Christian belief is acceptance of this story. As I put it earlier: the story of the Resurrection is not an (external) foundation of the Christian message, but an integral part of that message. Furthermore, it can be confidently imagined that those in Jesus' immediate entourage were in exceptional psychic states[35] in those days, both on account of the Passion and Crucifixion themselves and also on account of the tremendous prophecies associated with them. It is not hard to think that they had strange experiences which they found it natural to describe in the terms we find in the Gospels. The Emmaus incident, in particular, sounds very much like such a case. And remember again that Paul found it quite natural to put his strange and impressive experience on the road to Damascus on the same level as the experiences of the Apostles and others who claimed to have seen Jesus on and after that third day.[36]

Prophecies are typically mysterious; i.e. what is prophesied is typically a mystery. Such mysteries have a great affinity with riddles.[37] Wittgenstein uses the word in connection with the inconsistent accounts of Jesus' life in the four Gospels:

> Kierkegaard writes: If Christianity were so easy and cosy, why should God in his Scriptures have set Heaven and Earth in motion and threatened *eternal* punishments? – Question: But in that case why is this Scripture so unclear? If we want to warn someone of a terrible danger, do we go about it by telling him a riddle whose solution will be the warning? – But who is to say that the Scripture really is unclear? Isn't it possible that it was essential in this case to 'tell a riddle'? And that, on the other hand, giving a more direct warning would necessarily have had the *wrong* effect?[38]

His remarks can be applied more widely. For instance, the concept of the Incarnation, of God becoming man, can be regarded as a riddle. To say this is to say, amongst other things, that what baffles us about it is not lack of an explanation. It is rather bafflement as to how it is to be understood at all, so that we really have no clear idea *where we should look* for an explanation. If we can grasp that this is the situation, we may see that to learn from the concept we need, not to *get rid* of the puzzle (which is what an explanation tries to do), but to contemplate it, 'attend to it' (to use Simone Weil's phrase). That is to say, for example, we need to attend to the context – or contexts – of its application. For examples of such serious attention I would point in the direction of certain painters (Piero della Francesca), composers (Bach) and religious writers (Simone Weil) who have concentrated on the importance of the notion for the religious life. I would *not* include speculations about the precise mechanism of, for example, the Virgin Mary's impregnation in the category of 'serious attention', since they seem to me rather to *distract* attention from what is seriously at issue.[39]

The prophecy of the Resurrection is a riddle if ever there was one. It is no good saying that it is intended to be taken as 'literally true' since, as I suggested earlier, we really have no clear idea of what 'literally true' could *mean* in this connection. (This, of course, creates a difficulty for the claim that the Apostles were trying to deceive, since we cannot give a coherent account of *what falsehood* they were supposed to be trying to make people believe.) It is characteristic of a riddle that its 'solution' (in so far as it has one) lies in a quite different direction – perhaps even in quite a different dimension – from that in which, for one reason or another, we are inclined to look. The Apostles were (and so saw themselves) participants in the historical unwinding of the riddle of the prophesied resurrection from the dead of the Messiah. This 'unwinding' did not provide a *solution* to the mystery, or riddle, of the prophecy, but *deepened* it. I do not intend, in saying this, to suggest that it was in any way a retrograde step; on the contrary, my point is that the deepening of a mystery is to be found in a deepening of the religious reflection it gives rise to. If it had a 'solution', that would put an end to the very reflection it is intended to provoke! The mystery has of course continued to absorb people. I have given some examples of what I would regard as serious reflection. I would also include the prayers of the seriously faithful. And I include the sceptical, ironical Lessing, who took what he was writing about seriously even if he was unable to make it his own. He diagnosed his own inability here as due to the incommensurability between contingent historical truths and necessary truths of reason. What I have tried to show is that the intellectual difficulty Lessing had in mind was not quite what he took it to be, though he came closer to characterizing it than most. But I also think that Kierkegaard was clearly right in arguing that the main difficulty he faced was not in the ordinary sense an intellectual one at all.[40]

Emeritus, King's College, London, and the University of Illinois, Champaign-Urbana[41]

Notes

1 Ludwig Wittgenstein, *Culture and Value*, ed. G.E. von Wright, trans. Peter Winch (Chicago: University of Chicago Press, 1980), p. 73.
2 'Indeed, polemics were our Lessing's joy and so he never reflected for long whether his opponent was really worthy of him. In this way his polemics simply snatched many names from the jaws of well earned oblivion. He caught many tiny little writers as if in a web of the wittiest mockery, the most exquisite humour, and they are preserved in Lessing's works for ever like insects trapped in a piece of amber.' Translated by the author from Heinrich Heine, *Religion und Philosophie in Deutschland, Samtliche Werke in Vier Banden, Band III: Schriften zu Literatur und Politik I* (Munchen: winkler Verlag, 1992).
3 *Eine Duplik*, Vol. 8, p. 513. All page references are to *Gotthold Ephraim Lessings Werke*, ed. Klaus Bohnen and Arno Schilsen (Frankfurt am Main: Deutscher Klassike Verlag, 1993). All translations are by the author.
4 *Ibid.*, p. 517.
5 For purposes of this argument I shall not question it here either.
6 See *Gotthold Ephraim Lessings notige Antwort auf eine sehr unnotige Frage des Herrn Hauptpastor Goeze im Hamburg*, Vol. 9, pp. 429–34.
7 *Ibid.*, p. 62f.
8 *Axiomata*, VIII, vol. 9, p. 73.
9 This could also be translated 'the religion' (i.e. Christianity). The ambiguity is significant. It springs from the deistic element in Lessing's thinking: religions in general are expositions of certain 'universal truths of reason'.
10 *Ibid.*, p. 77.
11 *Ibid.*, p. 78.
12 *Ibid.*, p. 79f.
13 It may be objected that it is unfair to use such an example in view of Lessing's obvious deistic tendencies. In the writings under consideration, his attitude to such beliefs is certainly not one of *rejection*. Consider for instance the following from '*Der Beweis des Geistes und der Kraft*': *Das, das ist der garstige breite Graben, über den ich nicht kommen kann, so oft und ernstlich ich auch den Sprung versucht habe. Kann mir jemand hinuber helfen, der tue es, ich bitte ihn, ich beschwore ihn. Er verdient ein Gotteslohn an mir.* (This, this is the nasty wide ditch which I cannot get across, however often and seriously I have tried to make the leap. If anyone can help me across, let him do so. I beg him, I implore him. He will deserve a heavenly reward from me.) Vol. 8, p. 43f.
   This, concerning just such characteristic Christian revelations, is explicitly directed at the impossibility of deriving them from any merely historical premise, not against their truth as such. However, as Kierkegaard shows in the *Concluding Unscientific Postscript*, Lessing's irony must always be reckoned with, and the *tone* of the passage quoted certainly suggests a scepticism that goes well beyond that logical point. (It is a feature of Lessing's ironical treatment of Goeze for him to represent himself as a good Lutheran defending the pure doctrine against the heretical implications of Goeze's arguments.) Be that as it may, it is clearly *not* Lessing's business in the controversy with Goeze to reject any orthodox Christian belief and I shall consider his arguments within the framework of their presentation.
14 I think Kant makes a similar mistake in arguing that duty, because necessary, must also be universal. Kierkegaard, on the other hand, through the insight

which he (perhaps misleadingly) expresses as 'Truth is subjectivity' seems to avoid the mistake.

15   Vol. 8, p. 440.

16   Cf. Matthew 9: 32–4.

17   Mark 13: 22–23.

18   Flannery O'Connor, *The Complete Stories* (London: Faber & Faber, 1990). Asbury mistakenly thinking he is dying, has been reflecting agonizingly on his life. He stares at the ceiling where a leak 'had made a fierce bird with spread wings. It has an icicle crosswise in its beak and there were smaller icicles depending from its wings and tail. He had often had the illusion that it was in motion and about to descend mysteriously and set the icicle on its head' (pp. 365–6). Later, as the crisis in his illness passes, 'he felt the beginning of a chill, a chill so peculiar, so light, that it was like a warm ripple across a deeper sea of cold. His breath came short. The fierce bird which through the days of his childhood and the days of his illness had been poised over his head, waiting mysteriously, appeared all at once to be in motion. Asbury blanched and the last film of illusion was torn as if by a whirlwind from his eyes. He saw that for the rest of his days, frail, racked, but enduring, he would live in the face of a purifying terror. A feeble cry, a last impossible protest escaped him. But the Holy Ghost, emblazoned in ice instead of fire, continued, implacable, to descend' (p. 382).

19   My earlier example from Flannery O'Connor may illustrate this.

20   Vol. 9, p. 205.

21   Though in this case it seems to me questionable to rest such weight on 'our' (whose?) increased knowledge. Inhabitants of the Middle East at that time will have had a pretty good idea of what is and what is not possible with regard to resurrection. Presumably, in any case, the interval of three days between death and resurrection was introduced in order to emphasize the miraculous nature of the event.

22   An analogy (addressing no more than the limited point made in the text) would be the difference between assessing the veracity of a report of a really experienced occurrence and assessing the report of a dreamed experience – which might use the same words.

23   Luke 24: 13–33.

24   I am tempted to apply here St Jerome's equally remarkable exclamation concerning Paul's way with scriptural interpretation: *Paulus in testimoniis, quae sumit de veteri testamento, quam artifex, quam prudens, quam dissimulator est eijus quod agit!* (Quoted by Lessing in *Anti-Goeze*, V, Vol. 9, 206.)

25   Of course neither am I suggesting that this concept of an historical account is a modern invention. That would be a great injustice to, say, Thucydides! But this concept was not that informing the work of the Evangelists.

26   Matthew 27: 62–6.

27   A claim not made anywhere else.

28   *Anti-Goeze*, V, Vol. 9, p. 204.

29   Cf. my essay, 'Asking Too Many Questions', in T. Tessin and M. von der Ruhr (eds.), *Philosophy and the Grammar of Religious Belief* (London: Macmillan, 1995).

30   Think, for instance, of the contemporary struggle between Eugen Drewermann and Roman Catholic officialdom.

31   Wittgenstein, *Culture and Value*, p. 32.

32   *Anti-Goeze*, V, Vol. 9, pp. 240ff.

33   Cf. Matthew 1: 22, John 19: 24.

34 Acts 1: 15–26.
35 This is not an attempt at a psychological 'reduction'. Those exceptional psychic states would have been appropriately describable only in religious terms.
36 For a wonderfully imaginative evocation of the *kinds* of suggestion I have been making in this paragraph see Thomas Mann's tetralogy, *Josef und seine Bruder*. For those who, regrettably, cannot be persuaded to take on those four (in every sense) great volumes, I suggest Mann's short 'postscript', the novella *Das Gesetz*, the story of Moses; his realization of the Biblical accounts of the activities of the Angel of Death amongst the Egyptians is a particularly apt parallel.
37 On which see especially Cora Diamond's 'Riddles and Anselm's Riddle', in her *The Realistic Spirit* (Cambridge, Mass. and London: MIT Press, 1991).
38 *Culture and Value*, p. 31.
39 I recognize naturally that, in applying the word 'serious' as I do, I am speaking for myself and expressing an attitude which will by no means be universally shared. It is important to note this and also to note that such fundamental disagreements are inevitable. Everyone will have his or her own ideas about what is worth discussing and what isn't.
40 Søren Kierkegaard, *Concluding Unscientific Postscript*, trans. by David Swenson and Walter Lowrie (Princeton, NJ: Princeton University Press, 1941); Book Two, Part One, 'Something About Lessing'.
41 Peter Winch died in 1997.

10
'Is it the Same God?' Reflections on Continuity and Identity in Religious Language

Rowan Williams

'The question whether we are still talking about God now, or whether we are really worshipping God now, cannot be settled by referring to any object.'[1] This observation by Rush Rhees is in one way fairly obvious. If we think of circumstances where we ordinarily discuss identity and continuity, it is clear that some or most of the appeals we might make in such a context do not apply if we are talking about God. 'Is this the house where we used to stay on holiday when we were children? Yes, there's the boot scraper shaped like a pig at the front door.' 'This isn't the book I was looking for: that had a chapter on Hegel.' 'Is that the same John Smith who used to work at Harwell? His father had a mole upon his brow. – And so had mine.' Talking about God involves something more like the sort of question we might ask about, say, the performance of a play or a musical composition from an earlier and in important respects inaccessible age. Do we hear what Purcell heard? The cult of 'authentic' performance – with reconstructed period instruments, and so on – is not really much help: such a performance simply intensifies the strangeness of a piece, and thus takes us *further* from whatever may have been the experience of the original audience. And does the post-Freudian public see the same play as did the first audiences of *Hamlet* or *Measure for Measure*? Yes, at the level of the material text that is being enacted; the simple criteria for identity or continuity mentioned a moment ago are undoubtedly in place. But there are things we cannot not know as we watch or listen: inevitably, we hear certain words and 'read' certain actions as encoding matters that could not have been in the consciousness of writer or reader in the seventeenth century. Dewi Phillips's nicely titled essay on 'What the Complex did to Oedipus' is a reminder of the need to let a text *escape* at times from our hermeneutical lust and our unexamined or unsuspected suspicions.[2] But even this is to recognize, in effect, that we are not witnessing precisely the same 'enactment' that an earlier generation may have experienced. If we heed Phillips's cautions, we shall be playing off the modern and 'knowing' interpretation which is so tempting against a text that has to be rediscovered in its difference. Once again, we have reinforced the strangeness of the text and so moved further from what was happening for its first public.

Of course, to speak of the experiences of the original public might suggest the slightly bizarre idea that these were a bundle of mental happenings whose content could in principle be determined, even if in practice they were inaccessible. I mean rather by 'experiences' the range of possible connections an earlier audience would have been able to make, the sort of verbal and visual fields within which they might have been able to develop or follow up what had been said or shown. If we are interested in how an original performance was distinct from the performance we experience, we have to look into the question of what that other audience knew that we don't know – as well as what we know that they did not (remembering Eliot's caveat, 'they are what we know'). And without venturing too far into the turbulent waters that surround the question of the limits of interpretation and the authority of authorial meanings, I think it is essential to our own self-understanding as readers (in the widest sense) to gain some purchase on our own specificity; and that entails, at the very least, acquiring some grasp of where we differ from other readers and interpreters, including the 'original public'. While it might conceivably be said that it does not greatly matter whether we can say that we are attending to the 'same' work, or in what sense that is true if we do claim that we are, the reader with some sense of the *morality* of reading/interpreting is bound to be disturbed by the suggestion that she can cheerfully be blind to her own situatedness in such a way that the distance of the text from her is not allowed to establish itself. That a text can be cannibalized into an unproblematic contemporary frame of reference is not something easily reconcilable with any sense of what I have elsewhere called 'vitalizing difficulty' in the act of reading.

The point of these generalized reflections is to stress that the issues of identity and continuity in theological utterance are not completely *sui generis*. The question, 'Are we teaching what we always did? Is it the same God?', questions raised in acute form by various kinds of doctrinal revisionism, classically liberal or radically feminist, are at least a little bit like, 'Are we performing or witnessing the same play?' In both cases, the material identity of a script is certainly not a sufficient condition for a positive answer. And this suggests that the issue of continuity has to be addressed in connection with what an earlier generation knew, the connections they made. Affirming the importance of continuity, in other words, entails affirming the importance of a critical appropriation of the past – a *critical* appropriation, because the mere repetition of materially identical formulae will not provide adequate criteria. To ask what the first hearers and users of such formulae knew and therefore 'read' in the formulations can involve us in quite wide-ranging considerations of the factors that shape religious language. A *certain* measure of hermeneutical suspicion is actually necessary for any continuity that has substance and integrity to it, that does not effectively cannibalize the text in the way I have already described.

This is not at all a new perspective, nor is it one that denies 'revelatory' quality to doctrinal formulations. The classical period of doctrinal articulation, the age of the creeds and councils, certainly exhibited what is to us a startling confidence in the divine guidance granted to some very complicated and unedifying ecclesiastical gatherings in the business of formulating doctrinal agreements; but the period also saw the increasing acknowledgement of a systematic inadequacy in the language of doctrinal formulae, building up to the dramatic subversions of the pseudo-Dionysian corpus. In the controversy in the mid- to late fourth century over the teachings of Aetius and Eunomius, those who spoke for what was to be recognized as 'orthodoxy' freely expressed their unease with the claims made by their opponents to have access to the perfect verbal self-revelation of God (in the term *agennetos*, 'unbegotten', as the decisive and unimprovable description of the divine nature). In denying that any vocable could as such be the self-description of God, and in underlining the historical and pragmatic development of language about the divine, theologians such as Gregory of Nyssa were not proposing a relativizing of the claimed truth of credal articulation; they were doing something more like identifying the sort of use to which doctrinal propositions might be put. Were they held to give true information about the life of God? Yes; but that truth was not seen as a correspondence of word and object, expressible in any context by the simple assertion of a description or set of predicates. The question in this period is not whether or how language about God 'refers', but about how it operates in sustaining or furthering a particular kind of life in relation to or in the presence of God.[3]

Let me elaborate a little. Gregory Nazianzen, writing in the late summer or autumn of 380, in the course of a continuing doctrinal struggle against the views of the followers of Eunomius, asserts that philosophizing about God is not something that is the business of just anybody anywhere in any company. 'We need to reflect, learn how to know God, and "when we have seized the favourable moment, judge" the appropriateness or adequacy of theological utterance.'[4] We discuss these matters with those who have some experience of contemplation – or, at least, we make sure that we do not enter into discussion of complex matters with those who are spiritually naive or crude. As Gregory puts it, this is not a suitable matter for after-dinner speeches or for the pleasures of point-scoring. Speaking about God is bound up with the practices involved in knowing God – practices that, as Gregory makes clear later on, centre upon the radical stripping away of all concepts and images drawn from sense experience (which effectively means all determinate concepts and images whatsoever). Plato said that it was 'difficult to understand God and impossible to express God in words'; Gregory insists that it is impossible to express God, but 'more impossible' to conceive God.[5] In other words, our problem in speaking of God is not that we have experiences that we cannot put into words, but that *conceiving* God, being able to find a satisfactory definition, is not a possible way of thinking about our relation with God: God is not there for conceiving. This does not mean, as Gregory makes clear, that there are no 'characterizations' of God available to us; but the question, 'What sort of reality is divine reality?' is not one that we can intelligibly put. The kinds of question we might ask about a determinate reality within the systems of the universe are senseless when applied to that which we suppose to be the ground and context of every particular reality.

Later in this discourse, Gregory repeats that there is nothing that can be said about God's *phusis* or *ousia*, about the *kind* of reality we're dealing with.[6] Is this, he asks, simply a contingent matter, the result of the earthly limitations of our minds? His answer is interesting. If the substantial nature of God is ever discovered, it is only when the reasonable spirit in us is 'mingled' with its prototype, when the divine image in us arrives at the source and paradigm that is now the object of its desire or yearning (*ephesis*) and that is the condition where, in Paul's terms, we know as we are known. Evidently, this is *not* strictly an answer to the question as originally put. If we can ever be said to know the divine essence (and Gregory is cautious about making such a claim in plain words), it is only when the ordinary conditions for knowing definitions no longer apply, when the very character of our subjectivity is radically changed, when we 'know' in a way analogous to how we know ourselves, or when the restlessness of searching and finding out has disappeared. We are returned here to the point made at the beginning of the discourse, that we cannot speak of knowing God without discussing who is doing the supposed knowing, what context the matter is being raised in, and so on.

Gregory's text was of great importance in its own day, an age of passionate (even obsessive) concern with doctrinal exactitude; and its importance for the issues here under consideration is that it puts a serious question-mark against any claim that doctrinal continuity can be measured simply in terms of a continuing use of the same definitional formulae. On Gregory's premises, continuity would be adequately established only if we could show that doctrinal language was part of the same continuing practice or discipline, a practice designed to move us towards a particular kind of relation with God. Doctrinal language, in such a context, becomes less a way of *describing* a reality than a set of guidelines for what we might call 'coping' with a reality. These are the gestures you make; these are the verbal and imaginative moves that are appropriate when you have learned to 'read' the world in a certain way and to perceive bits of historical reality in a certain way. You could think of it in terms of the reading of a score: when you see *this*, this is the bowing or fingering that's appropriate in rendering aloud what's on the page in the notation. Or – with an analogy of Simone Weil in mind – these are the steps of the dance; when *this* is done, this is what *you* do.[7] Or even, these are the movements you make in your yoga exercise if *this* is what you're after. Words for God are prescribed as moves of this sort, moves that enable you to respond to the pressure and presence of the divine in ways that are coopera-tive rather than resistant, and to move forward in the direction of a desired state. And such prescribed verbal and imaginative moves are also, and cruci-ally, ways of thinking about, imagining and/or discovering roles and poss-ibilities for ourselves. Continuity would be not simply in the words used for God, but in the sense of what was imagined as possible and desirable for human subjects. The skill of making the appropriate gestures in respect of God would equally be a skill in nurturing one's own and others' human development according to a particular model of what human growth should involve. This is why the classical eastern Christian tradition lays such stress on the notion of *theosis* as integrating concerns about the divine and the human. Sharing by grace in the divine life (i.e. acquiring by the gift of God something of God's freedom from the conditioning of instinct, reaction, self-protection, and so on) is at once the goal of the believer's pilgrimage and a criterion for judging the adequacy of doctrinal formulation: does this or that statement allow for *theosis* to be presented as possible and intelligible? And this concern can also be traced indirectly in the kind of responses embodied in hymnody and art, or in the interpretation of saintly lives: the doctrinal formulations mould what is said or seen, what is picked out as significant in a life, how the goal of Christian life is imagined and expressed. To understand what the doctrinal expressions of the fourth and fifth centur-ies were about, it is necessary to look at the development, for instance, of Byzantine liturgy and iconography, to read the lives of the monastic saints of the early Byzantine period, and so on. *This* is how the dogmas are received, woven into the fabric of a corporate life at diverse levels. It is instructive to see how doctrine and iconography are interrelated in the period of the iconoclastic controversies; or to read a standard text of ascetical counsel, Cassian, say, or Nark the Ascetic, and note how the pattern of doctrine expressed in the Nicene and Chalcedonian definitions often unobtrusively colours the way in which the goal of the monk's life is pictured.[8]

This is a very large area of study, involving both the 'history of ideas' and the more suspicious interpretative disciplines of modern hermeneutics: we learn the meaning of doctrines also in seeing how they work into the distribution of power in a society, how they authorize or subvert (or both) the available possibilities in terms of social negotiation. The divergence between ideas of monarchy in Eastern and Western Christendom, the ten-sion between sacral and implicit contractual models expressed most fiercely in the *Libri Carolini*, with their strong polemic against Byzantine views of royal authority, has immediate roots in the iconoclast controversy, which in turn has roots in strictly Christological disputes.[9] My point is that all this should give a different slant to the question of continuity. We are not asking whether we still *say* the same things, nor whether we (privately?) *intend* the same things; nor are we looking for a similar or identical *experience* behind what we say and what our forebears said. We are looking at the range of expression made possible by particular doctrinal determinations, the styles of living and talking that are made sense of by the dogmas.

Thus, if we want to assess the degree of continuity or discontinuity in doctrine across the centuries, we need to come at it rather obliquely. We shall probably learn more from listening to popular hymns (and listening for what hymns are popular), looking out for the themes of visual and verbal religious art, and reflecting on what styles of Christian life are particularly prized than from trying to tease out explications from believers of how they as individuals understand doctrinal statements. Is the belief of a modern Roman Catholic, for example, in the divinity of Christ 'continuous' with the belief of a sixth-century Byzantine? Technically and verbally, yes, in so far as the modern Catholic belongs to a church still officially committed to the formulations of Chalcedon and takes part in a liturgy shaped in part by this theology. But she is likely to have experienced a style of catechesis that lays great stress upon the church's obligation to labour for social justice; she will be instinctively critical of the way authority operates in the Catholic Church and will probably be able to articulate a fairly robust view of the rights of the individual conscience; and the diet of hymnody she is used to will probably be heavily influenced by the prevailing sub-charismatic idiom, and will be largely composed of apostrophes to the Lord, with much emphasis upon his power and beauty. She is not very likely (even if she is a professed religious) to prize asceticism very highly, and will define the goal of Christian life more readily in terms of a faithful witness to God's love for the dispossessed than in terms of *theosis*. Is it the same God? Is the apparent continuity in doctrinal profession real?

As my sketchy characterization was meant to indicate, the answer isn't completely straightforward. Her accustomed style in hymnody presupposes, if it is to make any sense, a highish Christology, though not *necessarily* one identical with the decrees of Chalcedon. Her understanding of the 'option for the poor' is likely to be based on a slightly jejune picture of the nature of Jesus' teaching, which again assumes unspoken things about Jesus' authority. What she believes as to freedom of conscience and her suspicion of the *magisterium* will rest upon a blend of frankly Enlightenment assumptions with a stubborn sense that the character of the Christian narrative sits very uneasily with authoritarianism. In short, she is presupposing quite a lot that in fact derives from a doctrinal idiom pretty unfamiliar to her, and, if familiar, probably unappealing. There is more continuity than she realizes: remembering the famous phrase of Eliot once again ('We know so much more than our ancestors. Precisely; and *they* are what we know'), she 'knows' what kind of thing the classical doctrinal vision has in fact made possible.

Her informed reactions and imaginative constructs can be traced to the same roots as those of earlier generations.

But the case is more complex still. Her 'performances', in liturgy as in action outside the liturgy, will look remarkably different from what her forebears did. She will not approach the Eucharist with the sacred terror implicit in the words and practice of earlier Catholics, and, in common with most contemporary Catholics, she will be unfamiliar with the distinctive affective expressions and attitudes associated with the cultus of the Reserved Sacrament (as in Benediction), will have no particular devotion to the Sacred Heart, and will not interpret minor daily setbacks as occasions given for her to offer reparation for her sin and the sin of the world. From her conduct in the presence of the Sacrament, say, you would not be able to deduce in detail what her Church has taught for the best part of a thousand years. Is *this* how you behave in the presence of the incarnate Word? Her belief here is doubt-less *formally* continuous (she is not likely to want to engage in disputing the definitions of the Lateran Council on the presence of Christ in the conse-crated species), but it seems to prescribe or at least make available a far more modest range of behavioural response than would have been the case even fifty years ago. And this suggests that a set of responses once thought pretty well integral to belief in the revealed dispensation of Catholic Christianity has been lost. The Eastern Orthodox Christian prostrating before an icon of Christ inscribed with the words, *ho on*, the one who is, displays something of what Western Christian practice has lost hold of – just as, in more general terms, Western practice does not currently convey any conviction at all that what you do with your body, in private or public prayer by way of fasting or self-denial, is of much significance in your relation with God; which itself might raise a question about how 'incarnation' is being under-stood.

Are such losses, though, a real loss of the fundamental commitments that, as we have seen, inform her behaviour in other ways? Perhaps she would argue that an earlier generation actually failed to see just what the narratives did make possible; that it took a remarkably and shamefully long time for the Church to see that the gospel enabled not only a pietist critique of certain practices connected with slavery but a radical dismantling of the entire institution of slavery. A concern with freedom of conscience or with the emancipation of the dispossessed can surely turn out to be – given a fairly long wind – aspects of what the foundational models make possible (or imperative). And the history of frankly obsessive concerns with the physical conditions of piety, not to mention the servile and degrading models be-lieved appropriate for the conduct of worship, might suggest one of two conclusions: either the Christian narrative is to be held responsible for a fundamentally anti-humanist and even neurotic style of conduct; or the things that make these responses possible are not, after all, generated by the Christian narrative, but by the adoption of alien models.[10]

Fair enough. But I suspect that this reply cuts a few corners. It is certainly arguable that what the foundational narrative makes possible takes time to unfold – as the early and 'classical' developments of doctrinal formulation took time. Less straightforward is the claim that particular styles of devotional response, say, are simply alien importations. One has to ask what generated the import – just as one would in explaining why the modern Christian acceptance of liberty of conscience might be both an importation from the Enlightenment and capable of being traced to or justified in terms of a reading of the Christian story. The political rhetoric of the late Roman Empire provided a language and ritual characterized by a kind of extremism, by the hyperbole of distance or transcendence on the one hand and abasement and powerlessness on the other. In a different context, something very similar could be said about the rhetoric of the Tudor court in England and its echoes in the Book of Common Prayer. If theology and liturgy are looking for a language suitable for extremity, the extremity of a relation between the conditioned and the unconditioned, whether in the worshipper's approach to God or in the juxtaposition of divine and human in the person of the redeemer, there is to hand a cultural idiom that serves effectively. As such an idiom becomes more remote or embarrassing, the problem arises of how certain sorts of extreme situation can find expression. And I think that the cultural lack of a convincing language for non-negotiable authority and the kind of dependence expressed in adoration creates real difficulties for anyone concerned to say the same things as were said in the fourth and fifth centuries. The loss of the vehicle is also the loss of some part of the meaning; yet it is undoubtedly true that the vehicle may be at best ambiguous and at worst corrosive of the underlying narratives and images it serves. It has lost its innocence for us. The aporia that faces us is that the continuing use of particular idioms and customs risks forfeiting integrity as well as obscuring the new elements that have been found to be possible in the light of the narrative; yet their cessation leaves a gap in the continuity of meanings more serious than we might imagine.

Originally, the doctrinal pattern of Christian orthodoxy was thought and felt to require something of the baroque overstatement of the language of the absolutist court; it generated texts such as the Trisagion or the Carolingian *Laudes*, images such as the Pantocrator of Daphni or, some way down the road, Piero's Resurrection, words and images of terror and awe, deliberately invoking extremes in the confidence that the story and the doctrine licensed, or rather demanded, a playing with extremes. Liturgy, theology and Christian practice in the twentieth century have generally failed to produce a comparable language of extremity, largely because we are rightly and understandably wary of the ambiguities of the models used in the past. The tempting and, I believe, erroneous way out is to conclude that the extremity of classical art or liturgy or even physical discipline (prostration, genuflection, fasting) can be abandoned as culturally inappropriate, inaccessible, morally compromised, without any effect upon the content of what is doctrinally asserted. A simple sanitizing of practice fails to attend to the concrete process of the development of Christian language, to the question, 'What is it we are talking of if *this* is the language reached for, if this level of seriousness is evoked?' And this helps to explain the ways in which contemporary theologians may well turn to the extremity of some sorts of art, verbal and visual, in the hope of finding an appropriately difficult, distancing register. Like R.S. Thomas, we might think of those who 'sang their amens fiercely, narrow but saved in a way that men are not now'.[11]

Are we then fated to discontinuity? In some sense, yes; as we are, a modern audience watching *Measure for Measure*, incapable of feeling except in the weight of the actual words we hear what it might be like to consider chastity more important than life. But: 'except in the weight of the words'; it might be more important to *weigh* than to interpret. It is important like this; it makes this happen. Better these questions than simply the analysis of flawed and ambiguous motivation, with its assumption that somewhere there is an innocent language. It may be impossible to transcribe the fruits of the earlier reception of doctrine without apology or critique; but if the question is not raised of the level of importance shown in the words used and the gestures transmitted, it is inevitable that less will be said than before. And, while our conscientious modern Catholic is surely right in her contentions about how commitments to social radicalism are part of what the gospel makes possible, we would be justified in putting to her the question of whether this without attention to the baroque, the extreme, in her tradition, finally loses not only resonance but coherence. A discourse without attention to the roots of what I have been calling 'extremity' ultimately risks reducing the scope of what human beings may say and so may become; certain roles become unplayable. And while some, of course, can be seen as (at best) doubtfully compatible with the central assertions – for instance, the role of utter moral worthlessness, of being the object of inventive and irresistible divine anger – we should remember that doctrinal continuity requires a continuity in the range of human possibilities offered and specified by doctrinal formulation. This may not necessarily mean identity in concretizing these possibilities, but it should rule out at least some sorts of shrinkage in the scope of what is seen as the definitive and final goal of the believing life.

The continuing viability of a doctrinal formula has much to do with its continuing capacity to generate comparable responses, styles of life and language, as well as its capacity to generate new realizations. But what makes much contemporary discussion of the viability or intelligibility of traditional doctrinal formulae frustratingly difficult is a lack of concern with this area of what responses, what images of self and community, as well as of God, are bound up in the process of doctrinal articulation. The result of this inattention is the familiar polarization between what I would call revision-ism and positivism: on the one hand, the doctrine is said to be unintelligible or perhaps morally and politically ambiguous, requiring clarification or even purgation, and on the other, it is claimed to be, in its traditional shape and expression, irreformable and unimprovable. Neither strategy spends much time examining what role the formulae play in specifying the direction of Christian life, and whether this role is dispensable if the Christian 'style' of act and speech is to survive. Thinking back to Alistair Macintyre's remark about how vital traditions embody 'continuities of conflict',[12] we could say that continuity in doctrine entails continuity in concern about or debate about how the goals of redeemed human nature are to be imagined and constructed, given the character of our definitive Christian story.

I want to illustrate the impasse of some modern discussion in relation to a currently contentious question in which the opposition between revision-ists and positivists appears particularly sharp. Recent dogmatic theology has turned almost unprecedented attention upon the doctrine of the Trinity, and has often, in fairness, discussed it very much in tandem with issues about the nature of human community and communion, in a way that does indeed bring out the connection of the discourse with what is to be said about human goals. The work of someone like John Zizioulas is exemplary in this regard.[13] At the same time, however, feminist theology has insisted upon the ambiguous character of the formulation of Trinitarian doctrine, ascribing as it does an absolute ontological priority to a generative power clearly characterized as male. Here, surely, is one of the major ideological props of patriarchy, the systematic denial that woman is ever the author of meaning – the subject, not the object, in normative discourse. The Trinitar-ian formula, in liturgy and theology, must therefore come into question; certainly, as a liturgical (and therefore regular and accessible) convention, it cannot but invite critique and possible rejection.[14]

The defence that this is not the intent of the doctrine, or that this has not been the effect of the doctrine, is unsatisfactory. Conscious intent is not the issue; and the patriarchal register of an enormous quantity of Christian language should not seriously be in dispute, nor the malign effects of this on the experience of Christian women. But the simple positivist reply, popular in some American conservative circles, that God somehow *specifies* his name in the events of revelation, is worse than unsatisfactory, at least in the form in which it has been most sharply put in recent years.[15] It has the effect of bringing into clear focus precisely those elements of traditional doctrinal discourse that feminists find most questionable or offensive; and it is ironic that these are frequently the elements of the discourse that are most persistently relativized by formative theologians in the classical trad-ition. Thus the insistence of Athanasius and Gregory Nazianzen, for example, that the language of 'fatherhood' and 'sonship' had no specificity of gender, since that would be to introduce material terms into talking of the immaterial God, may not be a satisfactory answer to the contemporary feminist critique; but at least it attempts, in its own day, to block certain speculative flights that appear to have found their wings again in recent theology that claims to be 'traditional' in its Trinitarian perspectives.[16]

What seems to have gone wrong here – on both sides of the debate – is that there is an unwillingness to look at the words of Trinitarian definition in any but an abstract way. Both the feminist critic and the positivist defender react to the definitions as if what is unsaid in the context of, say, the fourth century dictates how meanings are to be construed in the twentieth; so that the silence of the doctrinal formulae in respect of feminine imagery takes on, for both, a portentous weight. Here, I think, we need to distinguish quite carefully between what this silence might tell us about a whole culture, even a whole idiom for talking about meaning and power, and what it might tell us about a particular set of doctrinal utterances. The feminist is right in saying that the silence is significant; but it is so as a silence *shared* throughout the discourses of the age in question. It is a silence very like the *articulacy* of the same period in producing images of distance and extremity, as discussed already, involved with a very complex network of modes for making sense. And this is not the network we (in modern North Atlantic society) habitually use, and both the silence and the articulacy have lost their innocence for us and become problematic. If it is true, as I suggested earlier, that our contemporary awkwardness or blankness in handling a language of 'extremity' means that we are in a very important respect not believing precisely the same things, and that the intention to believe the same should involve us in worrying about our prevailing rhetoric and the relative poverty of its range, then there are related consequences in respect of the silence of the tradition. For the fourth century (and subsequent centuries, virtually up to our own), silence in respect of the feminine was largely a matter of unconscious assumption, a 'natural' way of talking; but now that silence has been retrospectively identified as bound in with profoundly questionable practices of exclusion. It represents not nature but history, the realm of what could be otherwise. It has become a moral matter. Thus it is very easy to take particular samples of the discourse of a past age and subject them to moral scrutiny, so that they can be read as yet more flawed and oppressive instances of patriarchal evil.

The temptation, then, for someone who wants to defend their loyalty to the formulations of an earlier age, to preserve continuity and identity in theological utterance, is to argue that the silence of the traditional language is indeed significant, though not in the way the critic claims. It is significant in witnessing to mysterious determinations of the possibilities of theological language by the revealing God; silence about the feminine may not be a testimony to some strictly ontological privileging of the male in relation to God, but it is decreed as a condition of fidelity to what historical revelation enacts. It is a testimony to the concreteness of God's dealing with us in history and speech. This is a significant and serious theological point; but the way it is put in fact undercuts its own concern with the concrete by failing to see how the tradition's silence operates differently in different historical and cultural settings. It accepts the terms of its opponents, and so shares their misreading.

If silence in regard to the feminine becomes a thematic point, for good or ill, in our reading of doctrinal material, we become less sensitive to what it might be that a particular formulation is saying and not saying *in its specificity*. This is not to recommend a hermeneutic without suspicion or to proscribe the feminist critique; far from it. But in addition to the general identification of patriarchal distortion, and even the particular diagnosis of this in any one area of theological language, there remains the reading of the historical texts and practices with an eye to what they *deliberately* don't say and what they actually generate by way of imaginative engagement in their own world. Only when this task is undertaken (if my analysis so far has been correct) can we helpfully or adequately discuss issues of identity and continuity.

And what the theological tradition and its outworkings in the language of spirituality and liturgy seem to be concerned with is what I earlier identified as the centrality of *theosis* as the form of human destiny. More specifically: the Trinitarian language of the fourth century, especially in Athanasius and the Cappadocian Fathers, sought to define a particular relation, the relation believed to hold between God as source of all and God as embodied in the life of Jesus Christ. As articulated in the theology of the period and in the practices of worship and prayer, this was understood as a relation of *dependence* and also a relation of *equality*, an unrestricted sharing in the life of the source. This apparent paradox was glossed with reference to the narrative of Jesus, especially in the fourth gospel. But – again, if my analysis so far has been accurate – it was also a relation expressed and enacted in the practice of Christian life. The pattern of Christian faithfulness worked out in the practices of the first Christian centuries involved powerful affirmations about liberty in respect of particular political systems, the kind of liberty that issued in martyrdom; the Christian was someone whose definitions of *belonging* were not circumscribed by living in the Roman Empire, and whose meanings were not shaped by the sacred significance of the state and its ruler. Equally, the Christian was someone whose habitual language towards God was that of gratitude for wholly unearned favours, someone who regarded their present identity as grounded in divine gift rather than in moral or spiritual achievement. The goal of Christian existence was to come to the fullest possible assimilation to Christ; what was said about Christ was therefore shaped by the need to make sense of the kind of life and speech that the original event of Christ had made possible. The believer's relation to God transcribes (though imperfectly and in a temporally cumulative mode) the relation to God-as-source of God-as-saviour. In at least some degree, *this* is what the language of classical Trinitarian theology is trying to say. To concentrate on the genderedness of the terms as the key to reading the whole complex of concerns here will not tell you a great deal (because the skewing or imbalance of the discourse by patriarchy is not specific to *this* concrete piece of the territory).

This leaves us with a considerable problem, of course. Revisionist 'Trinitarian' formulae ('Creator, redeemer and sanctifier' and other variants) are manifestly discontinuous in what they affirm, since they contain nothing about the pivotal question of the relation to God-as-source that dominates classical Christian discussion; they simply enumerate divine activities which, in the traditional scheme, are shared between all three persons of the Trinity, and thus take us into a frame of reference significantly other than that of practically all earlier talking and practice in respect of the Trinity. This point has been made often enough in recent debate, as has the related point that a triad of terms specifying divine actions simply steps around the underlying issue of mutual 'definition' through relationship in the divine life (if God is eternally 'Father', then there is an eternal Son – one of the oldest arguments in this doctrinal tradition).[17] Because we have no gender-free language for the relation of 'generator' and 'generated' that is not uncomfortably abstract, there seems to be no straightforward way out. The replacing of 'Father' by 'Mother' doesn't really solve much: it introduces another gender-specific term, and does so at the cost of complicating the anchorage of trinitarian language in the language of Jesus.

But the point of this essay has really been to suggest that this problem presupposes a faulty view of how doctrinal speech works. There is little sense that the meanings of doctrinal formulation have to be learned within a temporally extended and semantically complex practice of word and deed; and there is a hidden assumption that the meanings that matter are those that appear at once by way of the immediately apprehended connotations of the words in question. There is an enormous issue here about the ways in which modern liturgical language shows its embarrassment with the temporal dimension, the construction of meaning *in* a necessarily protracted and carefully articulated process, both in the single act of worship and in the extended rhythm of the liturgical calendar.[18] In other words, there is a difficulty not simply about what traditional formulae mean, but about *how* they mean; and the model I have sketched earlier in this essay is evidently far from readily accessible to contemporary revisionists or contemporary positivists.

The conclusion is not a comfortable one. As with the language of 'extremity', of radical dependence and adoration, so with the language of Trinitarian relation: there is no way of resolving the difficulties they now seem to generate simply by working on the *words* involved. We cannot identify a tidy hard kernel of transferable information contingently encoded, so as to preserve a continuity of content in our religious discourse. We can do little

more than continue to listen for the meanings such words had by continuing some of the patterns of use within which, if at all, the question of
meaning is answered. And it may be that something will be made possible
for us too, out of such practice and out of such listening. But how very hard
it is, for theologian or philosopher these days, to believe that the difficulties
of words cannot be smoothed out by more words…

Bishop of Monmouth

Notes

1 Rush Rhees, *Without Answers* (London, 1969), p. 131.
2 D.Z. Phillips, *Through a Darkening Glass. Philosophy, Literature and Cultural Change* (Oxford: Basil Blackwell, 1982), pp. 82–8: in order to attend to the concreteness of the play 'one must put aside Freud's essentialist assumptions about sexuality, fathers, mothers, and children' (p. 88).
3 On the context of this, see, most conveniently, Andrew Louth, *The Origins of the Christian Mystical Tradition. From Plato to Denys* (Oxford, 1981), and Anthony Meredith, *The Cappadocians* (London, 1995).
4 Gregory of Nazianzen, First Theological Discourse, 3 (Gregoire de Nazianze, *Discours 27–34*, ed. Paul Gallay and Maurice Jourjon, Sources Chretiennes (Paris, 1978)), pp. 76–7.
5 Second Theological Discourse, 4, pp. 106–7, 108–9.
6 Second Theological Discourse, 17, pp. 134–7.
7 See Peter Winch, *Simone Weil. 'The Just Balance'* (Cambridge, 1989), ch. 4.
8 See, for example, the works of these two authors in *The Philokalia*, vol. 1, translated by G.E.H. Palmer, Philip Sherrard and Kallistos Ware (London, 1979).
9 Finely discussed in Judith Herrin, *The Formation of Christendom* (Oxford, 1987), pp. 437–40, and chapters 10 and 11, *passim*.
10 The whole notion of 'what a narrative makes possible' has been discussed with enormous sophistication by Michel de Certeau; see in particular, *La faiblesse de croire* (Paris, 1987), pp. 208–26, on the incomplete determinacy of what the narrative of Christ makes possible and the consequent need for an account of Christian truth that locates authority in a plurality of voices, each necessary to the others.
11 R.S. Thomas, 'The Chapel', in *Laboratories of the Spirit* (London, 1975), p. 19.
12 *After Virtue* (London, 1981), p. 206.
13 See, above all, *Being as Communion* (London, 1985).
14 The literature on this is now vast. Daphne Hamson's *After Christianity* (London, 1996) is an outstandingly powerful and thoroughgoing critique; but see also chapter 7 of Gail Ramshaw, *God Beyond Gender. Feminist Christian God-Language* (Minneapolis, 1995) and Brian Wren, *What Language Shall I Borrow? God-Talk in Worship: a Male Response to Feminist Theology* (London, 1989), especially pp. 115–22, and chapter 8, *passim*.
15 For this position, see several of the essays in Alvin F. Kimel, Jr. (ed.), *Speaking the Christian God. The Holy Trinity and the Challenge of Feminism* (Grand Rapids and London, 1992), especially those by the editor and Robert W. Jenson.
16 For Athanasius and Gregory, see the impeccably orthodox T.F. Torrance, *The Trinitarian Faith* (Edinburgh, 1988), p. 70, n. 64.

17 For some of this recent debate, see Torrance's essay in Kimel, *Speaking the Christian God*, especially pp. 141–2, and the essays by Janet Martin Soskice and Jane Williams, in Teresa Elwes (ed.), *Women's Voices. Essays in Contemporary Feminist Theology* (London, 1992).
18 Catherine Pickstock's *After Writing: Towards the Liturgical Consummation of Philosophy* (Oxford, 1997) is a particularly original and profound account of the problematic character of temporality in modern liturgy.

Part III
Philosophy of Literature and Education

11
The Mediation of Sense in Literature

Michael Weston

Dewi Phillips has characterized his work in moral philosophy as 'interventions in ethics', and no doubt we could describe his work in the philosophy of religion in similar terms. These 'interventions' are directed at the theoretical ambitions of philosophy and take the form of 'reminders', either 'teaching differences' or 'elucidating philosophically neglected perspectives',[1] which show that the generalizing character of theoretical accounts is, when confronted by the actuality of moral and religious language use, obscuring and confusing in relation to the phenomena it is intended to illuminate. From his earliest publications, this philosophical work has utilized detailed references to works of literature, a resource which, from the standpoint of theory, seems of questionable value.

Moral theory has characteristically wanted to give a general account of something called 'morality', to divine its logic and thus provide us with the true standard for moral action and so a guide to conduct. Sometimes this standard has been found externally to morality, in a reference to human good and harm, what is or is against any human being's interest. Sometimes it has been found internally, in the nature of the morally good action, as with Kant's account in terms of action for the sake of duty. For the moral theorist, the apparent variety of moralities and ways of living which history and contemporary life show us sets the problem his theory aims to resolve: without the true standard, we should not know how to judge this variety and so should not know what to do ourselves.

In terms of this theoretical ambition, references to literature seem of dubious value. Theory intends to determine the nature of morality and through this the criteria for moral action. Examples from literature can only provide data, either of our moral responses as readers or of the characters' responses to each other and their situations, which in either case awaits the formulation of the correct moral theory to determine its appropriateness. Non-literary examples would function just as well, indeed usually better. Our aim, after all, is to take our own intuitive moral responses, inquire as to their presuppositions, and then attempt to formulate an internal or external ground which would justify the greatest range of such responses or what appears the most central of them. The judgements we make about literary examples are not ones made to 'real' cases: they are second-rate evidence. And the judgements made by literary characters aren't ours in any case. Furthermore, we are often unsure how to describe in a determinate manner the situations presented in literature and even when we are, we are sometimes unsure what judgement to make about them, thus indicating our need for, rather than possession of, an adequate ethical theory! All in all, we would do better sticking to moral judgements we feel sure about, relating to simple cases we can clearly describe.

It may be suggested, however, that moral theory's attitude to literature needn't be negative. Martha Nussbaum, for example, has suggested we look at literature and philosophy as co-partners in a common inquiry to answer the question 'How should we live?' This question, asked by human beings about their own lives, must, she says, be both empirical and practical. There is no access to a position transcending the way the human condition has actually appeared to individual human beings so the inquiry must be based on such appearances, the *phainomena*. Furthermore, it is asked by human beings to determine the way they are to live themselves, and so it must be 'constrained, and appropriately constrained, by their hopes and fears for themselves, their sense of value, what they think they can live with'.[2] These empirical and practical restraints determine the nature of the inquiry. We are to survey 'the major alternative views about the good life' motivated by the desire for the practical truth about how to live. 'Truth' requires consistency, and practical truth community: we 'want to arrive at a view that is internally coherent, and also at one that is basically shared and sharable. Nothing else is non-negotiable, not even the precise interpretation of these regulative principles themselves.'[3] This procedure 'can be said to yield, in a perfectly recognizable sense, ethical truth'[4] and determines the respective roles of philosophy and literature in pursuit of such truth. In order for us to ask about any proposed answer to the question whether it could constitute practical truth, we have to ask whether we can live it, and in order to assess this we must see the way it would work out in life. We

> need to imagin[e] vividly what a life would look like both with and without that belief, allowing us in imagination and emotion to get a sense of what the cost for us would be if we gave it up. To get that kind of understanding of possibilities, an understanding that is both ethical and intellectual, we need literature in philosophy, for literature can show us in rich detail, as formal abstract argument cannot, what it is like to live in a certain way. In this sense literature, and our discourse about literature can be and is philosophy: it plays a part in our search for truth and for a good life.[5]

Literature is 'a source of a human sort of truth'.[6] Nussbaum, then, shares with moral theorists the conviction that there is a question 'How to live well' which is to be answered by an intellectual inquiry, but one which, being empirical and practical, involves literature as an essential element.

In looking for the standard for moral action and so the guide for our conduct, the traditional theorist separates himself from the particular moral concerns which characterize his life: they are to be judged by the results of his intellectual inquiry. Of course, those results must maintain some contact with our original intuitions, else they could hardly provide us with what we could recognize as a foundation for moral thinking. But which intuitions will turn out to be justifiable cannot be pre-judged. Similarly, in Nussbaum's inquiry, only the principles of consistency and the aim for community are 'non-negotiable': what we may recognize as constituting the good life after inquiry must maintain some continuity with our initial intuitions, but what that continuity will consist in cannot be assumed. Nussbaum's project, like that of the traditional theorist, involves a preconception that the moral values which we live (if we do) outside philosophy are in need of justification: we should have reasons for our values.

Against this picture, set that provided by Edith Wharton of Undine Spragg in *The Condition of the Country*, on which Phillips comments: 'Her values at any time are essentially transient, serving the constant need for new pleasures, new conquests ... With such an attitude she is condemned to perpetual rootlessness ... It is precisely because Undine Spragg has reasons for her values which are externally related to those values that we see in her a fundamental rootlessness in which no form of decency can grow or flourish.'[7] What is the point of such a 'reminder'? The theoretician might say that he has no wish to embrace Undine Spragg's criterion of 'new pleasures, new conquests', and in any case whether he did or not would be determined by his intellectual (or intellectual and imaginative) inquiry. But the 'reminder' isn't given to suggest a possible answer to the theoretician's question. It is rather intended to get us to recognize that the character of theorizing, of looking for such justification, is at odds with its own claim to continuity with moral seriousness.

To think our patterns of moral concern require a foundation or justification runs counter to that concern, or to what that concern may be. In terms of our moral understanding, which we show in being able to follow Wharton's novel, we can recognize that the individual who has reasons for the values she espouses is to be distinguished *morally* from the individual who rejects such reasons, whose reasons *are* her values. In recognizing this, we are returning the notion of 'reason' to moral life from the 'abstract reasonableness' of the theoretician, who must abstract the notion from our lived moral life since his inquiry is to stand in judgement on it. The theoretician's project could only produce an account of a life which is itself subject to moral criticism. In moral theories, language is 'on holiday': moral concepts are removed from the contexts where they have their use. They produce, then, a picture of a life which if lived would provide a context within which moral concepts could have only a deficient, parasitic role, of providing a moral veneer for other interests. The point of the reference to Undine Spragg is to return the notions of reason and justification to the moral context where they have their sense. This is not, of course, to deny that one can reflect on one's moral position. But what such 'reflection' amounts to has to be seen in terms of the use of the notion within moral cases. I may reflect on what counts as living in terms of certain values where this is unclear. Or I may reflect on the extent to which I can commit myself to certain values given my other commitments. Either way, the questioning proceeds in terms of values which provide the context for there being a 'question' and about which there isn't a problem – for the sense of 'problem' here is one with commitment. Or I may radically question moral values themselves. But such questioning proceeds itself from another perspective on life or is expressive of a loss of the sense of life, of despair. It does not constitute a privileged position from which moral values can themselves be judged.

Phillips contrasts the picture produced in terms of 'abstract reasonableness' with one formed in terms of 'moral reasons which are rooted in the ways people live and in their conceptions of what is important in life . . . The contrast depends on showing how much separates examples suggested by prevailing moral philosophies from other possibilities.'[8] When we return notions of reason and justification to moral life, we can see that the life of Undine Spragg is to be morally contrasted with the lives of those for whom their values are their reasons. And here Phillips refers to Countess Olenska in Wharton's *The Age of Innocence*. She flees from, and threatens to divorce, her husband. Newland Archer is sent by the influential families of New York to dissuade her from bringing scandal on herself and them. He is himself engaged to be married. Having put the case to the Countess, Archer finds himself in love with her and pleads for her to go away with him. But through his advocacy, Olenska has seen 'a moral reality in what to him was little more than decorum'.[9] She decides not to divorce and rejects Archer's proposal.

> Before Archer convinces her otherwise, the satisfaction of true love and her own happiness would have been of paramount importance to her. She would have described her elopement with Archer as a flight to freedom. But when she becomes aware of other values, values involving suffering, denial, endurance, discipline, she can no longer see things in that way. She says that her former way of looking at things is cheap by comparison. This judgement is not arrived at by cashing the two attitudes into a common coinage by which one can be demonstrated to be cheaper than the other . . . On the contrary, her judgement about her former attitude is intelligible only in terms of the new moral perspective she comes to embrace.[10]

When we return the notion of 'reason' to the moral context where it has its moral sense, we see that Olenska does not have 'reason' for her change, but that the change is her coming to have new reasons, a new conception of what counts as a reason for her. Moral change is not 'progress' (or 'decline') in terms of some unitary standard or conception of practical truth: it is coming to a new perspective on one's life, coming to see the value of different things. Olenska moves from valuing satisfying, genuine love, being frank and honest in one's relationships and the difficulties one may have with them, making up one's own mind and not paying too much attention to what one's parents or family have to say, on the one hand, to valuing family tradition, endurance, loyalty, faithfulness and subordinating one's own strongest desires, on the other. These perspectives on what is valuable in life are not subject to an impersonal standard or communally shared truth which can determine one as 'better' or 'truer' than the other. We see that 'truth' in its moral context is the truth of personal appropriation: to see certain values as 'true' is to take them as the measure for one's life.

The novel shows us the heterogeneity of morals, that moral change involves a change of perspective on one's own life, and that these values can be themselves the individual's reasons. Through engaging with the novel we can be reminded of what we know already in so far as we can use moral concepts and so read it. We can be recalled to, what we forget when we are tempted towards philosophical theorizing, the *lived* use of the notions of 'reason', 'truth', 'change', and so forth, in moral contexts. Philosophical theorizing abstracts these notions from those contexts since it aims to justify, or show to be unjustified, our moral practices. In producing such reminders, the philosopher is not, of course, endorsing or condemning his examples. In replacing the notions of 'reason' and 'truth' into their moral contexts, into the context of the significance an individual can see in one's own life, we see that it can be no part of the philosopher's task to determine the truth of such perspectives since 'truth' here is the truth of personal appropriation and not intellectual inquiry.

We can see why such 'reminders' should characteristically take a literary form. They are intended to bring the relevant notions back from the holiday of 'abstract reasonableness' to their use in moral life. Phillips's example of Olenska shows what it is to have reasons for one's moral values; it places the notion of 'reason' here within its lived context, and thereby shows the theoretical notion of having reason, justification, for our moral values to be an abstraction which has lost contact with the phenomena it claims to illuminate. What is needed to intervene in the theoretical ambition and its consequences is replacing the moral notions at issue within the context where they have their sense: in the significance which human beings find, or do not, in their lives. Phillips quotes Peter Winch: 'The seriousness of [moral] issues is not something we can add, or not, after the explanations of what these issues are, as a sort of emotional extra: it is something that "shows itself" . . . in the explanation of the issues.'[11] This seriousness is to be seen in an individual's life, in the way the issues are seen and in their ramifications for her other relationships, activities, and so on. To show this seriousness, and so to illuminate the nature of the *issues*, rather than just state them, requires, then, something like a story, the revelation of an individual's life at a particular juncture in a specific situation. This showing of an individual's life in the significance it has for her must, to be such a showing, command our attention, prompt our contemplation and emotional involvement. It must convince. And it is naturally to works of fiction which involve us in these ways that we would look for such reminders.

One way of 'combating utilitarianism', writes R.W. Beardsmore,

> would be to appeal to a work of literature like Faulkner's *Intruder in the Dust*. Faulkner's novel is not, of course, his greatest, and it is not always convincing, particularly in the later chapters, where he employs long polemical speeches by the lawyer Gavin Stevens to preach to the reader. What *is*, in my opinion, convincing (as in most of Faulkner's writing) is the portrayal of individual characters and their relationships. And it is such portrayals which can help break the hold on us of the abstract and mathematical account of human relationships embodied in the theory of utilitarianism . . . Unlike the relationship of a man's actions to the happiness of the greatest number (or some other variant), none of the relationships by which characters are impelled to act in Faulkner's novel, a man's relationship to his job, or to a particular human being (father, mother, friend), has any numerical or mathematical aspect.[12]

In recognizing this as a convincing portrayal of the lives of individuals and their relationships (if we do), we recognize the inadequacy of the categories of utilitarianism to account for them and that this inadequacy cannot show their irrationality as the claim of the utility principle to be the criterion of moral action would assert.

The recognition of the heterogeneity of morals which follows from replacing the notions of reason and truth into moral contexts doesn't mean, however, that we could understand anything whatever as the object of moral appraisal. In 'The Presumption of Theory', Phillips refers to Peter Winch's discussion of the notion of limiting conceptions in relation to human life. The very notion of human life is limited by the conceptions of birth, death and reproduction and it is to these that we look to gain a foothold in trying to understand the very various ways in which human beings find or fail to find sense in their lives. These limiting notions do not determine such perspectives, but rather 'their position as limits is shown by the role they play in that diversity'.[13] Thus in *From Fantasy to Faith*, he uses Hemingway's *The Old Man and the Sea* to remind his religiously inclined readers that non-religious moralities are possible. The Old Man has the values of a warrior, a hunter put to the test by the sea. The novel 'is a representation of life as a struggle against unconquerable natural forces in which a kind of victory is possible. It is an epic metaphor for life.'[14] The Old Man faces the forces of nature with awe, but this calls to him to become a hero, to triumph, temporarily, or be destroyed. We recognize this as a perspective within which human life can gain a sense: the Old Man has 'addressed life at certain of its limiting horizons'. He has referred life terminating in death to values whose point is not negated by death. He has turned 'from the temporal to the eternal'.[15]

The value of pitting his strength, his endurance and courage against nature is independent of the outcome since it is recognized that in the end destruction is inevitable. As Phillips notes about the Cossacks in Babel's stories later in the same chapter, within such perspectives we are called on to live proud and free, 'not humbling ourselves before gods or men. But we are called on, not only to live like men but to die like men.'[16] Such perspectives involve a glorification of the self, of the human, but one which is preserved from vainglory in its encompassing of death and injury. We may find such perspectives profoundly unattractive, of course, but such a judgement is one inevitably proceeding from another perspective. Changes in moral perspective both individually and culturally are not to be referred to some general standard. Old values die and are replaced by new ones, by different conceptions of what is important in life, without this constituting an 'objective' progress or decline. Yet such values, in order to give value to life, must relate to the limiting conceptions of the notion of human life. A way of life, in order to give reason to life, must not be valued for what is expected within life, within the temporal, but is rather that which gives the temporal its value. But this relation 'to the eternal' is itself historically contingent: it is possible for human life to cease to find significance in relation to such perspectives, to cease to be concerned in this sense with life as a whole. Then the picture painted by contemporary moral philosophy, of adherence to moral values depending on further reasons, would constitute a description of the culturally available possibilities in relation to what had been conceived as morality, whilst it could not, as it claimed to do, exhaust moral possibilities as such. Indeed, the dominance of such models in moral philosophy constitutes itself one of the forces in our culture working towards that end. If 'certain ways of regarding moral problems and difficulties are constantly ignored, misunderstood or misrepresented, those ways will sooner or later cease to be part of our conceptions of moral problems and difficulties'.[17]

Since the notion of the 'essence' of morality is a chimera, what is meant by 'moral', indeed, if anything is meant, is a matter of the use of the term, the role it plays in human life. Phillips is able to refer to certain moral possibilities shown to us in literature because these works still speak to us, because we still recognize these perspectives as living possibilities or related to ones which are. Such references can show us the contrast with the picture of human life contained in contemporary moral philosophies. But these poss- ibilities may cease to be so for us, or to stand in any meaningful relation to what we see as possible ways of life, precisely because the notion of the 'moral' has either radically altered or disappeared.

In both *Through a Darkening Glass* and *From Fantasy to Faith*, Phillips turns to Beckett's plays as 'an observation on a present state'[18] diagnosed as that in which such perspectives on life as a whole, in relation to the eternal, have been lost, but where the loss is still experienced, as absence. In *Waiting for Godot* this absence presents itself as a meaningless waiting. 'The objectless waiting that Beckett depicts gets its force by contrast with an absent mean- ing, an absence portrayed by memory of the past or inarticulate longing for the future.'[19] The absence of a relation to 'the eternal' in the sense of a perspective encompassing one's life as a whole has consequences for the conception of personal identity shown in the difficulties Beckett's characters have in recognizing and remembering each other. 'Moral considerations . . . enter into the determination of what does and does not constitute "the same" [person] and hence into what constitutes a justifiable claim on an- other. The characters in *Waiting for Godot* do not know any more what considerations should have weight in these matters.'[20] And in so far as this is no longer known, there are consequences for the language of emo- tions. 'What is it to commit oneself to someone divorced of all future implications? . . . One person would not recognise another as far as any claims are concerned from one day to the next. As Pozzo says, "I don't remember having met anyone yesterday. But tomorrow I won't remember having met any body today". Such an isolation of relationships from a yesterday and a tomorrow attempts to reduce human relations to the status of sensations . . . If this is what talk of love becomes – talk of a transient sensation [could] we not say that at least one concept of love has been forgotten?'[21] Beckett's play shows us life lived in the loss of a relation to the non-temporal, but where this absence is itself experienced, both in the pointless waiting and in the garbled memories of a religious and moral language which no longer make sense to his characters. 'Beckett . . . is con- cerned with a particular time, our time, and with what he thinks has happened in it.'[22] That we find Beckett's plays comic in recognizing the character of the 'waiting' and the garbled memories as garbled, shows we too have at least the memory of, and perhaps the desire for, other possibilities.

Moral philosophy and philosophizing about religion take place in a par- ticular historical setting. We are situated in a time when, if we recognize Beckett's depiction, the possibility of moral values and religious belief has itself become a question. Because there is no essence of morality independ- ent of how moral language is used, certain forms of such use that were once central, those concerned with making sense of one's life as a whole, may be forgotten. And since the human world within which we live is formed in terms of the concepts we use, that very world may come to preclude the application of terms in their previous meanings. What, for example, could it mean to commit oneself in love in circumstances where the relationships socially recognized are limited by temporal objectives, in a time, say, of 'serial monogamy'? Or what is it to see one's life in terms of vocation in a time of institutionalized 'labour flexibility' and the assessment of all occupations in terms of market outcomes?

If the occlusion of a relation to the non-temporal is transmuting what can be understood by our moral vocabulary, this cultural process is far advanced in relation to religion. In *From Fantasy to Faith*, Phillips quotes from Psalm 139 and remarks of the world of the psalmist that it is seen from the start as God's world. 'The movement of thought in the Old Testament is not from the world to God, but from God to the world.'[23] In such a world it would be senseless to ask for 'evidence for God'. But since the Renaissance this relation to the world and to human life has been under attack in terms of other, secular human values. It is in such a cultural setting that the need for evidence is felt both by those hostile to and those favourably disposed towards religion. In such circumstances attacks on and justifications for religion come to form the nature of philosophical engagement with religion.

Just as philosophy has seen its role in relation to morality as providing foundations or the revelation of its true nature, so too in relation to religion. The religious life of worshipping God, thanking God, trying to do God's will, and so on, surely rests on the assumption that there is a God to worship, thank and to will. Philosophy must, therefore, consider whether there are good reasons for believing that God exists. But just as the philosophical construal of morality as requiring reasons distorts moral life, so too does its reading of religious life as resting on an 'existence claim' which needs to be justified. Such a conception of 'God' removes the term from the context where it has had its use. If 'God exists' makes a claim about 'the way things really are', it could be false. But a religious believer isn't prepared to say 'I believe in God but maybe God does not exist'. To say 'God exists but might not have done' is to use the language of things in the world. Such a 'thing' is one of a kind. But God isn't one of a kind, and not a unique object either, since a unique object is only contingently so. 'God' is not, then, the name of an object whose existence is claimed by the believer. To come 'to believe in God' is not to come to believe that what one thought was false ('there is a God') is true according to standards already accepted, but of coming to live in a new form of language, to come to have new standards of what can be said, new conceptions of reasons and justification. 'Coming to believe' is 'conversion'. 'Belief' here is not an 'epistemic' notion. To believe in God is to be affectively disposed, whether in love, revolt, guilt, or whatever. As Kierkegaard reminded his age, Christianity is an existence communication, the communication of a way of living, one within which the conception of one's life and the world as a gift plays a central role, so that one has nothing by right but is saved by 'grace' alone.

Yet it has to be recognized that, just as there is no 'essence' of morality over and beyond the use of moral language, so too with religion. In so far as religion is interpreted in a particular way by both opponents and defenders, so certain possible understandings become hidden. 'Philosophical observations have a feedback into the language which is misunderstood, so that philosophical confusions themselves become a substantive part of what is believed. This has happened again and again in the philosophy of religion.'[24] The language in which religion is understood, in which the inheritance of religion is mediated to a contemporary audience, overwhelmingly characterizes it in compensatory terms. 'Things may not seem to make much sense from the perspective we are locked into here on earth. But there is a higher perspective, one which will make everything all right in the end.'[25] Arguments then take place as to whether there is or is not reason for believing in that higher perspective. The dominance of this understanding makes it difficult for other voices to be heard. Many 'are genuinely at home in the shabby language they employ when discussing religion or when acting for or against it . . . Individual voices may break through, but the likelihood is that they will seem forced, extreme, distorted, or even absurd.'[26]

Such voices are both literary and philosophical. The literary authors show possibilities of understanding religion, of mediating its sense in our world, which Phillips himself articulates in another way. *From Fantasy to Faith* passes from the compensatory understanding of religion to the possibilities shown by, for example, Flannery O'Connor and R.S. Thomas: 'The journey by which we have arrived at [these possibilities] has been both literary and philosophical. It is a journey, I believe, which must be undertaken by anyone seriously interested in the issues which confront philosophy and religion today.'[27] And in a reference to Flannery O'Connor in *Faith after Foundationalism* he compares the contemporary philosophical task of providing conceptual reminders to philosophy with that she faced as a Catholic writer, 'how to convey a religious perspective in literature in a pervasively secular American culture'.[28]

Religious sense must be mediated: the religious language inherited from our tradition must be understood and it must be applied in our contemporary situation. 'If religion has redeeming sense, it will have to be expressed in a pattern of meaning which informs everyday life. Only in this way can a timeless truth be said again effectively.'[29] In a society increasingly formed in terms of non-religious values and in which the dominant interpretation of religion is in compensatory terms, there are particular difficulties which attend this mediation. Literature attempting to convey a different understanding of what is involved in the religious life must take a disturbing form:

the preconceptions about what is to be valued and about what religion is must be upset. Phillips quotes Flannery O'Connor writing about her own work: 'The novelist with Christian concerns will find in modern life distortions which are repugnant to him, and his problem will be to make these appear as distortions to an audience which is used to seeing them as natural; and he may well be forced to take ever more violent means to get his vision across to his hostile audience . . . you have to make your vision apparent by shock – to the hard of hearing you shout, and for the almost-blind you draw large and startling figures.' The grotesquerie of which she was accused is rather a matter of using 'a certain distortion . . . to get at the truth'.[30]

The general difficulty of modernist forms of writing, of which Flannery O'Connor's shock tactics are an example, is a mark of the faithfulness of their response to the situation they address. Phillips quotes T.S. Eliot on the necessity of difficulty in modern poetry: 'The poet must become more and more comprehensive, more allusive, more indirect, in order to force, to dislocate if necessary, language into his meaning.'[31] If we are indeed living in an age when the conception of moral value is itself under threat, when the notion of a relation to the non-temporal is becoming difficult to apprehend and live, and when religion is being forgotten or transmuted into compensatory belief, then this must be reflected in the character of the writer's work. What a work of literature says cannot be separated from how it is said. If a writer wishes to convey the possibility of a moral or religious perspective in such a situation, the necessity to disrupt the preconceptions of the reader and the difficulties of conveying that vision will make writing something other than it could be in a more morally or religiously confident age. Or if a writer wishes to communicate the nature of our situation, in which moral and religious values are losing their hold and life exists only as their uncertain memory, as Beckett does, then this would have to be conveyed in forms which question notions fundamental to the conceptions of selfhood which those moral and religious values made possible. Inherited literary forms, concerned with character development or decline, and so involving a narrative structure reflecting the intelligible patterns of individual histories, cannot address a situation where the very conceptions of character and individual history have themselves become questionable.

Modern forms of writing can be 'difficult', however, in another way, one which, I think, Phillips does not directly address. Beckett's plays show us a time (and invite self-recognition on the part of the audience) when the very possibility of living in terms of our inherited moral and religious vocabularies has become problematic. Moral and religious traditions embody conceptions of the worthwhile life through which the individual can gain a sense of the significance of life as a whole and so a conception of the self, of her or his identity as an individual human being. In the context delineated in Beckett's plays, these fundamental concepts of the sense of life, of the self and personal identity are themselves destabilized. Such a situation may produce renewed efforts to articulate moral or religious perspectives. It may too result in a loss of a sense of the significance of life as a whole and a retreat into the pursuit of temporal objectives, a move Phillips sees reflected in the demands for the justification of moral and religious values we see in contemporary philosophy, where these justifications may become part of the transmutation of those vocabularies themselves. But equally it may produce an effort to articulate ways of living which are neither religious nor moral in the inherited sense of these terms, and which don't consist either simply in the pursuit of temporal goals.

Morality and religion have given us a sense of the significance of life as a whole by referring the temporality of life to a 'timeless' measure. Morality and religion have been opposed, however, at least from the Early German Romantic writings of Friedrich Schlegel, in the name of other ways of taking over this temporality. Nietzsche, for example, in proclaiming the death of God (which is the rejection of a relation to the 'timeless'), looked towards a form of life 'beyond good and evil'. To live one's life as 'becoming' is to live in terms of a future which is always open, and so requires a constant overcoming of the forces within oneself which make for fixity. Like Schlegel before him, Nietzsche often speaks of this in terms of creativity and the language of artistic production: 'The two futures of mankind: 1) constant growth of mediocrity, 2) conscious distinction, self-shaping'.[32] In Schlegel's novel *Lucinde* we are told that for one of the protagonists 'his life now came to be a work of art for him'.[33] Living as constant becoming, as the maintaining of the possibility of the always new, disrupts the unity of the self; 'of this only a mind is capable that contains within itself simultaneously a plurality of minds and a whole system of persons'.[34] Perhaps Lawrence's conception that 'my soul is a dark forest' and that 'gods, strange gods, come forth from the forest into the clearing of my known self, and then go back ... I must have the courage to let them come and go'[35] is analogous. Such values of creativity, the plurality of selves one may become, the passivity in responding to one's unknownness, and so forth, in setting themselves against the values of inherited moral and religious tradition, reject the notions of commitment and the unity of the self which the latter facilitate.

In post-Nietzschean thought, in Heidegger, Bataille, Blanchot and Derrida, for example, there are differing articulations of what living in terms of our temporality, without adherence to the notion of the eternal, can amount to. Both Bataille and Blanchot wrote 'fictions' which have an essential role in this articulation, and there is a tradition of 'avant-garde' literature, from Dada and surrealism on, concerned with the possibility of forms of living which take our temporality seriously without that seriousness involving a turn to 'the eternal'. Whatever one may think of such efforts, they are not attempts to live 'ethically' or 'religiously' in terms of other interests, nor are they a retreat to the pursuit of temporal objectives, and reminders of what moral and religious life can be can therefore have no purchase on them. Of course, they are open to ethical and religious criticism, and, to the extent that they claim a philosophical justification for their conceptions of life, to the charge of confusion. But their example should remind us that there may be possibilities of making sense of life beyond moral and religious categories: there is no essence of human life which makes these the only possibilities.

To the difficulties of getting oneself heard and finding the language to convey religious sense against dominant interpretations, the writer who wishes to convey a religious perspective on life faces the difficulty of its application in a world increasingly formed in accordance with different values. To recognize that a religion is a way of living, a way of relating in one's life to the limits of human existence, means that its concepts must be capable of expression in one's life. They must be mediated in words and action in terms of our world: we must be able to see what in these circumstances living in terms of God's grace and seeing the world as God's creation, as a gift of grace, can amount to. We cannot assume that because it was once clear what it was to live in these concepts, it is now. 'We may not know what hope, love or faith amount to. We cannot take it for granted that we do.'[36] In *Belief, Change and Forms of Life* Phillips mentions, for example, the challenge which changes in technology and their associated forms of activity pose to the intelligibility of seeing life in religious terms. Can the birth of a child be regarded as a gift from God when it is planned? Can a religious relation to death be actualized in the age of the motorized funeral cortège and cremation? Can the hills declare the glory of God when they are mined out of greed for gold?[37] As the transformation of the world in terms of other values increases, so too do the difficulties of applying religious concepts. What is it, we may ask now, to see life as God's gift in a time of genetic engineering where we face the prospect of designer babies? What does it mean to see the world as God's creation in a time of multinational agribusiness and the genetic alteration of plants and animals? Of course, this is not to say that religious sense may not be made of such a world, 'but at least there is a tension, a question to be resolved'.[38] It is important too to stress, what Phillips I think rarely does, that changes in the world that take place in terms of other forms of value can stimulate religious change, can be the occasion for a reconsideration of the application of religious terms and a coming to a new understanding of what living in terms of them requires. New religious thinking on gender relations, gay sexuality, the environment and the position of animals have all been prompted by the development of social movements which originally had little to do with religion.

It nevertheless remains the case that what is to count as applying religious concepts, of living in terms of them, is a question for us, and one which may appear increasingly insoluble. A writer's problem in conveying such a perspective now is precipitated by the problem of actually living in terms of such concepts. *R.S. Thomas: Poet of the Hidden God* shows us the poet making poetry out of his struggle to make religious sense of his life. The 'tensions in the poems are not to be resolved or tidied up. They reflect the poet's relation in verse to the questions which bear in on him.'[39] These questions are simultaneously ones of the sense of religious concepts and the sense of his life, since, as a priest, he is trying to live in terms of those concepts. Phillips speaks of a 'decisive drama' played out in the course of Thomas's poetry: 'It is the drama of concept formation in religion; the attempt to see what or how religious belief can inform human life.'[40] The difficulties the poet-priest faces are those of applying religious concepts to his life with the poverty-stricken Welsh peasants to whom he ministers. These difficulties would largely be present in any age since it is humanly difficult to apply the notions of 'praise' and 'God's will' to the sufferings of human life, although perhaps the presence of compensatory interpretations in philosophy and theology may make it more difficult to be clear to oneself just where the real, existential, difficulties lie.

But if the Christian is always to give thanks, the suffering and torment of the world presents a difficulty many will find insuperable. This is not an intellectual difficulty, since to speak of God's will is precisely to recognize the limits of the understanding: it is to speak of the givenness that confronts us after the understanding has done its work. 'Due attention will have to be given to a necessary compassion in face of suffering with its imperative to remove it, but due attention will have to be paid too to the fact that some suffering is necessary, defying all efforts at elimination.'[41] The poet 'shows us a religious faith which actually depends on embracing the mixed character of human life in a way which does not deny its character'.[42] Yet the attainment of such faith is essentially precarious, and the poetry expresses the poet's struggle with it. 'Struggle will always be part of faith, since the demands of faith ... are such that men will always wonder whether what they are giving themselves to is an illusion or not.'[43]

This is not an illusion that something exists when it doesn't, not a false belief held in circumstances where the believer is in a position to see its falsity but refuses. What is at issue, rather, is the question of whether it is an existential illusion, of whether anyone could relate to human suffering in this way without being self-deceived. Can one relate to one's own suffering in this way without it being a disguise for other motives, a self-hatred or a self-assertion over oneself (as Nietzsche thought)? Can one really relate to the sufferings of others in these terms without it being a mask for indifference or motivations even worse? Isn't the peasants' moral endurance in the face of their hardship a human response with which one can join in human solidarity? Isn't the striving after a religious perspective a desire to break with humanity (and what desires might disguise themselves here?)? The poetry of R.S. Thomas expresses the struggles of a life which, trying to live in religious categories, comes to see what the religious perspective demands and expresses the human conflicts and doubts in relation to these demands. But whereas these struggles would belong to Christian faith at any time, certain problems of the application of religious concepts are peculiar to ours. 'What can religion mean in a Benthamite culture dominated by the machine?'[44] The poet finds the mechanized world of agriculture that comes to characterize the life of the peasant presents problems of application he is unable confidently to resolve. Phillips remarks: 'The passages by which truth must be sought are narrower and narrower because the world which now awaits the mediation of religious sense is one which is increasingly resistant to it.'[45]

R.S. Thomas: Poet of the Hidden God is not a work of criticism. It neither attempts to situate Thomas in the context of Welsh or British poetry nor to show us the literary value of the poetry. The poetry's power as poetry is largely taken as read, or rather offered to us in quotation for our agreement in response. It is not an issue for the book. Rather, the book is an elucidation of a 'philosophically neglected perspective' through the presentation of that perspective in Thomas's poetry. The poet brings to language the experience of the individual trying to make religious sense of their own life in particular historical and social circumstances. This involves finding what sense religious concepts can have in those circumstances (what application they can have) which is at the same time discovering what sense his life can take, whether and how he can live religiously. In this way, the religious notions of the Hidden God, grace and God's will are placed within the context of use where they have their sense, in the struggle of the individual to see and live the significance of his or her own life. The philosopher in bringing out the nature of this lived context and the form which difficulties and resolutions can take there provides an articulation of a possibility of understanding religion which is forgotten by the dominant philosophical and popular voices of the age.

In the Preface, Phillips comments on the parallel between his and Thomas's tasks. Thomas is engaged with 'the struggle with the possibility of a satisfactory religious syntax in verse today. That struggle, unsurprisingly, shares many features of the thrusts and counter thrusts which have characterised the discussion of religion in contemporary philosophy.'[46] The poet's mediation of religious sense is to bring to language in verse the individual's struggle to make religious sense of his life today. The philosopher's commentary brings out the nature of this sense, articulates the context within which the concepts have their use and so their sense there. The success of such an elucidation reminds us at the same time, when impressed by philosophical theorizing about the significance of life, that we turn to literature to encounter the possibilities of meaning in human life, to see what those possibilities have been and to be confronted by the question of what can be made now, if anything, of the moral and religious vocabularies we have inherited. To engage with literature in this way is to contemplate the possibilities and impossibilities of sense for us now (which involves, of course, our active, concerned reading), to contribute to the mediation of these vocabularies in our own lives.

University of Essex

Notes

1   D.Z. Phillips, *Interventions in Ethics* (Basingstoke: Macmillan, 1992), p. xv.
2   Martha Nussbaum, *Love's Knowledge* (Oxford: Oxford University Press, 1990), p. 173.
3   *Ibid.*, p. 174.
4   *Ibid.*, p. 226.
5   *Ibid.*, p. 229.
6   *Ibid.*, p. 228.
7   Phillips, *Through a Darkening Glass* (Oxford: Oxford University Press, 1982), pp. 23–4.
8   *Ibid.*, p. 10.
9   *Ibid.*, p. 19.
10 *Ibid.*, pp. 22–3.
11 Phillips, *Interventions in Ethics*, p. 62.
12 R.W. Beardsmore, 'Literary Examples and Philosophical Confusion', in A. Phillips Griffiths (ed.), *Philosophy and Literature* (Cambridge: Cambridge University Press, 1984), pp. 70–1.
13 Phillips, *Interventions in Ethics*, p. 65.
14 Phillips, *From Fantasy to Faith* (Basingstoke: Macmillan, 1991), p. 140.
15 *Ibid.*
16 *Ibid.*, p. 154.
17 Phillips, *From Fantasy to Faith*, p. 47.
18 Phillips, *Through a Darkening Glass*, p. 119.
19 *Ibid.*, p. 121.
20 *Ibid.*, p. 126.
21 *Ibid.*, p. 125.
22 *Ibid.*, p. 127.
23 Phillips, *From Fantasy to Faith*, p. 1.
24 Phillips, *Belief, Change and Forms of Life* (Basingstoke: Macmillan, 1986), pp. 50–1.
25 Phillips, *From Fantasy to Faith*, p. 47.
26 *Ibid.*, p. 124.
27 *Ibid.*, pp. 220–21.
28 Phillips, *Faith after Foundationalism*, p. 311.
29 Phillips, *From Fantasy to Faith*, p. 9.
30 Phillips, *Faith after Foundationalism*, p. 317.
31 Phillips, *From Fantasy to Faith*, p. 3.
32 Friedrich Nietzsche, *The Will to Power*, trans. Walter Kaufmann (New York: Vintage, 1968), p. 500.
33 Friedrich Schlegel, *Lucinde and the Fragments*, trans. P. Firchow (Minneapolis: University of Minnesota Press, 1971), p. 47.
34 *Ibid.*, p. 92.

35 D.H. Lawrence, *Studies in Classic American Literature* (Harmondsworth: Penguin, 1971), p. 22.
36 Phillips, *From Fantasy to Faith*, p. 6.
37 Phillips, *Belief, Change and Forms of Life*, pp. 88–90.
38 *Ibid.*, p. 89.
39 Phillips, *R.S. Thomas: Poet of the Hidden God* (Basingstoke: Macmillan, 1986), p. 21.
40 *Ibid.*, p. 20.
41 *Ibid.*, p. 62.
42 *Ibid.*, p. 77.
43 *Ibid.*, p. 91.
44 *Ibid.*, p. 166.
45 *Ibid.*, p. 169.
46 *Ibid.*, p. xiii.

12
'That's it Exactly!'

Colin Lyas

When Leavis remarked that those who try to reduce the value of *Emma* to an aesthetic matter – a matter of formal qualities only – can give no account of why *Emma* is a great novel, he wished to stress what, alas, still needs stressing, namely, that the world of a literary work of art, and in particular of a novel, is an arena of moral activity. From that it follows that one simply could not understand many literary works of art if one were not a participant in some form of moral life. Moreover, a person following a narrative brings to it her or his moral commitments and some understanding of the nature of morality. If that understanding is defective, then the narrative will be misjudged. Thus, as Phillips points out, someone may mischaracterize the situation in Edith Wharton's *The Age of Innocence* through believing that the morality of old New York society must have been less liberating than a newer, and so more advanced morality, that puts personal happiness before duty. Another and, as we shall see, much more difficult case is one in which one's own, possibly excusable, moral inadequacies prevent one from characterizing and appreciating a work correctly. Someone who has overdosed on Baden-Powell is unlikely to see the xenophobia implicit in the works of Captain W.E. Johns. More complex perhaps is the case of someone taken in by Othello's final self-justificatory speech. A certain kind of Victorian critic, determined to impose views of Christian redemptive tragedy on that play, is bound to get it wrong. This is, indeed, simply a particular instance of the general truth that our preconceptions can cause us to mischaracterize what we encounter.

The notion that understanding a work of art may require an understanding of morality was, of course, a source of embarrassment to formalists who, like Clive Bell, wished to argue that to understand a work of art we need bring with us nothing from life, save a knowledge of form, colour and three-dimensional space. And when they classed an interest in the represented content of a painting as a literary interest this was intended as the derogatory characterization of that interest. For, on that view, literature, bound up as it is with human interest, is an impure art-form.

Few, save some musical purists, would now deny this moral prerequisite. The poverty of the literary criticism that has attempted to operate on the basis of a denial that works of art, and especially works of literature, require for their understanding an engagement with morality, speaks for itself. What remains ill understood, however, are the bilateral trading links that occur between the moral views of life embodied in all imaginative narratives, be they novel, film, dance or drama, and the moral views of life subscribed to, and brought to, those narratives by those who engage appreciatively with them. One of Dewi Phillips's great achievements is to have thought about these problems in a way that shows a notable and rare sensitivity to both the intricate task of interpreting imaginative narratives of widely different sorts and the task of understanding moral appraisal. I shall discuss some of those remarks, and I hope that the respect I feel for Dewi Phillips's work will be apparent in that discussion. The comparison between his writing on literature and what often now passes for literary criticism shows him to very substantial advantage. On a more personal note, I hope he will accept this essay as a kind of thanks for the hard thinking he has made me do, and also for the laughter and conviviality with which he has so often leavened that thinking.

What are some of the bilateral trading arrangements that exist between the morality of a work of art and the morality of the person engaging with that work? First, a work of art might effect a change in one's way of seeing something. Possessed of a knee-jerk disapproval of radicals one might, through a work of literature, simply come to a different understanding. That is no more surprising or problematic than that acquaintance with the life of the trenches which disinclined Owen or Thomas from continuing to feel and express heroic attitude to modern warfare. Of course this leaves open the problem, to which I return (and which is not in the end a problem just for aesthetics), of the source of one's assumption that one is changed for the better. I know of too many cases of students who have been converted to the views of Ayn Rand through reading *Atlas Shrugged* to be entirely happy with the thought that epiphanic artistic experiences are self-authenticating.

'That's right!'

I find a more interesting case to be the one in which Phillips talks of the work as 'reminding us' and in which the work occasions in us an experience that we articulate by exclaiming 'That's right!' The phenomenon may occur in many contexts and not only in art. We may so express ourselves: after struggling with a proof in mathematics; after wondering how to say a line in a play; on finding a solution when struggling with a compositional problem when painting; on seeing the aptness of a description of someone or something; on suddenly coming to see one's life as answering to a certain characterization; on suddenly seeing through someone; on suddenly seeing, as Glenn Miller did, what combination of instruments gave him the sound for which he had long sought; on suddenly seeing the face in a puzzle picture; after struggling with a thought in a seminar and having someone articulate it perfectly; on simply reading something, such as Bogart's advice to Lauren Bacall on how to cope with the death of a lover. Here are some particular cases from art, of a kind discussed in *Through a Darkening Glass*.

First we may feel that a work of art gives us a way of expressing what we already inchoately thought ourselves to be. That is why we exclaim, 'That's right!' Only after Dickens had written *David Copperfield* would it be possible for me to refer (whether rightly or wrongly) to the prime minister as the Uriah Heep of politics, and to hope that my audience might see him as an instance of a particular fictional realization of that kind of mixture of ingratiation and self-will used as a means to power and its retention.

Finally, an imaginative narrative may get us to see possibilities implicit in the morality to which we have subscribed. An example is the parable of the Good Samaritan, told to the lawyer who knew that he had to love his neighbour, but could not see what range of persons to include in that category. He came to see, through an imaginative narrative, that neighbours are not just fellow members of one's tribe.

The experiences, both artistic and non-artistic, reported by 'That's right!' seem to have an oddly double character. On the one hand, we feel something has been revealed to us: yet, on the other, we also feel we already knew it. How, though, could it be revealed if we already knew it? How could one say, with a sense of recognition, 'That is exactly what I was trying to say!' if one was not already, in some way, in possession of what one wanted to say? How could artists think such things as, 'Yes! that's the effect I was after!' if they did not already in some way know what effect was being sought? (And that carries with it the concomitant question why, if one knows already what one is after, does one have so much trouble producing it?)

The matter is an important one since these epiphanic experiences have been thought central to art in at least two ways. First, they occur when the artist is seeking the right word, the right combination of notes or the right compositional line. In this passage from the very end of *To the Lighthouse*, Lily Briscoe expresses how she feels when, of a sudden, light dawns and she resolves a compositional problem:

> She looked at her canvas; it was blurred. With a sudden intensity, as if she saw it clear for a second, she drew a line there, in the centre. It was done; it was finished. Yes, she thought, laying down the brush in extreme fatigue, I have had my vision.

Croce, indeed, made such experiences central to art. In Chapter 16 of *The Aesthetic* he writes:

Individual A seeks an expression for the impression he feels, or of which he has a presentiment but which he has not yet expressed. See him trying out different words and phrases which might give him the expression he seeks, which must be there, although he has not got hold of it yet. He tries a combination, m, and rejects it as inadequate, inexpressive, defective and ugly: he tries combination n, with the same outcome. He cannot see at all or he cannot see clearly. The expression still eludes him. After other vain attempts, in which he now draws near, now draws away from that towards which he strains, of a sudden he finds the form of the expression sought – (it almost seems that it forms spontaneously in him) – and lux facta est. He enjoys for an instant aesthetic pleasure or beauty. The ugly with its corresponding displeasure, was that aesthetic activity that did not succeed in conquering the obstacles that lay in its way: the beautiful is the expressive activity that now triumphantly unfolds itself.

Second, what innumerable people have valued in art is the way in which a work of art may bring to explicit and perfect articulation how, before its articulation, we already, but inchoately, felt the world and ourselves to be. So lovers appropriate Shakespeare sonnets, finding them exactly apt for their own expressive purposes; and those who have a sense of the losses of time might find this precisely articulated for them by Hardy's 'During Wind and Rain'. Similarly, after viewing a Turner painting, I might see a sunset and can now express myself by saying that the sunset is Turneresque. That is what Wollheim is in part after, when in his remarkable *The Mind and its Depths*, he speaks of the way in which projecting our inner lives onto some objective correlate helps to restore, or impose, order on to those internal lives. What could be more important than this? And what, if not art, is to do it? A passage from *Howards End* gives a perfect example of what I mean. In Chapter 5 Helen Schlegel's feelings as Beethoven's *Fifth Symphony* ends amid its 'roarings of superhuman joy' are characterized thus:

> Helen pushed her way out during the applause. She desired to be alone. The music had summed up to her all that had happened or could happen in her career. She read as a tangible statement, which could never be superseded. The notes meant this and that to her, and they could have no other meaning, and life could have no other meaning. She pushed right out of the building, and walked slowly down the outside staircase, breathing the autumnal air, and then she strolled home.

This reminds us that the inclination to say 'that's right', with its implications of finding a truth, arises as much in the case of music as it does in the case of the other arts. One can as well say 'My emotions are all Mahler's Ninth' as 'That sunset is Turneresque'.

Puzzles

Although 'epiphanic experiences' are familiar and of great importance, there are two things about them that can seem puzzling. One is put thus by Wittgenstein:

> One is tempted to use the following picture: what he really 'wanted to say', what he 'meant' was already present somewhere in his mind even before we gave it expression. (*Philosophical Investigations*, para. 334)

And:

> James, in writing of this subject, is really trying to say: 'What a remarkable experience. The word is not there yet, and yet in a certain sense is there, – or something is there, which cannot grow into anything but this word.' (*Investigations*, Part II, p. 219)

If I recognize something as what I wanted to say, I must already know that that is what I wanted to say. Then we are tempted to think of it already being in some occult place, the mind, and of bringing what we recognize in the expression up against it in order to check that it *is* what is already there. That model makes it mysterious, both where this occult place is, and, granted we do know already what we want to express, why we find it so hard to express it. Here the question for the more general philosophy of mind is seeing what is wrong with the notion of the mind as an occult room.

The second oddity is this: the feeling expressed by 'That's right!' seems to occur in a flash, in an epiphanic *moment*. But in many of the cases that occur in art, the consequences of that epiphany might be spread out in a life. And then we get the problem that puzzled Wittgenstein when he talked about suddenly coming to understand the meaning of a word. That process was presumably something that happened of a sudden. Yet the meaning of a word is spread out in its use. How, then, could some instantaneous process guarantee one an understanding of a use that might be extended into the far and indefinite future? Wittgenstein writes:

> But we understand the meaning of a word when we hear or say it; we grasp it in a flash, and what we grasp in this way is surely something different from the 'use' which is extended in time! (*Investigations*, para. 138)

Wittgenstein offers two comments. The first is that it is simply a mistake to think that the experience, for example, of recognizing that someone has expressed what one wanted to say, is a momentary experience, which, like, say, a stab of pain, could be entirely self-contained, being what it is regardless of what came before or after. One has to recognize that the true epiphanic experience is embedded in the life that precedes and follows it and gets its sense from its surroundings. He writes:

'You were interrupted a while ago; do you still know what you were going to say?' – If I do know now, and say it – does that mean that I had already thought it before, only not said it? No. Unless you take the certainty with which I continue the interrupted sentence as a criterion of the thought's already having been completed at that time. – But, of course, the situation and the thoughts which I had contained all sorts of things to help the continuation of the sentence. (*Investigations*, para. 633)

The words 'It's on the tip of my tongue' are no more the expression of an experience than 'Now I know how to go on' – We use them in certain situations, and they are surrounded by behaviour of a special kind, and also by some characteristic experiences. In particular they are frequently followed by finding the word.(*Investigations*, Part III, p. 219)

Imagine that someone who knew nothing of painting and lived where the sunsets were decidedly unTurneresque (say, Tampa) suddenly saw a Turner and had a feeling which he or she expressed by saying 'That's it', but never had any inclination subsequently to call sunsets 'Turneresque'. Here the mere sincere avowal of the feeling would not convince me that an act of epiphanic recognition had taken place, no more than I would take the fact that someone had had just the feelings or sensations that I had had when intending to play chess as evidence that she or he knew what it was to intend to play chess.

The second thing Wittgenstein says seems to me less helpful. Imagining someone puzzled about the epiphanic avowals: 'That's exactly what I was trying to say, exactly the word I was looking for!' – imagine him being reminded of the situations in which we use these expressions:

How do I find the 'right' word? How do I choose among words? Without doubt it is sometimes as if I were comparing them by fine differences of smell: That is too . . . that is too . . . this is the right one.

– But I do not always have to make judgements, give explanations; often I might only say: 'It simply isn't right yet'. I am dissatisfied, I go on looking. At last a word comes: 'That's it!' Sometimes I can say why. This is simply what searching, this is what finding, is like here. (*Investigations*, p. 218)

That, it seems to me, rightly reminds us of the situations in which we do talk of looking for the right word. But it seems not to address the question why we are so tempted to think of this as a sort of *recognition*. That unhelpfulness seems to be repeated in the following passage, whose terminal questions seem merely to express Wittgenstein's puzzlement about how to put the matter rather than to offer any solution:

> What happens when we make an effort – say in writing a letter – to find the right expression for our thoughts? – This phrase compares the process to one of translating or describing: the thoughts are already there (perhaps were there in advance) and we merely look for their expression. This picture is more or less appropriate in different cases. – But can't all sorts of things happen here? – I surrender to a mood and the expression comes. Or a picture occurs to me and I try to describe it. Or an English expression occurs to me and I try to hit on the corresponding German one. Or I make a gesture, and ask myself: What words correspond to this gesture? And so on. Now if it were asked: 'Do you have the thought before finding the expression?' what would one have to reply? And what, to the question: 'What did the thought consist in, as it existed before its expression?'
>
> (*Investigations*, para. 335)

Let us try this suggestion: the cases by which we are puzzled resemble a phenomenon with which we are familiar and by which we may be less puzzled. Thus, something may follow from two beliefs that I have, but I might not know that it follows, simply because I have had no occasion to put those two beliefs together as when I hold the belief that all warm-blooded creatures are mammals and the belief that whales are warm-blooded quite separately. When any two such beliefs are put together (and, in some cases, a novel might suggest that possibility to me) I immediately recognize that I am already committed to something by virtue of those beliefs. In that case I can understand both how I cannot formulate a proposition to myself and yet come to *recognize* it as one to which I am committed. (*Ad hominem* argument, sometimes mischaracterized as fallacious, seems to me to get its power just from this possibility.)

The 'right' in 'That's right!'

But in the context of *Through a Darkening Glass* there is a much deeper problem. For how, when we exclaim, 'Yes, that's it! That's right!', can we know that it is right? That is related to something that might cause unease about the way Phillips conducts his discussion in *Through a Darkening Glass*. For, in that work, there is a propensity to talk of moral views and views about morality as lacking in certain ways. Consider, for example, the view that the old New York morality explored by Edith Wharton is old hat and best got rid of. Phillips argues against any notion that change in morality is necessarily upward progress. We simply cannot say that an earlier morality which we do not share is defective simply because it is an earlier and possibly now abandoned morality. But then, the argument might go, either we abstain from commenting adversely on moralities that we do not share (in which case, what becomes of Phillips's criticisms, elsewhere in his work, of Ingmar Bergman's world picture), or we are owed some account of how we can adversely comment on moralities other than our own. And that account is certainly owed to us by Phillips, given both the frequency with which various moral perspectives are adversely characterized in *Through a Darkening Glass*, and given, too, his general claim that 'we do not have reasons for our values. Our values are our reasons'. If that is so, isn't any comment on a divergent morality *parti pris*?

How do we know, then, that what seems right to us is right? For couldn't one think that one had been brought to see oneself or the world rightly, and, indeed, live a whole life in the spirit of that revelation and, at the last, come to realize that this was not right? Is this any less possible than the feeling that one had, of a sudden, come to an understanding of the answer to a mathematical problem only to discover, alas, that one had not got the right answer at all? And couldn't someone think that she or he had found the solution to an artistic problem and others see that he or she had not? And couldn't the artist come to see that for him or herself at a later stage? And can't I think that someone's sincerely felt, dollar-laden post-*Atlas Shrugged* epiphanies are simply barmy?

So, Helen Schlegel's thinking that Beethoven had told her what her life was is compatible with her finding out, as that life continued, that he hadn't. Here, though, a real difficulty seems to emerge. For if Helen had found out that Beethoven had not revealed her life to her as it really is, it is presumably because, at some later time, she had a further epiphanic experience which revealed the falsity of what Beethoven had apparently revealed and the truth of something else. But then by parity of reasoning she could not trust that later epiphanic experience as genuinely revelatory. And then one might begin to wonder, if one cannot trust its revelations, what the value is of the claim that works of art have this revelatory power. For that is certainly what is claimed and certainly what Phillips claims when he speaks of literature in *Through a Darkening Glass* as a 'source of reminders' or revelations. Could someone, be that person the artist or one of the audience, think 'Yes! That's right! That's how I feel!' and be mistaken? Could an artist initially feel an inchoate restlessness, feel, subsequently, that a work expressed it clearly as Lily Briscoe in one of my earlier examples claimed to feel, and be wrong? Could a person, reading T.S. Eliot's 'The Love Song of J. Alfred Prufrock', think, 'Yes! that's me: I'm past it' and be wrong? In one of the few coherent discussions of this matter, indeed, one of the few discussions of any sort, John Benson suggests that if an expression feels wrong, it is wrong, and if it feels right, it is right (see his article in the *Philosophical Review*, 1967). Is this so?

Two cases need to be distinguished here. First, there is the case in which one inchoately feels past it, then feels, after reading a poem, that it precisely expresses that inchoate feeling, and yet is wrong in feeling, first inchoately and then articulately, that one is past it. Here the poem truly articulates what one inarticulately feels about oneself, only one is wrong in feeling that about oneself. Second, there is the more interesting possibility that one might be wrong in asserting, with a sense of recognition, that a poem expresses articulately one's inner life. One says, with a sense of either recognition or revelation, 'That expresses how it is with me!', when it does not. The first of these cases is certainly possible, and it raises problems, to which we shortly return, about the epiphanic status of art. But the latter case is both intriguing in its own right, as well as worrying for those who think that works of art can clarify, in a reminding way, our lives.

In the latter case, one possibility seems to me to be relatively uninteresting. I might carelessly (but sincerely, in the sense of having no intention to mislead, lie or whatever) say, perhaps at a Bergman film, 'Yes, that about sums up my world view', only to be subsequently persuaded that it does not. Wittgenstein remarks: 'it is the circumstances under which he had such an experience that justify him in saying in such a case that he understands'. And one of the circumstances seems to me to be how seriously the speaker took the matter. Did she or he, so to speak, shoot from the hip, speak hastily, carelessly, or whatever? And then I want to say that if a person speaks with due seriousness and consideration, attentively, let us say, then a gap cannot open between saying that a poem, say, expresses what we inchoately feel and what we in fact inchoately feel. That is the truth that Benson seems to me to have grasped. But that still leaves it open that both the inchoate and expressed belief or feeling about oneself, about the world, about what one wanted to say, about what would or would not work artistically in a certain picture, could simply be mistaken. In that case, one could say 'that's how it is (that's how the world is)' and be wrong, wrong not in describing one's feeling, inchoate or not, about how the world is, and asserting that the poem perfectly expresses this, but wrong in feeling that the world is so. Moreover, we can come to think that we erroneously believed ourselves to have had revelatory insights. What then becomes of the revelatory power of art?

Various possibilities exist here. One would be to invoke the notion, canvassed in Wittgenstein's *On Certainty*, that certain beliefs, like the belief that there are objects, are not to be doubted, but rather constitute a context in which doubt becomes possible. Similarly, one might say that a work of art might bring something home to us with such force that doubt is not something we could seriously entertain. After reading Tolstoy's short story about the matter, I might be so struck with the horror of prostitution that I could not seriously ever again engage with any work that was in any way sympathetic to that institution. But I am in sufficient doubt about what is going on in these discussions in *On Certainty* not to wish to exploit that possibility. Moreover that work seems to concede the possibility that our seemingly revelatory foundational experiences *can* come to be doubted, which rather shakes the foundations of any hope of having self-authenticating epiphanic experiences.

A second possibility is to claim that one can have a perfect title to say, on hearing the expression of a sentiment in a poem, 'That's exactly right', meaning by that that one thinks both that the poem gets it right and, moreover, that it exactly expresses what one inchoately felt, even if one later comes to feel that that didn't get it right. This seems to me to be of a piece with the claim that one can have a perfect title to say one is seeing a pig, even if that claim later turns out to be false. The error here is to believe that claims to have received revelations from art, like claims to see the world, require incorrigibility for their legitimacy. That is, for example, at odds with the fact that we may look back on the poems we loved in late adolescence and think of them as expressing a world view which is not so much false as inappropriate to our present condition. Yet we can still think them to be poems in which one really did once see something.

Art aside, however, the claim that revelation sorts with incorrigibility seems to me not to do justice to the fact that our moral views, and more generally our views of life, are constantly brought to the bar of experience and can alter in consequence. We can never be sure when this is going to happen. One example of this is the case in which my belief as to how one should comport oneself in the face of the death of someone loved may simply not be sustainable when that actually happens to me. We engage with each other in moral and kindred interchanges, interchanges which can effect a change in our views. These debates are complex, and the agreements and disagreements that are reached are often patchily overlapping and sometimes fugitive, as they must be since we all bring to these interchanges our individual and constantly updated psychological histories. This seems to me to happen both in ethics and in our engagements with the moral expressions of art. I bring to the work my present moral and metaphysical posture and a work can affect it, and later works may affect it yet again. At each stage I may feel a revelation. Although I must always be conscious that this revelation is at risk of what time and other insights may bring, I can still accept it, if I can live it.

Loosening up morality

These remarks touch on a thing that worries me a little about *Through a Darkening Glass*, for all that I admire the way it has illuminated a range of works of literature for me. For through it there seems to me to run an inclination to say that this or that moral perspective is right or wrong: Edith Wharton and Beckett, perhaps, right; Bergman, perhaps, wrong; R.S. Thomas, sometimes right and sometimes wrong. And one's wrong perspective can interfere with understanding. Given Phillips's dictum that 'we do not have reasons for our values, our values are our reasons', I have always wondered from what perspective these judgements were made and about their foundations. I now feel that we may need a greater degree of provisionality about morality than Phillips admits. I now wish to conclude with some remarks about that.

First, we should guard ourselves against having too austere a view of what counts as our morality in our involvement with art. One overly austere model might work like this: we are committed, say, to opposition to genocide (although western reaction to recent events in, say, Timor, might indicate that the commitment is lip-service). We then encounter a work expressing an endorsement of genocide. This repels us enough to prevent our enjoying whatever the work might have to offer were it, so to speak, on our side. That counts, for us, as a defect in the work. One possibly minor point of moral psychology is that such an account leaves out cases like 'Till Death Us Do Part' (or 'All in the Family' in its American incarnation). I became tired of hearing the righteous defending this as defeating evil with savage parody when it was obvious that a fair percentage of them (not to mention the public at large) were actually vicariously enjoying the saying of the unsayable. Indeed the very example of *The Triumph of the Will* brings before us the spectacle of the glamour of evil to which we may be attracted in the way in which we, as Plato claimed, cannot take our eyes off a repellent corpse. It simply will not do to represent our moral psychology as one that is simply switched off by the spectacle of that towards which we are at pains to voice our repugnance. We need a more sophisticated moral psychology if we are to understand the full extent of the dealings of art and morality with each other.

More importantly, the account, cast as it is in terms of being switched off by works that clash with our morality, leaves out any consideration of the fact that some of the very greatest of art enacts its programme in the very areas where our morality is not secure, however vehemently we may protest it is. To be sure, if I can 'inhabit' the work, to use Professor Hepburn's excellent word, then I'll like it better; and if I can't, I'll be to some extent turned aside from it. But this needs to be supplemented by some notion of being morally challenged by a work. Though I have some moral certainties, I do not have enough to prevent my experience of art from being not a matter of attraction and repulsion, but (and here I think of Kafka and Beckett, not to forget Genet and Robert Mapplethorpe) a matter of unsettled anxiety, the kind of anxiety, perhaps, felt by Huck Finn, trapped between a sense of duty to his racist society and his friendship with an escaped slave.

But there is another way in which an account of morality and its dealings with art may be too austere. It will be so if it concentrates on cases in which our attraction and repulsion to art is a matter of its according or not according with some moral principle to which we adhere. That certainly needs to be supplemented by a wider survey and aetiology of the ways in which we can be put off art. To take a few examples, I may, without this being strictly a moral matter, be put off by the pretentious (see *Lady Chatterley's Lover*), the banal (see Betjeman's Laureate verses), the mawkish (see Keats' 'Ode to Psyche'), the intellectually vague (see *Paradise Lost* and parts of *The Four Quartets*), or the infantilely lavatorial (see some of Picasso's later works and some of Swift's writings to Stella). Sometimes the failing might not be sufficient to prevent me from enjoying or even thinking highly of the work. What this suggests is that instead of taking on only the moral we should look more generally at the ways in which human qualities of a work of art may or may not make it possible for us to live with it.

That remark about human qualities brings me the full circle to my discontents with any formalism that ignores the connections between morality and art. Such a formalism is simply too unsubtle to help us with puzzles about our responses to art. Here is one example of a thing formalism could never account for. Kafka writes in the first sentence of *The Metamorphosis*:

> As Gregor Sarnsa awoke one morning from uneasy dreams he found himself transformed in his bed into a giant insect.

We can go along with a fictional world in which that sort of thing happens with no other sense of strain than the fictional world itself imposes on us, which, as Doctor Johnson found in the case of *King Lear*, might be pretty considerable.

> Then we hear at the end of *The Taming of the Shrew*:
> Thy husband is thy lord, thy life, thy keeper,
> Thy head, thy sovereign; one that cares for thee,
> And for thy maintenance commits his body
> To painful labour, both by sea and land;
> To watch the night in storms, the day in cold,
> While thou liest warm at home, secure and safe,
> And craves no other tribute at thy hands,
> But love, fair looks, and true obedience:
> To little payment for so great a debt...
> Such duty as the subject owes the prince,
> Even such a woman oweth to her husband.

And now it seems harder to go along with those words, as witness the desperate attempts of recent directors to salvage an ironic intention notably ill-evidenced in the original passage. There is an asymmetry between our willingness to accept works of art in which unlikely if not impossible events occur and our unwillingness to ascribe to works of art that differ morally from our own. We find it harder to go along with the fictional world in which Kate's words are spoken than the world of the metamorphosed Gregor.

I am sure that the reason we might recoil, if we do, from those words of *The Taming of the Shrew* is not that we might find it hard to empathise with a fictional speaker saying those things in a repressive fictional world. Rather it is that we suspect, or better fear, that these sentiments were shared by a real person in a real world, namely the person who wrote the play. What upsets our assessments is not the morality of people and societies in works of art but the attitudes often displayed, wittingly or not, by the creators of those works in their very real acts of creation. For a work of art cannot be immoral, as opposed to containing instances of immorality, unless the morality it contains, if only by omission, is endorsed. The morality of a work of art can only be the morality displayed in the real act of articulating that work. That makes it as much part of the work as any of its other properties. But to say that is to say that moral considerations and with them considerations of the truth of those considerations must enter into our assessments of art. And that makes nonsense of any formalism which tells us that to appreciate a work we need bring with us nothing from life.

University of Lancaster

13
Excellence and Elites: Sincerity, Rationality and Monitoring

Antony Flew

A comparatively small amount of the abundant published work of Dewi Phillips has been directed at what, since 1968, the year of student revolutions, has been going wrong in the educational world; the world which Tom Lehrer persuaded my generation to think of as Edbiz. But the quality of that work must make all of us who share Phillips's concerns regret that the quantity has not been greater, and produced over a longer period.

The first substantial contribution was 'Democratization: Some Themes in Unexamined Talk', published in the *British Journal of Educational Studies* in 1973. It starts with words well worth quoting: 'Socrates said that an unexamined life is not worth living. Certainly in philosophy, it could be said that unexamined talk is not worth saying...In education, time and time again, one can suffer from another outbreak of slogans which serves as a substitute for thought...It seems to me that much of the present day talk about democratization in education falls into the category of unexamined talk.'

The talk which Phillips there proceeded to examine and to discredit now has for us a period flavour. Thus Richard Atkinson is quoted as assuring readers of *The Times* of London that students 'hope to build a democratic alternative structure through which all, staff and students together, may gain control over their work situation, so making it relevant to contemporary educational needs'. Jack Straw, identified in that article as a former President of the National Union of Students but now better known as the British Foreign Secretary, was quoted as having maintained that: 'if the Universities cannot reform themselves we must ask whether it is not time for society to intervene and impose its values – of democracy and representative government – upon those institutions'.[1]

I have nothing to add or to object to in what Phillips wrote in that first of his education papers. So I will instead begin by noting something which I want to add and something to which I must object in two later papers, and then go on to expatiate on two topics suggested by his work in this area.

1

'Democratization: Some Themes in Unexamined Talk', a first blast, was
followed in 1974 by 'Another Outbreak of Misology', a response to what
had been presented as a polemic against that first blast. At one stage in this
response Phillips had to explain the difference between the respect to which
all human beings are entitled as such and 'those forms of respect which have
to be earned'. In view of the enormous effort which in recent years Departments, Schools and Colleges of Education appear to have devoted to indoc-
trinating aspirant teachers with the conviction that it is a prime duty to
promote self-respect in their pupils, it is most unfortunate that the staff of
these institutions should so generally have failed to appreciate that the only
firm ground for earned and deserved self-respect (which can in practice be
made available if not to absolutely all then at least to very nearly all children) is a mastery of what in the United Kingdom (UK) have traditionally
been called 'The Three R's' – reading, writing and arithmetic.[2] Notoriously,
this modest minimum objective is not at present being achieved by either
the US public school or the UK maintained school system. Actually to
achieve it will require teaching that is pedagogically effective rather than
merely 'progressive' and/or authoritatively recommended as 'best practice'.

The most recent relevant Phillips paper is 'Education and Magic' (1987),[3]
published in Roger Straughan and John Wilson (eds.) *Philosophers on Education*. Its thesis is that 'There is an internal relation between hard intellectual
labour and intellectual understanding. In other words, there is conceptual
confusion involved in the suggestion that understanding is contingently
related to the means by which it is achieved.'

If this thesis were correct, it would suggest an answer to the objection that
the supposedly intended and desired products of the Earth as 'a vale of soul-
making' might have been created by God directly. For perhaps there would
then be a similar internal relation between the troubles and temptations of
our lives on Earth and their ideal and divinely desired outcomes.[4] But
whatever the truth in that theological matter, Phillips surely failed to establish that 'there is conceptual confusion involved in the suggestion that
understanding is contingently related to the means by which it is achieved'.

For, after deploying several quotations from 'Goethe's Treatment of the
Faust Legend', Phillips concludes: 'Since understanding is not something
apart from its characteristic accompaniments in the lives of men, the patterns of behaviour in which it has its life, to search for understanding in
isolation from accompaniments and patterns is to search for something
which does not exist.' Perfectly true. And, as a matter of fact, no one has
ever been or is now able, without previous and preparatory intellectual
labour, to acquire the behavioural dispositions which are the essential
equipment of anyone who is to be truly said to understand. But that is not
to say that such understanding *logically* presupposes such hard intellectual

work. For it could be coherently suggested that someone might be effort-lessly endowed with that understanding. No one, for instance, has any difficulties in understanding the nature of the miracle by which, it has been alleged, Saint Francis Xavier suddenly became master of the Japanese language.

2

In September 1976 Phillips wrote a short piece in *The Times Higher Educational Supplement* under the title 'We Need a Concept of Failure'. He returned to this topic in the 1987 article on 'Education and Magic', considering 'the possibility that when intellectual competence is challenged by some form of examination, failure may be the result'. He goes on: 'There are those who would like to eliminate that possibility. For them, to say that a person has failed to reach an academic standard is to create an unnecessary elitism.' Phillips counters by saying that 'To criticise a work, even to say that it is deplorable is, in one sense, a compliment. The standard of the work may not be complimented, but the person criticised ... is not treated therapeutically as someone not up to hearing the news.' But he does not go on to ask what is meant by the word *elitism*, and what is supposed to be wrong with being an elitist.

In the UK, if not in the US, institutions are nowadays frequently de-nounced as elitist. There spokespersons for universities, which are supposed to be striving to remain or to become centres of excellence, can be heard shamefacedly explaining that, while not of course being elitist, they do nevertheless rather feel that some standards of academic quality ought to be maintained; and even perhaps – greatly daring – the better, the better. Yet before beginning to discuss the truth or falsity of any such accusations, and the guilt or innocence of any of those thus accused, we ought to insist upon receiving clear and definite answers to the two fundamental questions which Phillips did not, at least on that occasion, attempt to answer; the questions, that is to say, 'What is here meant by the word "elitism"?' and 'What is supposed to be wrong with being, in that sense, elitist?'[5]

Suppose we begin by following John Langshaw Austin's characteristic recommendation to 'work the dictionary'. It is, perhaps, significant that the particular form 'elitism' was not recorded in the great multi-volume *Oxford English Dictionary*.[6] Instead the word 'elite', as a substantive in current use, was listed as meaning: 'selection, chosen; in modern use, concretely, that which is chosen ... the chosen part or flower (of society, or any body or class of persons)'. The usages instanced were: 'the élite of the Russian nobil-ity' (1848); and 'the élite of a comparatively civilised generation' (1880). It was also noted that this English word is derived from the French 'élite'.

It is only in a supplementary volume,[7] first published in 1971, that the forms 'élitism' and 'élitist' find a place. Here more recent usages of 'élite' are cited, including some in which the reference was to 'ruling élites'. Note is also taken of an adjectival employment; as in 'an élite standing of timber'. 'Elitism' is now defined as 'Advocacy of, or reliance on the leadership and dominance of an *élite*... Hence *élitist*'. The first occurrence cited is in a 1950 statement that Freud 'shared with Nietzsche and Carlyle elements of an élitist position'. Next we have from R.N. Carew Hunt's 1957 *Guide to Communist Jargon* part of an explanation of 'Lenin's conception of the "narrow" party consisting of an *élite*, whose more highly developed class consciousness enables it to see further than those among whom it works'. Finally, after two citations from *New Left Review*, a journal founded – like the self-styled movement from which it took its title – in the later 1960s, there is something from a report which appeared in *New Scientist* during 1968. This told of someone lecturing about 'Elitism and Excellence', the excellence being that of the 'mathematically gifted and the élitism being the varying degrees of regard paid to that talent'.

Certainly that by now somewhat dated supplementary volume does suggest, among other things, a meaning which would make 'élitism' for me, if not for the editors of and contributors to *New Left Review*, a very bad word. For it suggests that we might define it as a general term for any doctrine or practice which demands or supports government by supposed experts, experts neither responsible to nor ejectable by the governed, experts prescribing what those subjects, altogether without reference to what they themselves may happen actually to want, are to be taken to need. Plato's Guardians – the philosopher-kings of *The Republic* – are the original paradigm case of such an absolute and irresponsible ruling elite; while, as the advocate of a system of this kind, Plato himself must correspondingly be recognized as the philosophical father of all elitism. In our own time, of course, by far the most important of such elites have been the controlling members of the Marxist-Leninist parties ruling so-called People's Democracies; while the most numerous and prominent elitists have been the rank and file members, the fellow-travellers and the other less committed sympathizers of such parties and their regimes.

Suppose that we do attempt to attach some sense of this sort to the words 'elitist' and 'elitism'. Then we shall be disturbed to discover that, whereas few if any of those in Edbiz who have in the last three decades been denounced as elitists could plausibly be accused of supporting or sympathizing with such regimes and such parties, some of those who have been most fervent in their denunciations both of elitism and of alleged élitists were at the time of these denunciations members or supporters of Leninist organizations.[8] So, although a definition along the lines suggested above would have for some of us a great attraction, and although it would also correspond closely with that provided in that 1971 *Supplement* to *The Oxford English Dictionary*, it surely could not constitute an adequate explication of what the Edbiz denouncers have had in mind.

A suggestion which appears more promising in this context was that made in the final citation from *New Scientist*, which associated the ideas of elitism and of excellence. Shortly after Margaret Thatcher was first appointed Secretary of State at what was at that time still called the Department of Education and Science (DES), she received what must have been a shocking lesson on the nature and purposes of the largest of the British teachers' unions, the National Union of Teachers (NUT).[9] For its weekly organ *The Teacher* for 26 June 1970, without actually going so far as to make explicit its own commitment to egalitarian mediocrity, nevertheless saw fit to warn her against 'those who preach the importance of excellence'. She was further instructed not to be tempted by 'arguments defending an elite in education'.[10]

In the same year the Editorial Introduction to a collection frankly entitled *The Red Papers*, proclaimed a similar doctrine: 'Elitist academic education fails because it fosters the values of competition rather than the values of co-operation.'[11] Waiving the question whether this editor was not really pointing to what was in his eyes an unacceptable cost rather than an educational failure, we have here to insist that to achieve excellence in any sphere is necessarily to excel and thus to become a member of an elite; although not of course of an elite which is powerful, irresponsible or otherwise especially privileged. As such, you cannot any longer be, in whatever is the relevant respect, equal to those who have not yet achieved this particular form of, or perhaps any form of, excellence. So, if we are going to have any excelling we are bound to have sets of persons who, with respect to that kind of excelling (though not necessarily in any other respects), constitute elites.

It is, therefore, small wonder that devotees of the Procrustean ideal of equality of outcome – an ideal which is often not systematically or at all distinguished from other different and in some cases practically incompatible egalitarian ideals[12] – should thus abhor all elites, and furiously repudiate the pursuit of excellence. For to excel just is to be, in whatever respect you are excelling, unequal to the average, to the statistically normal, to the possible competition. Any philosopher inclined to join the chorus denouncing excellence would do well to consider one of the obituary tributes paid to Wittgenstein: 'There are many sorts of human excellence. Not least among them is the excellence of one who devotes his whole life, giving up all else, to the attempt to do one thing supremely well.'[13]

There is perhaps less denunciation of elites and elitism and less explicit or implicit eschewing of excellence in the nineteen nineties than there was in the seventies and eighties. But the contradictions and the consequent calls for choices between incompatible alternatives will not go away. For instance, spokespersons for the [New] Labour Party constantly claim both that for them 'quality and equality go hand in hand' and that acceptably 'high educational standards' must always be 'not just for the few but for *all* pupils'. This irenic formulation collapses the crucial distinction: between, on the one hand, striving to ensure that all our children attain whatever levels of educational achievement they are severally capable of attaining; and, on the other hand, labouring to bring it about that all those children, often so very different both in their abilities and in their inclinations, achieve *one and the same high educational level*.

Once these rival educational ideals have been clearly formulated it becomes obvious that they actually are incompatible, as are the alternative institutional means suited to the securing of their realization. If the former is your end, then you will want to see a variety of specialist schools; and, at least whenever admission is not selective, a great deal of streaming and setting. (To stream is to divide an age cohort into two or more classes distinguished by the greater or lesser abilities of their members. To set is to make such divisions for the teaching of particular subjects.)

To the extent that the latter ideal is the one which you want to realize you will go for an all-inclusive state monopoly system. In this there would be only one type of school permitted; and that one in which all teaching of the correspondingly uniform and compulsory national curriculum would be in unstreamed, unsetted, mixed ability classes. It is surely significant that all of this, save for the explicit advocacy of a national curriculum, was clearly seen by Dennis Marsden (one of the militants of the Comprehensive Revolution) to be the outcome of the 'internal dynamic' of that revolution. His article maintaining this was entitled, with Procrustean menace, 'The Comprehensive School: Labour's Equality Machine'.[14] As he then went on to say, 'the community and the meritocratic schools represent quite different ideals – meritocrats and egalitarians will want to evaluate education, even the "development of talent", by different criteria'.

3

The Winter 1976 issue of the *New Universities Quarterly* contained a Critical Notice entitled 'Standards v. the New Egalitarianism' by Dewi Phillips. The book reviewed was by the present writer.[15] At that time, a quarter of a century ago, the new egalitarianism against which it polemicized was indeed fairly new. That book described the new egalitarianism as requiring the ignoring or even the denial of differences between individual talents and temperaments and achievements – and Phillips agreed with this description. It minimized or outright rejected all qualitative distinctions between cultures, whether these be the cultures of different societies or of different persons or groups within the same society. The notion of objective knowledge fell under the same ban. For were this to be admitted, it might serve as a basis for discrimination between superior and inferior, between those who actually do know and those who in truth do not. There was opposition to any form of testing which could reveal, and might perhaps encourage, differences in educational achievement. Since there can on these principles be no real and relevant difference between those qualified to teach and those still under instruction, there were demands that students should have a (if not *the*) deciding voice in the appointment of teachers and in the design of courses of study – demands which were in those days often urged in the name of academic freedom.

With the possible exception of the one mentioned last, all the elements in what was then the new egalitarianism appear still to be flourishing today. The essay which Phillips picked out as presenting the most formidable challenge to such ideas was one on 'Teaching and Testing'. That, he said, 'shows how there is an internal relation for teacher and pupil between the pursuit of a subject and some form of assessment of one's grasp of it. It would be logically contradictory if someone professed a serious interest in teaching or learning a subject, but no interest whatever in seeing whether an intellectual matter had been understood or not.'

It would indeed. Yet, as I discovered when I read an earlier version of that essay to audiences in two or three of the few teacher training institutions prepared to invite a notoriously 'right-wing' speaker, the very simple general principle involved – the general principle of which the version stated in 'Teaching and Testing' is a special case – is one which many people seem to have great difficulty in appreciating, a difficulty which apparently grew as they began to appreciate some of the (to them) disturbing implications of its acceptance. That general principle is that the sincere and wholehearted pursuit of any purpose whatsoever absolutely presupposes a real concern to discover how far that purpose has been and is being achieved. Furthermore, if the agent becomes aware that it is not being achieved, and shows no readiness to attempt alternative and hopefully more promising tactics, then we cannot allow that the task is still being pursued with the same sincerity of commitment and the same rationality as before.

Suppose, for instance, that someone claims to be in business in order to turn a profit, or to be playing some game in order to win. Then what credence could we give to these professions if there is no care to keep, in the one case, accounts and, in the other, the score? Descartes used to say that he preferred to judge what people sincerely believe by what they do rather than by what they say. The same shrewd principle applies equally well to the determination of true intentions and actual purposes, and of the rationality of their pursuit.

So let us now begin to apply this general principle to the operation of the state-maintained school system in the UK.[16] This system, though very different from the US public school system, is surely less unlike that than both are unlike the national school systems in most other First World countries. So to concentrate here in the former should still be usefully suggestive to those more familiar with the latter. The first point which needs to be made about the maintained school system in the UK is that, like the National

Health Service, it is a state monopoly. Both are, though they are rarely recognized as being, nationalized industries. Of course it might be said, very strictly speaking, that, since there are independent private schools catering for between six and seven per cent of each annual cohort of children, the state-maintained school system is not a monopoly. But is there any anti-monopoly legislation anywhere in the world which would not be activated long before any single supplier had achieved as much as a ninety per cent market share, and that even without taking account of the fact that this supplier operates a policy of predatory NOT-pricing?

   The second most remarkable fact about this particular nationalized industry is that no systematic attempt is or ever has been made to discover and to make known what its annual output is. For there never has been and still is not any system of comprehensive and compulsory school-leaving examinations. So anyone wishing to learn how many of our children are leaving school illiterate (or innumerate), for instance, has to find or make estimates based on surveys of those whose school years are behind them, together with the reported observations of employers or would-be employers.

   The traditional method for supervising and controlling this maintained school system, a method which began to change only with the passage of the 1988 Educational Reform Act, was to send into the school teams of Her (or, as the case might have been, His) Majesty's Inspectors of Schools, giving the schools to be inspected prior notice of their forthcoming inspections. Any school once inspected could look forward to several inspection-free years before the Inspectors called again. Such occasional inspections are in the nature of the case directed more at the *process* rather than at what is presumably the intended *product* of this industry, pupil knowledge. (This includes, of course, not only knowledge but also knowledge how.)[17]

   I described the fact that there never has been and still is not any comprehensive system of compulsory leaving examinations as the second most remarkable fact about this nationalized industry. The first most remarkable fact is that so little is ever made of that second most remarkable fact. For if any of those nationalized industries which were privatized during the Thatcher years had ever been managed in the way in which the maintained school system has traditionally been managed, then every Opposition, regardless of the party or parties of which it was constituted, would have been forever hounding and abusing the Government of the day for the egregious and wellnigh unbelievable negligence and incompetence of its management of that industry.[18]

   Anyone who has once realized the full enormity of this sustained refusal to attempt to measure the annual output will scarcely be surprised to discover a general failure to apply even the simplest of economic ideas in considerations of the workings of this industry. Most fundamentally, and most mistakenly, increases in resource input are simply assumed to be both the necessary and the sufficient conditions of increases in education output.

For instance, we find even Anthony Crosland writing (under the Administration in which during the 1960s he had served as Secretary of State at the DES) that 'expenditure on education rose from 4.8% of GNP to 6.1%. As a result all classes of the community enjoyed significantly more education than before'.[19] I can myself vouch for the fact that Crosland was an extremely able man who had, before becoming a professional politician, earned his living as an Economics Fellow of an Oxford college. So it is hard to believe that he could have been simply taking it for granted that – at least in this particular industry and under his own wise and careful administration – outputs were more or less precisely proportionate to inputs. Yet it is surely even harder to believe that Crosland could have failed to ask whether the 'steady reduction in the pupil/teacher ratio' on which he also prided himself was not perhaps (as he himself in any equally monopolistic enterprise which was under private ownership would surely have suggested it to be) a scandalous example of inefficiency and overstaffing?

It is not necessary here even to attempt to answer the question whether that was or is the truth. It is sufficient simply to say that the consensus, among those who have actually brought themselves to attend to the available research evidence, is that it has not been possible to demonstrate any significant increase in pupil learning over the range of class size between 20 and 40.[20] But even if we could give an affirmative answer to the primary question whether a reduction in the pupil/teacher ratio results in an improvement in pupil learning, we should still need to know the answer to a further question if we were going to consider the opportunity costs and so make economically rational decisions. That further question is the one with which the Irish poet William Butler Yeats reputedly responded to the news that he had won the Nobel Prize for Literature: 'How much? How much?'

That question is crucially relevant here. For those who are indeed sincerely and rationally dedicated to producing goods or services of any kind must be constantly concerned not just to maintain but to *improve* productivity. They will thus necessarily be straining to *economize*, which is to say, striving to deploy to maximum effect whatever resources from time to time become available to them. They will never forget or neglect the opportunity costs of inefficiency. For the wasteful and inefficient employment of any scarce resource always has opportunity costs, that is, the costs of forgone alternative employments of those wasted resources.

In the 1980 Parliamentary debate about education, a debate subsequent upon and shaped by an NUT 'Campaign against the Cuts' in tax-funded education spending – cuts which had allegedly followed the election of a new Conservative Administration – the Opposition motion took it absolutely for granted that the relations between input and output are here direct, constant and uniform: 'That this House', it began, 'recognising the direct relationship between the maintenance and enhancement of educational standards and an appropriate investment of resources...'; and so it went on (and on).

The Ministerial response, by Mark Carlisle, did at least mention value for money. It expressed 'confidence in the ability of the education service...to secure maximum educational value from the extensive resources which continue to be available to it'. Yet in the rest of his speech the Minister made no attempt to justify such confidence. Like so many of his predecessors in similar debates he could think only of offering formidable figures of increasing expenditure. 'Some 5.5 percent of the gross national product of this country, or twice what it was in 1950, today goes on education...In 1979–80 more was spent on the schools in real terms than ever before, twice as much in total and half as much again per pupil as twenty years ago. Much has gone on additional teachers and the reduction of the pupil/teacher ratio.'

That was all in 1979 and 1980. But similar observations apply to the similar series of advertisements published by the NUT in *The Times* during 1990–1. For, notwithstanding the widespread belief to the contrary, there were during the Thatcher years in fact no overall cuts in per pupil State spending under the budget heading 'Education'. On the contrary, according to the official statistics from the DES, given in a written Parliamentary answer, spending per pupil actually increased between 1979 and 1989 by 42 per cent *in real terms*. Speaking during the Budget debate on 7 December 1993, Education Secretary John Patten brought these figures up to date. Between 1983 and 1993 there had been an even greater increase in spending per pupil than that between 1979 and 1989 – an increase by not 42 per cent but 47 per cent, and again *in real terms*.

James Callaghan had, in 1976, as Prime Minister in the then Labour Administration, made at Ruskin College in Oxford a remarkable speech in which he spoke about educational problems, saying 'that those whose only answer to these problems is to call for more money will be disappointed. But that surely cannot be the end of the matter. There is a challenge to us all in these days and the challenge in education is *to examine its priorities and to secure as high efficiency as possible by the use of existing resources*' (emphasis added).[21]

Unfortunately, this speech seems to have had no lasting influence upon the Labour Party. For in its 1986 statement on education it asserted with invincible dogmatism that 'It has now been established once and for all that a decline in provision means lower educational standards.' Again in 1992 we find Ann Taylor, Labour's Education spokesperson, in her comment upon the strikingly superior examination performance of entrants from the independent schools,[22] asserting that 'this just demonstrates the importance of class sizes and the resources available to independent schools. If the government wants to produce the same results in state schools, it must give them more resources.'

It is tempting to respond to such remarks with a smile and a sigh: 'there is nothing so plain boring as the constant repetition of assertions that are not true, and . . . not even faintly sensible; if we can reduce this a bit, it will be all to the good'.[23] But such a protest in so practical a matter is much too gentle. For this blinkered and bigoted insistence that smaller classes and increased funding constitute the necessary and sufficient conditions of any and all improvement in pupil learning is an extravagant and irresponsible distraction from the task of developing and applying policies which actually will produce desperately needed improvement.[24]

4

It would be wrong to conclude the present essay without mentioning the possible effects upon the UK maintained school monopoly of the triumph of the [New] Labour Party in the General Election held on 1 May 1997. On 30 April 1997, the day before that triumph, the Leader of the then Opposition – Anthony Blair, who prefers to be called Tony Blair – had announced that 'some things the Conservatives got right. We will not change them . . . What counts is what works.'

In the years which have passed since that election there have been remarkable changes, if not yet in the actual performance of the monopoly, then at least in some of the reactions to it. For instance, on 24 June 1997, a mere eight weeks after that election, *The Guardian*, a newspaper which had often under Conservative Administrations behaved as if it were a house organ of the NUT, was lamenting that under those old regimes 'desks were swept away, blackboards removed, and children allowed to work at their own pace'. These methods, which *The Guardian* had so recently defended as truly progressive, had in fact, it now insisted, 'condemned hundreds and thousands of children to an illiterate and innumerate future'.

The teachers' unions made an equally sudden and complete reversal of position. For on the very same day Nigel de Gruchy, the General Secretary of the National Association of Schoolmasters/Union of Women Teachers (NASUWT), complained in *The Times* about 'the methods imposed on [teachers] in the 1960s and 1970s', which were, as he had now come to believe, 'either wrong in themselves' or 'impossible' to operate. Only twelve months earlier John Bangs, the Assistant Secretary of the NUT, was reported in *The Guardian* as describing Her Majesty's Chief Inspector of Schools as 'ignorant', on account of his belief that such methods were and are pedagogically less effective than those which he already was and still is recommending. Three months later *The Times* of 14 September 1996 had reported Douglas McAvoy as dismissing all such recommendations as the 'obsessions of far-right policy advisers'.[25]

Most remarkable of all is the apparent transformation of David Blunkett, the [New] Labour Minister of State. *The Spectator* for 18 April 1998 carried an article on 'Blunkett Past and Present', which claimed that he had in his time as Leader of the Sheffield City Council been a Procrustean and hardline militant of the comprehensive revolution. He responded in a long letter from the House of Commons, which was published in *The Spectator* for 25 April 1998. Allowing that 'it is difficult for some (present-day) Tories to accept that a Labour government is taking real action to improve standards or to promote diversity', he went on to say:

> Literacy and numeracy are my top priorities. That is why I have set minimum standards and expectations for schools. It is why, for the first time in recent years, I have published a framework which ensures that children learn phonics in the early years, as well as having clear instruction in grammar and spelling. It is why we will ensure that the skill of mental arithmetic is a part of our numeracy strategy. It is hardly 'social engineering' to expect children leaving primary school to have a better grasp of the basics than has been deemed acceptable in recent years... I am very clearly committed to diversity in education. That is why I have accelerated the specialist school programme, so that there will be 450 schools specialising in technology, languages, arts and sports by 2002. It is also why we are introducing three categories of schools – including foundation schools, which we have worked closely with grant-maintained schools[26] to develop – rather than one.
>
> Our programme is designed to raise standards in state schools significantly. It is backed by extra resources and clear targets, as well as my own personal commitment and that of the Prime Minister. I have never argued that equality of outcome is desirable or achievable. I do believe, however, that education is the best way to provide equality of opportunities and thus lift people out of poverty so that they have the opportunity to earn and help themselves and their families.

University of Reading, Emeritus

Notes

1   Was Straw, like most left-thinking people – or in this case, unthinking people – outraged when, in an interview with *Woman's Own* on 31 October 1978, Margaret Thatcher repudiated such hypostatizations of society: 'I don't believe in Society. There is no such thing, only individual people, and there are families'? I suspect that he was, even if he has perhaps by now learnt better.
2   The success of the campaign to promote pupil self-esteem in the USA – or perhaps only the lack of any need for such a campaign! – is epitomized in the following quotation from Thomas Sowell, *Inside American Education: The Decline, the Deception, the Dogmas* (New York: The Free Press, 1993): 'Perhaps nothing so captures what is wrong with American schools as the results of an international study of 13-year-olds, which found that Koreans ranked first in mathematics and Amer-

icans last. When asked if they were "good at mathematics", only 23 percent of the Korean youngsters said "yes" – compared with 68 percent of American 13-year-olds' (p. 3).

3 *Philosophers on Education*, ed. Roger Straughan and John Wilson (London: Macmillan, 1987).

4 Those who share my own interest in such questions may wish to refer to 'Divine Omnipotence and Human Freedom', in Antony Flew and Alastair MacIntyre (eds.), *New Essays in Philosophical Theology* (London: SCM Press, 1956). The most lamentable of the still uncorrected corrigenda in that article is the misapplication to St Augustine of the motto sentence.

5 Parallel questions ought to be asked and answered – yet almost never are – before anyone is ostracized as a racist. See, for instance, 'Three Concepts of Racism', in Antony Flew, *Atheistic Humanism* (Buffalo, NY: Prometheus, 1993). There is an earlier, Anglocentric version of the same paper in Antony Flew, *Power to the Parents: Reversing Educational Decline* (London: Sherwood, 1987).

6 That is a publication which in its original form is to be found only in major institutional libraries. In 1971, however, its publishers – the Oxford University Press – issued a *Compact Edition of the Oxford English Dictionary* in two India paper volumes.

7 This is uniform in format with, and is presented as a supplementary third volume of that *Compact Edition*.

8 Consider, for instance, the personnel listed in the Tables of Contents of such once widely circulated and influential works as David Rubinstein and Colin Stoneman (eds.), *Education for Democracy* (Harmondsworth: Penguin, 1970) and David Rubinstein, *Education and Equality* (Harmondsworth: Penguin, 1979).

9 American readers will no doubt notice strong similarities between the NUT and both the American Federation of Teachers and the National Educational Association. But the NUT certainly exercises less general political influence than either. For more information see Fred Naylor and John Marks, 'The National Union of Teachers – Professional Association or Trade Union or...?', in Caroline Cox and John Marks (eds.), *The Right to Learn* (London: Centre for Policy Studies, 1982), pp. 119–34.

10 We should ponder the significance of the fact that objections to elites of excellence seem to be urged only in Edbiz, never in sport. Football supporters, for instance, are eager for the teams which they support to become football elites.

11 John Hemming (ed.), *The Red Papers* (London: Islander, 1970), p. 2. It should perhaps be explained that this title was chosen in reaction against a series of *Black Papers*. The members of this series, of which the first was published in 1969, were all collections of short papers attacking what were seen by those promoting these tendencies as educationally progressive but by their opponents as anti-educational. The authors were most strongly opposed to the Labour Party's drive to dissolve the traditional grammar and other selective schools and to replace them by common schools – called comprehensive as not selecting their intakes.

12 Compare Antony Flew, *The Politics of Procrustes: Contradictions of Enforced Equality* (London, and Buffalo, NY: Temple Smith, and Prometheus, 1981), Chapter II.

13 D.A.T. Gasking and A.C. Jackson, 'Ludwig Wittgenstein', in *The Australasian Journal of Philosophy* for 1951.

14 In Rubinstein and Stoneman (1970). The two passages quoted are at pp. 139 and 140.

15   Antony Flew, *Sociology, Equality and Education* (London: Macmillan, 1976).
16   It is applied more extensively in Antony Flew, *Thinking about Social Thinking* (Buffalo, NY: Prometheus, second edition, 1995).
17   This important distinction is developed in Gilbert Ryle, *The Concept of Mind* (London: Hutchinson, 1949), Chapter II. Another Rylean distinction which ought to be introduced into the philosophy of education is that between task words, such as 'looking' and 'listening', and achievement words, such as 'seeing' and 'hearing'. For the word 'teach' has both task and achievement uses. Teachers and especially teachers' unions have a very understandable preference for having the performance of teachers judged by the time and effort which they devote to the task rather than by the achievement of pupil learning actually effected by this devotion.
18   I have often wondered why people are so slow to recognize this disquieting analogy. When I was one of the graduate students supervised by Gilbert Ryle we all used to make much of a categorical distinction between those things which could and those which could not be hit with a hammer. So perhaps there is some reluctance to apply standards appropriate to industries producing things which can be hit with a hammer to one producing things which cannot be so treated. But electricity, gas and water – which at one time were all produced in the UK by nationalized industries – are almost as elusive to such treatment as knowledge.
19   C.A.R. Crosland, *Socialism Now, and Other Essays* (London: Cape, 1974), p. 200.
20   The *locus classicus* appears to be G. Glass, L. Cahen, M. Smith and N. Philby, *School Class Size: Research and Policy* (Beverly Hills: Sage, 1982). Another slightly more recent classic is E. Hanushek, 'The Economics of Schooling: Production and Efficiency in Public Schools', *Journal of Economic Literature* (September 1986, Volume XXIV). He updated this with 'The Impact of Differential Expenditures on School Performance', *Educational Researcher* (May 1989, Volume 18) and again with 'Assessing the Effects of School Resources on Student Performance: An Update' (Summer 1997, Volume 19, Number 2). For a demolition of the popular misinterpretation of the exceptionally large Tennessee experiment, see S.J. Prais, 'Class-size and Learning: The Tennessee experiment – what follows?' in the *Oxford Review of Education*, XXII 4, pp. 399–414.
21   For the background of this speech and for its practical impact or lack of it, see Antony Flew, *Shephard's Warning: Setting Schools Back on Course* (London: Adam Smith Institute, 1994), pp. 40–4. The reason for the apparently misspelt title was that before its publication an announcement was made that Gillian Shephard was shortly to become Secretary of State at what was then in process of becoming no longer the DES but the Department of Education and Employment (DEE).
22   She had, before becoming a Member of Parliament, been an official of the NUT.
23   J.L. Austin, *Sense and Sensibilia* (Oxford: Clarendon, 1962), p. 5.
24   For a sympathetic critique of the reform efforts of the Conservative Administration elected in 1987 and 1992, and for further information on what made and still makes reforms so very necessary, see *Shephard's Warning: Setting Schools Back on Course*. For a much less sympathetic treatment of anything Conservative, but for much more and more up-to-date information about the condition of the maintained school monopoly, see Melanie Phillips, *All Must Have Prizes* (London: Little, Brown, 1996).
25   I find it very difficult to convince myself that these approvals and disapprovals of alternative methods of teaching, which can be so suddenly and so inexplicably

reversed, spring from a simple and a non-political concern for the educational welfare of children.

26 Grant-maintained schools are a sort of semi-independent state school introduced by the 1987 Conservative Administration and to which before the 1997 election the Labour Party had been vehemently opposed.

An Afterword

A Brief History of Philosophy in Wales and Phillips's Contribution to Philosophy in the Welsh Language

Walford Gealy

Wales has produced very few, if indeed any, philosophers of importance. Even more relevant to our present deliberations is the fact that no Welshman has made a significant contribution to philosophy through the medium of the Welsh language. I do not know of a single piece of philosophy, written originally in Welsh, which has been translated into any other language. If Welshmen have contributed anything at all to philosophy, they have done so in either the Latin or the English tongue. Of course, I am presupposing that there is a distinction between contributing to philosophy as a major historical and intellectual discipline, and contributing to a discussion of philosophical issues within a specific and restricted context – such as the Welsh situation as it is, with its minority language and culture. There is, and there has been over the centuries, particularly during the last two hundred years, some discussion of philosophical issues in the Welsh language. But this, it seems to me, does not amount to anything more than that – simply a discussion of some philosophical ideas, current or common in European thought, but without any original contribution being made, or having been made, to that European tradition in the Welsh language. There isn't such a thing as a Welsh philosophical tradition.

The absence of such a tradition requires an explanation as much as if the opposite were true. Why is it that the Welsh have made such little impact in this particular field? Anyone familiar with Welsh history will not find it difficult to discover reasons. Most historians of Wales would probably agree that the three most important factors in the history of Wales have been, first, religion, second, the proximity and politics of England and, third, but probably largely insignificant in this context, the physical character of the Welsh landscape. Has any, or all, of these factors anything to do with the absence of a philosophical tradition in Wales?

Religion as a way of life and theology as an intellectual preoccupation have almost always dominated the lives and thought of Welsh people. The

Welsh have often compared their fate and culture with that of another minority people – the Hebrews of the Old Testament. The Hebrews in Biblical times formed a small theocentric community, occupied a small strip of land, and they were politically almost continuously under the thumb of some alien imperial power. Wales is similarly a small territory, occupied by people that have been for most of their history profoundly religious, and, for almost a thousand years, deeply troubled, if not wholly controlled politically, by its larger national neighbour, the English.

Wales has always been a land in which religion has played a central role in the lives of its people. There is superabundance of archaeological evidence which clearly demonstrates that, even in pre-historic times, the early inhabitants of Wales, the Iberians and the Celts, were deeply religious. After the advent of Christianity, first the Celtic Church, then later, the Catholic Church and, since the Protestant Reformation, the Scriptures, have all in their turn been the predominant influences on Welsh culture. And like the Hebrews, the Welsh have been relative strangers to the Greeks. Wales has been the land of the poet and the prophet rather than of the philosopher and the intellectual speculator. (Of course, I do not wish to imply that religion necessarily precludes philosophical activity. Indeed, there is some evidence that suggests that in the late Middle Ages, for instance, when Wales was part of a largely unified Christendom, there were some Welsh philosophical theologians who had a European reputation.) This is partly due not only to the fact that there is a strong bardic tradition in Wales, but also to the fact that quite soon after the Protestant Reformation and the translation of the Bible into Welsh in 1588, a Bible-oriented Nonconformity became deeply rooted here in Wales, and this religious movement does not seem to have been instrumental in fostering or encouraging philosophical activity. It is only since the second half of the nineteenth century, when liberal theology and higher Biblical criticism became fashionable (and, coincidentally, when Wales first had a University of its own), that philosophy became more of a preoccupation of Welsh intellectuals. Hence, during that crucial era that saw the emergence of both Continental Rationalism and British Empiricism, the Welsh were immersed in a Protestant, Bible-centred Puritanism. I suspect that today, such a religion would be branded as 'fundamentalist'. It was a religion that demanded the submission of the whole person, both will and intellect, to the will and commands of God as revealed in what were regarded as infallible Scriptures. It was thought that philosophy could be, at best, of little use, and at worst, a positive impediment to living a holy life – for man's reason, unaided and unsanctified by faith, had been badly affected by the fall of Adam. Indeed, such views are still held quite commonly by some religious believers in Wales.

Then there is what may be called 'the English factor' that has affected Welsh history. The geographical proximity of Wales to England, the strength of the English State, the English language and the richness of English culture (in an intellectual sense of culture?), the annexation of Wales to England in the sixteenth century, and the subsequent destruction, or Anglicization, of whatever educational institutions existed in Wales – all these elements have contributed to the fact that the Welsh language in Wales, in the last four hundred years, has had but an inferior role in every aspect of Welsh life except in religion. Welsh as a language, since the Acts of Annexation of 1536 and 1543, never had any official role or any legal status even within Wales, until, roughly, thirty years ago. And from Tudor times, when Grammar schools were first established in Wales, the medium of instruction in such schools was, at first, Latin and later English – and never was any discipline at any time taught through the medium of Welsh. Indeed, the Welsh language was, for a period, proscribed altogether in Welsh schools. As recently as the second half of the nineteenth century, it was even a punishable offence for a Welsh child to speak his or her native tongue, not only within the classroom but even within the precincts of the school. This proscription is usually referred to as 'the Welsh Not'. One of Wales's few philosophers of some repute, Sir Henry Jones (1852–1922), testifies in his autobiography, *Old Memories*, that at his own village's primary school in his time, the barbaric punishment of caning children for speaking Welsh in school was regularly administered by the head teacher.

Gradually, from the eighteenth century onwards, the Welsh and Welshness became increasingly identified with rural, peasant life, and with religion in the form of Welsh Nonconformity, with its chapels, the Bible, the pulpit and Sunday schools. Englishness was connected with the establishment, the Church and State, with officialdom, with law and the courts, and with education and scholarship. The divide was deep and often bitter. These were conditions that made it virtually impossible for any Welsh-language educational system to develop – at least from the direction of the State. If there was Welsh scholarship, it was invariably tied to religion. Only in the twentieth century did we begin to experience something of a renaissance in Welsh consciousness and confidence, and only very recently indeed, within the last twenty or thirty years or so, has Welsh become a medium of instruction in almost every subject, and at any educational level, including university level. In contrast, for most of the first half of this century, even Welsh literature was taught through the medium of English in the Colleges of the University of Wales! What hope was there for any contribution to philosophy in the Welsh language!

Yet it was against such a background that some Welsh-speaking philosophers, mainly professors and teachers at the University of Wales, moved to establish a forum to discuss philosophy through the medium of Welsh. And for such a purpose the Philosophical Section of the Guild of Graduates of the University of Wales was established in 1931. These philosophers established an annual philosophical conference, and for the first time in our history, a Welsh-language philosophy journal, *Efrydiau Athronyddol* (Philosophical

Studies), which was first published in 1938 and published annually ever since. The task of doing philosophy through the medium of Welsh inevitably involved many innovations, such as the coining of an appropriate terminology in the language, particularly in logic and epistemology, translating into Welsh important philosophical texts, such as Plato's Dialogues, and, of course, producing original philosophical texts and papers in the language. Several of Plato's works, including *The Republic, Gorgias, The Apology, Crito and Euthyphro*, have been translated into Welsh. Aristotle's *Ethics*, St Augustine's *Confessions*, St Anselm's *Proslogion* and Descartes' *Meditations* have also been translated, as well as sections of the writings of Aquinas, Kant and Wittgenstein. Several Welsh-language textbooks have been published on the history of philosophy, on individual philosophers such as Hume, Hegel, Marx and Wittgenstein, and on aspects of philosophy such as ethics, politics and the philosophy of religion. And there was, until very recently, a full-time Welsh-language teacher of philosophy at the University College of Wales, Aberystwyth.

However, those ardent and determined Welsh-speaking philosophers of the early 1930s were not only interested in contemporary philosophy, but they were equally keen to examine the whole of Welsh literature from a philosophical standpoint, in order to see how much philosophy lay hidden, perhaps, beneath the surface. Their question was: To what extent had European philosophical thought influenced Welsh writers and thinkers? In this connection, there has been less success, both in terms of the amount of work that has been done, and in terms of any positive results from what work has been done. Of course, the task is huge, and it is an interdisciplinary task. For although there is no shortage of Welsh historians and Welsh literary scholars, there is a shortage of such scholars who are equally interested in the European philosophical tradition. And similarly, there is a shortage of Welsh-speaking philosophers who are as thoroughly well versed in Welsh literature as they are in the developments in philosophy in Europe. Some work has been done in this important field, but very much more still remains to be undertaken.

But what of Welsh thought in earlier times, before the political assimilation of Wales into England? Welsh is one of the oldest living languages in Europe and Welsh literature extends back as far as the sixth century. But for over a whole millennium, from the sixth to the sixteenth century, this literary tradition was dominated by the poet – particularly so during the latter part of this era, the period of the *Gogynfeirdd* (the early bards) which extends from *c*. 1100 until the demise of the practice called *'clera'* – that custom of the professional bard moving from one aristocratic household to another to entertain their Welsh-speaking hosts and patrons with their strict-metre (*cynghanedd*) poetry. Yet one finds it difficult to see any trace of philosophy in the works of these poets. The earliest Welsh poets, Taliesin and Aneirin, for instance, who belong to the sixth century, were preoccupied with themes such as war, death, mourning and nature, and their writing is almost wholly elegiac in character. Later poetry, while often concerned with similar themes, is more positive, religious and eulogistic. But, as far as I am able to discern, it contains nothing that may be properly called 'philosophy'. This is not unexpected, however, as the primary function of these poets was to entertain their noble lords.

Of course, there was a considerable amount of Welsh prose too written during this period, the most important of which includes the Laws of Hywel Dda (Hywel the Good, King of Wales in the first half of the tenth century); the famous twelve tales called 'Y mabinogion', first written in the eleventh century but whose origins, in part, may even be pre-Christian. And several of the famous Arthurian legends were written during this period, and also numerous biographies of earlier Welsh saints, which were written by some Cistercian monks who settled in Wales in the twelfth century. And not least of the creations of the same monks and friars, we have the invaluable history of the period called *Brut y Tywysogyon* (Chronicle of the Princes). Again, it is difficult to call anything in this body of literature by the name 'philosophy', although the moral reasoning, values and priorities of the Laws of Hywel Dda are very interesting. But no one, as yet, has examined these laws from the standpoint of ethics or of jurisprudence.

As it has been already intimated, there were Welsh scholars in the Middle Ages who may be called 'philosophers' – at least to the extent that theology and philosophy were, in that period, inseparable disciplines. But the literary language of such scholars was, of course, Latin and not Welsh. Such scholars include, for instance, in the twelfth century, a Welsh bishop, from the northeast Wales diocese of St Asaph, named Adam. He was one of the ablest of Peter Lombard's students at Paris; and at the third Lateran Council (1179) it was Adam who was called upon to defend the views of his teacher. In the following two centuries, Wales produced the so-called four 'Wallensis brothers', two of whom achieved considerable academic fame. Sion Gymro (John Wallensis), who flourished *c.* 1260–83, became head of the Franciscan Order at both Oxford and Paris. He was the author of several theological works, and was regarded by many as a leading European scholar of his day. Tomos Gymro (Thomas Waleys), who flourished in the first half of the fourteenth century, also taught at Oxford. He once had a face-to-face theological disputation with a contemporary Avignon pope. His work is said to have been much admired by Roger Bacon and Robert Grosseteste.

There were other Welsh scholars too, like Henry de Gower, probably a Swansea man, who became Chancellor of the University of Oxford, and later, bishop of the diocese of St David. And there is the celebrated pseudo-historian and author of *Historia Regum Britanniae*, Siffre o Fynwy (Geoffrey of Monmouth). But, unfortunately, arguably the most influential Welsh writer of the late Middle Ages, *Gerallt Gymro* (Giraldus Cambrensis, *c.*1146–1223), whose knowledge of Classical poetry was second to none, and who travelled

three times to Rome to plead for the autonomy of the Welsh Church from
the see of Canterbury, and who contributed most to our understanding of
his contemporary Wales (and Ireland), appears to have had no training at all
in philosophy. Despite his unquestionable scholarship, he appears to have
been a most gullible and credulous person. His *Itinerarium Kambriae*, for
instance, is full of tales which defy belief. Or is one being too critical? It is
just possible that believing what we regard as utter fantasy was quite normal
for them in their more mysterious world.

In the sixteenth century, the Tudor king of England, Henry VIII, annexed
Wales to England and English became the official language of Wales – with
devastating cultural consequences. For during the preceding five centuries,
Wales had one of the richest bardic traditions in the whole of Europe,
fostered and patronized by the Welsh-speaking aristocracy. But after annexation, the sons of the Welsh-speaking aristocracy migrated to England, to
the new centre of political power. Consequently, their patronage of the
bards ceased. A leading contemporary English historian, Christopher Hill,
has recently written of this emigration in terms of 'a cultural influx' from
Wales to England, which 'may have been a bad thing for Wales. But it was
certainly very good for England.' He mentions John Donne, George Herbert,
and his brother Lord Herbert of Cherbury, Thomas Traherne, Inigo Jones,
Robert Recorde and John Dee, among several others, as Welshmen or men of
Welsh extraction, who flourished in England as an immediate consequence
of the conditions and opportunities created by annexation.

Perhaps even of greater and more permanent devastation to the Welsh
culture was the dissolution of the monasteries, particularly of the Cistercian
monasteries, which also had become centres of Welsh literary activity, and
institutions which patronized the Welsh bards. No one knows how many
unique and invaluable Welsh-language manuscripts were lost for ever to
posterity as a result of that fanatical act of the destruction of the monasteries. Furthermore, despite the aspirations of such a monarch as Llywelyn Fawr
(Llewelyn the Great), who died in 1240, and those of the 'rebel prince'
Owain Glyndwr (Owain Glendower), who died in 1416, Wales was united
with England before it had established any national educational institutions
that could be called, or develop into, universities or higher education estab-
lishments. And Welsh culture inevitably suffered as a result of this. Hence, in
general, until the establishment of university colleges in Wales in the second
half of the nineteenth century, if Welsh sons were to receive a university
education, they would have to be sent away from home – either to Oxbridge,
Belfast, Scotland or to the continent of Europe. And, if they did well at these
educational institutions, and unless they were clerics, they tended to spend
the rest of their professional lives outside Wales due to the lack of opportunities for such scholars within Wales itself. It is also the case that some Welsh
scholars of the Tudor period were devout Catholics, and after the passing of
the 1559 law making Elizabeth I head of the Church of England, many of the

ablest Catholic scholars in Wales fled to the continent for fear of persecution. These included the bishop elect of Bangor, Morys Clynnog (*c.* 1525–81), the author of a short Welsh book entitled *Athravaeth Grisrnogavl* (Christian Doctrine), and Gruffydd Robert (*c.* 1522–*c.*1600) who became Divinity Canon of the Cathedral of Milan, and who wrote a short treatise in Welsh entitled *Y Drych Crisrianogawl* (The Christian Mirror).

The reign of the Tudors largely coincided with the Renaissance in England and Wales. And Welsh Renaissance scholars devoted most of their energies to translating the Bible in Welsh – the single greatest contribution to Welsh culture in any period, and almost certainly the act that has preserved the Welsh language and with it, the strength of Welsh identity. (The third factor alluded to above, that of the Welsh landscape, is a relevant consideration in this context. Mountains tend to divide and isolate communities from each other, particularly so in pre-industrial times. It is not unreasonable to assume that without some common unifying element, the Welsh language would have fragmented into a multiplicity of different dialects that would not have been strong enough to withstand the pressures of Anglicization. Welsh, like Cornish, would have ceased as a living language. But the Welsh Bible, together with the Circulatory Schools of the eighteenth century, preserved the unity of the language.) Apart from the translating of the Bible, the Welsh Christian humanists of the period were lovers of works of grammar and of dictionaries, and several were produced in the Welsh language. The greatest optimist of the period must have been William Salesbury, who not only translated the New Testament into Welsh and produced a Welsh–English dictionary 'moche necessary to all suche Welshemen as wil spedly learne the englyshe tongue', but he also produced in 1550 *A briefe and a playne introduction teaching how to pronounce the letters in the British Tong (now com'enly called Walsh)* to assist Englishmen to learn Welsh! I am certain that a second edition of this volume was never published!

In the seventeenth century many famous Welsh literary figures embraced Puritanism, and as a consequence, poetry gave way to prose. Not that these Puritans were against poetry *per se*, but they urgently wanted to proselytize their faith, and that in the simple, effective, direct language of prose. Among these prose writers, one Morgan Llwyd (1619–59) has often been hailed by many Welsh thinkers as a philosopher. Certainly, Llwyd was a considerable literary scholar and the ablest writer of Welsh prose of his time. But first and foremost, he was a theologian who had been deeply influenced by the writings of the Lutheran mystic Jakob Boehme. There is, however, in Llwyd's writings, an analysis of the human personality. Man, according to Llwyd, is not only body, soul and spirit, but beyond or beneath all these three levels of humanity is 'the root and depth ('y *gwreiddyn a'r gwaelodl*) of all being – that level of unity, or of potential unity, of the human with the divine.' The body is regarded by Llwyd as merely the external shell of a person, and it is the level of discontent, irritation and even contention. To move inward to the concerns of the soul, and then to that of the spirit, is to move away from conflict and distress. But it is only when the root or depth of one's being is discovered that peace and salvation are gained. Such is Llwyd's analysis. This description, however, is not philosophical but religious, and is both theologically motivated and dogmatically asserted. Llwyd's analysis cannot be compared, say, with the philosophical analysis of his slightly older contemporary, Descartes. Indeed, both religiously and intellectually, Llwyd has much more in common with that other outstanding French thinker of the same period, Blaise Pascal.

Before the instituting of university colleges in Wales, four Welshmen (contingently, all from different centuries) had to a greater or lesser degree reputations as philosophers – and all of them lived most, if not all, of their lives outside Wales, received their higher education outside Wales, and wrote hardly any philosophy in Welsh. They are John Dee (1527–1608), Lord Herbert of Cherbury (1583–1648), Richard Price (1723–91) and Sir Henry Jones. Probably, only John Dee, who was born in London, was not able to speak Welsh. (But he was as deeply conscious of his Welshness and Welsh ancestry as any of the others. He himself created a family tree that purports that he descended directly from Rhodri Mawr – Rhodri the Great, King of all Wales, who died in 877.) Lord Cherbury was born in Montgomery and was taught Welsh as a child. And so was Richard Price, possibly the greatest Welsh philosopher of all time. He was the son of a Welsh dissenting minister of religion, and he received his early education in two small Nonconformist religious academies in Wales (first at Pentwyn, Llanon, near Lianefli, and then at Liwynliwyd in Breconshire – where he may have shared a desk with, arguably, Wales's greatest son, William Williams, Pantycelyn, author of hundreds of Welsh hymns and of the famous English hymn 'Guide me, O Thou great Jehovah'). Unfortunately, Price lost his mother in his early teens and this untimely loss meant that he spent most of the rest of his life away from his native Wales. He may, as a result, have lost much contact with his country and its language. There is no evidence that Price wrote anything at all in Welsh. The last of the four, Sir Henry Jones, 'the cobbler-philosopher', was the most deeply rooted Welshman of these thinkers, but it was in Scotland that he received most of his university education and where he spent most of his academic life. He had a greater opportunity than any of the others to contribute to Welsh philosophy. For by the time he had finished his academic training, the University of Wales had been established, and Jones taught philosophy, briefly at Aberystwyth, and then held the chair of philosophy, again briefly, at Bangor before he settled permanently in Scotland. Yet the sum total of his legacy in Welsh is four articles in *Y Traethodydd* (see below), a short volume entitled *Dinasyddiaeth Bur* (True Citizenship), based on a series of six lectures which Sir Henry once gave to the slate workers of North Wales, published by the workers union, and a sixty-eight page pamphlet in which Jones prognosticates on the political future of his country. However, these Welsh-language publications have as much, if not more, to do with practical politics and religion as with political philosophy and the philosophy of religion.

These four thinkers not only wrote hardly anything in Welsh, but one would find it difficult to say that there is anything that is distinctly Welsh about their thinking. Their combined works do not constitute anything like a Welsh philosophical tradition. There are no indications, for instance, that Lord Herbert was influenced intellectually in any way by Dee – even though there was a long and close friendship between the Dee and Herbert families. Neither is it possible to say, for instance, that Jones was influenced by Price, or that Price was influenced by Herbert of Cherbury. There is no continuity of ideas at all in the writings of these thinkers. They are four individuals who happened to be Welsh by birth, but their philosophical views are dependent more on their English, Scottish and European heritage than on any discussion of philosophical ideas current in the land of their fathers.

Hence, it may be safely concluded from the evidence available that there is no such thing as a Welsh Philosophical Tradition. It is certainly true that in comparison with, say, Scotland (a country that has only around twice the population of Wales and which also, in time, like Wales, became part of the United Kingdom), Wales can be proud of very little in terms of philosophical achievement. But Scotland has, in contrast to Wales, a very old university tradition and, of course, philosophy has traditionally been a university discipline. Furthermore, the exclusion from Oxbridge, until late in the nineteenth century, of the sons of religious Dissenters, further reduced opportunities for Welshmen, particularly, as has already been noted, as the Welsh were in their religious convictions so deeply Nonconformist.

But with the growth of this Nonconformity, and with it the need to train Nonconformist ministers, there grew in Wales a large number of religious academies and denominational colleges to fulfil this specific task. And from the second half of the seventeenth century until the establishment of the university colleges in Wales, leading Welsh academics were teachers at these academies. Places such as Brynllywarch, Ystrad Wallter, Caerfyrddin (Caernarthen), Llwynllwyd, Y Fenni (Abergavenny) and Aberhonddi (Brecon), where these academies and colleges existed, were of central importance to Welsh culture during this period. And one has to mention Tewkesbury (just the other side of the river Severn) where a Cardiganshire man, Samuel Jones, had his academy. This Samuel Jones trained many famous Welshmen for the ministry, and he could also name among his English students people who achieved subsequent fame and authority in England and beyond – people like Thomas Secker (who became Archbishop of Canterbury), Nathaniel Lardner, Samuel Chandler and, perhaps, his most famous pupil of all, Bishop Butler. (Also at one time at this Tewkesbury academy there was another Samuel Jones, a student, who in later years became a tutor to the young Richard Price at Penllwyn.) It has been alleged that the educational standard of this Tewkesbury Academy was higher than that at Oxford during the corresponding period. Of course, these Welsh and border-country academies were theological institutions with a religious *raison d'être* and not nurseries for young philosophers. But they were virtually the only institutions that gave any chance for sons of ordinary Welsh peasants and workers to gain some higher education, even though, again, English was the medium of instruction in all but one of these institutions. Often the teachers at these institutions complained that they wasted so much time in teaching English to monoglot Welshmen, but such was the climate of the period that it was unthinkable that education could be through the medium of Welsh! How servile a people can become!

Of course, there were several grammar schools in Wales, the earliest of which were established in the Tudor era. But they were not Welsh-medium schools at all. After the Latin period, English became the medium of instruction and the Welsh language had no function whatsoever in these schools. They were also expensive and normally only children of the more privileged classes were able to profit from them, even though, exceptionally, they had places for 'poor scholars'. These grammar schools served the establishment well. The establishment was Anglican, and Anglicanism rapidly grew to represent Englishness in the minds of the majority of Welshmen. It may be stated as a generalization that for two whole centuries, from the late seventeenth to late in the nineteenth, Welshness was inseparable from Nonconformity and its accompanying educational institutions. Indeed, Nonconformity became almost synonymous with Welshness. But it would be a travesty of the truth to claim that there were no Welsh-speaking Anglican scholars, or that Wales was not in any way deeply indebted to Anglican institutions. Indeed, two of the most important Welsh prose writers of the eighteenth century, Ellis Wynne (1670/1–1734) and Theophilus Evans (1693–1767) were both Anglican priests. And Wales owes an incalculable debt to one Anglican priest, Gruffith Jones, Llanddowror (1683–1761), who is thought by many to be the greatest Welshman of the eighteenth century. Through his enthusiasm for religion and education, he founded the Welsh Circulating Schools throughout the country – with the result that by the end of the eighteenth century the Welsh were, probably, the most literate people in the whole of Europe. Still, as Nonconformity grew stronger, particularly after the Methodist revival in the eighteenth century, the gulf between Anglicanism and Englishness on the one hand, and Nonconformity and Welshness on the other, widened. And by the nineteenth century Anglicanism in Wales was represented more by people like the English-speaking Isaac Williams (1802–65), sometime Dean of Trinity College, Oxford, and a prominent member of the Oxford Movement. But the Welsh-speaking people of Wales (who up to the middle of the nineteenth century were in the majority in Wales) seldom looked towards Anglicanism for direction but rather to the principals and professors of the

Nonconformist educational institutions and to the men they prepared for the chapel pulpit. From these institutions there also came a profusion of publications – particularly in the form of Biblical exegeses for use in the numerically strong, adult Sunday schools of Wales, and the regular weekly evening Bible classes. There were also hundreds of biographies and auto-biographies of preachers, and endless books of collected sermons. Yet one will have difficulty in finding a single volume of philosophy in Welsh amongst this proliferation of writing.

Much research from a philosophical standpoint still needs to be done into the writings of the leaders of these Nonconformist colleges. They were well-educated men and many would have been at least influenced by the philo-sophical developments in Europe. It is a well-known fact that philosophy was an integral part of the syllabuses of these academies, with Plato's *Republic* and Aristotle's *Nicomachean Ethics* regarded as essential texts. Towards the end of the nineteenth century, some other favourite texts were Butler's *Analogy* and *Sermons*, Masson's *Recent British Philosophy*, Jonathan Edwards's *Freedom of the Will* along with the works of others such as Hamilton, Reid and Calderwood – works that underline the Scottish influence on these academies. However, from the evidence surveyed, these Welsh teachers did not themselves write a great deal of philosophy. As an estimate, no more than a total of fifty articles on philosophical topics were written and pub-lished in Welsh-language journals in the whole of the nineteenth century, and most of these articles are closely related to either religious issues, such as the notion of immortality and the freedom of the will (a bitter dispute between Calvinists and Armenians had raged in Wales for well over a cen-tury), or to ethical matters. And no more than two or three philosophy books were published, and that only in the last decade of the last century. Furthermore, there was hardly anything at all produced on epistemology, or logic, or even on political philosophy. And in terms of the content of what was produced, the articles tended to be descriptive or critical of other people's systems rather than expressions of an author's original ideas. At best, there is only original criticism of other people's beliefs and systems. Welsh writers were not metaphysical system-builders themselves. Yet even though by the end of the nineteenth century there was much more philo-sophical activity in Welsh, unfortunately Wales did not produce anyone of the calibre of Richard Price.

Of the intellectual leaders of Nonconformity in Wales in the nineteenth century, many Welsh scholars maintain that Lewis Edwards was by far Wales's most perceptive thinker. He was a graduate and an honorary DD of the University of Edinburgh, and was for a period of fifty years, principal of the Calvinistic Methodist College at Bala. (He was also the father of Thomas Charles Edwards, the first Principal of Aberystwyth University College.) He wrote several influential theological works, the most well known being, *Athrawiaeth yr Iawn* (Doctrine of Atonement), which was written in the form of a dialogue between teacher and pupil. It was a treatise deeply influenced by Anselm's *Cur Deus Homo* and was unquestionably the single most influential Welsh theological work of the last century. But together with two other prominent Welshmen of the time, Lewis Edwards established in 1845 a Welsh journal named *Y Traethodydd* (The Essayist) for promoting discussion in the Welsh language of 'religion, theology, philosophy and literature'. This was Lewis Edwards' greatest legacy to the Welsh people, for this journal still survives as, arguably, the most prestigious of all Welsh-language journals, and one to which Phillips has often contributed in recent times. It was in this journal that most philosophical material written in Welsh in the nineteenth century was published, and Lewis Edwards himself contributed to it several articles on philosophical topics. Lewis had a particular admiration for Kant, particularly Kant's ethics, and a number of Lewis's articles in the journal elucidate different aspects of Kant's philosophy.

With the establishment of university colleges in Wales, the denominational colleges moved closer to these new centres of academic excellence, and the situation in relation to philosophy was gradually transformed. Even before receiving its charter to give degrees of its own, we see the University Colleges of Wales influencing students. For instance, one of the first students to graduate at Aberystwyth was David Adams. He graduated in 1877 with a London university degree. His fame in Wales today rests on his book, *Yr Hên a'r Newydd mewn Diwinyddiaeth* (The Old and New in Theology), which represents his attempt to portray Christianity as the most developed form of religion, using Hegel's concepts of thesis, antithesis and synthesis as a philosophical framework for his analysis. Even here, there is no originality of thought, as Hegel's work was well known, and the application of Hegelian principles to religious thought had been adopted by several English and Scottish theologians earlier in the same century. It was clearly enunciated in the writings of, for example, J.R. Illingworth and the Caird brothers.

In time, departments and chairs of philosophy were established within the University Colleges of Wales, and several of these chairs have been occupied by Welsh-speaking thinkers who have contributed substantially to a discussion of philosophy in the language – people like the late Professors R.I. Aaron, H.D. Lewis and Phillips's predecessor in the chair at Swansea, J.R. Jones. All three came from a common strong Nonconformist background: Aaron was a Baptist deacon, Lewis was the son of a Presbyterian minister and Jones was a Presbyterian lay preacher. I suspect that all three started doing philosophy in their adolescence in their respective Sunday schools and Bible classes where discussion of topics such as individual freedom and divine foreknowledge, the problem of suffering, the meaning of concepts such as salvation, redemption and forgiveness, would have been a natural part of their religious education. Had these thinkers been born a generation or so earlier, they would have probably been ministers of religion or theologians. But a university education in Wales introduced them to philosophy and, more significantly, enabled them to become professional philosophers in Wales itself.

Furthermore, all three were not only Welsh speakers, but were Welshmen who were committed to all things Welsh. Aaron and Lewis were, for instance, founder members of the Philosophical Section of the Guild of Graduates of the University of Wales. As already mentioned, soon after its formation this Welsh philosophical society established a Welsh-language philosophy journal, *Efrydiau Athronyddol*. Aaron was, for over two decades, its editor. Lewis was the secretary of the society for many years, and Jones its treasurer. This trinity of thinkers represents the best of this early period of Welsh-language philosophy in Wales since the establishment of the Welsh University. All three were, philosophically speaking, in the modern British empiricist tradition. Each gained some recognition outside Wales as philosophers: Aaron for his work and commentary on Locke, Lewis for his philosophy of religion and, despite his empiricism, his defence of Cartesian dualism. Jones's main philosophical preoccupation was with the question of personal identity. Jones, of course, after coming to Swansea, renounced his empiricism and espoused the standpoint of the later Wittgenstein.

In more recent years, 'the Swansea School of Philosophy' has emerged. The person primarily responsible for this development was Rush Rhees, who spent almost the whole of his professional life at Swansea. He was not a Welshman, even though he was of Welsh descent – a fact that he was very much aware of – and it is possible that he remained in Wales because he identified himself with the Welsh. His most famous pupil is Professor Phillips, and also, possibly, the ablest Welsh-speaking philosopher of this century, and the most prolific too – although H.D. Lewis is also a contender for this last title. Of course, it important to bear in mind that in this century in particular, the linguistic situation in Wales has changed entirely and Welsh-speakers now represent only slightly less than 20 per cent of the whole population of Wales. This means that there are far more non-Welsh-speaking Welsh philosophers than Welsh-speaking philosophers. Some of these Anglo-Welsh philosophers have achieved considerable distinction in their time, and among the more famous of them is the late Professor H.H. Price, who occupied a chair of philosophy at Oxford in the twentieth century.

Phillips shares much in common with Aaron, Lewis and Jones. He too comes from a strong Welsh Nonconformist tradition, and one of his brothers, Cadfan, was a Welsh Congregationalist minister. Phillips himself was, for a brief period, a Congregational pastor. And, like the other three, he was introduced to discussions of difficult theological concepts and issues quite early in his teens, so it is little wonder that his main interest is the philosophy of religion. Furthermore, those who have heard Phillips lecture, and who also know of the wealth of the Welsh pulpit tradition and oratory, cannot but conclude that the latter's influence is clearly detectable in Phillips's inimitable style and excellence of delivery.

Anyone who has taken any interest at all in Phillips's writings will know that he has published some material in Welsh. The titles of the two books that he has published in Welsh, *Athronyddu am Grefydd* (Philosophizing about Religion) and *Dramau Gwenlyn Parry* (The Plays of Gwenlyn Parry – which has just recently been republished with additions) have appeared regularly in the list of his publications. These two relatively short volumes in Welsh, as opposed to at least thirteen volumes in English, do not appear to represent a significant contribution to Welsh thought. But several factors need to be borne in mind. First, Wales is by today a bilingual country, and everything which Phillips has written in English is thus accessible to Welsh-speaking readers. Secondly, less than half a million people out of a total population of 2.7 million living in Wales now speak the Welsh language. And of any country, it may be asked what proportion of the population is really interested in philosophical issues? Thirdly, and much more significantly, Phillips's contribution to philosophy in Welsh is much greater than what these two volumes suggest. Much more important than his two books is his large number of articles in Welsh. In all, he has published around thirty articles, excluding a large number of reviews, in his mother-tongue over a period of almost forty years. (To repeat, during the whole of the nineteenth century only around fifty philosophical articles were published in Welsh.) His book, *Athronyddu am Grefydd*, published in 1974, is a short collection of eight of his Welsh articles which had already appeared in Welsh language journals. And his other Welsh book, first published in 1982, *Dramau Gwenlyn Parry* (Gwenlyn Parry's Plays) contains, apart from the introductory essay, five other essays on five of the plays of Parry, and three of these essays had already appeared as articles in other Welsh publications. But the two volumes represent less than a third of Phillips's total output in Welsh. Phillips also edited a book entitled *Saith Ysgrif ar Grefydd* (Seven Short Essays on Religion) which is, as the title suggests, a collection of seven Welsh essays on religion written by different Welsh scholars, including one essay by Phillips himself.

Not all of Phillips's articles in Welsh are of equal philosophical weight, and for the good reason that he has written sometimes to larger and sometimes to more exclusive audiences. The journals in which the articles have appeared is an indication of the philosophical importance of their content. There are only three Welsh-medium journals that are apt places to publish thoroughgoing philosophical articles, and they are, in order of their philosophical importance, *Efrydiau Athronyddol* (Philosophical Studies), *Y Traethodydd* (The Essayist), and *Diwinyddiaeth* (Theology). The first and the last of these journals are, respectively, the official organs of the Philosophical Section and the Theological Section of the Guild of Graduates of the University of Wales, and both journals are published annually. The *Traethodydd*, a quarterly journal, has been referred to above. Other publications referred to below such as *Y Tyst* (The Witness – a Congregationalist publication), *Barn*

(Opinion) and *Y Faner* (The Banner) are (or were) lesser weekly or monthly journals designed for a wider audience of readers.

Here is a list of Phillips's philosophically more important articles in chronological order of their first publication.

1958 'Cyfiawnhau Crefydd' (Justifying Religion), in *Y Traethodydd* and republished in *Athronyddu am Grefydd*.

1961 'Y syniad o fywyd tragwyddol' (The concept of eternal life) in *Y Dysgedydd* and republished in *Athronyddu am Grefydd*.

1964 'Credu neu Beidio' (Believing or Not Believing) in *Barn*.

'Rhyddid a Chaethiwed mewn Moesoldeb' (Freedom and Slavery in Morality) in *Y Dysgedydd* (The Educator, a Welsh Congregationalist publication).

1965 'Personoliaeth a Rheswm mewn Moeseg' (Personality and Reason in Ethics) in *Efrydiau Athronyddol*.

Yr Argyfwng Gwacter Ystyr' (The Crisis of Meaninglessness) in *Y Traethodydd* and republished in *Athronyddu am Grefydd*

1967 'Angau a Thragwyddoldeb' (Death and Eternity) in *Saith Ysgrif ar Grefydd* and republished in *Athronyddu am Grefydd*.

1968 'Credu ac Anghredu' (Belief and Unbelief) in *Diwinyddiaeth* and republished in *Athronyddu am Grefydd*.

1969 'Gwirionedd, Ystyr a Chrefydd' (Truth, Meaning and Religion) in *Diwinyddiaeth* and republished in *Athronyddu am Grefydd*.

'Byd y Saer Doliau' (The world of the doll-maker) in *Ysgrifau Beirniadol IV* (Critical Essays, Volume IV – a prestigious series of essays on Welsh literature edited by a leading Welsh scholar, Caerwyn Williams F.B.A.. Prof. Williams was the editor of Y *Traethodydd* for thirty years) and republished in *Dramau Gwenlyn Parry* ('Y Saer Doliau' is the title of a play by Gwenlyn Parry).

1970 'Unamuno a Gelynion Athroniaeth' (Unamuno and the Enemies of Philosophy) in Y *Traethodydd*.

'J.R. Jones: Yr Athro ar Athronydd' (J.R. Jones: The Teacher and the Philosopher) in *Y Traethodydd*.

1971 'Crefydd a Metaffiseg' (Religion and Metaphysics) in *Efrydiau Athronyddol* and republished in *Athronyddu am Grefydd*.

1972 'Y Gymdogaeth Ddynol' (The Human Community) in *Efrydiau Athronyddol*.

1975 'Dadl: Beth yw pwrpas llenydda? gyda Bobi Jones' (A debate on 'What is the purpose of literary activity?' with Bobi Jones. Professor Bobi Jones FBA was, until his retirement in 1988, Professor of Welsh Language and Literature at Aberystwyth) in *Y Traethodydd*.

1977 'Chwant a Serch' (Lust and Love) in *Efrydiau Athronyddol*.

1978 'Ty ar y Tywod' (A House on the Sand).

'Y Ffin: Rhwng Ystyr a Diddymdra' (The Border: Between Sense and Nihilism) in two editions of the weekly Welsh journal *Y Faner* (The Banner).

Both papers were republished in the volume *Dramau Gwenlyn Parry* ('Ty ar y Tywod' and 'Y Ffin' are the titles of plays by Gwenlyn Parry).

1979 'Crisnogaeth a Diwyiliant' (Christianity and Culture) in *Y Traethodydd*.

Trafodaeth: Dylanwad Wittgenstein ar Athroniaeth Crefydd: Ateb i'r Beirniaid' (A Discussion: The Influence of Wittgenstein on the Philosophy of Religion: A reply to the Critics) in *Efrydiau Athronyddol*.

1981 'Ysbrydoliaeth' (Inspiration) (A symposium with Rev. Professor J. Heywood Thomas) in *Efrydiau Athronyddol*.

1983 'Ai bod yn naif yw ceisio bod yn ddiduedd?' (Is it naive to seek to be impartial?) in *Y Traethodydd*.

'Ffydd yr Athronydd – Eglurder neu Atebion?' (The Faith of the Philosopher – Clarity or Answers?) in *Efrydiau Athronyddol*. (The whole of this issue of *Efrydiau Athronyddol* was dedicated to the study of Phillips's thought, with four other contributors evaluating different aspects of Phillips's writings.)

1984 'Ffrindiau Cleanthes' (Cleanthess Friends) in *Y Traethodydd*.

1985 'Gemau jaith, Ymatebion Cyntefig a'r Awydd am Fetaffiseg' (Language Games, Primitive Reactions and the Desire for Metaphysics) in *Y Traethodydd*.

1989 'Fy Nghymydog a'm Cymdogion' (My Neighbour and my Neighbours) in *Efrydiau Athronyddol*.

1993 'Pam Achub Iaith?' (Why Save a Language?) in *Efrydiau Athronyddol*.

1996 'Pan Edrychwyf ar Nefoedd', *Y Traethodydd*.

'Heb Fyn i'r Unlle', *Yr Aradr*.

1997 'Y Duwiau a Ni', *Efrydiau Athronyddol*.

1998 'Ôl y Duwiau: Jane Gruffydd a *Traed Mewn Cyffion*', *Efrydiau Athronyddol*.

2001 'Y Cyn-Socratiaid', *Efrydiau Athronyddol*.

It will be clearly evident to those familiar with Phillips's English publications, even from the titles of the above papers, that they echo the same themes and concerns that we find in his English works. Phillips's main philosophical preoccupations, in Welsh as in English, have been with issues in the philosophy of religion, followed closely by those in ethics. Literature is also important for Phillips not only from an aesthetic standpoint, but as a philosophical medium that draws our attention to the variety of human situations and the diversity of our experiences, and hence as a corrective to any form of logical essentialism. If one were to look for differences in Phillips's contributions in the two languages, it would appear that even a greater proportion of his writings in Welsh is on issues in the philosophy of religion. However, as in his English works, so much of his Welsh writings represent responses by him to what other thinkers and writers have said and published. Phillips has always thrived on criticism – both of his own works by other writers, to which he normally responds with avidity, and criticism of any suggestion of conceptual confusion in the writings of others. He is a fair if a severe critic, and this has been such a positive and creative factor in Welsh circles. For, it has to be confessed, in a small linguistic community there is a danger of paying too much respect to those who have made their reputations, and to accept too uncritically on their authority, that such and such is the case. That *used* to be the situation in the philosophical sessions of the University of Wales Guild of Graduates Society – until Phillips came along! 'What has Professor so and so to say on this issue?' And Professor so and so would respond to such an invitation to give his unchallenged judgement on the matter. Phillips changed all that. Truth or clarity must never be sacrificed in the interest of not offending reputations. The essence of philosophy is discussion and Phillips reacted with courage and passion against the rather sterile and authoritarian manner in which some of the discussions used to be conducted at the Welsh-language conferences. And this kind of response is equally behind much of his writings. For instance, the late Professor J.R. Jones, once head of the department of which Phillips was a member, contributed an essay entitled 'Gwirionedd ac Ystyr' (Truth and Meaning) to the book *Saith Ysgrif ar Grefydd*; and the same author, in 1964, published a booklet entitled *Yr Argyfwng Gwacter Ystyr* (The Crisis of Meaninglessness). The logical assumptions and reasoning in both these writing are attacked without fear or favour in Phillips's articles 'Gwirionedd, Ystyr a Chrefydd' and 'Yr Argyfwng Gwacter Ystyr' respectively. The articles, 'Trafodaeth: Dylanwad Wittgenstein ar Athroniaeth Crefydd' and 'Gemau iaith, Ymatebion Cyntefig a'r awydd am Fetaffiseg' are attempts by Phillips to answer my own attacks on his account of the nature of religious belief – an attack which Phillips allowed to spill over into English in his book *Belief, Change and Forms of Life*. The article 'Cyfellion Cleanthes' is another outspoken attack on the ethical standpoint of another professional Welsh philosopher. Two of Phillips's articles listed above discuss the views of Emeritus Professor Bobi Jones. Jones is a Welsh poet and a literary critic with deep evangelical convictions. He also adheres to a Calvinistic foundationalist philosophical position and appears to have been influenced by the writings of Alvin Plantinga – and inevitably, Phillips has made his opposition to Jones's foundationalist beliefs clear in his Welsh publications.

   Phillips's love of literature, particularly of English literature, is reflected clearly in his writings, and particularly so in such works as *Through a Darkening Glass, R.S. Thomas: Poet of the Hidden God*, and *From Fantasy to Faith*. His interest in Welsh literature is reflected in his volume *Dramau Gwenlyn Parry*. In this collection of essays, Phillips examines the religious outlooks represented by the various characters in Parry's plays. Or, perhaps it would be more accurate to state that the religious standpoint of the playwright himself is under Phillips's scrutiny. Gwenlyn Parry (1932–91) was a school teacher who developed a love for the theatre and ultimately became the head of the Drama department of the BBC in Wales. He wrote several one-act plays and several longer plays, and it is these longer plays that aroused Phillips's interest. They are all plays with a religious or quasi-religious theme and Phillips's central contention is that there is some development to be perceived in the author's own understanding of the erosion in the significance of the language of religion in our increasingly secular society. For instance, in the first of Parry's longer plays, Y *Saer Doliau*, the language of religion is intelligible enough for the chief character in the play, Ifans, and his spirituality is real. But unfortunately, when Ifans is challenged by a young modern secularist, he fails to respond, and he cannot cope with the attacks. Phillips's own response to this common phenomenon of modernism attacking religion – a response frequently echoed in his philosophy papers – is that the modernist attack is itself grounded in conceptual confusion. Hence, according to Phillips, Ifans's real failure is not his inability to answer the questions, but rather his inability to perceive that the questions are themselves the result of confused thinking about religion. In subsequent plays, such as *Ty ar y Tywod* and *Y Ffin*, according to Phillips's interpretation, the significance of religious language is seen by Parry to be further eroded in the Welsh community and there is an accompanying breakdown in human relationships. And in one of Parry's last plays, *Y Twr*, we have a picture of a wholly godless and secular society in which the characters are completely alienated from each other. The last of Parry's plays which Phillips examines in his volume, is called *Sal*. This play is based on a true story from late in the last century, about a young Welsh girl named Sarah Jacob. It was claimed that Sarah was miraculously sustained, for, it was alleged, she did not eat or drink at all for two whole years. The story ended tragically in the death of the girl and her parents were subsequently prosecuted and imprisoned for causing her death. This play, according to Phillips, is not so much on the notion of the erosion of the sense of religion, but rather, on the idea of a debased religion, or superstition. This is a different form of the lack of genuine spirituality, and the *Sal* phenomenon belongs 'more to the occult than to religion'.

The issues raised by Parry in these plays are important and are connected with the effects, particularly on Welsh rural life, of the pressures exerted by rapid changes brought about by technology and increasing bureaucracy. These changes tend to destroy the old sense of community, and human beings become increasingly alienated from each other. The plays themselves describe real social phenomena. But Parry does not provide anything more than a vivid description of these social changes. It is Phillips's interpretation of the plays that has depth and not the plays themselves. Parry knew of the decline in religion in Wales, and he was aware that this was partly a consequence of scientism. He had read John Robinson's *Honest to God* and had been impressed by that book. But he would not have seen, say, that modernists' attacks on religion are based on conceptual confusion. That is Phillips's claim. And what we have in *Sal* is a simple, effective account of the tragic story of Sarah Jacob. It is Phillips who sees the play as examining the idea of a depraved form of religion. But, unfortunately, I do not share in Phillips's admiration for the work of Parry, and in my view, Phillips has too elevated an opinion of Parry's intellectual powers. Parry's plays cannot be compared with those of the best of Welsh playwrights in the twentieth century, such as Saunders Lewis and Emyr Humphreys. Neither was Parry in the same literary league or of the same intellectual stature as, say, the Anglo-Welsh poet R.S. Thomas, whose poetry Phillips so rightly admires.

In contemporary Wales, non-Welsh speakers are often heard asking sceptical questions about the value of Welsh-language intellectual activities. For instance, why should Phillips, and the handful of other Welsh-speaking philosophers, bother to discuss philosophy through the medium of Welsh? Are they not all bilingual? And would it not be the case that philosophizing in English would mean that no non-Welsh speaker would be excluded from any discussion? In one of his more recent Welsh-language publications (*Efrydiau Athronyddol*, 1992) Phillips addressed issues raised by such questions. This paper is entitled *Pam Achub Iaith?* (Why save a language?). The issue of the preservation of the Welsh language is currently a crucial one in Wales. Indeed, Welsh speakers have been anxious about the decline of the language for a considerable time. But in 1962 Wales's greatest *littérateur* of this century, Saunders Lewis, in a radio lecture entitled *Tynged yr Iaith Gymraeg* (The Fate of the Welsh Language) argued that unless radical, and indeed, revolutionary measures were adopted, the Welsh language would cease to be a viable, living language before the end of the twentieth century. This lecture led to the establishment of a movement called *Cymdeithas yr Iaith Gymraeg* (The Welsh Language Society), which subsequently has been in the forefront of a campaign of civil disobedience in order to draw the attention of those in power to the demise of the language, its lack of any legal status, and its neglect in public life. To many Welsh speakers, the Welsh language is the most significant, if not the only, criterion of Welsh identity. For them, to destroy the language is to destroy the definitive element of Welsh identity. Professor J.R. Jones was one who maintained such a position, and he published several essays and pamphlets on the issue. He also delivered several lectures in support of the Welsh Language Society's campaign.

Inevitably, this stance has provoked bitter reactions in some quarters in Wales. The Welsh who have lost the language often perceive it as divisive and merely the means of ensuring privileges and preference in terms of jobs for the elite who are fluent in the language. And the inevitable cynical questions arise, 'Why do you want to save the language anyway?' Would not the Welsh be better off with a single language? Would not that unite Wales as a country? Would it not immerse the Welsh in a richer English culture? Far from being a tragedy, the death of the language would be most beneficial – socially, politically and culturally. Faced with such an attack, the Welsh have been tempted to answer the question, 'Why save the language?' by providing reasons for doing so. We want to save the language because . . . followed by a diversity of reasons. This strategy, Phillips argues, is based on a confusion. The confusion is partly based on a failure to distinguish between the respective roles of the first language and that of second languages in our lives. Our first language, the mother tongue, is as natural as our lives, as our breathing and walking. It is given to us. And there is no sense in asking, 'Why do we speak this language?' In this matter, we have no choice. The whole conception of purpose is irrelevant in this context – as irrelevant as it is to speak of the purpose of falling in love. But in relation to any second language, the question of why was it learnt in the first place, or spoken, is an intelligible question, and people may give a multiplicity of different answers. Phillips's point is that the confused Welsh speaker, by giving reasons for speaking his mother tongue, fails to see that its role in his life is different from any of the roles of a second language in his life.

But the confusion is not only made by the Welsh speaker. The confusion is also present in the challenger's initial question, 'Why do you speak Welsh?' By asking the question, the questioner already perceives of a person's natural tongue in terms of a second language. It never occurs to, say, an Englishman, to ask 'Why do I speak English?' That *is* his language.

The importance of the role of the first language in our lives can be fully appreciated, Phillips argues, only if we take on board the significance of what Wittgenstein has taught us about the nature of language. Part of Phillips's paper is an attack on the erroneous Lockean conception of language, in which language is seen merely as an instrument of communication. In this empirical philosophy, we already know or understand the world through 'ideas', and we require language only to communicate those ideas with each other. In this philosophy, any one language will do the job, and that equally well. There is here no essential connection between understanding our world and the language we use. But what Wittgenstein showed is that without the language there is no understanding. We see, or rather, we understand what we see, through our language. Our world and our understanding of that world are logically inseparable from the language we use to speak of that world. And if Welsh is my language then I see my world through that language. In that language 'I live and move and have my being'. And Phillips further underlines Wittgenstein's point that language is not merely a matter of the correct use of signs. Language and life's activities are inseparable. To speak of one's language is to speak of what we do, of how we act, of the practices in our lives.

Of course, as Phillips points out, the significance of language may be wholly understood. But that does not mean that, inevitably, people will want the language saved. On the contrary, it is because some people appreciate the importance of language that they will want to see the language destroyed. Those who have understood the inextricable connection between language and culture may want to destroy the language, for in so doing they will achieve their end of genocide. The moral issue of respect for a language and its accompanying culture is another issue altogether. And, towards the end of the paper, Phillips shows how much contempt still exists for the Welsh language in real terms, and in practical situations – such as the failure to secure the continuing of the teaching of philosophy through the medium of Welsh anywhere in the University of Wales. Yet respect, if it is real, must be understood in such pragmatic terms.

It is accepted that the notion of choice is irrelevant in relation to the first language. I did not choose to speak Welsh and, in fact, neither did my parents choose to teach that language to me either. Welsh was their language. But with English as an increasingly omnipresent language in the culture, parental choice is real. All Welsh-speaking parents are bilingual; there are no monoglot adult Welsh-speakers. Hence such parents may choose the first language of their children, and the sad story in Wales is that the Welsh themselves have lost their self-respect to such a degree that they often opt for English. There are, even today, Welsh-speaking professional philosophers who will have nothing to do with philosophy in Welsh. This can mean nothing else than a total lack of respect for the Welsh language and Welsh culture. As we have seen, there are historical reasons for this lack of self-respect, and preserving this self-respect is not easy in a bilingual society with English being such a dominant language and influence. Every request made in Welsh at any shop counter in Wales is a political act that needs courage. It was J.R. Jones who coined the expression 'genocide by assimilation' to describe what has happened, and is happening in Wales. It is a bitter and painful experience.

Phillips's constant and consistent contributions to philosophy in Welsh is indicative of the thoroughness of his Welshness and his respect for his native culture. And in our minority situation his work is invaluable, and that not only in terms of the quantity of the material that he has published (he has published more on the subject in Welsh than any other individual at any time in Welsh history) but also in terms of its excellence. The Welsh have recognized this in the only uniquely Welsh way possible for Welsh speakers to honour such a contribution – by making Phillips an honorary member of the highest order of the Bardic Circle, that of the White Robe, of the National Eisteddfod of Wales. Assessing the long-term significance of Phillips's work is an altogether much more complex matter which depends on a multiplicity of factors, such as how pervasive and permanent Wittgenstein's influence will be on philosophy in general, and on how far Phillips's work will be perceived to be an accurate working out of the implications of Wittgenstein's later philosophy, particularly in the context of the philosophy of religion. But from a Welsh standpoint, no one in the future will be able to give an account of philosophy in Wales without paying substantial attention to Phillips's work.

University of Wales, Aberystwyth

D.Z. Phillips: Publications

Books

The Concept of Prayer, Routledge and Schocken Books, 1965; Blackwell and
  Seabury Press, 1981.
Moral Practices (with H.O. Mounce), Routledge and Schocken Books, 1969.
Faith and Philosophical Enquiry, Routledge and Schocken Books, 1970.
Death and Immortality, Macmillan and Humanities Press, 1970.
Sense and Delusion (with Ilham Dilman), Routledge and Humanities Press,
  1971.
Athronyddu Am Grefydd, Gomer Press, 1974.
Religion without Explanation, Blackwell and St. Martin's Press, 1976.
Through a Darkening Glass: Philosophy, Literature and Cultural Change, Black-
  well and University of Notre Dame Press, 1982.
Dramau Gwenlyn Parry, Pantycelyn Press, 1982; 2nd edn 1995.
Belief, Change and Forms of Life, Macmillan and Humanities Press, 1986.
R.S. Thomas: Poet of the Hidden God, Macmillan and Princeton Theological
  Monograph Series, Pickwick, 1986.
Faith after Foundationalism, Routledge, 1988; Westview Press, 1995.
From Fantasy to Faith, Macmillan and St. Martin's Press, 1991.
Interventions in Ethics, Macmillan and SUNY Press, 1992.
Wittgenstein and Religion, Macmillan and St. Martin's Press, 1993.
Writers of Wales: J.R. Jones, University of Wales Press, 1995.
Introducing Philosophy: The Challenge of Scepticism, Blackwell, 1996; rep. 1997.
Recovering Religious Concepts, Macmillan, 1999.
Philosophy's Cool Place, Cornell University Press, 1999.
Recovering Religious Concepts, Macmillan and St. Martin's Press, 2000.
Filosofi – en presentation: Skepticismens utmaning (Swedish translation by Yrsa
  Neuman and Lars Hertzberg of *Introducing Philosophy: The Challenge of
  Scepticism*, 1996) 2000.
Religion and the Hermeneutics of Contemplation, Cambridge University Press,
  2001.

Edited books

Religion and Understanding (with Introduction), Blackwell and Macmillan, 1967.
Saith Ysgrif Ar Grefydd, Gee Press, 1967.
J.L. Stocks, *Morality and Purpose* (with Introduction), Routledge and Schocken Books, 1969.
Rush Rhees, *Without Answers*, Routledge and Schocken Books, 1969.
John Anderson, *Education and Inquiry*, Blackwell and Barnes and Noble, 1980.
Jakob Fries, *Dialogues on Morality and Religion*, Blackwell and Barnes and Noble, 1982.
Peter Winch, *Wittgenstein: Attention to Particulars: Essays in Honour of Rush Rhees* (with Introduction), Macmillan and St. Martin's Press, 1989.
Religion and Morality (with Introduction and 'Voices in Discussion'), Macmillan and St. Martin's Press, 1996.
Can Religion Be Explained Away? (with Introduction and 'Voices in Discussion'), Macmillan and St. Martin's Press, 1996.
Rush Rhees, *On Religion and Philosophy* (assisted by Mario von der Ruhr) (with Introduction), Cambridge University Press, 1997.
Rush Rhees, *Wittgenstein and the Possibility of Discourse* (with Biographical Sketch and Introduction), Cambridge University Press, 1998.
Timothy Tessin, *Religion without Transcendence?* (with Introduction and 'Voices in Discussion'), Macmillan and St. Martin's Press, 1997.
Rush Rhees, *Moral Questions* (with Introduction), Macmillan, 1999.
with Timothy Tessin, *Religion and Hume's Legacy* (with Introduction and 'Voices in Discussion'), Macmillan and St. Martin's Press, 1999.
Rush Rhees, *Discussions of Simone Weil* (assisted by Mario von der Ruhr), SUNY Press, 1999.
with Timothy Tessin, *Kant and Kierkegaard on Religion*, Macmillan and St. Martin's Press, 2000.
Studies in Ethics and the Philosophy of Religion, 1968–1974, Routledge and Shocken Books.
Values and Philosophical Inquiry, 1976–1986, Blackwell.
Philosophy of Religion in the 21st Century (with Timothy Tessin), Palgrave, 2001.

General editor

Philosophical Investigations, 1982–, Blackwell journal.
Swansea Studies in Philosophy, 1990, Macmillan.
Claremont Studies in the Philosophy of Religion, 1993, Macmillan and St. Martin's Press.

Contributions to books, papers, critical notices and reviews

1958

'Duw A'i Greadigaeth', *Y Dysgedydd*, May
'Cyfiawnhau Crefydd', *Y Traethodydd*

1959

'Gwybodaeth Wyddonol a Chrefydd', *Y Dysgedydd*, January and February

1963

'Can Theology Be Taught?', *The Universities Quarterly*
'Philosophy, Theology and the Reality of God', *Philosophical Quarterly*
Review of John Macmurray's *Religion, Art and Science. Philosophical Quarterly*

1964

'Moral and Religious Conceptions of Duty: An Analysis', *Mind*
'The Possibilities of Moral Advice', *Analysis*
'Rhyddid a Chaethiwed Mewn Moeseg', *Y Traethodydd*
Review of John Baillie's *The Sense of the Presence of God, Philosophical Quarterly*
'Does it Pay to be Good?', *Proceedings of the Aristotelian Society*, 1964–5
'Yr Argyfwng Gwacter Ystyr', *Y Traethodydd*
'Personoliaeth a Rheswm Mewn Moeseg', *Efrydiau Athronyddol*
'On Morality's Having a Point' (with H.O. Mounce), *Philosophy*
'Meaning and Belief', *The Listener*
Review of Axel Hagerstrom's *Philosophy and Religion*
Review of Henry David Aiken's *Reason and Conduct: Near Bearings in Moral Philosophy, Philosophy*

1966

'God and Ought', in *Christian Ethics and Contemporary Philosophy*, ed. I.T. Ramsey, SCM Press and Macmillan
'On the Christian Concept of Love', in *Christian Ethics and Contemporary Philosophy*, ed. I.T. Ramsey, SCM Press and Macmillan
'Religion and Epistemology: Some Contemporary Confusions', *Australasian Journal of Philosophy*
'La Prière transforme le monde. De quelques différences entre superstition et prière de demand' (trans. of chapter Six of *The Concept of Prayer* by J. Godin) in Cahiers 'Lumen Vitae', *Le Psychologie Religieuse* IV, ed. J. Godin
Review of H.D. Lewis, *Philosophy of Religion. Efrydiau Athronyddol*

1967

'Moral and Religious Conceptions of Duty', in *Religion and Understanding*, ed. D.Z. Phillips, Blackwell and Macmillan (reprint from 1964)
'Faith, Scepticism and Religious Understanding', in *Religion and Understanding*, ed. D.Z. Phillips, Blackwell and Macmillan
'Angau a Thragwyddoldeb', in *Saith Ysgrif Ar Grefydd*, ed. D.Z. Phillips, Gee Press
'Remorse Without Repudiation' (with H.S. Price), *Analysis*
'From World to God?', *Aristotelian Society Supplementary Volume*
'Faith and Philosophy', *The Universities Quarterly*
Review of L.M. Loring's *Two Kinds of Values*. *Philosophy*

1968

'Does it Pay to be Good?' in *Ethics*, ed. Gerald Dworkin and Judith Jarvis Thompson, Harper and Row (reprint from 1964)
'Byd y Saer Doliau', in *Ysgrifau Beirniadol IV*, ed. J.B. Caerwyn Williams, Gee Press
'Religious Belief and Philosophical Enquiry', *Theology*
'Miss Anscombe's Grocer', *Analysis*
'Subjectivity and Religious Truth in Kierkegaard', *Sophia*
'Credu ac Anghredu', *Diwinyddiaeth*
'Letter to the Editor: The Entry of the Philosophers', *Times Literary Supplement*
Review of George C. Kerner's *The Revolution in Ethical Theory*. *Philosophy*
Review of Julian Marias' *Migel de Unamuno*, and Allan Lacy's *Miguel de Unamuno: The Rhetoric of Existence*. *Philosophical Quarterly*

1969

'Subjectivity and Religious Truth in Kierkegaard', in *Philosophy Today* No. 2, ed. Jerry H. Gill, Macmillan. See 'Subjectivity and Religious Truth in Kierkegaard' (1968)
'On Morality's Having a Point' (with H.O. Mounce), in *The Is/Ought Question*, ed. W.D. Hudson, Macmillan (reprints from 1965 and 1964 respectively)
'The Possibilities of Moral Advice', in *The Is/Ought Question*, ed. W.D. Hudson, Macmillan (reprints from 1965 and 1964 respectively)
'Wisdom's Gods', *Philosophical Quarterly*
'The Limitations of Miss Anscombe's Grocer', *Analysis*
'Gwirionedd, Ystyr a Chrefydd', *Diwinyddiaeth*

1970

'Religious Beliefs and Language Games'/'Religiose Uberzeugung und Sprachspiel', *Ratio* XII/I

'Philosophy and Religious Education', *British Journal of Educational Studies*
'Belief and Loss of Belief' (with J.R. Jones)
'Unamuno A Gelynion Athroniaeth', *Y Traethodydd*
Review of Renford Bambrough's *Reason, Truth and God. Philosophical Books*

1971

'Religious Beliefs and Language Games', in *Oxford Readings in the Philosophy of Religion*, ed. B. Mitchell, Oxford University Press (reprint from 1970)
'Crefydd a Metaffiseg', *Efrydiau Athronyddol*
'Some Limits to Moral Endeavour', Inaugural Lecture, University College of Swansea

1972

'On Morality's Having a Point' (with H.O. Mounce), in *Fundamental Problems of Philosophy*, ed O. Hanfling, Blackwell and Open University (see 'On Morality's Having a Point', 1965)
'Moral Presuppositions and Literary Criticism', *The Human World*
'Y Gymdogaeth Ddynol', *Efrydiau Athronyddol*
' "Rhagluniaeth yn Dy Law": Darlun Sy'n Darfod', *Y Tyst*, February and May
'On Morality's Having a Point' (with H.O. Mounce), in *Problems of Moral Philosophy*, ed. Paul Taylor, Dickenson Publishing Co., California (see 'On Morality's Having a Point', 1965)

1973

'Allegiance and Change in Morality: A Study in Contrasts', Royal Institute of Philosophy Lectures Vol. 6, *Philosophy and the Arts*, ed. G. Vesey, Macmillan and St. Martin's Press
'Philosophy, Theology and the Reality of God', in *Philosophy of Religion: Selected Readings*, ed. William L. Rowe and William J. Wainwright, Harcourt Brace Jovanovich (reprint from 1963)
'Democratisation: Some Themes in Unexamined Talk', *British Journal of Education Studies* Vol. XXI

1974

'Religiose Uberzeugung und Sprachspiel', in *Sprachlogik des Glaubens*, ed. Ingolf Dalferth, Chr Kaiser Verlag, 1974 (reprint from 1970)
'Iaith a Chrefydd', *Y Tyst*, May
'Another Outbreak of Misology', *Education for Teaching*
Review of Gregor Malantschuck's *Kierkegaard's Thought. Mind*
Review of H.H. Price's *Essays in the Philosophy of Religion. Journal of Philosophy*

1975

'Belief and Loss of Belief' (with J.R. Jones), in *The Logic of God*, ed. Malcolm L. Diamond and Thomas V. Litzenburg Jr, Bobbs-Merrill (reprint from 1970)

'Beth yw Pwrpas Llenydda?', *Y Traethodydd*
Review of Keith Ward's *The Concept of God. Philosophical Books*
Review of Michael Durrant's *The Logical Status of 'God' and the Function of Theological Sentences*, Kai Nielsen's *Scepticism*, and Ninian Smart's *The Phenomenon of Religion. Mind*

1976

'Philosophers, Religion and Conceptual Change', in *The Challenge of Religion Today*, ed. J. King Farlow, Canadian Contemporary Philosophy Series, Science History Publications, New York
'We Need a Concept of Failure', *Times Higher Education Supplement*
'Infinite Approximation', *Journal of the American Academy of Religion*
Review of James Wm McClendon, Jr and James M. Smith's *Understanding Religious Convictions. International Studies in Philosophy/Studi Internazionali di Filosofia*
'Standards v The New Egalitarianism'. Review of Antony Flew's *New Studies in Practical Philosophy, Sociology, Equality and Education. New Universities Quarterly*

1977

'The Problem of Evil' and 'Postscript', in *Reason and Religion*, ed. S.C. Brown, Cornell University Press
'In Search of the Moral "Must": Mrs Foot's Fugitive Thought', *Philosophical Quarterly*
'On Wanting to Compare Wittgenstein and Zen', *Philosophy*
'Serch a Chwant', *Efrydiau Athronyddol*
'Ethics, Apologetics and the Metaphysical Man', *Sophia*
'Moral Philosophy in Practice'. Cassette. Discussion with H.O. Mounce on moral issues and the diversity of possible moral traditions with Godfrey Vesey, Open University
Review of H.J. McCloskey's *God and Evil. Mind*
Review of David Miller's *Social Justice. Philosophical Quarterly*

1978

'Iaith Ysbrydolrwydd', *Y Traethodydd*
'A Freedom to Communicate: Censorship and the Life of the Intellect', *New Universities Quarterly*
'Dramau Gwenlyn Parry – I', *Y Faner*, November and December
'Dramau Gwenlyn Parry – II', *Y Faner*, December
Review of Aurel Kolnai's *Ethics, Value and Reality: Selected Papers. Philosophical Quarterly*
Review of Gilbert Harman's *The Nature of Morality. Philosophical Quarterly*

Review of Henry Leroy Finch's *Wittgenstein – The Later Philosophy: An Exposition of the 'Philosophical Investigations'* and Garth L. Hallett's *A Companion to Wittgenstein's 'Philosophical Investigations', Philosophical Books*

1979

'Is Moral Education Really Necessary?', *British Journal of Educational Studies*
'Cristionogaeth a Diwylliant', *Y Traethodydd*
'Alienation and the Sociologising of Meaning', *Proceedings of the Aristotelian Society*
'Do Moral Considerations Override Others?', *Philosophical Quarterly*
'Bywyd y Pypedau – I', *Taliesin*
'Can There be a Christian Philosophy?', *Perkins Journal*, Summer
'Dylanwad Wittgenstein ar Athroniaeth Crefydd', *Efrydiau Athronyddol*

1980

'Knowledge, Patience and Faust', *The Yale Review*
'Philosophy and Commitment', *Metaphilosophy*
'Not in Front of the Children: Children and the Heterogeneity of Morals', *The Journal of Philosophy of Education*
'Bywyd y Pypedau – II', *Taliesin*
'An Argument from Extreme Cases?', *Philosophical Investigations*
Review of Stuart Hampshire, ed., *Public and Private Morality. Philosophical Quarterly*

1981

'Belief, Change and Forms of Life', in *The Autonomy of Religious Belief*, ed. F. Crosson, University of Notre Dame Press
'God and Ought', in *Divine Commands and Morality*, ed. Paul Helm, Oxford University Press (reprint from 1966)
'Wittgenstein's Full Stop', in *Perspectives on the Philosophy of Wittgenstein*, ed. I. Block, Blackwell
'Bad Faith and Sartre's Waiter', *Philosophy*
'Ysbrydoliaeth', *Efrydiau Athronyddol*
Review of Basil Mitchell's *Morality: Religious and Secular. Philosophical Quarterly*
Review of Walter Kaufmann's *Existentialism, Religion and Death. Scottish Journal of Religious Studies*

1982

'Can You be a Professional Friend?', *The Gadfly*
'Ai Bod yn Naif yw Ceisio Bod yn Ddi-Duedd?', *Y Traethodydd*
'In all Probability'. Review of Richard Swinburne's *Faith and Reason. Times Literary Supplement*

Review of David Lyons, ed., *Rights. Review of Metaphysics*

1983

'Eglurdeb Neu Atebion?', *Efrydiau Athronyddol*
'Primitive Reactions and the Reactions of Primitives', Marett Lecture, Exeter College, Oxford

1984

'The Devil's Disguises: Philosophy of Religion, "Objectivity" and "Cultural Divergence"', in *Objectivity and Cultural Change*, ed. S. Brown, Royal Institute of Philosophy Lectures Vol. 17, Cambridge University Press
'Mystery and Mediation: Reflections on Flannery O'Connor and Joan Didion', in *Images in Belief and Literature*, ed. D. Jasper, Macmillan
'Ffrindiau Cleanthes', *Y Traethodydd*
'Grace and Works', *Philosophic Exchange*
'A. MacIntyre's *After Virtue*', Critical Notice, *Mind*
Review of Alastair Hannay's *Kierkegaard. Mind*
Review of O.K. Bouwsma's *Without Proof or Evidence. Scottish Journal of Religious Studies*

1985

'The Friends of Cleanthes', *Modern Theology*
'Grace and Works', *Philosophic Exchange*, 1984–85
Celfyddyd: A Oes Rhagoriaeth?
'Art and the Possibility of Excellence', The Sir Ben Bowen Thomas Lecture, 1984, Arts Council of North Wales
Critical Notice of Leonard Angel's *The Silence of the Mystic. Canadian Journal of Philosophy*
'The Grammar of Religious Conviction'. Review of Stephen R.L. Clark's *From Athens to Jerusalem: The Love of Wisdom and the Love of God. Times Literary Supplement*
Review of A. Phillips Griffith, ed., *Philosophy and Literature. Philosophical Books*

1986

'Religious Beliefs and Language-Games', in *Ludwig Wittgenstein: Critical Assessments*, ed. S.G. Shanker, Croom Helm (reprint from 1970)
'On Wanting to Compare Wittgenstein with Zen', in *Ludwig Wittgenstein: Critical Assessments*, ed. S.G. Shanker, Croom Helm (reprint from 1977)
Primitive Reactions and the Reactions of Primitives: The 1983 Marett Lecture, *Religious Studies*
Critical Notice of C. Stephen Evans' *Kierkegaard's Fragments and Postscripts* and H.A. Nielsen's *Where the Passion Is: A Reading of Kierkegaard's Philosophical Fragments. Philosophical Investigations*

'Have You Missed Your Connection?'. Review of Don Cupitt's *Life Lines*. *Times Literary Supplement*
'A Natural Transcendence'. Review of Fergus Kerr's *Theology after Wittgenstein* and Joseph Runzo's *Reason, Relativism and God*. *Times Literary Supplement*

1987

'The Problem of Evil', in *Philosophy of Religion: An Anthology*, ed. Louis P. Pojman, Wadsworth Publishing Co. (reprint from 1977)
'Education and Magic', in *Philosophers on Education*, ed. Roger Straughan and John Wilson, Macmillan
'The Friends of Cleanthes: A Correction', *Modern Theology*
Review of Edward L. Schoen's *Religious Explanations: A Model from the Sciences*. *Religious Studies*

1988

'Grammarians and Guardians', in *The Grammar of the Heart*, ed. R.H. Bell, Harper and Row
'Lindbeck's Audience', *Modern Theology*
'On Not Understanding God', *Archivio di Filosofia*, Vol. LVI
'Advice to Philosophers who are Christians', *New Blackfriars*
Review of Peter Winch's *Trying to Make Sense*. *Religious Studies*
Review of H. Morris-Jones, *Durkheim. Efrydiau Athronyddol*

1989

'The Presumption of Theory', in *Value and Understanding: Essays for Peter Winch*, ed. R. Gaita, Routledge
'How Lucky Can You Get?', in *Wittgenstein: Attention to Particulars: Essays in Honour of Rush Rhees*, Macmillan
'William James and the Notion of Two Worlds', in *Religion, Reason and the Self: Essays in Honour of Hywel D. Lewis*, ed. S.R. Sutherland and T.A. Roberts, University of Wales Press
'Searle on Language Games and Religion', *Tijschrift voor Filosofie*
'My Neighbour and My Neighbours', *Philosophical Investigations*
'What Can We Expect From Ethics', *Proceedings Aristotelian Society*, Supp. Vol. LXIII
'Fy Nghymydog a'm Cymdogion', *Efrydiau Athronyddol*
Review of Oswald Hanfling's *The Quest for Meaning* and Oswald Hanfling, ed., *Life and Meaning: A Reader. Philosophy*

1990

'Y Duw Cudd' (with M. Wynn Thomas and Gwyn Erfyl), in *R.S. Thomas, V Cawr Awenydd*, ed. M. Wynn Thomas, Gomer Press
'From Coffee to Carmelites', *Philosophy*
'Sublime Existence', *Archivio di Filosofia*

Review of Charles L. Creegan's *Wittgenstein and Kierkegaard, Individuality and Philosophical Method. Modern Theology*

1991

'Religion in Wittgenstein's Mirror', in *Wittgenstein Centenary Essays*, ed. A. Phillips Griffiths, *Royal Institute of Philosophy Lectures* Vol. 28, Cambridge University Press
'Faith, Scepticism and Religious Understanding', in *Contemporary Classics in Philosophy of Religion*, ed. Ann Loades and Loyal D. Rue, Open Court (reprint from 1967)
'Eternal Life and the Immortality of the Soul', in *Contemporary Classics in Philosophy of Religion*, ed. Ann Loades and Loyal D. Rue, Open Court (reprint from *Death and Immortality*, 1970)
'Waiting for the Vanishing Shed', *Philosophy and Theology*, Vol. V
'Poetry and Philosophy, A Reply', *The New Welsh Review*, Vol. III

1992

'Faith, Scepticism and Religious Understanding', in *Contemporary Perspectives on Religious Epistemology*, ed. R. Douglas Geivett and Brendan Sweetman, Oxford University Press (reprint from 1967)
'Between Faith and Metaphysics', in *Christian Faith and Philosophical Theology: Essays in Honour of Vincent Brummer*, ed. Gijsbert van den Brink, Luco J. van den Brom and Marcel Sarot, Pharos
'Authorship and Authenticity: Kierkegaard and Wittgenstein', *Midwest Studies in Philosophy: The Wittgenstein Legacy*, ed. Peter A. French, Theodore E. Uehling Jr and Howard K. Wettstein, University of Notre Dame Press
'Creencias religiosas y juegos de lenguaje', *Creencia y racionalidad. Lectures de filosofia de la religion*, ed. Enrique Romerales, Madrid: Consejo Superior de Investigaciones Cientificas, Barcelona: Anthropos (see 'Religious Belief and Language Games', 1970)
'Ethics and Anna Karenina', *Literature and Ethics*, Proceedings of the Norwegian Academy of Science and Letters, Oslo
'Scripture, Speech and Sin', *Archivio di Filosofia*
Review of A.P. Shooman, *The Metaphysics of Religious Belief. Efrydiau Athronyddol*

1993

'God and Concept-formation in Simone Weil', in *Simone Weil's Philosophy of Culture*, ed. R.H. Bell, Cambridge University Press
'On Really Believing', in *Is God Real?*, ed. Joseph Runzo, Macmillan and St. Martin's Press
'How Real is Realism', in *Is God Real?*, ed. Joseph Runzo, Macmillan and St. Martin's Press

'Great Expectations', in *Is God Real?*, ed. Joseph Runzo, Macmillan and St. Martin's Press
'Ten Questions for Psychoanalysis', *Philosophy*
'Miracles and Open-Door Epistemology', *Scottish Journal of Religious Studies*
'On His Knees With His Eyes Open' (Review of R.S. Thomas's Poetry), *The New Welsh Review*
'Pam Achub Jaith?', *Efrydiau Athronyddol*
Review of M. Jamie Ferreira's *Transforming Vision: Imagination and Will in Kierkegaardian Faith*. *Philosophical Investigations*
Review of Nelson Pike's *Mystic Union: An Essay in the Phenomenology of Mysticism*. *Philosophical Books*
Review of John V. Canfield's *The Looking-Glass Self*. *Philosophical Investigations*
Review of Bruce D. Marshall, ed., *Theology and Dialogue: Essays in Conversation with George Lindbeck*. *Scottish Journal of Theology*
Review of Christina Howells, ed., *The Cambridge Companion to Sartre*. *The Expository Times*

1994

'Introduction: Piety, Theism and Philosophy', in *Theism: Traditional Theism and its Modern Alternatives*, Aarhus University Press
'Philosophy and Religious Education', reprinted in *Christian Perspectives on Christian Education*, ed. J. Astley and L.J. Francis, Gracewing
'Reclaiming the Conversations of Mankind', *Philosophy*
'Glaucon's Challenges', *Philosophical Investigations*
'Authority and Revelation', *Archivio di Filosofia*
'Pwy Oedd J.R. Jones?', *Barn*
Review of Richard Fleming's *The State of Philosophy: An Invitation to a Reading in Three Parts of Stanley Cavell's 'The Claim of Reason'* and Ronald E. Hustwit's *Something about O. K. Bouwsma*. *Philosophical Investigations*
Review of M.J.J. Buuren's *Waiting: The Religious Poetry of R. S. Thomas, Welsh Poet and Priest* and R.S. Thomas's *Frieze*. *The New Welsh Review*

1995

'Y Gymdogaeth Ddynol', in *Y Meddwl Cymreig*, ed. W.J. Rees, University of Wales Press
'Kolakowski on Religion and Morality', in *Veritas filia temporis? Philosophie historie zwischen Wahrheit und Geschichte*, ed. R.W. Puster, Berlin and New York
'At the Mercy of Method', in *Philosophy and the Grammar of Religious Belief*, ed. Timothy Tessin and Mario von der Ruhr, London and New York: Macmillan and St. Martin's Press
'Where Are the Gods Now?', in *Relativism and Religion*, ed. Charles M. Lewis, Macmillan

'Philosophers' Clothes', in *Relativism and Religion*, ed. Charles M. Lewis, Macmillan
'On Giving Practice its Due – A Reply', *Religious Studies*
'Epistemic Practices – A Reply to William Wainwright', *Topoi*
'Can Which Good Man Know Himself: Reply', *Philosophical Investigations*
'The World and "I"', *Philosophical Investigations*
'Dislocating the Soul', *Religious Studies*
'Mysticism and Epistemology: One Devil of a Problem', *Faith and Philosophy*

1996

'Wittgenstein, Religion and Anglo-American Philosophical Culture', in *Wittgenstein and the Philosophy of Culture*, Proceedings of the 18th International Wittgenstein Symposium 1995, ed. K.S. Johannessen and T. Nordenstam, Verlag Hölder-Pichler-Tempsky, Vienna
'Dislocating the Soul', in *Can Religion Be Explained Away?*, ed. D.Z. Phillips, Macmillan and St. Martin's Press (reprint from 1995)
'Suspended from Heaven: Ethics, Religion and Modernity', *Archivio di Filosofia*
'Pan Edrychwyf ar y Nefoedd', *Y Traethodydd*
'Heb Fynd I'r Unlle', *Yr Aradr*
(Ed.) Rush Rhees, 'On Editing Wittgenstein', *Philosophical Investigations*
Critical Notice of Stephen Mulhall, *Stanley Cavell, Philosophy's Recounting of the Ordinary. Philosophical Investigations*
Review of Terrence W. Tilley, *The Wisdom of Religious Commitment. International Journal for Philosophy of Religion*

1997

'In the Beginning was the Proposition – in the Beginning was the Choice – in the Beginning was the Dance', *Mid-West Studies in Philosophy*
'Ethics and Humanistic Ethics – A Reply to Dilman', in *Commonality and Particularity in Ethics*, ed. Lilli Alanen, S. Heinamaa, T. Wallgren, Macmillan and St. Martin's Press
'Notes on a "Monstrous Illusion"', in *Philosophy and Theological Discourse*, ed. Stephen T. Davis, Macmillan and St. Martin's Press
'Die Moglichkeit der Rede: Zu Rhees' Kritik der Philosophischen Untersuchungen Wittgensteins' (trans. Geert-Lueke Lueken), *Kommunikationsversuche Theorien der Kommunikation*, Leipzig
'Y Duwiau a Ni', *Efrydiau Athronyddol*
'Obituary Peter Winch 1926–1997', *Philosophical Investigations*
(Ed.), Rush Rhees, 'Language as Emerging from Instinctive Behaviour', *Philosophical Investigations*
Review of Stephen N. Williams, *Revelation and Reconciliation. Efrydiau Athronyddol*

1998

'Moral Philosophy: The Arrogance of Solitary Intellect?', in *Critical Reflections on Bioethics*, ed. Martyn Evans, JAI Press
'Who Do You Say that I Am', in *Archivio de Filosofia*, ed. M.M. Olivetti, CEDAM-CASA, Editrice Dott Antonio Milani
'Ôl y Duwiau: Jane Gruffydd a *Traed Mewn Cyffion*', *Efrydiau Athronyddol*
Review of Philip L. Quinn and Charles Taliaferro, eds., *A Companion to Philosophy of Religion. International Journal for Philosophy of Religion*
Review of Jeff Jordan and Daniel Howard Snyder, eds., in *Ethics*
Review of Richard Messer, *Does God's Existence Need Proof? International Studies in Philosophy*

1999

Filosofi – en presentation: Skepticismens Utmaning (Introducing Philosophy: The Challenge of Scepticism), Swedish translation by Yrsa Neuman and Lars Hertzberg, Daidalos
'Is Hume's "True Religion" a Religious Belief?', in *Religion and Hume's Legacy*, ed. D.Z. Phillips and Timothy Tessin, Macmillan and St. Martin's Press
'Reflecting on Identity and Change', Introduction to *Identity and Change in the Christian Tradition*, ed. Marcel Sarot and Gisbert van den Brink, Peter Lang
'Religieuze overtuigingen en taalspelen' ('Religious Beliefs and Language-Games'), in *Rationaliteit en religieus vertrouwen*, ed. Paul Cortois and Walter Van Herek
'What Can We Say about Morality and Religion?', *Miscellania Bulgaria*
'Belief and Conceptual Analysis – Where Are We Going?', *Cuaderno Gris*
'Rush Rhees, Athroniaeth a Chrefydd', *Efrydiau Athronyddol*
'Trust It!', *Bijdragen. International Journal in Philosophy and Religion*
Review of Timothy Gould, *Hearing Things: Voice and Method in the Writing of Stanley Cavell. Philosophical Investigations*

2000

'Four Reasons for not Getting Nervous', in *Post-Theism: Reframing the Judaeo-Christian Tradition*, ed. A.L. Morendrijk, H.A. Krop and H. de Vries, Peeters Publishers
'Self-Deception and Freedom in Kierkegaard's Purity of Heart', in *Kierkegaard and Freedom*, ed. James Giles, Palgrave
'Practices, Practice and Superstition', *Journal of the American Academy of Religion*
'Beyond Rules', *History of the Human Sciences*

2001

'Intersubjectivity, Religion and Philosophical Method', *Archivo di Filosofia*

'What Even God Cannot Tell Us: Realism versus Metaphysical Realism', *Faith and Philosophy*
'Y Cyn-Socratiaid', *Efrydiau Athronyddol*
'Yspryd y Gair: R.S. Thomas Fel Bardd Crefyddol', *Y Traethodydd*
(Ed.) Rush Rhees, 'Notes on Four Conversations with Wittgenstein', *Faith and Philosophy*
(Ed.) Peter Winch, 'What Can Philosophy Say to Religion?', *Faith and Philosophy*

2002

'Rationality, Trust and Religious Trust', *Philosophical Investigations*
'Ethics and Faith and "What Can be Said"', *Wittgenstein: A Critical Reader*, ed. H.-J. Glock, Blackwell
'Theism without Theodicy', 'Criticism' and 'Reply to Critics', in *Encountering Evil*, ed. Stephen T. Davis, Westminster Press
(Ed.) Rush Rhees, 'Numbers; Concept-Formation; Time Reactions; Induction; Causality; Conversations with Wittgenstein', *Philosophical Investigations*
(Ed.) Peter Winch, 'How is Political Authority Possible?', *Philosophical Investigations*
'Winch and Romanticism', *Philosophy*

Forthcoming

'"Just Say the Word", Logical and Magical Conceptions in Religion', in *Religion and Wittgenstein's Legacy*, ed. D.Z. Phillips and Mario van der Ruhr, Palgrave
'Wittgensteinianism', in *Handbook for Philosophy of Religion*, ed. William J. Wainwright, Oxford University Press
'Kierkegaard and Loves that Blossom', in *Kierkegaard's 'Works of Love'*, ed. Ingolf Dalferth, Mohr Siebeck

This bibliography has been formed from two Bibliographies by Eddie Yeghiayan and Helen Baldwin respectively. We acknowledge their help with gratitude.